Elvis Costello, Joni Mitchell, and the Torch Song Tradition

Elvis Costello, Joni Mitchell, and the Torch Song Tradition

LARRY DAVID SMITH

Westport, Connecticut
London

Library of Congress Cataloging-in-Publication Data

Smith, Larry David.
   Elvis Costello, Joni Mitchell, and the torch song tradition / Larry David Smith.
      p. cm.
   Includes bibliographical references (p.) and index.
   ISBN 0-275-97392-1 (alk. paper)
      1. Costello, Elvis—Criticism and interpretation.   2. Mitchell, Joni—Criticism and
   interpretation.   3. Popular music—Analysis, appreciation.   4. Long songs—History and
   criticism.   I. Title.
   ML400.S658   2004
   782.42164′092′2—dc22   2003068713

British Library Cataloguing in Publication Data is available.

Library of Congress Catalog Card Number: 2003068713
ISBN: 0-275-97392-1

First published in 2004

Praeger Publishers, 88 Post Road West, Westport, CT 06881
An imprint of Greenwood Publishing Group, Inc.
www.praeger.com

Printed in the United States of America

ᵉ paper used in this book complies with the
ᵗanent Paper Standard issued by the National
ᵗmation Standards Organization (Z39.48-1984).

ᵗ 7 6 5 4 3 2 1

In Memory of Edith Elizabeth Love

Contents

Preface

This is the third volume of a continuing exploration into the practice of songwriting. Merging auteur theory and narrative criticism, I've examined one songwriter's career in terms of his narrative tendencies and professional negotiations (Pete Townshend), and I've compared two songwriters' contributions to the Woody Guthrie celebrity-singer-songwriter tradition of American song (Bob Dylan and Bruce Springsteen). Here I apply the technique to Joni Mitchell's and Elvis Costello's careers as I consider these two artists' lifeworks and their impact on the melodramatic love story known as the torch song. These books represent an effort to build a body of knowledge in a systematic way, so I occasionally use my previous findings regarding Dylan, Springsteen, and Townshend to make sense of my current observations. The auteur–narrative framework is a fine hammer for pounding away on the unique artistic role that emerged with the celebrity-singer-songwriter in the mid-twentieth century. The celebrity-singer-songwriter composite changed the musical world and, as this book hopefully demonstrates, shifted the content and style of specific musical genres.

Of course, I must pause to thank the many wonderful people who have contributed to this work. Heartfelt thanks go out to Glenda and Wayne Hall, Michael Holmes, Nicola Joss, and Pete Townshend. I would also like to thank the city of Memphis, Tennessee, for providing a magical workplace throughout this book's development. The stars align in a special way over the Holy City of American Music. Please, go there and feel it. Memphis features the world's greatest radio station (WEVL), a storied musical history, and some of the most colorful characters you'll *ever* meet (thanks, Richard Owen!). Thank you, Memphis! May your future be as bright as your past.

Speaking of special people and places, words fail my efforts to thank Eric Levy. Eric is more than my editor; he is a dear friend who truly cares about *me* as much as my work. Thanks, Eric. Maybe I can go to war for *you* sometime. And thanks to everybody at Praeger for their continued belief in these projects. A very special thanks also to Joni Mitchell, Christy Ikner, and all the fine people at Sony/ATV Publishing in Nashville. Another special thank you to Elvis Costello, Gigi Lam, and the people at BMG Music in Beverly Hills and London.

Finally. Finally. After using my experiences with her wonderful boogie-woogie piano playing to close my two previous books on songwriting, it is high time to give it up for the keyboard player. This one's for you, Mom. I bet they're dancin' all over heaven as you continue to play the devil's music Up There. Thanks for the continued inspiration. I think that it's fitting to dedicate a book on love songs to the greatest love of all: a boy's love for his mother. Bang it out, Momma. I can *still* hear you.

Introduction

When music historians speak of the "love song" as a songwriting theme, their thoughts instantly turn to the troubadours of southern France and their pivotal contributions to that genre's development. As eleventh-century popular music crawled away from the Church's shadows and toward such secular notions as love and happiness, these Provencal poets paved the way. How important are the Provencal troubadours to art history? Consider Reverend H. J. Chaytor's comments from his 1912 book, *The Troubadours*: "Few literatures have exerted so profound an influence upon the literary history of other peoples as the poetry of the troubadours." There seems to be a strong case to be made in support of Chaytor's claim. After all, the romantic poetry that flowed from the pens of French poets who dared to comment publicly on that which had been *so* private for *so* long was quite an artistic innovation as well as a literary invitation for "other peoples" to do the same. Just as Chaytor suggests, the troubadours appealed to more than their audiences' hearts. They unshackled the literature of the Western world, initiated secular commentary on human affairs, and introduced music with a recognizable personality.

Though they typically concentrated on romance, Chaytor reports the troubadours' subject matter included "Not only love, but all social and political questions of the age. . . . They satirised political and religious opponents, preached crusades, sang funeral laments upon the death of famous patrons, and the support of their poetical powers was often in demand by princes and nobles involved in a struggle." Clearly, these celebrity tunesmiths were harbingers of free speech, daring to explore controversies and personalities that had heretofore been off-limits. While contemporary events may have captured their attentions from time to time (and lined their pocketbooks), love dominated the troubadours' work. What made this poetry so timeless? James Wilhelm's answer is compelling: "Because these elements are . . . an essential part of the human apparatus, and by no means monopolized by Christians or members of any other religion or culture. One has every reason to believe, without checking, that natives in the jungle and Eskimos tell their beloveds that they will follow them over the hills and vales and any other appropriate parts of the local landscapes." Love knows no boundaries, and the troubadours charted romantic courses that transcended borders, creeds, or social affiliations. Assuredly, they chronicled "an essential part of the human apparatus." They told the stories of love.

The communicative practices through which the troubadours plied their trade were hierarchal in nature. Once more, we turn to Reverend Chaytor:

> A famous troubadour usually circulated his poems by the mouth of a *joglar* (Northern French, *jongleur*), who recited them at different courts and was often sent long distances by his master for this purpose. A joglar of originality might rise to the position of a troubadour, and a troubadour who fell upon evil days might sink to the profession of joglar. Hence there was naturally some confusion between the troubadour and joglar, and poets sometimes combined the two functions.

Thus, from the outset, we have a division of roles as writers differentiated themselves from performers, singers aspired to the greater status that accompanied authorship, successful practitioners suffered at the hands of "evil days" (critics? industry pressure??), *poets* occasionally synthesized the two jobs, and competition was naturally rampant. Moreover, the potential conflict between pleasing patrons and satisfying creative impulses required writers to negotiate their financial conditions and their art's contents. From its beginnings, we see that the musical world was a complicated, competitive, and conditional place.

To prosper in such an environment, stylistic innovation quickly became necessary. Lyrical nuances, vocal tricks, instrumental prowess, performance skills, and thematic flexibility defined the troubadours and incited even more competition. Wilhelm charts the careers of seven troubadours who achieved celebrity status and established the creative baseline for those who followed. He begins with Duke William of Aquitaine, the world's first—and perhaps greatest—troubadour. William was quite a character. His voice represented "an outcry against the vulgar spiritualism of his day" as he decried "the hypocrites who tried to conceal their real selves under the cloaks of sanctity." William aggressively confronted the system and enjoyed himself, to everyone's annoyance. He may be the musical world's first rock-and-roll star. Next, we have Marcabrun (who "carried sermons to the court"), Jaufre Rudel (who challenged the "mournful and pessimistic" work of his time), Bernart de Ventadorn (who had "one of the best senses of humor in medieval literature"), the Countess of Dia (who "sang in measures that are comparable with the best work of the men of her day"), Bertran de Born (who was a poet of war), and Peire Cardenal, who appeared toward the end of southern France's glory age and chronicled its demise through dour, bitter poetry. What characters. What work. Wilhelm sums up their significance:

> The troubadours did not leave us tourist guidebooks any more than they left candid memoirs of their sex lives or propaganda pieces about the superiority of women. They did, however, leave us their poetry, and this heritage binds them to us directly. Peire Cardenal cries out against the Church and conservatism in general in precisely the same way that Joan Baez and Bob Dylan are coherent spokesmen for modern liberal ideals. Bernart de Ventadorn manipulates the age-old tropes bequeathed him with the same sort of assured hand that Cole Porter and Lorenz Hart used in reworking the stock materials of their day. The Countess of Dia is quite comprehensible in the context of Billie Holliday [sic] and Helen Morgan; her torch may be less intense, but it is held equally high. Even in the consciously artistic work of the Beatles and the Supremes and our other modern troubadours from Liverpool and Detroit and Nashville, we can hear the age-old cries issuing forth in the same general atmosphere of hand-clapping, footstomping, and hilarity—call it "joy" or plain old "fun."

Those "age-old cries" may involve joy, pain, fun, or despair, but when they stoke the fires of love, they report on an essential element of the human experience through the language and sounds of their times—stylistic tendencies that continually influence the art form's maturation.

Just as quickly as the love song emerged, unimaginative songwriting dominated the genre. Wilhelm's troubadours may have achieved stylistic notoriety, but mainstream writers wallowed in trite expressions and mundane metaphors. As twentieth-century songwriters massaged the love song, searching for some unique sentiment or insight, they encountered the same limitations that hounded their French predecessors. Philip Furia explains:

> Such a constraint of subject matter put Tin Pan Alley lyricists in the same straightjacket as their medieval ancestors, the troubadours of Provence, who, after all, invented this thing called romantic love. To the modern reader, who looks to poetry for original insight, sincerely expressed, popular song lyrics, like medieval *chansons*, "all sound the same . . . sweet but bland repetitions of the few basic clichés of courtly love." What such readers miss is the cleverness, the inventiveness and, in the best sense of the word, artifice, that displays itself by ringing endless changes upon what are indeed the tiredest clichés, the tireder the better for the skillful artificers of Provence. In the lyrics of Tin Pan Alley, similarly, we must listen, not for new ideas or deep emotion, but for the deftness with which the lyricist solves the problem posed by a song of the 1930s: "What Can You Say in a Love Song That Hasn't Been Said Before?"

While many Tin Pan Alley writers searched for adroit ways to communicate "I love you in 32 bars," a few pursued alternative formulas. One possibility involved the creation of musical hybrids that synthesized the strengths of existing genres into new forms. Furia describes one innovation that emerged from the prohibition era nightclubs in which Tin Pan Alley writers slowly transformed blues and jazz compositions into popular songs. The "hot tunes and torch songs" of the Harlem nightclubs "could sometimes inspire a talented lyricist to come up with a sensuously vernacular setting that set nightclub songs apart from theater or film songs of the period." With that, the "torch song" was born.

Alec Wilder maintains the torch song arrived via Spencer Williams's 1915 tune "I Ain't Got Nobody," and its "new, more personal point of view." Such an outlook dismissed the tired clichés that dominated contemporary love songs in favor of personal melodrama and intimate detail. Furia writes how the torch song was refined by singers such as Billie Holiday, Lena Horne, and Peggy Lee, who learned how to give a song "the full-flame treatment." One of the problems associated with this new genre involved the difficulty in collaboration since lyricists were brought in to devise words for already existing—and occasionally popular—jazz tunes. Consequently, the words often lacked development or inspiration. Though the compositional process was weird initially, the new genre prospered. Masterpieces such as Gillespie and Coots's (of "Santa Claus Is Coming to Town") "You Go to My Head," Brent and Dennis's "Angel Eyes," and Mercer and Arlen's "One for My Baby" demonstrate the early torch song's melodramatic power.

The advent of the celebrity-singer-songwriter changed everything. With talented innovators such as Jimmie Rodgers, Woody Guthrie, and Hank Williams, the composer-lyricist-performer roles converged into a single musical entity. The celebrity-singer-songwriter composite sparked the rebirth of songs with public personalities as it retrieved that tradition from the dusty court chambers that time forgot. To the extent that William of Aquitaine projected his personality through his thoughts about love, war, and gardening, Woody Guthrie would do the same. To the degree that Jaufre Rudel confronted his contemporaries' "mournful and pessimistic" work, Hank Williams enriched his songs through his rebellious honky-tonk persona. Accompanying that musical evolution was the torch song's liberation from the smoke-filled corridors of bar life and its introduction to radio, recording, and mass audiences. Smoke-free versions of Frank Sinatra renditions of Sammy Cahn songs were suddenly available to anyone with a phonograph or radio. Do as music does, mix it all together, and a new variation emerged: torch songs with celebrity personalities.

Here we consider two celebrity-singer-songwriters who write of "social and political questions," who satirize "political and religious opponents," and, occasionally, who advocate "crusades," all the while consistently mining the rich vein of human relationships—exploring what the natives in the jungle, the Eskimos, hippies, and punks call "love." By bringing their celebrity personalities to their work, Joni Mitchell and Elvis Costello created more than songs about this or that; they generated a public dialogue about their subjects in a manner that transcends the context of performance or means of reception. Like the troubadours of old, they brought personalities to their work in a fashion that made it original and memorable. Unlike the troubadours of old, they performed their work before international audiences who instantly praised or damned their efforts. The threat of "evil days" was ubiquitous. Their creative–commercial challenges were constant. Their responses to their artistic situations created bodies of work as daring as any Provencal poet's. And their efforts brought *personality* to a song form that had previously known only a *context*. The results may not be as musically precise as the lyricist-composer-performer composition, but they involve distinctive artistic signatures nonetheless. The following pages use auteur theory and narrative techniques to examine Mitchell's and Costello's oeuvres in terms of the stories they told throughout their careers, the stylistic tendencies that organize those expressions, and their subsequent contributions to the torch tradition. Joni Mitchell's Earth Mother manifesto and Elvis Costello's Citizen Elvis editorials represent narrative superstructures through which these writers cast tales of love, war, peace, politics, fashion, fascism, and house pets in a manner consistent with their stated artistic philosophies and creative goals. In so doing, they advanced the concept of the celebrity-singer-songwriter, created an extraordinary body of art, and contributed to the torch song's thematic development. We begin with peace, love, freedom, and The Garden of Eden just off Sisotowbell Lane.

PART I

Joni Mitchell

INTRODUCTION

The December 16, 1974, issue of *Time* features as its cover story an article on the "women of rock" with an emphasis on "Rock 'n' Roll's Leading Lady"—Joni Mitchell. The article concentrates on Mitchell, but also contains interviews with Maria Muldaur, Bonnie Raitt, and Linda Ronstadt as well as commentary on the careers of female artists Carole King, Carly Simon, and Wendy Waldman. David DeVoss paints a grim picture of the Rock Women: "Caught in the wink of a photographer's lens, they stand together smiling, rock-'n'-roll women in sequined chiffon and funky jeans. But they pay dearly for success. The rock business is a road business. Once the euphoria of the first room-service sirloin evaporates, they inherit a numbing chronology of concrete tunnels, cold buffets and limousine-driving dopers." DeVoss's cynicism is just warming up: "It is a life where one is seldom alone but usually lonely. There are plenty of men, but they are mostly grinning sycophants or lecherous disc jockeys. Yet it is almost impossible to retire; the thrill of recognition quickly becomes an opiate." Among talk of Simon's and King's disdain for the "rock life," Raitt's commitment to a modest lifestyle that stresses her music, and Ronstadt's commercial success, DeVoss shares an account of "dinner at Joni's" in which rock's leading lady prepared "three meticulously cooked courses" that were eagerly consumed while the "spiced apple dumplings cool on the sideboard." Not only does Mitchell cook a mighty fine meal, but her boyfriend leaves the table to grab a beer and watch a football game while our hostess cleans her kitchen.

This was the leading lady of rock.

In December 1974 Bob Dylan was hard at work in Minneapolis, Minnesota, recasting much of what was to become *Blood on the Tracks*. Dylan was, no doubt, the "leading man" of rock since he had that year completed the most profitable tour ever staged to that point in popular music history. His comeback album, *Planet Waves*, the "Tour '74" experience with The Band, and his highly anticipated new record certainly placed him atop the musical world. Yet could you imagine *Time* sending a correspondent out to Dylan's house to watch him mow the lawn, fix his kid's bike, or wash the car? Could you imagine *Time* cooing over the toy chest Dylan just finished in his woodshop as his wife stops by to pick up the credit card to go shopping at Victoria's Secret? Do you get my drift here? As Mitchell complained to David Wild in 1997: "They tend to lump me always with groups of women. I always thought, 'They don't put Dylan with the Men of Rock; why do they do that to me with women?'" She has a compelling point.

DeVoss opens his exposé on rock's leading lady in this fashion: "When Myrtle Anderson's daughter Joan lived at home in Saskatoon, Sask., she was a rebel. She danced the wicked twist, ignored her math, spent Saturdays sketching Indians and communed only with her celluloid idol James Dean. But Mrs. Anderson's girl turned out different from most of the teen-agers living for the rock-'n'-roll scene. She learned to play the guitar and discovered that she had a fluent talent for words." He describes Mitchell as a "creative force of unrivaled stature in the mercurial world of rock" who represents a "focal point for elegance in a profession of rumpled informality." According to the *Time* reporter: "Everyone seems to know Joni. She is the rural neophyte waiting in a subway, a free spirit drinking Greek wine in the moonlight, an organic Earth Mother dispensing fresh bread and herb tea, and the reticent feminist who by trial and error has charted the male as well as the female ego."

This was the leading lady of rock.

This is Joni Mitchell's problem. While DeVoss opens the piece with a genderless description (young Joan was a rebel, admired Dean, played guitar, and wrote songs), he gradually drifts into a sexist portrayal that is apparently unavoidable. Rock men also cope with cold food, sycophantic personalities, cheap people, and boredom. Rock men may also be refined, popular, free-spirited, and nurturing. What, then, is the point? The fact that Joni Mitchell was the first female to excel among the growing number of celebrity–singer–songwriters is the most obvious explanation. From that vantage point, her gender is unavoidable. She was the first of her kind.

DeVoss also exposes Joni Mitchell's relationship to her work. When he reports that our leading lady "believes in a male muse named Art" and that "Art" represents her "shrine of creativity," he reveals an artistic attitude that never, ever wanes. When Mitchell told DeVoss "I feel like I'm married to this guy named Art . . . I'm responsible to my Art above all else," she demonstrated her dedication to her creative work. Whether she is painting, drawing, knitting, or playing music, Mitchell pursues an artistic agenda that may—or may not—agree with the commercial industry that markets her work. She is responsible only to her Art. She is as relentlessly rebellious as any artist at any time.

One thing is certain: Joni Mitchell is neither the greatest female singer-songwriter ever, nor the greatest right-handed female singer-songwriter, nor the greatest blonde right-handed female singer-songwriter; rather, she is one of the greatest singer-songwriters, *period*. Though widely misunderstood, her songwriting and sonic innovations blazed new trails for musicians to follow. *After* Joni Mitchell, writers freely probed their personal experiences or their individual perceptions as a pathway to expressions that embellished those insights for their audiences. *After* Joni Mitchell, "world music" emerged as an essential element of the musical landscape. Joni Mitchell's pioneering songwriting and musical innovations exist independently of her gender, and to qualify her contributions in those terms is more than misleading, it is downright insulting.

Evidence of her success exists in the recognition Mitchell has received over the years. Her many awards include *Billboard*'s Century Award, the National Academy of Songwriters' Lifetime Achievement Award, the Canadian Governor-General's Performing Arts Award, the Swedish Polar Music Award (the first woman), election to the Rock and Roll Hall of Fame, the ASCAP Founders Award, the Orville H. Gibson Guitar Award, election to the Songwriters Hall of Fame, Grammy Awards, Geminis (Canadian Emmy), the Saskatchewan Recording Industry Association's Lifetime Achievement Award, and more. Though she has not received the academic or journalistic attention of her Rock Spouse (Mr. Dylan), all the musical world pales in comparison to Dylanology, anyway. Biographers Karen O'Brien and Brian Hinton join scores of dedicated fans and their prodigious web sites to build an impressive account of one of popular music's more frustrated legends.

The following chapters chronicle a songwriter who dared to probe her life experiences for useful insights that she could share with others. She saw *that* as her "job." More often than not, these sentiments massaged the frail conditions that surround romantic relationships. In so doing, Mitchell revised and extended the torch tradition's melodramatic imperative by associating a personality with those intimate offerings. Her "confessional" songwriting—regardless of its autobiographical qualities—changed the practice of songwriting in general, and embellished the torch strategy in particular. That her accomplishments are so often characterized by her gender is unfortunate if for no other reason than that Mitchell herself disdains the practice. That outlook is evident in a story she shared with Chip Stern when she described her greatest compliment: "You know, in my entire adult life, my favorite compliment—and I think a true compliment should be inspiring, not just flattering—was received from a blind black piano player. And what he said was 'Joni, thank you for your music—it is genderless and raceless.'"

While her music may prove to be "genderless and raceless," its emotional depth invokes the torch tradition's melodramatic sentimentality in a compelling fashion. To be sure, her "confessional" writing style is a funda-mental element of the torch formula. Furthermore, Mitchell's status as a celebrity-singer-songwriter elevated the author's role in these emotional renderings. Unlike Billie Holiday or Frank Sinatra, once Mitchell bled onstage, her audience followed her home, hoping to watch her bleed more in private and, therefore, enrich their own lives through her sacrifice. In many respects, Mitchell's tale is an odd story that offers meaningful insights into artist-audience-industry relations. Although her art may be genderless, our Earth Mother's story is dominated by gender. When considered together, Mitchell's life and art demonstrate the emotional power of the torch song—a power with serious consequences for artists and their art.

CHAPTER 1

The Artist

Joni Mitchell's life story is a fascinating tale of potent prophecy, brutal illness, righteous rebellion, inspired determination, frustrated celebrity, and bitter indignation. These traits float in and out of Mitchell's life, and at times dominate her biography. Occasionally, these qualities overlap in powerful ways, as in the case of her inspired battle with polio, or her predictable musical pioneering, or her wrathful reactions to celebrity hypocrisies and industrial abuses. The one constant ingredient in all of these matters, however, is her *intensity*. Joni Mitchell's career is a testament to a creative passion that defines her very being. For one who emerged in an era of peace and love platitudes and their nondirective philosophies, Mitchell is a fierce artistic force with little patience for personal, interpersonal, or commercial compromise. From the moment of her birth, it seems, Mitchell has been driven by her muse and its restless need for diverse expression—regardless of the personal or professional consequences. These characteristics have spawned musical innovation, personal sacrifice, professional recognition, audience admiration, audience rejection, and industrial recrimination in varying fashions. Though born with an undeniable talent, Joni Mitchell has endured an unrelenting battle for artistic freedom and integrity.

Let us begin our story with potent prophecy and the wonderful tale of "tea leaf" prognostication, Canadian style. When schoolteacher–turned–bank teller Myrtle "Mickey" Marguerite McKee accompanied a friend to high tea at Regina's finest hotel, she humored herself by allowing a gypsy to read the tea leaves that adorned her empty cup. When the gypsy announced that Miss McKee would be married within a month, bear a child within a year, and die a long and agonizing death, well, what could she do but laugh? It was wartime (1942–43), and eligible bachelors were few and far between across Canada's great plains. Chalk one up for the gypsy: Myrtle met Flight Lieutenant William Andrew Anderson within two weeks of the reading, married him almost immediately (within the required month), and gave birth to his child, Roberta Joan Anderson, on November 7, 1943 (within the allotted year). Fortunately, as of this writing, Myrtle has lived a long and prosperous life with no sign of the third prediction in sight. It appears she works quite hard to take care of herself. Can you blame her?

The prophesied one was born in Fort Macleod, Alberta, and her description of her hometown to *Billboard*'s Timothy White says much about the eyes through which she views her world: "Fort Macleod was coming out of the Great Depression and into the war, so every house was weathered-out and derelict-looking with no paint on it. There had been a drought, too, so gardens were nonexistent. Some of the people who had no money for paint would try to brighten things up by stuccoing their houses with chicken feed and broken brown glass, and blue bottle glass." There she describes her earliest memory: "Above my crib as a baby was a roll-up blind. This was a poor household, and they had those kind of blinds that came in beige and dark green. This one was dark green, and it was perforated and cracked in a lot of places from frequent rolling. I can remember lying in my crib, seeing the filtered little stream of light and the fluffs of dust floating in it. I was 1½, and that's my earliest memory." The attentive youngster with a sharp eye for detail accompanied her parents to Calgary, back to the Regina area, and finally to a new house in Maidstone, where her father obtained work as the manager of a small grocery. While growing up in Maidstone, young Joan viewed the world from a window that overlooked the railroad tracks, and she would await and greet the daily train as it passed through. Years—actually decades—later, the train's engineer recalled his daily wave from the fair-haired maiden perched above the tracks. All indications suggest the Andersons were a small, happy family laboring to make ends meet in postwar western Canada.

Eventually, the family landed in North Battleford, where Mr. Anderson managed another grocery in the same chain of stores (OK Economy). Music emerged as one of the family's principal forms of recreation: Bill played trumpet in the North Battleford Kinsmen's Band, the family enjoyed a small but invaluable record collection, and a department store listening booth provided a dream station for young Joan's imagination. Mitchell told Dave DiMartino that there were five records played in heavy rotation in her house: two trumpet-based recordings for her father (Harry James and Leroy Anderson), a *Clair de Lune* record for her mom, and a couple of children's records. The real musical adventure involved the department store booth, where the youngster listened to her beloved Rachmaninoff's *Rhapsody on a Theme of Paganini* and the varied sounds of the day. Joining Rachmaninoff on Joan's hit list was French singer Edith Piaf. She described her first encounter with Piaf for Robert Hilburn in 1991: "I remember the first time I heard her. It was a recording of 'Les Trois Cloches'—'The Jimmy Brown Song'—and my hair stood on end. Her voice just thrilled my soul."

Artistic expression (e.g., drawing, painting, pressed-flower scrapbooks) and imaginative games (e.g., dressing up, role-playing) were what the kids had in North Battleford, and Joan was an active participant in her own way. She described her childhood for Jenny Boyd: "I was a painter always—I had difficulty playing with the other children in the neighborhood, just because my games they couldn't get in on. . . . Since mainly the kids were athletic . . . they were hardy, robust, physical, not very creative." She recalled the "creative people" in the town "studied classical piano or classical voice, so I had a lot of friends who were considered the singers."

Although Joan naturally aligned herself with the creative people in her town, Karen O'Brien writes of her continual efforts to join the "athletic" kids and their raucous games. In particular, she wanted to play "cowboys and Indians" with the boys, but was frustrated by her relegation to predetermined "girls' roles." In defiance, she persuaded her parents to purchase a Roy Rogers outfit that she felt would guarantee her admission to the game on her terms. She would not be denied. She refused to occupy her designated place. She did what she felt was necessary to overcome an unfair situation. She laid the foundation for her life.

Boy games aside, art was an essential part of Joan's youth. O'Brien claims she wrote her first song at age seven (titled "Robin Walk"), and her experiences with a neighbor heightened her artistic fantasies, as she related to *Maclean's* Malka Maron in 1974:

> I always had star eyes, I think, always interested in glamour. I had one very creative friend whom I played with a lot and we used to put on circuses together, and he also played brilliant piano for his age when he was a young boy. I used to dance around the room and say that I was going to be a great ballerina and he was going to be a great composer, or that he was going to be a great writer and I was going to illustrate his books. My first experience with music was at this boy's house, because he played piano and they had old instruments like auto harps lying around. It was playing his piano that made me want to have one of my own to mess with, but then, as soon as I expressed interest, they gave me lessons and that killed it completely.

Lessons would always prove difficult for the pugnacious personality who preferred individual eccentricity over systematic instruction. From the outset, Joan Anderson carried her Roy Rogers outfit wherever she was challenged by the status quo. If the rules denied entrance, those rules were tested. Her initial piano lessons offer a concrete example of this lifelong penchant for rebellion. She told Penny Valentine:

> I was constantly rapped on the knuckles at piano lessons because I'd listen to what the teacher played and I'd remember it. So I never learned to sight

read properly and she'd bust me on it. I'd fake it—like I'd read the music and it wouldn't be quite right, there was a certain amount of improvisation in it. And she'd say "those notes aren't in there." That kind of killed my interest in piano for a good 15 years or so. From the beginning I really wanted to mess around and create, find the colours the piano had buried in it. You know, I always feel like such an irresponsible creature.

Here we have the crux of Joni Mitchell's creative worldview: "Find the colors the piano had buried in it." This innocent comment captures her career as none other. Her musical life has been dedicated to that simple ambition.

Whether irresponsible or irrepressible, Joan Anderson experienced her life's greatest challenges early on as she battled poor health. Her extensive 1995 interview in *Billboard* chronicles how her appendix burst at age three, her bouts with German *and* red measles, her experiences with chickenpox *and* scarlet fever, and her recurring tonsillitis. None of these medical happenings compare to her 1953 bout with polio. The landmark *Billboard* interview captures Mitchell's recollections in sharp, characteristic detail:

I vividly remember the day I got polio. I was 9 years old, and I dressed myself that morning in pegged gray slacks, a red and white gingham blouse with a sailor collar, and a blue sweater. I looked in the mirror, and I don't know what I saw—dark circles under my eyes or a slight swelling in my face—but I said to myself, "You look like a woman today." After I got outside, I was walking along with a school friend, and at the third block I sat down on this little lawn and said, "I must have rheumatism," because I'd seen my grandmother aching and having to be lifted out of the bathtub. I complained a bit more but still went and spent the day in school. Next day I woke and my mom said, "Get up, come!" I said, "I can't." She didn't believe me and yanked me out of bed, and I collapsed. They rushed me to the St. Paul's Hospital in Saskatoon. The infectious part of the disease lasts two weeks, and it twisted my spine severely forward in a curvature called lordosis, and then back to the right in a lateral curve called scoliosis, so that I was unable to stand. One leg was impaired, but the muscles didn't atrophy, so there was no withering, thank God. I was put in the children's ward, and with Christmas rolling up it became apparent I wasn't going home. Someone sent me a coloring book with pictures of old-fashioned English carolers and the lyrics to all these Christmas carols. I had ulcers in my mouth that they'd come and swab [with] an antibacterial solution called gentian violet and they'd leave the swabs behind, so I used the swabs to color the carolers purple. And I sang the carols to get my spirits up. My mother came with a little mask on . . . and put a little Christmas tree in my room with some ornaments. The first night they allowed me to leave it lit an hour after lights out. And I said to the little tree, "I am not a cripple," and I said a prayer, some kind of pact, a barter with God for my legs, my singing.

What a story! Notice the little girl's tenacity as well as the artist's sharp attention to detail. Can *you* remember what you were wearing on *any* morning of your ninth year on this earth? Her drive. Her spirit. Her personal strength. All of these lifelong traits are rooted in this pivotal life battle with one of the most dreaded of all diseases. Sources report how the youngster endured deep massages and scalding compresses, yet she managed to fetch good from evil and paint with the swabs left behind after treatments. Her interview with Cameron Crowe discusses her principal coping mechanisms:

> I guess I really started singing when I had polio. . . . I was nine, and they put me in a polio ward over Christmas. They said I might not walk again, and that I would not be able to go home for Christmas. I wouldn't go for it. So I started to sing Christmas carols and I used to sing them real loud. When the nurse came into the room I would sing *louder*. The boy in the bed next to me, you know, used to complain. And I discovered I was a ham. That was the first time I started to sing for people.

Young Joan wisely struck a personal deal that if she could walk, she would sing. She described her pledge to Chip Stern: "I kind of made a promise to my Christmas tree, that if I could get up and walk that I would pay it back somehow. So when I got out of the hospital I joined the church choir. . . . I don't think I lasted too long in the choir, but I did learn to smoke there." Years later, she looked back on the experience and its impact on her life for Robert Hilburn: "I had a strong will. But also, being so confined, I think I developed an inner life. I'd imagine all kinds of stories and pictures and scenes in my head—just look at the ceiling and think it was a screen."

After spending her tenth birthday and Christmas in the hospital, Joan returned to North Battleford, where she joined her mother (remember, an ex-teacher) in a vigorous battle to regain her health and continue her education at home. When Joan was eleven, the family moved to Saskatoon. There her determined recovery continued, she excelled in her art classes, and, apparently, she survived her remaining schoolwork. The biographers tell us about influential teachers such as Arthur Kratzman (who instructed the youngster, "If you can paint with a brush, you can paint with words") and Henry Bonli (whose last name inspired the shift from "Joan" to "Joni" since she admired his signature on his paintings), who shaped the emerging artist in powerful ways. In high school, Anderson's passions were music, writing, and fashion. She joined a creative writing group that met after school, she painted props for school plays, she wrote a fashion column for the school newspaper, and—in an extremely clever move—she drew portraits of renowned mathematicians for her math teacher and created charts for biology classes as a way to negotiate her way through classes. She described her school years for *People*'s Michael Small:

> I was always the school artist. I did the backdrops for plays, illustrated the yearbook and the school newspaper and wrote a little column called Fads and

Fashions. I'd advise people to paste silver stars on their blue suede shoes, or I wrote that girls should wear their father's ties to school. . . . I used to lie up at night and listen to the Hit Parade under the covers. Then in the morning, I'd drag myself to school. But I couldn't see what school had to do with my adult life.

That attitude manifested in her grades. Although her writing demonstrated her creativity (she penned a poem titled "The Fishbowl," in which she portrays the horror of celebrity life for her tenth-grade teacher), her course work more than suffered. Her resourcefulness, however, enabled her development outside the classroom. She collected albums by winning dance contests (a *major* victory for a polio victim), made a Christmas card in exchange for Miles Davis records, and painted a mural for a jazz enthusiast who paid her with jazz recordings. Through it all, an industrious, resourceful, determined personality was systematically formed. Her friends referred to her as a "Good-Time Charlie" (according to a 1991 interview with David Wild), and her love of Chuck Berry–style rock and roll facilitated her intense desire to dance, as she related to Chip Stern in 1995:

> That became kind of my reason to be. And specially the jukebox at the Avenue H swimming pool and the jukebox at the CM Lunch, which was on the west side of town, where I was forbidden to go. . . . Then there was this group of guys: They were my dance partners—we used to call them Ocean's 11. Three or four of them went to New York City and came back with scruffy little goatees, and berets and striped T-shirts. . . . We used to go out in the bush and drink beer and put our cars in a circle and turn all the radios on at once and dance wildly in the stubble.

Among the revelry, she attended her first concert, featuring Ray Charles, and overcame her reluctant parents' concerns about her attire, according to a 2002 interview with Wild: "I went and bought some rhinestones, and I clipped rhinestones down the side of my slim jims, they called them, these black pants. And I borrowed my dad's jacket. My mother wasn't going to let me go out of the house dressed like that." Another memorable occasion involved a promotion for a Johnny Cash recording, as Cash recounted in Colin Escott's book on Sun Records:

> Dan Bass, the promo man for Quality Records . . . set up a Teenage Queen contest in every city. I flew into a new city each morning and did radio and television interviews. Then in the afternoon I signed records at record shops. My last promo appearance of the day, before the arrival of the Teenage Queen contestants, was to draw a name out of a box at a large department store's record counter and name the Teenage Queen and the runner up. . . . In the city of Saskatoon, the Teenage Queen died tragically, leaving the runner up to be enthroned. That runner up was already writing songs and singing. Her name was Joni Mitchell.

Though it is doubtful that she was writing, singing, or calling herself "Joni Mitchell" at that time, such an event must surely have fed those "star eyes" in an inspiring fashion.

Despite all the fun, Mitchell conveys mixed emotions about her formal education. In 1972, she told Penny Valentine: "It's like I came through the school systems completely unscathed in a way, and completely unlearned in another way. Which makes me feel terribly ignorant." On another occasion, she offered this detailed account of her schooling to Cameron Crowe:

> I was a bad student. I finally flunked out in the twelfth grade. I went back later and picked up the subjects that I lost. I do have my high-school diploma—I figured I needed that much, just in case. College was not too interesting to me. The way I saw the educational system from an early age was that it taught you what to think, not how to think. There was no liberty, really, for free thinking. You were being trained to fit into a society where free thinking was a nuisance. I liked some of my teachers very much, but I had no interest in their subjects. So I would appease them—I think they perceived that I was not a dummy, although my report card didn't look like it. I would line the math room with ink drawings and portraits of the mathematicians. I did a tree of life for my biology teacher. I was always staying late at the school, down on my knees painting something.

Notice the intense rebellion, the focused determination, and clever resourcefulness of our "Good-Time Charlie" as she pursued *her* agenda within the context of one of society's major institutional environments.

Anderson's emerging musical tastes involved jazz (Lambert, Hendricks, and Ross's *The Hottest New Sound in Jazz* was an early and permanent favorite) and, of course, Chuck Berry–style rock and roll. Interestingly, she dismissed the emerging folk trend as boring, "pseudo-intellectual nonsense" (according to O'Brien). Then, things changed, as she recounted for Sankey Phillips in 1977:

> I went to a coffeehouse to hear some jazz, because my friends were interested in jazz and I was kind of curious to find out what it was all about—I was still a rock and roller, teenybop go-to-the-dances-on-Saturday-night type. Anyway, that night there was no jazz, there was this terrible folk singer. I didn't enjoy it at all, but I kept going down there. . . . And I found there were some things I liked. I liked a group that was very Kingston Trio-ish; they were local, and they were very amusing—it was really funny to hear comedy in music. I wanted the leader to teach me how to play the guitar, but he wouldn't, so I went out and bought myself a ukulele because my mother thought that guitar . . . she thought that guitar music was sort of associated with country and western, which was sort of hillbillyish—so she said "No guitar!"

Despite her mother's protestations, her interest was piqued, the introverted portion of her personality revealed itself, and the aspiring artist discovered yet another avenue for her expressive needs.

While saving money for college, Joni Anderson modeled, worked as a waitress, and eventually found herself on stage at the Louis Riel coffeehouse in Saskatoon with her baritone ukulele. She taught herself to play guitar thanks to a Pete Seeger instructional record—which she no doubt played while wearing her Roy Rogers outfit and, once again, denied the boys their chauvinistic prerogatives. As she mastered the instrument, she encountered difficulties with her left hand as the result of her polio. Consequently, she developed an unconventional method of playing that relied on a host of unique tunings that would one day be her sonic trademark.

With these events, Anderson walked off the dance floor, turned increasingly introspective, and embraced folk music and its emerging lifestyles. While performing at a party, she was noticed by people who worked for a television station in northern Saskatchewan (Prince Albert's CKBI-TV); they promptly enlisted the beautiful, poised blonde to perform on a half-hour variety program. Anderson agreed, and played six songs on her ukulele. As the saying goes, with that, a star was born.

Anderson ventured to Calgary and the Alberta College of Art in the fall of 1963. There, predictably, she rebelled against her teachers' methods of instruction, performed in coffeehouses, and dated fellow art student Brad MacMath. The couple left Calgary in the summer of 1964 and traveled to Toronto. During the journey, O'Brien reports, Anderson wrote her second first song ("Day After Day"), attended an annual folk festival (the Mariposa Folk Festival), and obtained a sales job in the women's wear department at Sears. The bohemian couple lived a communal lifestyle, sharing living quarters where and when they could. The $160 musicians' union dues required to work the Toronto folk circuit was a huge—seemingly insurmountable—burden and prohibited Anderson from playing the city's more profitable venues. Therefore, she obtained scab work where she could—typically, for scab wages. MacMath apparently tired of the hippie lifestyle and left a pregnant Anderson to struggle in Toronto. Kelly Dale Anderson was born on February 19, 1965, and her mother faced the possibility of raising the child in less than ideal conditions. Since her family and friends back home knew nothing of the pregnancy, Anderson dealt with her situation to the best of her ability. In June 1965, she met a 29-year-old American folk singer from Detroit and, after a 36-hour courtship, Charles Mitchell proposed to the young mother. Implicit in their arrangement was the understanding that Kelly—currently in the care of temporary foster parents—would join the couple once they settled in Detroit. Married and living in Detroit, the new Joni Mitchell quickly discovered that her new husband had no intention of raising Kelly, a situation that forced Mrs. Mitchell to allow her daughter to be permanently adopted. Contrary to Charles Mitchell's comments or uninformed gossip, Joni Mitchell did *not* abandon her daughter for her career. Her concerns for her child's well-being dictated the decision—

a pivotal life happening that would haunt her for the next 30 years. She stated her case for Edna Gundersen:

> I was very stoic about it. I blocked out the day that I signed the papers. I must have been quasi-hysterical. It says in the file that it was "very difficult for mother emotionally." I don't even remember. I was made to feel ashamed, but I don't have any guilt about that loss and the ugly gantlet of opinion you first walk through. I couldn't find another way. I had no money to put a roof over my head or feed myself, let alone buy diapers, and no one to ask help from. And I was wildly independent. I married [folk singer] Chuck Mitchell, and he said he didn't want to raise another person's child, so I had to give her up.

Few life events compare with such an experience. Mitchell's agony would continuously surface in her work.

Young Kelly was not the only birth from early 1965; Mitchell's songwriting emerged along with the infant. In the video *Woman of Heart and Mind*, Mitchell reports Kelly's birth inspired her pen: "I started to develop my own private world, and also because I was disturbed." After hearing Bob Dylan's "Positively 4th Street" later that year, the enterprising artist placed another iron in her creative fire. In the *Woman* video she explains that she always loved the "crooner era" but felt the words were too simple. She preferred writing with more "poetic description"; therefore, she was attracted to the "more storytelling quality of Dylan's work." She continues: "Bob Dylan inspired me with the idea of personal narrative . . . he would speak as if to one person in a song . . . such a personal, strong statement. . . . His influence was to personalize my work." So, once she heard "4th Street," she acknowledged "that was the key" that "opens all the doors . . . we can write about anything." Her response was not to copy Dylan, but to use his technique to her own ends: "The thing that I was reluctant to let go of was the melodic, harmonic sense. Whereas Dylan . . . you could speak in paragraphs, but it was for the sacrifice of the music. You get the plateaus upon which to speak. So it was my job to distill a hybrid that allowed for a certain amount of melodic movement and harmonic movement but with a certain amount of plateaus in order to make the longer statement . . . to say more."

While her writing flourished, the Mitchells performed around the Midwest, Canada, and the American east coast. New compositions such as "Urge for Going" and "The Circle Game" appeared on stage and during radio interviews as the musical world took notice of a formidable talent with impressive looks. By late 1966, O'Brien tells us, Mitchell's "days as a folkie interpreter were over" as she focused on her songwriting and performed her original compositions before a more than receptive audience. Performers such as Tom Rush, Buffy Sainte-Marie, Ian and Sylvia, Dave Van Ronk, Canadian country singer George Hamilton IV, and English folk-rock act Fairport Convention performed and recorded Joni Mitchell songs. By all accounts, Mitchell's Canadian roots fed her pen, as she told *Sounds*: "The land has a rich melancholy about it. Not in the summer because it's usually very clear, but in the spring and winter it's very brooding and it's conducive to a certain kind of thinking." In a 1966 article by the hometown Saskatoon paper, an unnamed reporter elaborates on that thesis:

> Much of Joni's material was inspired by her impressions of life on the Prairies. The haunting lyrics of "Urge for Going", she explained, stemmed from the effect the bitter western winter has on prairie residents, and their wish to escape the cold. Another song, "What Will You Give Me", describes in nostalgic terms the longing of a prairie native who is far away from home, in a moment of regret. The Mitchells both agreed Saskatoon and the Prairies contained much that was esthetically beautiful, and Joni said she hopes to continue writing songs based on her Saskatchewan background, and her love of the flat western landscape.

(On other occasions, Mitchell claimed "Urge" chronicles the dying folk music scene.) As the writing prospered, Charles Mitchell offered his greatest contribution to his wife's life when he encouraged her to form her own publishing company to protect her work. It was a decision that would guarantee Joni Mitchell's financial security.

The Mitchells ended their marriage in early 1967 and Joni relocated to the Chelsea area of New York City. It was a lonely, trying time hawking her wares on the road, as she recalled for the *Los Angeles Times*:

> It was a lonely job. You'd go into a town and have nothing to do except the shows and then you'd be on the road again, but it was good in a way because it gave me the time to write. I learned the purpose of melancholy too . . . that grieving and sorrow are highly underrated in this culture. In a 9 to 5 job, you are not allowed to really savor your emotions, but on your own, you have time to live with them, and I was on my own. I wrote a lot of the songs that appeared on the first three albums during that time.

Mitchell resisted securing a manager for some time, but her arrival in the Big Apple prompted her to consider Bob Dylan's manager, Albert Grossman, as a possible choice. When that failed to materialize, Mitchell eventually turned to Elliot Roberts for management. Roberts—an enterprising manager of comic acts—was associated with music entrepreneur David Geffen. In 1974, Roberts offered his first impression of his new client for the aforementioned *Time* cover story: "She was a jumble of creative clutter with a guitar case full of napkins, road maps and scraps of paper all covered with lyrics." Though Mitchell had strong reservations about securing the services of "Mr. Ten Percent" due to her ever-present feelings of rebellious, self-supporting determination, she relented and hired the fun-loving Roberts. Mitchell needed a recording contract, and Roberts approached a number of

New York–based record labels in pursuit of an arrangement that granted complete creative control to his client (including album cover design). *This* was a prodigious request that eventually found a home on the west coast and the Los Angeles–based Warner Brothers label. Roberts's leverage was enhanced by the number of artists recording Mitchell's songs, but it required special concessions to grant *complete* creative control to an unproven artist. Roberts told O'Brien: "That was the hard part. They were not used to anyone saying, 'It has nothing to do with the money, we need creative control.' We had a long-term goal, Joan had a long-term goal and knew how her record should sound. She hadn't learned the craft yet but she knew she was going to."

With an unusual recording contract, an enterprising and dedicated manager, and a stable of strong songs available, Joni Mitchell and rookie producer David Crosby set about the task of constructing a debut album. Mitchell met Crosby while performing in south Florida and they became personally and professionally involved; hence, when he expressed an interest in producing Mitchell's first album, his request was granted. Crosby—an accomplished musician—implemented a nondirective production strategy that allowed Mitchell free rein over the material and its arrangement. Such a plan not only appealed to an artist with strong memories of piano teachers and their strictly applied rulers, it also initiated a lifelong solo act in the recording studio. Crosby represents Mitchell's first—and last—"producer"; the determined, rebellious art student would forever bake her cake and eat it, too (there are only a few exceptions to this rule). Few artists are as strong-willed as Joni Mitchell. Although she met Henry Lewy during these original sessions and initiated a long-term relationship with the engineer, she would refrain from securing an official producer for her records. She explained her stance to Karen O'Brien:

> If you're in art school, nobody would come up and put a mark on your canvas. It is my work and be damned if anybody is going to put a mark on it. Whatever your reason to make it something else, it isn't my music and if it isn't my music, then I'm being slapped by my piano teacher again. You're going to kill my love of it and it won't go the distance. I knew what a good performance was, so in order to protect my music for the second time, I worked with just an engineer. He's like a print puller.

Future strategies aside, Crosby entered the studio with a plan. With the current folk-rock trends dominating the contemporary music scene, Crosby was determined to keep the "rock" out of Joni Mitchell's "folk," and he succeeded. While production problems plagued the project (e.g., tape hiss, poor levels), Crosby overcame them and *Joni Mitchell* or *Song to a Seagull* was issued in March 1968. The album, dedicated to Arthur Kratzman, has ten songs divided into two parts ("I Came to the City" and "Out of the City and

Down to the Seaside") and features only two musicians: Mitchell and bassist Stephen Stills. Crosby's efforts to issue a minimalist version of his client's rich talent were successful. As an aside, Mitchell claims that "20 to 30 songs" from her stage act were omitted from the album and, as she told William Ruhlmann, have never been recorded (e.g., comedic songs such as "Dr. Junk the Dentist Man"). Crosby's tenure as Mitchell's producer may have been short-lived, but his contributions to the focus achieved on her initial recording should not be minimized.

Mitchell toured vigorously in support of the record, continued to profit from the significant success other singers achieved with her songs, purchased a home in Laurel Canyon, and managed her professional affairs with the fierce determination of a polio survivor. *Melody Maker*'s Karl Dallas offers this assessment of Mitchell's writing on *Seagull*: "Talking to Joni Mitchell about her songs is rather like talking to someone you just met about the most intimate secrets of her life. Like peeping in a window on someone and then discussing with her what you have seen. Her songs are so personal." The view that Mitchell deployed an innovative "confessional" approach to songwriting quickly gained momentum.

Mitchell's self-produced second album, *Clouds*, appeared in May 1969 (and won a Grammy for Best Folk Recording); she wrote the definitive anthem for the '60s counterculture that summer (1969's "Woodstock"); performed on tour before huge (and unnerving) audiences in sprawling venues; released her third album, *Ladies of the Canyon*, in April 1970; and achieved a defining moment in songwriting history with June 1971's *Blue*. With *Blue*, Mitchell solidified her status as a confessional, autobiographical writer with the courage of her convictions unleashing an unbridled honesty. *Rolling Stone*'s Timothy Crouse captures the essence of Mitchell's work with this insightful commentary:

> More than ever, Joni risks using details that might be construed as trivial in order to paint a vivid self portrait. She refuses to mask her real face behind imagery, as her fellow autobiographers James Taylor and Cat Stevens sometimes do. In portraying herself so starkly, she has risked the ridiculous to achieve the sublime. The results, though, are seldom ridiculous; on *Blue* she has matched her popular music skills with the purity and honesty of what was once called folk music and through the blend she has given us some of the most beautiful moments in recent popular music.

Such songwriting tactics may have provided beautiful moments for the art form, but it also invited a downright dysfunctional response from audiences whose uncontrollable codependencies gradually proved problematic. The level of vicarious suffering inspired by *Blue* represented an artistic double-edged sword. Joni Mitchell—like her contemporary Pete Townshend—fell into an artistic trap in which the compelling self-revelations that fueled her writing eventually oppressed her. She dutifully searched for a remedy that would enable her to share her observations without forsaking her privacy. The "Joni Mitchell Cult," as Lynn Van Matre labeled the phenomenon, was becoming quite a burden for the idealistic, determined, and now frustrated celebrity. Honesty may not always be the best artistic policy.

Complementing the unanticipated response Mitchell received for her heartfelt revelations was the unrestrained sexism that surrounded her professional life. Her record company's use of sexist slogans to promote her work joined a downright hypocritical music press in flaunting Mitchell's gender for, at times, promotional reasons and, at others, sensational reporting. The author of "The Fishbowl" was experiencing what she prophesied in the tenth grade, and it produced yet another reason for a professional hiatus from that deceitful scene. While our polio survivor represents the quintessence of personal resolve, the commentary propagated by publications such as *Rolling Stone* not only injured an extraordinarily powerful individual, it raised *serious* questions about the publication's credibility—questions that have gone unresolved to this day.

Not surprisingly, Mitchell left Laurel Canyon for her native Canada, moving north of Vancouver to Half Moon Bay. She was simply overwhelmed by the abusive world of celebrity and in need of reorientation. She described her rationale to the *Los Angeles Times*:

> I was really disillusioned—by my own generation and where I could see it was headed. I had to go back and spend time among slithery and furry things. I just had to be away from people, had to reinvent myself, discover myself, sort out things. Inside, you have all the tendencies of the world . . . tendencies towards good, tendencies towards evil. So you have to sort it out, get over the shock that these things are in you and figure out which ones you want to try to use.

In the *Woman* video, Mitchell labels her respite an "attempt to get back to The Garden." Fortunately, her plan worked, and she recounted her moment of revitalization for a February 1987 *Musician* article:

> One day about a year after I started my retreat in Canada I went out swimming. I jumped off a rock into this dark emerald green water with yellow kelp in it and purple starfish at the bottom. It was very beautiful, and as I broke up to the surface of the water, which was black and reflective, I started laughing. Joy had just suddenly come over me, you know? And I remember that as a turning point. First feeling like a loony because I was out there laughing all by myself in this beautiful environment. . . . And then, right on top of it, was the realization that whatever my social burdens were, my inner happiness was still intact.

While frolicking in the black waters of Half Moon Bay and recovering from the hypocrisies of a convoluted industry, Mitchell wrote the bulk of the material for her fifth album, November 1972's *For the Roses*—the artist's first recording for her new label, David Geffen's Asylum Records. Mitchell traveled to Canada in search of renewal, and her plan worked. As she confides in the *Woman* video, "Depression can be the sand that makes the pearl."

Roses' pop sounds and media diatribes signaled a new direction—both sonically and lyrically—for the universally acknowledged confessional poet. That trend culminated in Mitchell's strongest-selling album, 1974's *Court and Spark*. *Court* represents Mitchell's first recording with a full band (the fusion jazz group the L.A. Express) as well as her shift toward jazz. The album's success extends beyond its sales or its four Grammy nominations in that it introduced a more comfortable artist, one free of her perceived burdens and relishing the company of musicians capable of following her enigmatic musical urges. She discussed the state-of-Joni with *Maclean's*:

> Well, I really don't feel I've scratched the surface of my music. I'm not all that confident about my words. Thematically I think that I'm running out of things which I feel are important enough to describe verbally. I really think that as you get older life's experience becomes more; I begin to see the paradoxes resolved. It's almost like most things that I would once dwell on and explore for an hour, I would shrug my shoulders to now. In your twenties things are still profound and being uncovered. However, I think there's a way to keep that alive if you don't start putting up too many blocks. I feel that my music will continue to grow . . . and I also continue to draw, and that also is in a stage of growth, it hasn't stagnated yet. And I hope to bring all these things together. . . . There's a lot of things I'd like to do, so I still feel young as an artist. I don't feel like my best work is behind me. I feel as if it's still in front.

Full of creative energy, honest to a fault, and inspired by her musical expansion into jazz, Mitchell followed *Court* with 1974's live double album *Miles of Aisles* (also featuring Tom Scott and the L.A. Express), in which she recast significant portions of her catalog through the jazz sensibilities that emerged with *Court*. Obviously smitten with the jazz bug that was as much a part of her musical past as her frustrations with piano lessons, Mitchell issued a series of adventurous, jazz-oriented explorations that lost any commercial ground she had gained with *Court*. November 1975's *The Hissing of Summer Lawns*, November 1976's *Hejira*, December 1977's *Don Juan's Reckless Daughter*, and June 1979's *Mingus* trade *Court and Spark*'s accessibility for expressive idiosyncrasy. Here Mitchell's muse yields blends of obscurity and poignancy through improvisational sounds that support esoteric expression—regardless of the costs. Audiences seeking life-influencing prescriptions for living were stonewalled by dense observations void of the author's—or anybody else's—blood. For most of these projects, Mitchell closed her diary and opened her book of traveling short stories and observational poetry. It was a decisively bold, rebellious, determined act that was—literally—years ahead of the "world music" surge that soon followed. In 1985, Mitchell explained her shift to jazz to *Musician*'s Bill Flanagan:

I had no choice but to go with jazz musicians—I tried to play with all of the rock bands that were the usual sections for James Taylor when we made our transition from folk to folk rock. They couldn't play my music because it's so eccentric. . . . Finally one bass player said, "Joni, you know really you should be playing with jazz musicians." People used to call my harmony weird. In context of today's pop music it's really not weird, but it was much broader polyphonic harmony than was prevalent ten, fifteen years ago. Now, much of it has been assimilated. . . . So that's when I started playing with the L.A. Express and while they could play the changes, a jazz drum kit is light compared to a rock 'n' roll kit. The two camps were so orthodox then. They didn't like each other. . . . So I had no choice but to play with the virtuosity available. Just people who could understand these little rhythm changes. Otherwise, I was going to have to play by myself.

She had other reasons as well, as these remarks to Kristine McKenna indicate: "One of the things that attracted me to the jazz world was the fact that many jazz people didn't know who I was and there was no phenomenon surrounding me there—I found that delicious. I also like the fact that the jazz world allows you to grow old gracefully, whereas pop music is completely aligned with youth." Joni Mitchell was in her creative element with this series of recordings. As we shall soon discover, the poignant participant–commentator of the '60s bohemian experiment rebounded from the abuses hurled upon her by deploying the skills she mastered during the Christmas of 1953. Instead of singing Christmas carols at the top of her lungs, she let loose the jazz demons that roamed her musical brain and, in so doing, issued a writ of defiance to the musical world. The child who quietly promised "I will not be a cripple" issued yet another proclamation to her oppressors. This period of exploratory music concludes with the live set *Shadows and Light*, released in September 1980 (a live album again punctuates an artistic phase). She looked back on her explorations in the 1985 Flanagan interview: "So I'm a person without a country now. All because I'm an eclectic, I like a lot of different kinds of music. So I went through this kind of persecution which culminated with the *Mingus* album, because when I moved to do that the jazz camp was all up in arms, considered me an *opportunist*. Little did they know that album cost me everything."

With a loss of radio play and a diminishing audience, Mitchell followed her "eclectic" period with October 1982's *Wild Things Run Fast*—a record biographer Karen O'Brien designates as the oeuvre's "Joni loves Larry" entry. In November 1982 Mitchell married bass player/producer Larry Klein, and *Wild Things* conveys the bliss that accompanies romantic engagement. With a new husband/collaborator, a revised musical strategy (stressing concrete pop over abstract jazz), and a new record label (Geffen Records), Mitchell relaxed her touring schedule after a grinding 1983 international tour. The relationship with Klein proved to be a genuine elixir.

"Joni loves Larry" enjoyed a short run; 1985's *Dog Eat Dog* turns from public proclamations of romantic rapture to public denunciations of societal issues. Enlisting the voices of popular singers such as Michael McDonald, Don Henley, and James Taylor, *Dog* spans the sonic gap between pop and fusion jazz with lyrics that attack perceived injustices in an uneven manner. Synthesizer wizard Thomas Dolby joined a production process that deployed the current technology to Mitchell's always carefully designed ends. Predictably, Dolby struggled in vain to assume the reins over the record's production, which, in turn, contributed to the project's disjointed qualities. All sources agree that *Dog Eat Dog* was one of Mitchell's more difficult endeavors. Dolby had to learn the essential lesson that nobody paints on Joni Mitchell's canvas but Joni Mitchell. Painting is not a team sport.

The topical shift signaled by *Dog* was accompanied by Elliot Roberts's departure from the Mitchell operation. Furthermore, Mitchell and Klein narrowly escaped serious injury in an automobile accident in the fall of 1985, she appeared at the Farm Aid benefit that September, and in June 1986, she performed at the Amnesty International "Conspiracy of Hope" benefit. Although she was still appearing at select charity events, Mitchell's touring diminished considerably—the remnants of polio proved prohibitive to extensive tours. Years before the "duet" recording strategy was popularized by Frank Sinatra and Tony Bennett, Mitchell advanced the trend introduced in *Dog* with March 1988's *Chalk Mark in a Rain Storm*. Musical luminaries Peter Gabriel, Don Henley, Billy Idol, Willie Nelson, and Tom Petty add their distinctive voices to world music rhythms in songs that follow *Dog*'s exploration of contemporary social issues. Nominated for a Grammy for Best Female Pop Vocal, the album extended Mitchell's role as a social commentator.

After performing "Goodbye Blue Sky" for Roger Waters's June 21, 1990, production of *The Wall* in Berlin, Mitchell returned to her personal portrait songwriting method with February 1991's *Night Ride Home* and October 1994's *Turbulent Indigo*. These blends of autobiography and focused commentary explore youthful memories, personal experiences, and candid observations through friendly, accessible musical structures that heighten the artist's lyrical reflections. *Indigo*—nominated for two Grammy Awards (Best Pop Album and Artwork)—also involved Mitchell's departure from David Geffen's operation and her return to Warner Brothers' Reprise label. Placing the icing on this record's transitional cake, she divorced Larry Klein just before the *Indigo* sessions began (though they continued to record the album together!).

In 1996, Mitchell presented the musical world her first "greatest hits" package; the mischievously arranged *Hits* and *Misses* dual release. The strategy involved an account of Mitchell's widely acknowledged "hits" as well as a separately packaged presentation of *her* carefully selected not-so-hits. The songs' arrangement, the cover art—virtually everything about the project—communicated the everlasting impact of her piano teacher's ruler as Mitchell rebuked the system in favor of her artistic agenda (if only she had worn her Roy Rogers outfit on the cover). Notice, however, that the auteur did not force her "misses" on her audience, only on her *new* record company.

Spring 1997 was a highly publicized, emotional time for Joni Mitchell as she was reunited with her daughter after over 30 years of separation. Kilauren Andrea Christy Gibb used the sketchy information provided by Canadian authorities in conjunction with specific knowledge obtained from friends of friends to determine that her birth mother was, in fact, a famous folksinger from Saskatoon. Several attempts at contacting the auteur's management yielded a phone message from a stunned, elated Mitchell who announced to *Maclean's* Brian Johnson: "I've had pain and joy in my life, but nothing like this. It's an unparalleled emotional feeling." Kilauren and her young son traveled to Los Angeles and a 30-year void was filled, as Mitchell told James Riginato: "Up until then [the reunion], I didn't have my feet on the ground. There was a big hole in me. You can't believe the emotional complexity of what I went through." The story received much publicity and those accounts pointed the need for serious revisions in the adoption policies of the United States and Canada.

A revitalized Joni Mitchell issued her last album of original material in 1998 with *Taming the Tiger*. *Tiger*'s blend of autobiography and societal/music industry commentary represents a compelling capstone to a career dedicated to a painfully honest exploration of those topics. Her difficulties with the music business are all too evident on this record. From this, one may conclude that Joni Mitchell's uncompromising battles with the industry that markets her art have taken their toll. *Taming the Tiger* unveils one unhappy camper. In any event, Mitchell toured in support of *Tiger* with a fascinating triple bill involving Van Morrison and Bob Dylan. She also recorded the video *Joni Mitchell: Painting with Words and Music*, in 1998. And she appeared at 1998's "Day in the Garden" festival on Max Yasgur's fabled farm—unlike the original event when her management held her in New York in order to appear on *The Dick Cavett Show* that Monday.

The year 2000 witnessed Mitchell's release of a series of torch standards (mixed with two of her compositions) arranged to chronicle a relationship's life cycle. The marvelously orchestrated *Both Sides Now* features a 70-piece orchestra as it reveals Mitchell's vast musical knowledge, her commitment to the torch genre, and her reluctance to pen new material. She explained the latter point to Robert Hilburn and the *Los Angeles Times*:

> My music is drawn from my [feelings] and I just didn't want to be a social commentator at this time. I feel these are difficult times and we all need to

develop some sort of . . . discipline or soul nourishment or strength to deal with all the problems facing the world, problems that are coming to a head in every department. Even I wouldn't want to hear an album of that stuff right now. I just feel my point of view is too realistic and reality is too bleak.

O'Brien reports *Both Sides* (winner of two Grammy Awards) was the first installment of an orchestral trilogy involving 2002's *Travelogue* and, eventually, a collection of traditional Christmas songs that would, indeed, take Mitchell's singing career full circle. Obviously, none of the project contains new material. Still, *Travelogue*, released in November 2002, is an impressive, richly orchestrated treatment of the Mitchell canon that heightens the dramatic impact of the original compositions while the auteur's seasoned voice superimposes an aura of reflection on the proceedings. In particular, the songs' contributions to the torch tradition are on display in these theatrical arrangements that occasionally transform the original work into a more mature reading.

After *Travelogue*'s release, Mitchell boldly announced to James Riginato: "These are my last two records. I'm quitting after this, because the business has made itself so repugnant to me." The widely reported outburst prompted a disclaimer from the angry auteur that appeared in—of all places—the *Toronto Star*:

I don't want songs to be disposable. Instead of being swayed to demographic and marketing procedures, it has to mean something. Music is too calculated now. It's good for aerobics, but it isn't moving. . . . The artist's job is to sit on the sidelines. We're supposed to be outcasts. An artist is not a politician. We have to be non-partisan, skeptical. . . . I threatened to quit because I was pissed off, and with good reason. I don't think I can quit, but in order to write again, there's going to have to be a real shift in me. Where that will come from, I don't know.

While it is trite to say that only time will reveal if Joni Mitchell will discover the personal "shift" that enables her pen, it is safe to say that her career is so full of misunderstanding, mislabeling, and misinterpretation that such a revitalization may be quite doubtful. The incongruities between Mitchell's agenda and her industry's program are so pronounced that they appear insurmountable. Mitchell told Kristine McKenna in 1988: "I'm a composer, not a pop star that can be decorated into fashion. . . . I've come to accept that I must write what I feel when I feel it and can only do what is given to me." But that is not how her industry perceives her. Her compositional explorations have fallen upon deaf industrial ears; her experiments have yielded marginal results for the money changers and, therefore, receive minimal encouragement—even though they pioneered a musical path that has proven to be extremely profitable. Does Mitchell deny this? Absolutely not. As these 1991 remarks to David Wild indicate, she fully understands what has transpired:

> I paid a big price for doing what I've done. I started working in a genre that was neither this nor that. People didn't know where I fit in anymore, so they didn't play me at all. And so I disappeared. I lost my ability to broadcast, my public access. It was worth it. I would do it all over again in a minute for the musical education. But, of *course*, it hurt. Your records are like your kids. And you want to say, "Don't bloody my baby's nose when I send him to school, because he's a *nice* kid. You just don't *understand* him. He's a little different, but if you try, you'll like him."

At that point in time, Mitchell remained cautiously optimistic about her creative future: "Well, the thing is, I *never* wanted to turn into a human jukebox. I haven't used all of my ideas yet. There's a possibility that I can continue to invent new music up into my eighties—like a legitimate composer. But I'm working in a pop field, and whether they're going to allow an older woman to do that is an open question. It requires a loyal, interested audience who believes in my talent." We may only hope Mitchell's octogenarian ambitions are fruitful.

Regrettably, one pivotal consideration in Mitchell's artistic future involves her health. The wear and tear of her youth's physical battles have left conditions that threaten her vitality. She explained her predicament to Janice Dunn in 1994: "I have post-polio syndrome, which is like multiple sclerosis. Victoria Williams and I were comparing notes, and the two diseases are very similar. It's a deterioration of the nervous system. We're still mobile, but depending on the rate of deterioration, the muscles seize up and just don't work. So it's a magical mystery tour—you don't know what lies ahead of you." In 1995, she discussed her health with *Vogue* and, once again, demonstrated the institutional rebellion that fueled her creative career:

> Basically, what the AMA says is "Lie down and die." But over there in mystery land where I've chosen my medical aid, there's hope. I'm in the hands of two kinds of occult types who give me energy transfusions by pointing their fingers at me. I've got this Chinese guy who's trying to address my DNA and tell it that nothing ever happened. Well, maybe he can do it. I give him faith, because faith is luminous. . . . The polio survivor is a stubborn creature. I'm in good spirits, and high spirits is how I beat it before.

Evidence of that last point appears in these colorful comments to Iain Blair in 1988: "I'll be one of those frail people that lives to be 102, full of complaints and poking you with a cane. I'm actually looking forward to that, and I already have a cane collection. As soon as I go lame, which is inevitable, I'm gonna start swinging it at people."

Something tells me that that last remark is yet another potent prophecy. A life filled with brutal illness, righteous rebellion, inspired determination, frustrated celebrity, and bitter indignation has yielded art that is by turns inspiring, exhausting, exhilarating, depressing, pioneering, and self-defeating. As artists of the '60s enter their sixties, the industry that transformed the 1960s' youthful declarations of institutional freedom and interpersonal responsibility into financial empires now wrestles with artists offering seasoned observations on timeless issues in a less profitable market. The industry has failed its artists, and the bitterness that flows from that failure consumes more than Joni Mitchell's muse—it threatens an entire generation's creativity. Mitchell's outspoken commentary follows her musical impulse in that she once again pioneers a rebellious response to her professional environment. Where does this resolve come from? What forces could see her through life-threatening illness, personal betrayal, audience abandonment, and industrial sexism? *That* is our next topic.

CHAPTER 2

The Impulse

The artistic philosophy that guides Joni Mitchell's work is a coherent, conscious, and concentrated manifestation of the creative impulse that motivates and sustains her career. The creative influences from her youth complement a natural inclination toward intense, probing expressions to render a consistent approach to the songwriting process. Correspondingly, her rebellious, determined, and decidedly idiosyncratic attitude toward commercial music also reflects that creative imperative and its professional resolve. Mitchell's philosophy of song, her perceived relationship with her audience, and the compositional process that flows from those starting points work in a creative harmony that is as inspiring for our auteur as it can be frustrating for the industry that supports her. Mitchell's impulses yield creative imperatives that take her far and wide in their intuitive adventures—often into uncharted or underdeveloped areas of the musical world. Her approach is as distinctive as her commitment is unshakable; as industry executive Joe Smith said of his charge: "You don't tell Joni Mitchell what to do." The following pages reveal that while no one may tell Mitchell "what" to do, her creative impulse deploys a standard repertoire of songwriting techniques that respond to a guiding philosophy on a remarkably consistent basis. As usual, there is method to the auteur's madness.

We begin with definitions. One fact is absolutely certain: Joni Mitchell relishes the concept of "art." In 1979, she told *Rolling Stone*: "Some people get nervous about that word. Art. They think it's a pretentious word from the giddyap. To me, words are only symbols, and the word *art* has never lost its vitality. It still has meaning to me. Love lost its meaning to me. God lost its meaning to me. But art never lost its meaning. I always knew what I meant by art." She conveys that understanding via precise—and prescriptive—

commentary about artists and their labors. Although she joked with Bill Flanagan that "writers are a cruel lot . . . they just raid life," those raids serve specific functions in the idealistic auteur's mind. On one occasion, she told Robert Hilburn that an artist "should be an antenna for the culture," while on another, she related to Bell and Sexton: "The introspective artist is like a canary in a coal mine in that they are the first to feel things. If they are worth a salt, they should turn a jaundiced eye toward society and look for a vaccine. That's the difference between artists and stars. Stars are only concerned with twinkling." This notion of art's social responsibilities is the foundation upon which Mitchell's creative ambitions rest, as she discussed in detail with Jenny Boyd:

> On a spiritual or a human level, I have felt that it was perhaps my role on occasion to pass on anything I learned that was helpful to me on the route to fulfillment or happy life [even if what she must share is a negative self disclosure, she must share]. . . . By giving the listener an opportunity then to either identify, in which case if he sees that in himself he'll be richer for it, or if he doesn't have the courage to do that or the ability, then he can always say, "That's what she is." So I feel that the best of me and the most illuminating things I discover should go into the work. I feel a social responsibility to that; I think I know my role. I'm a witness. I'm to document my experiences in one way or another.

As our witness pursues her role and its perceived responsibilities, she shapes her work with certain guiding principles in mind. First, as her 1991 interview with David Wild indicates, the work must be "genderless": "For a while it was assumed that I was writing *women's* songs. Then men began to notice that they saw themselves in the songs, too. A good piece of art should be androgynous. I'm not a feminist. That's too divisional for me." Next, it should aspire to a holistic perspective that conveys a balanced sentiment, as she explained to *Musician* in 1988: "A work of art should have something for the intellect; should certainly contain something for feeling people; it should contain some kind of brief clear insight . . . and . . . a certain attention to sensual detail in the lyric."

A genderless, balanced work of art pursues specific objectives that not only invoke her guiding artistic philosophy but also coordinate the mechanical procedures that represent her compositional process. Our discussion of Mitchell's creative objectives begins with her pragmatic views regarding artistic innovation. Her remarks to Cameron Crowe are unequivocal: "Here's the thing. . . . You have two options. You can stay the same and protect the formula that gave you your initial success. They're going to crucify you for staying the same. If you change, they're going to crucify you for changing. But staying the same is boring. And change is interesting. So of the two options . . . I'd rather be crucified for changing." Almost ten years later, she cast the same sentiment in simpler terms for *Musician*: "I'm just a fresh-ness freak. I'm never bored because I'm always searching for something fresh." Such aspirations seem so simple on the surface. What artist would not seek to enliven his or her work with "fresh" approaches to that craft? Why would innovation be feared or shunned?

Mitchell is precise on this matter: The fear of failure is perhaps the most debilitating phenomenon that an artist may face. She explained this crucial point to Jenny Boyd:

> You have to able to go out on a limb. What keeps a lot of people from being creative is the fear of failure. In creativity, the accidents and the mistakes and the coincidences—that's what keeps some people from being creative. They're afraid to take chances. They might even be considered creative by some people, but at best they're just copycats. They hear that, they like it, they'll make something like it, they can do that. But to innovate, you have to have a certain kind of fearlessness. I think it helps if at an early age you got used to being shunned and you survived that. If you had to fight some things in your childhood, you now can stand alone.

Our polio survivor expanded her point in these remarks to Chip Stern:

> I think it's very important to teach people to take the risk, and view failure as one step towards success. You should not be afraid to fail, especially if you want something fresh. Say you have five solutions to a problem, and all of them are commonplace. Well, throw it into randomness. Often, out of the chaos, come these great juxtapositions. I do it with film, I do it by twiddling the strings into a different tuning—I throw it open to the cosmos. Then when you discover something that has an element of divine intervention, it's like a blessing—and it's real exciting. And it also restores your faith in the greater ether. It draws you into a state where synchronicity can come in.

This sincere belief in a controlling synchronicity is tied directly to the social responsibility clause of her guiding artistic philosophy. That Mitchell fear-lessly pursues a creative karma that opens the door to artistic innovation is certain. Strive for androgynous, balanced, socially responsible art in a brave but assured fashion, and success—creative success—will reveal it-self to you. You may have to fight for it, but if you believe, you may suc-ceed. Evidence of this perspective exists in Mitchell's interview with Iain Blair in which she discusses how *she* evaluates *her* work: "I don't . . . see some records as being better or worse than others. I just see them as a natural fluid progression in my relentless pursuit of perfection, and it's more a case of correcting what I feel are my mistakes, not necessarily what was criti-cized by the press." The formula is straightforward: To do fresh, innovative things in a socially responsible, balanced way, one must dare to pioneer. Courage and personal integrity enable a progressive, innovative "pursuit of perfection"—a perfection that has nothing to do with the music industry's commercial objectives.

We should pause here and remember that Mitchell's art involves more than songwriting. In fact, as we shall discover, she is, first and foremost, a *painter*. Karen O'Brien cites Mitchell's view on the distinction between her writing and her painting: "The difference is I write my frustration and I paint my joy." Elsewhere, she told Vic Garbarini: "If I experience something, it will make a better painting than it will a song. For instance, about a month ago I finished driving across the prairie, where I had grown up. When I got back, I started painting enormous collagelike landscapes of the memory of that vastness. Then I thought, 'Ah, this could be an album cover. I better write a song called 'Prairie Roads'!'" In all cases, her personal ambition remains constant, as these comments to Penny Valentine indicate: "Whatever I've made—whether it's a painting, a song, or even a sweater—it changes my mood. I'm pleased with myself that I've made something." For Joni Mitchell, that pleasure is increased if that "something" is innovative, balanced, unifying, and responsible.

The creative influences that shaped Mitchell's natural gifts echo these sentiments. First, of course, are her public school teachers, Arthur Kratzman and Henry Bonli. The former inspired Mitchell to paint with words, while the latter encouraged her to paint, period. To reinforce her natural rebellion and her hard-won individualism, Mitchell looked to "monsters" who were "restless," as she explained to David Wild: "Most of my heroes are monsters, unfortunately, and they are men. Separating their personalities from their art, Miles Davis and Picasso have always been my major heroes because we have this one thing in common: They were restless. I don't know any women role models for that." In 1994, she said to Janice Dunn: "I'll tell you what's knocked my socks off: Edith Piaf, Billie Holiday, Miles Davis, Pablo Picasso, Chuck Berry." Annie Ross of Lambert, Hendricks, and Ross (in particular, *The Hottest New Sound in Jazz* album) inspired Mitchell to the point where she covered Ross's "Twisted" in her landmark 1974 work, *Court and Spark*.

With regard to Mitchell's writing, she cites two major influences. She described the first to Barney Hoskyns: "I'm influenced by Shakespeare, not so much by the reading of him as by the idea that the language should be trippingly on the tongue, and also by the concept of the dark soliloquy, with a lot of human meat on it. Obviously it has to be more economical and direct, and that's Dylan's influence on me." Bob Dylan may be *the* major influence on Joni Mitchell's work. When Cameron Crowe inquired about the confluence of influences that shaped her career, Mitchell responded:

> It was a hobby that mushroomed. I was grateful to make one record. All I knew was, whatever it was that I felt was the weak link in the previous project gave me my inspiration for the next one. I wrote poetry and I painted all my life. I

always wanted to play music and dabbled with it, but I never thought of putting them all together. It never occurred to me. It wasn't until Dylan began to write poetic songs that it occurred to me you could actually *sing* those poems.

For Mitchell, as we observed in our biography section, Dylan's "Positively 4th Street" introduced anger into the songwriting formula in a fashion that motivated her to take her personal poetry and share it. Although the artistic philosophy that supports Dylan's work in no way resembles Mitchell's nurturing perspective, his pioneering response to his creative situation most certainly fueled Mitchell's emerging quest.

Turning to Mitchell's concept of "song" and its specific requirements, we immediately notice a direct reiteration of her artistic philosophy. First, we should understand that the auteur is "obsessed with pushing the parameters of what entails a pop song" (she is, again, fearless) and that her intuitive drive is unashamedly curious ("I don't know where I'm going. I never do."). Flowing from that starting point is her perceived role in the musical world. She told Divina Infusino: "I'm not a pop star. The role of pop stars is to present themselves as larger than life, more desirable than anyone. Pop is an illusionary world. They don't present their human foibles. That's the realm of art and literature. I'm an artist working in a pop arena." As she functions as an artist in the pop arena, she maintains a clear image of her vocation, reiterating the witness role to Alan Jackson ("My job as I see it is to be a witness. I am a witness to my times."). But our witness offers not raw testimony while she pushes the parameters of pop songs. She discussed her position in Bill Flanagan's book on songwriting:

> In my job I have the luxury of creating a soliloquy that I think is valuable at the time. So out of the nonsense that pours from my pen, I have to do my own censorship based on what I want to put into the world. What do I think is nurturing, what do I think is valuable. . . . Obviously not all of what a person is, feels, thinks is *worthy* of putting in a song. You don't have to display your asshole side anymore than you have to limit yourself to only heroic roles. I guess the best of it would be to chronicle as much as possible the heroic parts of your thinking as well as your frailties, so you give a balanced picture. That's what makes a good part in any art form. Otherwise it becomes caricature.

Notice the consistency of her commentary and its insistence on a nurturing soliloquy—perhaps even a *dark* soliloquy—which presents a *balanced* picture that avoids mockery. Essential to that process, that interview reports, is a sharp eye toward editing: "Writing can be a focusing exercise, to cut through your own layers. . . . You get to second guess, to get clear of yourself, to get closer to what you really mean . . . in songs you can get as close as possible to the point where there's less room for misinterpretation. But no matter how clear you get it, it's always going to be reinterpreted as people bring their own life experience to it."

Subsequently, as our nurturing narrator sharpens her views in a socially responsible manner, she is consciously aware that audiences will do with her balanced picture what they will. Here is where Mitchell's views gain in complexity as she entertains the precarious relationship between a song's author, its singer, and its audience. She communicated her stance to *Musician*'s Matt Resnicoff. When Resnicoff inquired what she meant by a particular project, Mitchell fired back:

> The people who will enjoy the record won't think about what *I meant*; they'll hold it up and it'll be like a mirror. Any time a singer sings—any singer in the *world*—they're acting. And sometimes in the course of performance something strikes against the actor's life, and it becomes vital. But art is artifice no matter how much of your life you put in. . . . Every time you sing it you don't relive it. An old song can die on you. The point is, do *you* see yourself in it? Does the mirror show you screwing up, and perhaps set you on a course to changing that? Or do you see another person suffering like you did and it brings a *comfort* to your sorrow?

Mitchell expanded her views on "method acting" and its relationship to singers and authors in these remarks to the *Boston Globe*'s Matthew Gilbert:

> It makes no difference if it's you or not. It's life. You can play any character with vitality. Whether you take your libretto from someone else's experience or from your own, you take it because you understand it. Because you've been through it. . . . When Nat King Cole used to sing, they didn't think, "Oh, that's Nat singing about himself." Something terrible has happened between the song and the audience since those days. Too much attention has been given to the artist, and not enough to the song.

These comments take us to one of the more intriguing aspects of Joni Mitchell's career and her relationship with her perceived audience. To be sure, if a song is designed to nurture the listener in some fashion, the author must maintain some mental construction of the intended audience. With notions of social responsibility and emotional nourishment guiding her pen, how does the auteur relate to her audience? Initially, she enjoyed performing before small club audiences. That changed. She told Steve Pond: "The thing that made my early work easy for people is that they could see themselves in the songs. . . . But people were getting obsessed with the state of my psychology, so I thought if I removed the *I*, it'd make my poetry more accessible. It had the opposite effect. They needed me to be their safety valve, and when I took the *I* out, they thought I was getting haughty." Now this has all the makings of a serious dilemma for a socially conscious artist attempting to create nurturing, balanced work for her audience. The more they idolized her, the more she revealed. When that grew too taxing and she shifted tactics from the experiential "I" to the reportorial "you," she perceived a backlash, even though her noble creative objectives remained constant. Crowd Joan Anderson in such a fashion and prepare yourself for a serious dose of rebellion, as these comments to *Vogue* suggest: "People like me to suffer, to bleed for them. That's how I entered the arena, and that's how people want me to remain. But I can't pander to public opinion." Over time, Mitchell discovered a personal compromise regarding her relationship with her perceived audience; nevertheless, this situation presented a serious dilemma for quite some time. Had Mitchell not actively massaged the social responsibility clause of her artistic philosophy, she would never have had to endure such scrutiny. But she did, so she did.

When we turn to Mitchell's compositional process and the means through which she articulates her balanced, nurturing expressions, we quickly return to the fact that the auteur is a painter. All of her creative strategies flow from that spring. Consequently, she uses ensemble methods to build her musical work. That is, she collects a number of intuitive leaps on a given topic and then systematically arranges their articulation. Her compositional strategy is a remarkable blend of spontaneous intuition and deliberate arrangement. Our auteur is more than precise in her discussion of this process. First, as she related to Leonard Feather, the process is predicated on inspiration, not craft: "See, I can only work from inspiration. I have a certain amount of craft, granted, but I cannot work only from craft. A piece that is merely craft doesn't mean anything to me. It has to be inspired." At the heart of that inspiration are the artist's intuitive powers, as this 1983 *Musician* interview reveals: "I work from intuition, so I'm always flying blind and looking to be thrilled. Waiting for the magic to happen. I think it's easier to recognize the truly spectacular from an intuitive position than from your intellect, which is linear, dealing only with knowledge of the past projected into the future." Later, she added: "Intellect comes in paragraphs, ya-da-ya-da-ya-da, and intuition comes ZAP!, like a bolt of lightning. It comes as a pill, and then has to be translated from an impulse into language by the intellect." When the intuitive impulse is "translated" by the "intellect," it undergoes the various tests posed by Mitchell's artistic philosophy: Is the subsequent language balanced, nurturing, and useful?

Once the process of assembling these lyrical and sonic intuitions begins, the painter emerges. She described her method to Feather: "I approach it very paintingly, metaphorically . . . I see music very graphically in my head—in my own graph, not in the existing systemized graph—and I, in a way, analyze it or interpret it, or evaluate it in terms of a visual abstraction inside my mind's eye." Most of the time, the words lead the way, as she told John Ephland: "I am first responsible to my words." On other occasions, the melody may arrive first and she appropriates words within that sonic framework. In all cases, it is a process of systematic assembly. She explained to

Michael Small: "Writing a song is like doing a crossword puzzle. Though you can't get too literary, I do push vocabulary a little bit. It's a gift when the words come."

Later I shall discuss Mitchell's studio work in more detail, but at this point notice the consistent application of her guiding artistic philosophy, its clear-cut definitions of song, and the striking blend of intuitive pragmatism that controls the compositional process. While intuition may "ZAP!" its way into Mitchell's consciousness at any moment, she may carry that inspiration around for an extended period, waiting for the proper vehicle to unpack the expression, as she conveyed to *Vanity Fair*: "There are images I carry for a long time before I find the artistic receptacle, the proper scenario to let them into." Her interview with Sankey Phillips used the song "Urge for Going" as an example of her approach. She reported that she came up with the song title, and then:

> I forgot about the line, and then one day I was cleaning out my guitar case which is usually full of scrap songs . . . and I came across that piece of paper. I used to clean the case out every so often, and read all the notes over—and I would sometimes find something where I couldn't even remember what the original thought was . . . but the line would stir up a whole fresh idea, completely new.

Originally, "Urge" represented an obituary for the folk music scene until time passed, the seasons changed, she wanted to escape the cold weather, and the song came to embrace that.

With such a dynamic inventive process controlling the compositional effort, Mitchell refrains from bringing demo recordings to the studio to guide the production process. She explained to Daniel Levitin: "In a sense I never make demos because the demos are always incorporated into the final piece. It varies from project to project, but for many albums, I would lay down my voice and piano, or voice and guitar. That's my sketch. From that I know where the 'height' has to come in, and where the 'depth' has to come in. I imagine my cast of characters, my guest performers, and I add them last." (Here we clearly see the painter at work.) Mitchell's interview with Jeffrey Rodgers precisely demonstrates the ensemble qualities of the auteur's metaphorical method of composition:

> Sometimes the words come first, and then it's easier, because you know exactly what melodic inflection is needed. Given the melody first, you can say, for instance, "OK, in the A section, I can get away with narrative, descriptive. In the B, I can only speak directly, because of the way the chords are moving. I have to make a direct statement. And in the C section, the chords are so sincere and heartrending that what I say has to be kind of profound, even to myself." Theatrically speaking, the scene is scored—now you have to put in the dialogue . . . even though I may have written the text symmetrically verse

to verse to verse, in terms of syncopation I'll sing a slightly different melody to make the emphasis fall on the correct word in the sentence, as you would in spoken English.

Should this process of assembly break down and Mitchell's intuitions fail to connect, no worries—the painter has a plan for that, too. Karen O'Brien cites Mitchell's remedy for writer's block: "When I get writer's block, I don't panic—I just pick up a brush. It's like crop rotation. It keeps the soil fertile." Joni Mitchell has a plan.

Nowhere is Mitchell's discussion of her compositional process more comprehensive than in her extended comments to Jenny Boyd. There Mitchell brings her painting and music into a focused discussion of creative method. She begins with her painting:

> When I paint for long hours, my mind stills. If you hooked me up to a meter, I don't know what you'd find, but maybe it's like a dream state. It goes very abstract. The dialogue is absolutely still, it's like Zen no mind. You hear electrical synapses, which could be cosmic electricity, snapping, and occasionally up into that void, in the Zen no mind, comes a command, "Red in the upper-left-hand corner." There's no afterthought, because ego is the afterthought; you paint red in the upper-left-hand corner, and then it all goes back into the zone again. You achieve that sometimes in music. I think I achieve it in the loneliness of the night just playing my guitar repetitiously. The mantra of it, the drone of it will get you there.

In the *Woman of Heart and Mind* video Graham Nash claims Mitchell "channels" when she writes. When applied to writing, the key is self-knowledge, she explained: "To know yourself is to know the world; everything, good, bad, and indifferent is in each one of us to varying degrees, so the more you know about that, the more you know about that which is external. So in that way, the writing process is fantastic psychotherapy—if you can survive. But it is tricky." To solidify her point, Mitchell recalled writing a song that was "so dense with imagery that for me it was thrilling," but it was "hard for me to sift through it." Suddenly, a "line" appeared "that was like a gift," in that it just "flowed out." Mitchell "drew back and said 'thank you' to the room" since the line "just came out and said so much, I felt, so economically." She continued: "I'd been grinding the gray matter trying to get this thing to come, and maybe I then just relaxed or something. Whatever it was, when it poured out it did seem like it was a gift. There are pieces in a song that just seem to pour out in spite of you. I mean, you're the witness but the language does seem to come from someplace else." She summarized her position in this way:

> If you're too reasonable, then creativity won't come around in you, because then you're not intuitive, and it requires a great deal of intuition. You need a

bit of all of it: you need to be emotional, otherwise your work will be chilly. If you're too emotional, your work will be all over the place. You need to be rational for linear, architectural, orderly, structural work, but if you stay there too long, the stuff will be chilly. You need some clarity to make the thing pertinent.

Here, again, is an artist with a plan. She knows what she wants, she understands patience, and she has developed a procedure to achieve her goals. She is a painter who has co-opted the skills associated with that craft and systematically applied them to another. Her goal is a nurturing, balanced, but not necessarily autobiographical truth, as she told Timothy White: "In a certain way, I do see myself as an eyewitness reporter. Some of my things are purely fictional, though, in that I begin from an eyewitness vignette to depict it. . . . We're talking about art's artifice here, and it has its own truth. It's not necessarily a literal truth. It's a creative truth, a larger truth." Indeed, a socially responsible "creative truth" that may or may not have a direct relationship to Mitchell's life constitutes the crux of her creative ambition. She described her objective to Edna Gundersen: "I'm always trying to expose a universal truth. It's easy for me to use myself as subject matter because I can take it. Most people don't like portraits unless they flatter them. Some themes require stirring up and sustaining an emotion that isn't a fun companion." Moreover, in the *Woman of Heart and Mind* video Mitchell states it succinctly; she probes the subjective in pursuit of the universal. As all of these comments indicate, whether autobiographical or fictional, Joni Mitchell's art is genuine. Regardless of whether she is "reporting" or "editorializing," she tries to nurture, to remain socially responsible, and in general to be positive. Later in life, when these goals seem too distant to obtain, the auteur refrains from writing—a response that is predictable only because it is a direct manifestation of her stated artistic philosophy.

Refusing to pander to her audience or her industry has had serious consequences for our idealistic, duty-bound auteur. Along with wealth and fame, Mitchell's career has brought her deep-seated frustrations that, at times, seem to dominate her. Her complaint is quite evident in her 1979 *Rolling Stone* interview:

> If I experience any frustration, it's the frustration of being misunderstood. But that's what stardom is—a glorious misunderstanding. All the way along, I *know* that some of these projects are eccentric. I *know* that there are parts that are experimental, and some of them are half-baked. I certainly have been pushing the limits and—even for myself—not all of my experiments are completely successful. But they lay the groundwork for further developments. Sooner or later, some of those experiments will come to fruition. So I have to lay out a certain amount of my growing pains in public.

Almost 20 years later, her comments to *Vanity Fair* restate that view: "It's a very frustrating thing to try to make enduring literature and real music in a world that is suspicious of it and wants to call it pretentious. I've tried to make music that was enduring and classical with lyrics of the same standard, and I've been a recipient of prejudice as a result of it. America cheats on its exams. It likes copycats, it likes mediocrity."

Mitchell might qualify her comments about America's preference for copycats or mediocrity, but she will never back down from her views about the music industry. With time, anxieties over her audience dissipate somewhat, yet her anger with the music industry continues to intensify. In 1991, she told David Wild: "It's a *horrible* job. People don't realize how horrible it is. Making music is great. The exploitation of it is horrible." In 1994, she told Robert Hilburn: "People don't understand how distasteful it is to the artistic temperament to be pulled through the business like we are forced to. . . . It threatens the creativity. It cheapens. It slanders. It assumes. . . . You are subject to the printed opinions of jackasses. . . . It is a heartbreaking gantlet young artists have to run." And in 2002, David Wild once again witnesses Mitchell's wrath:

> So I would never take another deal in the record business, which means I may not record again, or I have to figure out a way to sell over the Net or do something else. But I'd be damned if I'll line their pockets. . . . I hope it all goes down the crapper. It's top-heavy, it's wasteful. It's an insane business. Now, this is all calculated music. It's calculated for sales, it's sonically calculated, it's rudely calculated. I'm ashamed to be part of the music business. You know, I just think it's a cesspool.

I think it is safe to say that Mitchell feels her industry does not share her socially responsible, nurturing point of view about art. Our interpretation of the oeuvre reveals where this attitude emerged and why it has affected Mitchell to the extent that it has; nevertheless, her perspective is crystal clear. In his book, *Rock Lives*, Timothy White cites Mitchell's assessment of the delicate balance an artist must achieve in order to remain productive: "You wonder about people who made a fortune, and you always think they drank it up or they stuck it up their nose. That's not usually what brings on the decline. It's usually the battle to keep your creative child alive while keeping your business shark alive. You have to develop cunning, and shrewdness, and other things which are not well suited to the arts."

That last phrase captures it all. Joni Mitchell's respect for and dedication to the "arts" is an all-consuming passion. She considers creativity to be a "gift" that must be applied in a socially responsible fashion. To take the product of that gift and distort or contort it for financial gain is blasphemous. And the polio victim who cut a heavenly deal with her Christmas tree will have none of that—it is a breach of her wedding vows to her

Art. Disrespect the gift as an artist, and the muse will forsake you. Divorce is inevitable. Disrespect the gift as an industry, and Joni Mitchell will crucify you. Her passions, her commitments, her beliefs run so deep that she would have no choice. It would be her duty to respond. I mean, just look at her descriptors! A creative "child"—innocent, receptive, defenseless—versus a business "shark"—predatory, vicious, unrelenting. That metaphor falls a hair short of the balanced, maternal, healthy outlook that edits Joni Mitchell's inspirations and characterizes her marriage to Art. The following pages will reveal just exactly how that came to pass.

CHAPTER 3

The Oeuvre

From matters of biography, creative development, and artistic orientation we now turn to the lifework and Joni Mitchell's oeuvre. Here we witness the convergence of personal history, creative method, and professional philosophy within the art. To be sure, Joni Mitchell is a natural product of her times. From nature she received her talent—a creative impulse that manifests in multiple forms. Whether she is painting, writing, photographing, sewing, or cooking, Mitchell approaches that creative act as an "artist" with a firm commitment to the aesthetic objectives she associates with that work. She is a slave to her aesthetic vision. From her environment she absorbed a perspective on life—an idealistic, nurturing outlook that projects an unashamed sincerity. As much as any artist from any time, Joni Mitchell was a True Believer in a social movement that eventually abused her for her dedication. Initially, Mitchell's idealism fueled her pen, but as time passed and those dreams disintegrated one by one, that pen chronicled their passing just as fiercely as her early work heralded their potential. As we are about to discover, our polio survivor will don her Roy Rogers outfit and combat the music industry, journalists, audiences, colleagues, and total strangers with the rebellious determination of her youthful bouts with piano teachers and chauvinistic playmates. There are times when the difference between Joni Mitchell's art and Joni Mitchell vanishes. The axiom "Trust the art, not the artist" disappears, for she *is* her art. Such raw, unfiltered honesty proved to be as costly as it was innovative.

Professionally, Mitchell's worldview forced her into the compromising realm of creative submission. As she surrendered to her perceived audience's needs by offering her heartfelt interpretations of the events before her, she revised the methods of songwriting—especially as the practice applied to the new breed of celebrity-singer-songwriters that followed Bob Dylan's ascendance. Her widely acclaimed "confessions" blazed a trail that married personal commentary and public personality (regardless of their auto-biographical relevance). Again, songs were more than words and music; they were *messages* from *celebrities*. In sharpening that connection, Mitchell did two things: First, she stepped directly into the trap that Bob Dylan deftly avoided when he shifted from "message music" to idiosyncratic expression; second, she changed songwriting in terms of the celebrity-singer-songwriter composite. Individual *expressions* quickly evolved into packaged *messages*. Like an actor or a commentator known for a particular role or political stance, and unable to shake that perceived persona, Mitchell was pigeon-holed by her public and, predictably, she rebelled. Nevertheless, while she fought with music companies and dysfunctional audiences, she never, ever abdicated the sincerity that guided her songwriting. To the degree that her work earnestly pleads for love, faith, and community, it genuinely damns those who harbor the materialistic, abusive practices that prohibited her ideals from achieving realities. The key word here is *passion*.

Mitchell's lifework unfolds in three phases: a participant-commentator period that extends from 1968's *Song to a Seagull* through 1974's *Court and Spark* (including 1969's *Clouds*, 1970's *Ladies of the Canyon*, 1971's *Blue*, and 1972's *For the Roses*); a sonic explorer era that ranges from 1975's *The Hiss-ing of Summer Lawns* through 1979's *Mingus* (including 1976's *Hejira* and 1977's *Don Juan's Reckless Daughter*); and a seasoned commentator phase that opens with 1982's *Wild Things Run Fast* and closes with 1998's *Taming the Tiger* (including 1985's *Dog Eat Dog*, 1988's *Chalk Mark in a Rain Storm*, 1991's *Night Ride Home*, and 1994's *Turbulent Indigo*). Throughout this three-part journey we witness a host of sonic innovations that deploy the diverse sounds of world music years before they occupied the musical mainstream. Moreover, her strategic blend of character and scenic portraits, life celebra-tions and complaints, social commentary, introspection, and confrontational rebellion is systematically applied across the oeuvre. In other words, the music explores a vast array of sonic possibilities, but the lyrics focus on specific, recurring topics that are of concern to the auteur. Joni Mitchell maintains that the *gift* that is her talent contains a *duty* to share her obser-vations on life in a sincere and forthright manner. Those observations may praise, plead, prick, pontificate, punish, or personalize their subject mat-ter; in all cases, however, they remain relentlessly nurturing. Mitchell may scold, yet those admonitions honor her life's ideals in a dutiful—almost maternal—fashion. That passion yields a depth of conviction that, for good or ill, separates Mitchell from her songwriting peers. It also reflects an ar-tistic philosophy that occasionally conflicts with her industry's commercial agenda. In all cases, as we move through 30 years of work, notice the stub-born courage that enabled a ten-year-old girl to declare to the world that she would never be a "cripple." Such fierce determination may have proved costly for the artist's career, but it transformed songwriting for all those who followed.

THE PARTICIPANT-COMMENTATOR PHASE

As media technologies developed throughout the twentieth century, certain individuals emerged who were particularly well-suited to the challenges posed by their specific medium. What Franklin Roosevelt was to radio, Orson Welles was to film, John Kennedy was to television, and Bob Dylan was to popular music. Each performer had what seems to be the perfect crystallization of talent to media form: Roosevelt's commanding voice suited the airwaves the way Welles's cinematic creativity, Kennedy's visual coolness, and Dylan's rebellious personality set performance standards for film, television, and music. Each was perfect for his medium—a mode of public communication that highlighted specific strengths while simultaneously hiding equally compelling weaknesses.

Joni Mitchell is this type of media pioneer. She, too, represented that magical combination of timing and talent which opened the way for the introspective songwriting that was to follow. But Mitchell was more than a celebrity-singer-songwriter, she was a spokesperson for a particular way of life. Like Woody Guthrie, Hank Williams, or Loretta Lynn, Mitchell's songs chronicled a lifestyle, its philosophy, and ambitions that she then personified in performance. Joni Mitchell was the poster person for the peace and love movement; a role that required her to act naturally and advocate positions that were genuinely close to her heart. To claim that her ascendance had anything to do with her gender is more than simpleminded, it is downright inaccurate. Yes, Mitchell's voice, beauty, and personality represent feminine ideals. Yes, those traits fed the marketing mechanisms that dominate her field. But her work is no more gender bound than Lorenz Hart's, Cole Porter's, or Hank Williams's writings. What Joni Mitchell espouses has to do with *people*, regardless of their gender or sexual orientation. While she may assume a decidedly feminine point of view from time to time, her work speaks to a generation, its lifestyles and its fantasies, as well as its relationship to the varied institutions that define society. Mitchell most assuredly *is* a woman, but her art transcends gender in all-too-obvious ways.

While beautiful women with pretty voices are as much a part of music history as cellos, flutes, guitars, and moneychangers, the beautiful woman-celebrity-singer-songwriter composite was a powerful innovation in the latter portion of the '60s. I mean, what a combination! Although Elvis Presley represented a commanding synthesis of looks and talent, he did not write. His *actions* motivated a generation, not his *words*. Mitchell did it all. She was the quintessential flower child, blessing all while damning none (well, almost none). Her voice, physical presence, and lyrical content all worked in harmony to promote the peace and love worldview in what would have to be considered an unprecedented fashion. Our opening phase of Mitchell's work chronicles the budding auteur's participation in the social movement that birthed her. Mitchell's writings represent a commentary on her times as she issues a "hippie manifesto" via 1968's *Song to a Seagull*, reiterates those stances with *Clouds* and *Ladies of the Canyon*, turns slightly introspective with *Blue*, pauses to contemplate her situation with 1972's *For the Roses*, and concludes the period with the 1974 commercial powerhouse, the comprehensive *Court and Spark*. The passion of Mitchell's convictions is on display during this phase of her career to an extent that one is hardly surprised by the intensity of her response when these ideals disintegrated.

Our musical expedition into America's peace and love era begins with a fine combination of wide-eyed wonder and mature insight. Mitchell has repeatedly claimed to be a variety of ages all at once. She maintains she is part child, part adolescent, part adult, and part senior citizen with various situations arousing responses from a particular part of that complex personality. Such an argument gains credibility through the songwriting on *Seagull*. The album's ten songs (running 38:10) represent a prequel of stories to come as they convey the youthful joys of a night out on the loving, caring, happy-go-lucky town (the first of many "travelogues"); ponder the loss of a treasured loved one (the initial entries of a soon-to-be-thoroughly-mined genre); discuss the pitfalls of urban life (ditto); and, offer the first of a lifelong series of portraits that emphasize points of relevance to that moment in time. *Seagull*—dedicated to former schoolteacher Arthur Kratzman—is a hippie manifesto that captures the joy and exhilaration of a lifestyle that would crash and burn almost as soon as it was born.

The record's themes seem to rest on "Cactus Tree" and its portrayal of the '60's relational dilemma: how to balance sincere feelings of love and adoration with intense desires for personal freedom. Can you have one without forsaking the other? Subsequently, "Tree" introduces one of the oeuvre's foundational narrative forms, the love challenge. The song's many characters—a sailor, an outdoorsman, a businessman, an anxious urban lady, a woman with many suitors—long for love and wrestle with its particulars. The song effortlessly balances cross-generational notions about traditional relationships with new perspectives on personal freedom. From there we have installments of romantic complaint ("I Had a King" and "The Pirate of Penance"), life celebrations ("Night in the City" and "Sisotowbell Lane"), urban anxieties (the complaints that are "Nathan La Franeer" and "Song to a Seagull"), and heartfelt portraits with a thematic point ("Michael from Mountains," "Marcie," and "The Dawntreader"). Throughout, Mitchell's child gazes at all the wonderful colors and activities, her adolescent ponders her adult future, and her senior citizen warns of impending dangers.

The portraits offer considerable depth as we consider the situations surrounding Mr. Perfect (the ideal man who is "Michael"), Miss Disappointed (the sad state "Marcie" endures), and Mr. Escape (the "Dawntreader" and its seafaring invitation). "Michael" is the perfect man who awakens his love with candy, frolics in the rain, protects his love from the elements, and is nurturing beyond belief. Yet he is preoccupied with *his* freedom and his mountains—the quintessential hippie fantasy. "Marcie," on the other hand, is not faring that well. This sad, touching portrait features a woman in waiting, to no avail. Here Mitchell introduces a duality strategy that consistently reappears throughout the oeuvre. Using red and green, she paints a portrait that communicates images of sweet/sour, autumn/summer, stop/go, angry/jealous as they relate to Marcie's disintegrating emotional state. The descriptions are rich, revealing, and remorseful. Between these two extremes is "Dawntreader" (a name producer David Crosby considered for his boat) and its account of life on the open seas. Mitchell describes her character's seafaring lover, his invitation to escape, and her powerful peace and love fantasies (while watching her lover/sailor sleep, the character envisions a world of love, peace, and happy children). Each song consists of simple language, vivid descriptions, and coherent emotional portrayals that communicate the moral of the story in a direct manner.

In thematic contrast, we have the urban complaints and their anxieties about potential threats to the peace and love ideal. These concerns appear in both a direct ("Nathan") and an indirect manner ("Seagull"). In the former, Mitchell uses a cab ride to the airport to portray the dreary, impersonal, money-hungry ways of the city. Our narrator describes a grim urban scene of loud alarms, gangs, strip joints, dirty landscapes, and evil greed. Our narrator certainly aspires to something better. The indirect expression, "Seagull," uses a free-flying seagull metaphor to contrast the hells of urban life. The narrator's dream of joining the flock and escaping the repressive city is more than apparent. In the city, dreams sink like stones cast into the water—it is ceaselessly oppressive. Both accounts paint a grim picture of the dreaded concrete jungle and its institutional threats to the freedoms espoused by the peace and love rhetoric. That Mitchell divided the record's two sides into different "parts" (part 1: "I Came to the City" and part 2: "Out of the City and Down to the Seaside") once more demonstrates an urban–nature duality that hovers over both this project and the hippie fantasy.

Proving that attitude can be everything, Mitchell pauses to celebrate city life in "Night in the City." This is the first of the oeuvre's life celebration songs in which the author points to simple pleasures such as running down a crowded street, waving to friends, kissing strangers, dancing the night away, and passing flowers out to people. The threats posed by the concrete jungle are nowhere in sight—it is all one big urban festival. Those simple pleasures recur in "Sisotowbell" and its life-in-paradise celebration of a peaceful place where neighbors exchange stories, rock away in their rocking chairs, and eat healthy food; the poets sing; and life is more than grand. Should you, for some reason, travel to the city, no worries, you will receive a hero's welcome upon your return to paradise. The fact that Mitchell placed

"Sisotowbell" (the beginning of part 2) immediately after "Nathan La Franeer" (the end of part 1) demonstrates a strategic use of contrasting images to establish or reinforce her point—another songwriting tactic that recurs throughout the lifework.

The relational complaints (or elegies) use two strategies as well. The direct but accepting account of impossible love in "King" and the cloudy tale of what appears to be relational revenge in "Penance" relate Mitchell's capacity to massage the same topic from different angles. With "I Had a King" we observe how Mitchell accepts a failed romance without blame—he was from one era, she from another. This, too, is a steady staple from Mitchell's work in that she rarely attacks *individuals* in songs of love lost. She may rail against situations or characteristics, but rare, indeed, is the personal attack. Although our cheating pirate appears to get his in the end, the odd story contained in "Penance" is so indirect that any sense of revenge or attack is muted. The song does establish one of Mitchell's recurring motifs through its use of layered voices. This sonic strategy pulls the curtain back to reveal the painter behind the songwriting.

Song to a Seagull is a simple, minimalist presentation of the peace and love worldview—just as producer David Crosby planned it. It is also a thematic and musical overview of things to come. Mitchell described the project's sonic simplicity to Les Brown in a manner that, once more, shows the painter at work with her musical brush: "If I'd recorded a year ago . . . I would have used lots of orchestration. No one would have let me put out an acoustic album. They would have said it's like having a whole paintbox and using only brown. But today is a better time to be recording. It's like in fashion. There's no real style right now. You find who you are and you dress accordingly." Mitchell's metaphors, it appears, are controlling. Throughout her career, we shall observe how she characterizes her work in terms of painting, fashion, architecture, or film.

That simplicity does not end with production matters. Her comments to Karl Dallas indicate the sources of her songs' subject matter: "I'm the girl in all these songs. And the first song in the album, 'I Had a King,' is about the breakup of my marriage." After that autobiographical admission, she continued: "The album does tell a story, though not necessarily in chronological order. Certainly the songs aren't placed in the chronological order that I wrote them. As we were working on it, songs came up that would fit in. And since it was finished, I've written others that could go into the sequence, too." With time, they do. More important, these admissions of autobiography will taint all subsequent readings of her work. Despite the fact that "Marcie" is clearly a portrait of someone else, and contemporary pirates and talking birds are rare finds, journalists and fans will bend, distort, and convolute Mitchell's writings to suit their interpretive ends. For example, consider Brown's conclusion for *Rolling Stone*: "Joni Mitchell leaps from image to image but seldom leaves you hanging. Occasionally her

lyrics seem to lose relevance and become frosting without any cake, but then
she's like a sand dune: you like the idea of her." The "idea of" Joni Mitchell
would soon be the controlling element in any consideration of her art. The
use of a real cab driver's name ("Nathan La Franeer"), references to David
Crosby's boat ("The Dawntreader"—it wound up with a different name), and
other incidentals inspired legions of fans and journalists to search and
search for biographical clues—regardless of their relevance to the song's
point.

Mitchell's claim that other songs were written that fit into the *Seagull*
sequence was substantiated by her next album, 1969's *Clouds*. The self-
produced sophomore entry featured *Seagull* engineer Henry Lewy at the
controls for another ten-track project (running 37:42)—this time dedicated
to Mitchell's grandmother, Sadie J. McKee. *Clouds* both builds upon and
departs from *Seagull*'s starting point as it extends the love challenge, life
celebration, and portrait narrative strategies while also adding new story
forms and the oeuvre's first piece of impressionism. This smooth, coherent
work tells its stories through clear, accessible songs that rely on direct,
understandable language. Although Paul Rothchild produced the opening
track ("Tin Angel"), the Mitchell–Lewy team is firmly in control as the
painter and her print-pulling engineer weave their production magic once
more.

The life celebration portrayed in "Chelsea Morning" represents the photo
negative of "Night in the City," in that our life revelers now adore the morning hours and the array of colors and sounds that usher in each new day.
The simple joys of living are presented in terms of happy scenes, rich colors, and vivid descriptions. The song is an aural smiley face that communicates how life is beautiful when viewed so simply. Few songs are as
cheerful, and hopeful, as this light, airy account of the hippie fantasy and
its eternal, natural bliss. Mitchell's voice and distinctive guitar tunings play
significant roles in the song's joyous representation of street life. She described the song's origins for Robert Hilburn in 1996: "I wrote that in Philadelphia after some girls who worked in this club where I was playing
. . . found all this colored slag glass in an ally. We collected a lot of it and
built these glass mobiles with copper wire and coat hangers. I took mine
back to New York and put them in my window. . . . The sun would hit the
mobile and send these moving colors all around the room. As a young girl,
I found that to be a thing of beauty."

The portrait ("Roses Blue"), love challenges ("Tin Angel," "I Don't Know
Where I Stand," and "The Gallery"), and testimonials ("I Think I Understand" and "Both Sides, Now") build directly on *Seagull*. Affairs of the heart
are seen in terms of the challenges they pose as opposed to simply staring
into the romantic abyss. Key to the love challenge story is the measure of
hope portrayed in the song. For instance, "Angel" charts the change from
one relationship to the next as the narrator expresses little remorse over

the loss of one love and little joy over the arrival of the next. Instead, she merely acknowledges that her new love interest has his challenges—as they all do—and how she plans to meet those needs (there is more than a little bit of *Wizard of Oz* imagery here). Similarly, "I Don't Know" finds the narrator uncertain of her position in the relationship, but seemingly optimistic. The song is rich in colorful detail as the young hippie braids flowers in her hair, thrills at the sound of her lover's voice, and anticipates the arrival of a new morning (the song oozes peace and love imagery). As you listen, you can literally *see* Mitchell's character practicing writing "I Love You" in her finest script with a serene smile on her lips and the sun glistening off her long, flower-braided hair. In many respects, it seems as though the same character has somehow magically entered "The Gallery" as she tenderly embraces her lover's romantic history and naively ponders her role in his love life. Yet, our narrator is no fool—just a touch innocent—as she senses that all may not be what it appears to be. These characters are most certainly youthful, optimistic, and occasionally, naive, yet you just know that they all *believe* that everything is going to work out *perfectly*.

The portrait-testimonial connection is intriguing. The portrait of Gypsy Rose ("Roses Blue") is loaded with detail about our gypsy's mysterious ways that will confound you, abuse you, but never truly comfort you. Mitchell denounces the self-subjugation that accompanies any reliance on card readings, zodiac interpretations, magical potions, or any other quick fix, and instead advocates a simple dose of any "Night in the City" or "Chelsea Morning." That is, your laughter will set you free. Forget about gypsies, priests, soothsayers—just believe in yourself, our hippie rhetorician urges. This type of prescription for living also appears in the oeuvre's first installments of the testimonial narrative strategy. After establishing that Rose is a ruse, Mitchell advocates facing—and respecting—your fears ("I Think I Understand") and understanding your lifelong illusions ("Both Sides"). "Both Sides" is a beautifully constructed song that presents the hard lessons earned from experiences with clouds, love, and life. Here Mitchell urges us to lose our illusions, face our ignorance, open our hearts, and accept life's challenges with a healthy respect for our fears. This is powerful stuff that certainly involves the wise, senior citizen portion of the auteur's multiaged personality. Just when you thought all that hippie rhetoric was full of vacuous platitudes! She offered this explanation of the song's origins to Robert Hilburn: "I was reading Saul Bellow's 'Henderson the Rain King' on a plane and early in the book Henderson . . . is also up in a plane. He's on his way to Africa and he looks down and sees these clouds. I put down the book, looked out the window and saw clouds too, and I immediately started writing the song."

Speaking of aging, the lifework's first piece of narrative impressionism, "Songs to Aging Children Come," foreshadows a major recurring theme in the Mitchell canon. (The narrative impressionism songwriting strategy was

oneered by Bob Dylan and involves the use of recurring tag lines, choruses,
musical punctuation to create the illusion of narrative coherence when,
fact, no narrative structure exists.) Quirky imagery, rushed people, whis-
ng birds, and lunar activities fill this highly repetitive offering from the
ild portion of Mitchell's personality. Although appearing to be artsy for
e sake of appearing artsy, the song introduces one of the songwriter's life-
ng themes in a fashion that honestly communicates her confusion over
ing. There is, however, nothing confusing about *Clouds'* two remaining
tries, the personal complaint "That Song About the Midway" and the
euvre's most direct antiwar song, "The Fiddle and the Drum." Just as
ging Children" introduces the aging theme, "Midway" subtly previews a
usic business angst theme. What starts out as a portrait of a roustabout
d his free-spirited ways suddenly uses those traits to contrast the
arrator's situation. He is running around the world enjoying his freedom
hile she is running out of professional gas. The narrator is tired and en-
ous of our roustabout's freedom, but she does not say why she is tired
in any way attack the music business; she just contrasts his freedom with
er perceived subjugation. Once again, we witness Mitchell's "contrast" or
uality writing strategy at work.

"Fiddle" is a powerful song. Mitchell's a cappella presentation of the Earth
other's response to the war is moving and entirely consistent with the
aracterizations in the life celebrations. That is, she wants to *help*, not
ondemn, those involved in the conflict. She acknowledges that much of the
ouble is earned, yet she offers her understanding and comfort in spite of
all. Despite all of the problems the country faces, she still sees the good-
ess in America's heart and longs to help the country return to its peace-
l, loving ways. One gains the impression that if only the country would
pen its eyes to a cheery Chelsea morning or experience an invigorating
ight on the town or face—and respect—its fears or just acknowledge the
lusions that can confuse anybody, everything could return to normal, and
e war could end. This may seem like a naive pipe dream to cynics, yet
r Mitchell a return to these nurturing first principles was no fantasy, illu-
on, or magical concoction—it was the real deal: a genuine invitation to
eturn to the Garden of Eden (located just off Sisotowbell Lane) and its loving
mplicity.

That Joni Mitchell actually believed her rhetoric is clear in her third al-
um, 1970's *Ladies of the Canyon*. This time the Mitchell-Lewy team gener-
ted a 12-song work (running 44:59) that represents yet another installment
the author's unfolding hippie manifesto. Again, what to many may have
een viewed as peace and love platitudes are articulated in a truly heart-
lt fashion. (Don't be cynical!) The ongoing effort to discover personal iden-
ty *outside* the context of institutional/societal labels represents the crux of
is portion of Mitchell's manifesto. Let there be no doubt, this is a *coherent*
tatement that introduces a variety of instruments to achieve a fuller sound

as it pursues the self-understanding that is essential if one is to escape the "circle game" of youth.

First, we gain another glimpse of The Garden just off Sisotowbell Lane as we visit the joyous happenings in Morgantown. Again, we worship the morning hours as "Morning Morgantown" portrays the happy-go-lucky ways of Chelsea, the "love everybody" enthusiasm of "Night in the City," and the serenity of "Sisotowbell" all in one, very special, *Pleasantville* moment. THIS IS THE GARDEN: a simple, loving, nurturing existence where *acceptance* is the guiding creed, judgments are reserved for the afterlife, and the butterflies are as big as your head. From there, *Ladies of the Canyon* focuses on specific threats to The Garden through a series of societal complaints ("The Arrangement," "Big Yellow Taxi," and "Woodstock"), a series of classic Mitchell portraits that stroke various notions ("For Free," "Ladies of the Canyon," and "Circle Game"), and a series of love challenges that address different stages of the mating game ("Conversation," "Willy," "Rainy Night House," "The Priest," and "Blue Boy").

We open with the societal complaints. While "Woodstock" is, literally, a hymn for the cause and a call to action regarding a return to simplicity (and—as a sidebar—a celebration of the music festival), the need for that action is established in the woeful "Arrangement" and driven home in "Big Yellow Taxi." Of course, "Woodstock" deals with the war (where even *bigger* butterflies emerge), but it also deals with the search for self, concerns over the environment, and the magical qualities of human life. Things are *bad*, man, and if we fail to sidestep the devil's trap, all could be lost. So celebrate with the music, discover your identity, and join your brothers and sisters in a triumphant return to the Original Home. This is, in every respect, a battle of ultimate good vs. ultimate evil. Its status as an anthem for the peace and love era is much deserved—it is a topical masterpiece.

"The Arrangement" is a simple little dirge. Here Mitchell portrays another life of endless possibilities lost to the evils of consumerism. There is more to life than high-rise offices, swimming pools, credit cards, and trophy wives, and Mitchell leaves us with the compelling understanding that some "arrangements" are, indeed, bad deals. This simple little dirge is perhaps the oeuvre's most significant song. Throughout Joni Mitchell's lifework she will point to the lessons communicated via "The Arrangement" as the Great Satan that inhibits our return to The Garden. Our greed, with its corresponding commercialism, is our prison, and our Earth Mother will continually invoke her hippie manifesto by denouncing the commercial devils and advocating a return to loving simplicity. This is the one theme that never dies. The war ends, show business is just another personal pain, but the commercial abuses and manipulations that threaten love, family, and the environment are never dismissed. That Mitchell actually *believed* in the worldview she espoused through her art is evident in the intensity of her emotions and her relentless treatment of the topic.

Although "Taxi" also invokes images of appreciation for important things that have slipped through our greedy fingers (she claims she wrote the song in Hawaii after opening a hotel window and seeing a huge parking lot eating up much of her otherwise glorious view), its significance to the oeuvre lies not in its thematic content but in its narrative strategy. Joining "That Song About the Midway," "Taxi" follows a narrative scheme in which the author introduces one topic, contemplates the moral of that story, and closes by applying the principle to another context. Just as "Midway" praises the roustabout's freedom before lamenting her perceived subjugation, "Taxi" rails against environmental abuses, notes how you never appreciate something until it is taken away from you, and concludes by applying that notion to her love life. We start on one narrative terrain and end on another, but the story's moral holds true. Occasionally, Mitchell uses this tactic in a doughnut framework in which one scenario opens and closes the song, with the middle portion featuring another application of the principle in question. In many respects, "Taxi" echoes "The Arrangement"—one day you will miss the simple things in life.

The portraits reinforce that realization: Money corrupts and complicates the beautiful, simple practice of music making (the music biz complaint, "For Free"); the "Ladies of the Canyon" prosper in their quaint but nurturing lifestyles; and life spins around as we age ("The Circle Game"). In the latter number, Mitchell seems to argue that if you understand what is happening, you can step off the carousel of youth and gain your adult freedom. Each portrait features either an explicit or an implicit point that somehow, someway, leads back to the highly desired simplicities of The Garden and its magical, nurturing, inexpensive pleasures.

Five of this record's 12 songs deal with Mitchell's "love challenge" narrative. "Conversation" presents an emerging love triangle in which the narrator has designs on a man who is abused by his wife. Their friendly, nurturing conversations may pave the way to his eventual escape from Evil Woman to Earth Mother. Those maternal instincts are on display in "Willy" as well. Here we have a man who has been burned by love, but our narrator is patient, loving, and willing to accept the challenge of bringing him along. Our remaining love challenges posit questions of personal identity ("Rainy Night House"), ponder the various tests love poses ("The Priest"), and contemplate the potential failure to reach love's potential (the very sketchy "Blue Boy"). Questions of commitment, patience, identity, and perseverance dominate these challenges of the heart.

With that, our three-album manifesto reaches its conclusion. From *Seagull*'s dreamy intuitions, to *Clouds*' pointed reiterations, to *Ladies*' comprehensive summary, Joni Mitchell has constructed her artistic baseline. Appreciate The Garden and its colorful wonders ("Night," "Sisotowbell," "Chelsea," and "Morgantown"); discover your true self and accept your limitations ("I Think I Understand" and "Both Sides"); reject simple remedies or solutions ("Roses Blue"); face love and its challenges ("Cactus Tree," "Tin Angel," "Willy," and more); understand the Devil, his offer, and its consequences ("Song to a Seagull," "The Fiddle," "The Arrangement," "Woodstock," and "Big Yellow Taxi"), and you may be able to enjoy yourself, others, and nature's wonders without the constrictions imposed by society's evil loan-sharking gatekeepers. It is, in every respect, a simple vision of love, acceptance, and mutual admiration for the uncomplicated wonders of life. In short, our peace and love poster person points her nurturing finger at her adoring audience and announces, "I Want You," with all the sincerity one expects from the highly acclaimed Earth Mother of her time. This is quite a responsibility. If Mitchell's audience responds in kind, no doubt it will all be worth the effort; if not, Earth Mother's passions will most certainly erupt once more.

With 1971's *Blue* our nurturing spokesperson turns away from her lessons for aging children and toward affairs of the heart. By all accounts, *Blue* is a watershed record. This is, assuredly, an album with a *serious* reputation. It is credited with changing songwriting forever by elevating the "confession" as a vehicle for self-disclosures that make songs more intimate, more touching. The Mitchell-Lewy production team's fourth album once again contains ten tracks (running 36:13) and Lewy's comments to Steve Pond indicate the intimacy that surrounded the venture: "We went into the studio, locked all the doors and didn't let anybody in. . . . When that album came out, we knew we had something." And they did, as Timothy White's comments in *Billboard* report: "A million-seller . . . at a time when such feats were exceptional, 'Blue' remains the vocal, lyrical, and compositional equal of any celebrated album of rock's first 40 years, whether it be 'Blonde on Blonde,' 'Rubber Soul,' 'Pet Sounds,' 'Tapestry,' 'The Joshua Tree,' or 'Diva.'" As I said, this is an album with a *serious* reputation.

While the confessional dimension is certainly present and the album's sonic qualities are definitely pensive, I am not certain that this album is as "blue" as *everybody* says it is. Thematically, the record is quite diverse. It contains a love celebration ("My Old Man"), three love struggles ("All I Want," "This Flight Tonight," and "A Case of You"), two personal complaints ("River" and "The Last Time I Saw Richard"), a tribute (the portrait "Little Green"), a piece of narrative impressionism ("Blue"), and two trademark Mitchell travelogues ("Carey" and "California"). One could hardly call "My Old Man" anything but a joyous account of a loving relationship. The couple is infatuated with one another (when he leaves, she just dies), they are committed to one another (and, therefore, do not require any official sanctions—i.e., marriage), and happy as could be. Obviously, the couple lives on Sisotowbell Lane! This song may appear on *Blue*, but it is light, airy, and full of the kind of love advocated by the Earth Mother's established manifesto. Correspondingly, the love struggles are actually quite positive in their perspectives on love, the travelogues are bouncy and bright, and though

Mitchell does pause to share personal observations on love and war, she is—for the most part—darned positive.

Consider the three love struggles, for example. The opening track, "All I Want," is certainly a struggle as the narrator desires a resolution to the couple's problems so everybody may live happily ever after. She is neither angry nor complaining. She accepts her role in the situation. She just wants *everybody* to be happy. Our Earth Mother carries those sentiments into "This Flight Tonight," except this time she has committed a mistake: She got mad and left town. The song features lots of standard Mitchell descriptions that have little to do with the story as the narrator explains her predicament. She does not complain or attack her lover; in fact, she is (of course) quite nurturing as she hopes he is warm, that his car is OK, and that everything will be just fine once they are back together. She just got mad and left— only to return with a heart full of love. "A Case of You" also chronicles a bittersweet love full of struggle. But again, no putdowns or recriminations, just an admission of struggle. Our narrator does not just desire her lover, she wants *a lot* of him (an entire case, to be accurate). She wants to drink him as she would a vintage wine—savoring every drop, dreading the end of the bottle, yet willing to pop another cork. To be sure, these songs discuss the struggles loving relationships occasionally bring, but they are a rather light shade of blue—full of hope, optimism, and, ultimately, commitment.

This optimism continues in the personal complaints as well. In "Richard," the narrator denies his cynicism, and even when she sits in the bar by herself (just as he predicted), she declares her situation to be merely a phase that she must endure. Things will get better. Of that, she is certain. A similar scenario unfolds in "River" as our central character denounces her business, regrets a failed romance, admits to deep dissatisfaction with the status quo, and aspires to escape. It is one sad Christmas, indeed. However, there is the implicit belief that skating away on the much-desired frozen waterway will take her someplace better—the grass is greener downstream (or is it upstream?), our narrator seems to believe. These songs *sound* horribly blue, yet their stories hold out hope.

The title cut and the tribute certainly contribute to this overall *feel*, but once more, let us examine the specifics. "Blue" abounds with potential metaphors; still, the song is more a series of impressions (not a word game) that suggest hard times without any specifics. The song neither praises nor blames, although it does question a lifestyle based on self-abuse. It is, in a word, *cryptic*. "Little Green" does not share that trait. Without prior knowledge, much of this would prove difficult to unpack; nevertheless, it is most certainly a tribute to a child. The narrator tells the child about living and hopes the little girl enjoys a wonderful life. The song is tender, loving, and completely void of any negativity (no complaints, laments, or attacks). If you know about Mitchell's daughter, odds are you will make the song darker than it really is. Yes, Mitchell was probably wrestling with her past (the song was written—and often performed—long before it was recorded), but without prior knowledge, it is no confession, but just an Earth Mother prayer for a life full of butterscotch sunrises.

The only blue I sense in the travelogues would be the Carolina blue skies that provide the light, pleasant settings for these bouncy, fun tunes about adventures in far-off lands. "Carey" features a series of fun-filled romps with Carey. The narrator may have issues with Carey, but they are clearly beside the point: Let's dance! Our quintessential folk track, "California," is a more complicated song. Although it is part tribute to California and part societal complaint about the war, it is mostly a series of travel scenes with observations about France, life on a Greek island, and a trip to Spain. Each time, our narrator gets homesick and longs for the Golden State. Identity issues seem to lurk within her plea for acceptance, yet this is most certainly a thematic aside. Problems exist in these stories, but they are not their central organizing features.

Blue, then, is in the eye of the beholder. Do not let the dark sounds fool you! Mitchell's comments about the recording process and her self-concept certainly suggest that this was a blue period for her personally, as these 1985 remarks to Bill Flanagan indicate: "That album is probably the purest emotional record that I will ever make in my life. . . . All I knew was that everything became kind of transparent. I could see through myself so clearly. And I saw others so clearly that I couldn't be *around* people." On another occasion, she told Cameron Crowe: "At that point in my life, I had no personal defenses. I felt like a cellophane wrapper on a pack of cigarettes. I felt like I had absolutely no secrets from the world and I couldn't pretend in my life to be strong. Or to be happy. But the advantage of it in the music was that there were no defenses there either." Somewhere, someplace there is a 45-minute version of the song "Blue." There has to be, since the sentiments cited above (and there are many more such comments) fail to measure up to the songs. "Old Man," "Carey," "California," and even "Little Green" just do not follow that perspective. Something else is going on here. Mitchell's intense anxieties over her relationship with her audience, the demands of performance, and her growing understanding of the music industry are tickling her rebelliousness and ushering in discomfort. In fact, Joni Mitchell may just be sonically restless, as she confided in this long commentary to Penny Valentine after *Blue*'s release:

> Like Miles Davis always has a band that are [sic] really great, but are [sic] cushions for him you know. That sounds very egotistical that I should want that, but this time I really want to do something different. Like the music is already a growth, a progression from "Blue", the approach is stronger and melodically it's stronger, I think that will be noticeable whether I make a sparse record as I did with "Blue" or not. But I feel I want to go in all directions right

now, like a mad thing right! I'd think "this is really rock and roll, this song, isn't it?" and I see it with French horns and everything and I really have to hold myself back, or I'll just have a monstrosity on my hands. No, I don't feel trapped in this held back careful image. I could sing much stronger than I do you know, especially on the low register. I've got a voice I haven't used yet and haven't developed, which is very deep and strong and could carry over a loud band. And I'm very tempted to go in that direction experimentally. But rushing ahead of ideas is bad. An idea must grow at its own pace. If you push it and it's not ready, it'll just fall apart.

It is not easy to be a genuine Earth Mother. To fake it is to fail. To sincerely strive to offer nurturing, positive statements of unconditional love for total strangers is a tough narrative row to hoe—especially when you stand onstage or in the studio by yourself. Perhaps Mitchell's growing predicament was best expressed by Kris Kristofferson after hearing *Blue* when he pleaded with the auteur, "Joni, save something for yourself." Apparently, as we are about to discover, Mitchell took that advice to heart.

The post-*Blue* period of Mitchell's career was a confusing time for the internationally successful artist. She sold her house, donned her metaphorical skates, and raced up that "River" to her native Canada in order to regroup and reinvigorate her art. She explained her situation to Timothy White in his 1990 book: "*For the Roses* was written in retreat, and it's nearly all piano songs. I was building a house in the northern British Columbia forestry, with the rustle of the arbutus trees at night finding its way into the music. There was moonlight coming down on black water; it was a very solitary period. It was melancholy exile; there was a sense of failure to it." Why? Why would someone who just completed a million-seller record, who had legions of loyal (albeit overly dependent) fans, and who seemingly had the musical world in her hip pocket feel as though she had failed? How could this be?

Whether Mitchell was suffering from romantic disappointment, an idealistic reckoning, or a music business epiphany, she moved to Canada, got in touch with nature, and churned out a series of songs that foreshadow the future while clinging to the past. The Mitchell-Lewy team's fifth album, 1972's *For the Roses*, contains 12 songs (running 40:40) that explore tried-and-true themes via a slight sonic twist. The news here involves the new musical platforms Mitchell is developing. The saxophone in "Cold Blue Steel and Sweet Fire," the jazzy sounds of "Barangrill," the full band in "Blonde in the Bleachers," and the theatrical orchestrations in "Judgement of the Moon and Stars (Ludwig's Tune)" take us a long way from the lone figure at the piano or with the guitar. Just as she told Penny Valentine, Mitchell's musical interests are drifting back to her youth, reorganizing and moving—ever so slowly—in a new direction.

Another major shift on *Roses* involves the increase in the auteur's narrative impressionism. Five of the album's 12 tracks deploy this songwriting strategy: "Banquet," "Cold Blue Steel," "Barangrill," "Electricity," and "Judgement of the Moon." Classic Mitchell descriptions are crammed together into collages that go nowhere while their flowing images run amok. Often, there are not-too-cryptic show business, relational, or show business relationship complaints placed neatly amongst the droves of images. For example, in "Banquet" we experience a series of metaphoric vignettes featuring scenes of the seaside, seagulls, and ocean-side activities that are blended into a banquet scenario where inequity abounds (the big dog eats in a big way while others starve). The song marches to its own symbolic logic, yet the stench of show business abuse is certainly strong. These idiosyncratic images reappear in "Electricity" and "Judgement" through their home repair metaphors and cryptic tributes, respectively. Nothing ever happens, just more images and metaphors. That trait holds for the sonic explosions that are "Cold Blue" and "Barangrill" as well. "Cold Blue" reads like a chapter from Bob Dylan's *Tarantula* with its weird-named characters and chaotic scenes, while "Barangrill" offers "Chelsea"-like descriptions that center around a restaurant scene. Nothing happens here, either; just more and more images. As we shall discover as we move through the lifework, whenever Earth Mother is confused or working her way through something, her impressionism increases and her "confessional" prescriptions wane. In any event, as you listen to these songs, you feel an onslaught of impressionistic jazz moving right around the corner. Once more, just as she reported to Valentine, she is allowing her sonic urges to gestate, birthing no sound before its time.

The remaining songs ponder a steady flow of relational ills that seem to involve romance and business. The record features a relational complaint ("Lesson in Survival"), two professional complaints ("For the Roses" and "Blonde in the Bleachers"), a testimonial or self-portrait ("Let the Wind Carry Me"), and three love struggles: "See You Sometime," the metaphoric "You Turn Me On, I'm a Radio," and "Woman of Heart and Soul." The apparent personal detail in "See You" portrays a woman who is angry, but desirous of her man, while the heavy complaints in "Woman of Heart" push her agenda and ambitions (there is a flash of maternal angst present), but it eventually yields to a sense of struggle over her man's rock-and-roll lifestyle. Both songs contain not-too-cryptic complaints about the music industry and celebrity lifestyles. On the other hand, "You Turn Me On" applies a radio metaphor to a love struggle. The track is a great little pop song with an ingenious metaphoric hook as the narrator urges her audience (i.e., her lover) to tune in to the comforts of love as she promises to lift his spirits from dawn to dusk. Still, if it all becomes too great a hassle, just change the station, baby.

The hints of industry complaint that float throughout the love struggles blossom into frontal attacks with "For the Roses" and "Blonde." In the former, the narrator offers testimony regarding how something so natural, so wonderful has turned out so badly (shades of "For Free"). In particular, the song rants about the music press and its efforts to crucify artists (literally!). In the latter, the focus is on the rock-and-roll road lifestyle, groupies, and the vacuous qualities of it all. In both tracks, an aura of relational unrest abounds. Though I avoid commenting about a given song's intended target, the presence of "See You," "Woman of Heart," "Roses," and "Blonde" on one record indicates that Mitchell's feelings for her rock-and-roll beau are all-consuming—there is a definite thread running through these songs. Still, Mitchell spends little to no time complaining or crying; rather, she is usually supportive of her partner (though decrying his lifestyle), understanding of their competing agendas, and willing to work at the relationship. At times it seems as though our Earth Mother is doggone angry, yet wants to tuck you in bed and darn your clothes.

Relational survival seems doubtful in the album's lone romantic complaint ("Lessons"). This track charts a relational downturn that has affected the narrator to the point where she perceives she is a burden to her friends— "survival" seems unlikely in this woeful tale. Finally, all the talk about Mitchell's autobiographical writing gets a solid boost with the self-portrait "Let the Wind Carry Me." A family portrait featuring mom, pop, and rebellious daughter sets up a testimonial about the torn emotions associated with her career and her maternal ambitions. Earth Mother is struggling with her biological clock and her wild artistic urges. The song goes out of its way to be autobiographical, therefore, you *have* to consider it to be a genuine "statement."

For the Roses is autobiographical, enigmatic, and the wave of the sonic future. It is most assuredly a transitional work. To me, this is *by far* the most confessional record to date. Whereas previous records either hinted at autobiographical confession or opened the door for that interpretation, this record screams confession so that it may be heard over the ocean tides and the rustling trees. Mitchell is upset with the moneychangers, disgusted with the decadence of the rock lifestyle, disappointed over her failed relationship with a fellow music professional, and openly contemplating a shift in life direction. She packed up her emotions, skated upstream to her native Canada, and wallowed in her perceived situation. Perhaps the project proved therapeutic in that instead of attempting to nurture her audience, she labored to care for herself, exorcise her anxieties, and cleanse her soul. Whatever the case, her strategy apparently worked, for Joni Mitchell is about to give up her tenure as Jesus and concentrate on becoming Miles Davis.

The participant-commentator phase of the auteur's lifework concludes with her strongest-selling album, 1974's *Court and Spark*. That *Court* represents a significant sonic turning point in Mitchell's career is indisputable. And it is not that she uses her first full band (Tom Scott and the LA Express) that makes this album's sound so distinctive; rather, it is the way the record incorporates that rich, full, balanced sound of her acoustic recordings within a full band setting. *Court and Spark* is a stellar recording achievement by Mitchell and Henry Lewy. The album's 11 tracks (running 36:58) offer Mitchell's first recorded cover song (Ross and Grey's delightful "Twisted"), three narrative vignettes or scenic portraits ("Court and Spark," "People's Parties," and "Raised on Robbery"), a portrait ("Free Man in Paris"), a testimonial ("Down to You"), a love challenge ("Help Me"), a relational plea ("The Same Situation"), a relational struggle ("Car on a Hill"), a relational complaint ("Just Like This Train"), and a personal complaint ("Trouble Child"). In many respects, the project is a thematic sampler that dutifully closes an innovative era of songwriting (only Mitchell's impressionism and societal and professional complaints are absent on this pop tour de force).

Thematically, we begin with the three vignettes in which Mitchell takes a scene, identifies its characters, and describes what transpires. These scenic portraits do not offer any morals, lessons, or prescriptions—they merely embellish that particular scene and allow it to play out. For instance, "Court" traces a cloudy moment in which a stranger appears at the narrator's doorstep, she recognizes him from someplace, he delivers his testimony, and he is reportedly prepared for love. The scene just ends; nothing happens. Similarly, "Parties" offers a full, colorful description of people at a party, their varied traits, and their games. The portrayal contains some judgments about the party's activities—that is for certain—but it mainly focuses on interpretive reporting and the narrator's sudden desire for an improved sense of humor. Both songs contain brief glimpses of a larger story. Our third scenic portrait, "Raised," in no way shares this cloudy quality. Instead, we are treated to a masterpiece of humorous storytelling. This account of a pickup scene at a hotel bar contains vivid descriptions, hilarious dialogue (several cute culinary metaphors), and raucous sounds that make for a strong single release. Though void of any heavy-handed commentary, deep lamentations, or Earth Mother prescriptions, the song does what it does extremely well. Here, Mitchell's writing is rich, funny, and entertaining—literally something she *never* does, even though she is quite good at this form of narrative songwriting.

That writing style is also evident in "Free Man in Paris." In this instance we have a blend of character portrait, travelogue, and music business angst all rolled into one smooth, coherent presentation. Interestingly, the song opens with the central character addressing someone in a conversation and continues with his self-important diatribe. Only in Paris can the powerful music mogul relax, we are told. Mitchell deftly manages to stroke her music business anxieties through the words of a character who personifies the essence of her complaint. She explained the song's origins to Robert Hilburn: "I wrote that in Paris for David Geffen, taking a lot of it from the things he said. . . . He didn't like it at the time. He begged me to take it off the record."

From there, we turn to what could easily be assembled into a relational life cycle set. First is the love challenge "Help Me" and its account of the narrator's struggle with that delicate balance between a romantic ambition and individual freedom. The narrator wants to take that leap, but her experience prompts hesitance. The "Cactus Tree" rhetoric is once more challenged by love, and Mitchell's character pleads for assistance in her ongoing struggle with her emotions. Still, there is absolutely no doubt that she will accept that love challenge. Next, we move to the relational plea "Same Situation" and its prayer for true love in a fake world. Our narrator is insecure, tired, and a little bit desperate for lasting, meaningful love. This song is an unadulterated plea for Divine Intervention. Here, too, the "Cactus Tree" dilemma looms in the background as the character prays for love *and* the time away from her career to enjoy the bliss. Her explanation of the song's origins are fascinating, as she told Hilburn: "I don't want to name names . . . but basically it is a portrait of a Hollywood bachelor and the parade of women through his life. . . . So many women have been in this position . . . being vulnerable at a time when you need affection or are searching for love, and you fall into the company of a Don Juan." From a challenge and a plea, we turn to the inevitable struggle and "Car on a Hill." This character takes the plunge, and insecurities quickly follow due to her inattentive lover. Our narrator sits at home, awaiting her tardy boyfriend's arrival—wondering. Throughout, we hear the piercing lament regarding a love that started with so much promise, only to return to the anxious insecurity that always lurks around the relational corner. Few songs assume this particular characterological stance, and Mitchell's poignant writing captures her character's perspective in a compelling manner.

At this point, *Court* pauses for an insightful—and depressing—testimony: The powerful "Down to You." This seasoned, slightly cynical testimony charts how lovers come and go like fashion, how disappointment abounds, and how it all comes down to a questionable stranger at the bar. A temporary lapse of reason yields another disappointing realization, however; the narrator condemns neither her lovers nor their actions as she seems to accept her situation and its dire conditions. She walks down the street on one of those butterscotch Chelsea mornings, and it rips *her* heart out. Not all laughing lovers have laughing lover audiences, and this song presents the other side of the Sisotowbell coin. The song concludes with its yin-yang logic, an acceptance of life's uneven qualities, and the resignation of acceptance. Earth Mother tells it like it is, in her own Earth Mother way.

Our two remaining story forms lodge complaints of a personal ("Trouble") and relational ("Just Like") nature. In "Just Like" the narrator uses a train trip as a vehicle to complain about her troubled love life. Superb descriptions of the train station's occupants join accounts of the trip and its sights to frame the central character's love complaints. Not even a high-speed locomotive can deliver you from love's wrath, we are seemingly told. The complaint thematic widens its net and hauls in a school of negativity with

"Trouble Child." This character is worn out from her failures and distrustful of everybody. Religion, the gypsy's tarot cards—nothing works for this person. Betrayal is ubiquitous. There is no apparent resolution in sight. "They" (whoever "they" are) are going to get you. You may venture over to the "Down To You" pickup station, this song seems to say, but everything there just adds to more "trouble." The quiet optimism from "Last Time I Saw Richard" is gone. To end this record with Ross and Grey's "Twisted" was a humanitarian act.

This phase of Mitchell's work concludes, as all of her phases do, with a live album. Her first live work, 1974's *Miles of Aisles*, features Tom Scott and the LA Express and, in some instances, fairly radical revisions of her work to date. The 18 tracks offer two new songs ("Jericho" and "Love or Money") and a variety of tunes from days gone by—only one of which appears on *Court*. In some cases, the jazz influence sharpens the recast song; in others, the revision falls flat. Nevertheless, the record captures Mitchell (her between-song dialogue is refreshing), her adoring audience (and in one instance, their dialogue as well), and her new musical direction for posterity. Perhaps *Rolling Stone*'s Stephen Davis describes the record best: "After a couple of hearings, the songs begin to blur into a sameness. Perhaps it is a sameness of mood and tone, and not of style and tangible content. In any case, much of the material here is beautiful, replete with the patented Mitchell tension. And a word for engineer Henry Lewy—the sound is terrific, the best reproduced concert album I've heard."

That "sameness of mood and tone" is about to become a thing of the past. The transition that began with *For the Roses* blossoms with *Court* and *Miles of Aisles*. The key is *Court and Spark* and its sonically liberating, thematically depressing body of work. When considered in light of the other entries in this phase of the auteur's career, you just *know* these stories are going to take their toll. What began with the wide-eyed innocence of a hippie-go-lucky night out on the town or a dreamlike morning in Morgantown ends up in a smoke-filled bar with slim possibilities lurking over your shoulder, hoping for a few free drinks and a guiltless rendezvous. The nurturing character who once beheld a king now beholds a constant stranger. Once Michael came down from his mountain and rode in Nathan La Franeer's cab, he quickly bolted out of town—probably on David Crosby's yacht. The ladies of the canyon are more than a distant memory for the character riding on that train looking at beautiful sights through tear-filled eyes. Yep, they say, you take things for granted until they are gone. Then what do you do? Do you continue to wallow in the muddy muck of memories or do you give up, move up to Canada, and howl with the wolves? Joni Mitchell wisely discovered another option. She called time out, allowed her Earth Mother responsibilities a brief four-album respite, and became a Black Man.

THE SONIC EXPLORER PERIOD

The "sonic explorer" phase of Joni Mitchell's lifework demonstrates the extent to which she was, in fact, a media pioneer of the magnitude of those talented innovators I mentioned in the previous section. During this portion of her career, the auteur wrestles with her Earth Mother manifesto, advances the musical shift that occurs on *Court* and *Miles of Aisles*, and, in so doing, alienates her record company and a large portion of her fan base. Sonically, this facet of the work applies Arthur Kratzman's advice to yet another creative domain as Mitchell not only paints with words, she paints with sounds as well. Many of the songs from this era feature layers and layers and layers of voices, instrumentation, and sound effects as our painter moves her sonic substances around her musical canvas, searching for that magical combination of aural textures and colors. Though widely condemned for her musical adventures, in this period, she blazes a trail for the world music explosion that would eventually follow.

Lyrically, the sonic explorer phase presents a search for a metaphysical resolution to the auteur's idealistic dilemma. As her manifesto's goals of individual freedom and relational stability fade into the realities of materialistic imprisonment (as predicted in "The Arrangement"), Mitchell negotiates her way through the transition. Initially, she appears to be confused by the dream's failure to materialize—and she shares that, too. With our opening installment, *The Hissing of Summer Lawns*, we see that symbolic playfulness may actually represent symbolic confusion. As her utopian ideals disintegrate, Mitchell explores certain recurring emotional situations, searching for a fitting response. Those inquiries pause with *Hejira* and Mitchell's amorous detoxification. Love, once more, has failed the artist, and in response, she road trips her way through an internal struggle that crystallizes in a specific set of realizations concerning her manifesto's condition. With *Don Juan's Reckless Daughter* we reach a pivotal turning point in which Mitchell examines a dream vs. reality struggle as she looks back on her fantasy-filled youth, contemplates the state-of-the-dying-dream, and projects where "The Arrangement" will take you: the conspicuous consumption capital for retiring consumers, Miami. Suddenly, it appears, Mitchell turns a corner, steps away from the mess, and honors Charles Mingus. Musically, the auteur ventured where she was destined to go. Lyrically, she entered a place beyond her wildest dreams. Earth Mother is not going to take the disintegration of her prescriptive worldview lightly; rest assured, we are going to hear about her disappointment. With time she will not only acknowledge that her perspective failed, she will dutifully explain why. But first, let the jazz winds carry you where they may as our sonic explorer enjoys a musical reprieve that soothes her anxieties, releases her audience, and disappoints her industry.

The Hissing of Summer Lawns (released in November 1975) is our seventh Mitchell–Henry Lewy production and features a host of talented musicians (e.g., Larry Carlton, Wilton Felder, John Guerin, Joe Sample, James Taylor, and more). In any protracted career, there are musical departures from an artist's previous works and, occasionally, there are *musical departures*. Anyone who purchased this record anticipating another "Raised on Robbery" or "Car on a Hill" is probably still in shock. Of the record's ten tracks (running 42:38), seven involve the narrative impressionism strategy ("The Jungle Line," "Don't Interrupt the Sorrow," "Shades of Scarlet Conquering," "The Hissing of Summer Lawns," "The Boho Dance," "Sweet Bird," and "Shadows and Light"), with one patented life celebration ("In France They Kiss on Main Street") and two portraits—the relational portrait "Edith and the Kingpin," and the scenic portrait "Harry's House—Centerpiece" (featuring a sample of the Johnny Mandel–Jon Hendricks song "Centerpiece"). To begin, we pause to consider the rare edition of Joni Mitchell's liner notes that accompany this project: "This record is a total work conceived graphically, musically, lyrically and accidentally—as a whole. The performances were guided by the compositional structures and the audibly inspired beauty of every player. The whole unfolded like a mystery."

Mystery or not, this record is an act of rebellion. Though sonically beautiful, most of this album marches to its own drum. The impressionism is full of negativity. Occasionally tracks such as "Hissing" or "Boho" begin with little Mitchell short stories before taking off on impressionistic junkets to uncertain destinations. The moral of the story, while there, is often buried (which, in turn, invites over-reading). Although Mitchell's descriptive powers continue to impress, she crams many of these phrases together in fairly chaotic ways. Often, the music follows that lead in a style which moves one to conclude that something is about to erupt here. This record is, in every respect, yet another transitional piece. We begin with Mitchell's impressionism.

With the sonic textures of a Tom Waits song, "The Jungle Line" comes as close to pure wordplay as any Mitchell composition ever will. Jungle rhythms provide a context for jumbled images that dance all over the auteur's musical canvas. Though the number approaches one of Mitchell's standard vignettes (a waitress scene), it quickly bounces off to another image. The wordplay dance continues with "Don't Interrupt" and its evasive internal logic. The song contains witches, references to foreign lands, concerns for The Original Sin (more Eden angst), God/Santa Claus metaphors, and a cloudy hint of escape. Rebellion is certainly in the house, but the specifics escape me. It is another invitation into the interpretive abyss. That trend dissipates with "Shades of Scarlet Conquering" and its return to the ladies of the canyon from days gone by. In this case, these characters have grown darker, more demanding, and considerably more materialistic. This impressionistic denunciation of materialistic women offers a pretty grim account of that lifestyle. Is Mitchell saying "I told you so"? That negativity advances in the title cut, as what opens with typical Mitchell descriptions of suburban living suddenly shifts into dense scenes full of imagery but with no action. There appears to be quite a bit of relational deterioration present, but Mitchell's point is conveyed in such a cryptic, idiosyncratic fashion that any message is buried. That narrative strategy is in evidence in "Boho" as well. Here another coherent scenario opens a song (this time, a nostalgic account of Mitchell's New York days) before shifting into more obscurity. Just as relational deterioration seems to float through "Hissing," celebrity angst appears through scenes featuring a well-dressed lady with a run in her hose, a priest with dark ambitions, and other random descriptions that appear for no apparent reason. We have, then, a cast of characters without a plot. The rain of impressionistic complaint continues with "Sweet Bird" and its blend of negativity concerning aging and celebrity. The "sweet bird" (of youth?) seems to have a grand time, and the narrator is pretty upset about it. Finally, we close this round of impressionism with a hymn. "Shadows" contains God, the devil, coal miners, and music critics, along with various references to right and wrong that are all woven together in a call-and-response, choirlike manner. This one is difficult to unpack, yet you know something is working itself out in this concluding statement. When we consider this portion of the oeuvre as a whole, "Shadows and Light" may preview the duality theme that occurs in a more direct manner later in the sonic explorer phase. For instance, the devil/snake vs. God/eagle imagery recurs in "Don Juan's Reckless Daughter." Again, Mitchell is wrestling with her Earth Mother values here and, it seems, attempting to reconcile certain metaphysical incongruities.

In complete contrast to these impressionistic songs are the two portraits. With "Edith" a smooth, jazzy sonic platform projects a Mitchell short story about a drug dealer and his eye candy. The "Kingpin" scopes "Edith" out, picks her up, and takes her home, and a snow-blind Edith wonders about it all. The song is direct, coherent, and rather depressing. The depression continues with "The Arrangement, Revisited" and "Harry's House." This mini-opera features a short story about domestic relations that pauses for a jazzy lounge tune ("Centerpiece") before concluding with a not-too-blissful scene. Mitchell's observational powers are on display here as she unpacks one of her trademark complaints: "The Arrangement" is bogus. The trophy wife suggestion that accompanies the inclusion of "Centerpiece" indicates how some trophies are lacking in permanence. "Edith" and "Harry" demonstrate Mitchell's continued ability to weave tight tales when she wants; even though her traditional optimism is nowhere in sight. Edith and Harry just do not fare very well in these songs.

Equally reminiscent of narrative days gone by is the opening track, the life celebration "In France They Kiss on Main Street." This song reveals the extent to which Mitchell still longs to assemble her "Ocean's 11" cast out in the bush, circle the cars, crank up the radios, and dance. "In France" goes nowhere and does little besides relate the "let's party" sentimentality that runs throughout Mitchell's lifework. Again, foreign scenes are used as a context for directionless celebration. It is all one big party in another foreign land. Earth Mother's passport is well worn, indeed.

And it is the only party in this suburban environment that is *The Hissing of Summer Lawns*. They may kiss on main street Over There, but Over Here our materialism is causing us to feed on ourselves. This "Jungle Line" is about as angst-ridden as it gets, as Mitchell's impressions paint bleak pictures of a dream in decline; moreover, when she pauses for narrative precision, she unveils the horrors of the cocaine/swimming pool lifestyle and its less-than-temporary rewards. Through it all, we sample doses of celebrity angst and music business anxieties. When "Shadows and Light" takes aim at critics (seeming to lump them in with famed judge Cain), we somehow find ourselves contemplating images of a pugilistic Mitchell pounding on her piano teacher or some other authority figure for their constricting attitudes. Mitchell's rebellion is festering, itching to attack and damn those who threaten her peace and love idealism with their cheesy materialism. She is also frustrated by her industry and its patrons. Why so much anger? Well, consider these two reviews of *Hissing* for insight into this mounting confrontation.

In his *Washington Post* review, Larry Rohter expresses his displeasure with Mitchell's characterizations, claiming her characters are not "hurting for money" as they "vacation in Paris, shop at Bloomingdale's when they're in New York, [and] party at night in the slickest discos." For Rohter, the auteur "takes a tone that is smug, sometimes so smug that it is downright irritating." Yet, he continues: "What redeems the album are cool and jazzy melodies and some of the best songs about women and men that Mitchell has ever written." Sharing the mixed response is *Rolling Stone*'s Stephen Holden. Holden opens with the confused view that Mitchell has moved "beyond personal confession into the realm of social philosophy" (as we know, Mitchell's confessions *involved* her social philosophy) before he praises her "eye for detail" that he considers to be "at once so precise and so panoramic" with its "cerebral" accounts of its subject matter. After celebrating the writing, however, Holden attacks the music: "If *The Hissing of Summer Lawns* offers substantial literature, it is set to insubstantial music." He argues the music is "self-indulgent" and the songs are "as pretentiously chic as they are boring." Holden closes by encouraging readers to read the lyrics first and appreciate the poetry before listening to Mitchell's sonic "experiment."

For two critics to disagree over a work's strengths and weaknesses is in no way uncommon. The tone of the disagreement, though, is another matter. No doubt, Rohter hates Scott Fitzgerald's work, and Holden never purchased a Miles Davis record, since artists who explore affluent lifestyles or alternative sounds are considered to be smug and pretentious. As Mitchell's audience consumed these wisdoms, they too, echoed such sentiments, and Earth Mother, unfortunately, was listening. Why these individuals refused to listen to what she *said* in those songs is beyond me. Do they think Mitchell is *praising* the lifestyles of the rich and famous? Did anyone notice what she *said* about elite vacationers or wealthy shoppers or money-hungry suburbanites? Now, what would you expect Joni Mitchell to do with such knowledge? I bet I know what her piano teacher would say. The auteur will respond to these and other charges, but first she has some personal business to handle.

Joni Mitchell's solemn personal oath to never, ever repeat herself is on display with the on-the-road-with-Joni travelogue, *Hejira*. The project neither leaps back to her pre-*Court* past nor explodes into an uncharted musical area; instead, it strikes a compromise that emphasizes a state-of-the-artist message. Her eighth studio recording contains nine songs (running 52:05) that explore traditional thematic territory through an expanded autobiographical style and a more laid-back sonic strategy that stresses Mitchell's unique guitar tunings. Mitchell and Henry "Inspirational" Lewy (according to the liner notes) are joined once more by Larry Carlton, John Guerin, Tom Scott and other members of the LA Express, as well as famed bassist Jaco Pastorius and fellow Canadian Neil Young for a more subtle presentation of Mitchell's emerging musical style.

The album's title is an Arabic term for an exodus or flight from persecution. Mitchell told Cameron Crowe that the term connotes "running away honorably," as she explained her personal application: "It dealt with the leaving of a relationship, but without the sense of failure that accompanied the breakup of my previous relationships. I felt that it was not necessarily anybody's fault. It was a new attitude." Years later, she described the project to Dave DiMartino as simply "The poet took over the singer." With *Hejira*, the Earth Mother's metaphysical quest for a resolution to her ongoing struggle with ideals and realities pauses to embrace a series of personal issues of consequence for the auteur. That one song mentions her *by name* ("Blue Motel Room") and another is full of hometown references ("Song for Sharon") must have intrigued scores of fans hoping for a good old dose of accessible self-revelation. In many respects, *this* is the *real Blue*. The confessions that everyone claimed were on *Blue* are actually on *Hejira* in great abundance.

When compared to *Hissing*'s abstractions, *Hejira* is tamely concrete. It offers three relational complaints (the on-the-road-with-lost-love episodes "Amelia" and "Hejira," as well as the letter to hometown Sharon), two personal complaints ("Black Crow" and "Refuge of the Road"), two relational struggles ("Coyote" and "Blue Motel Room"), and two portraits, "Furry Sings the Blues" (with its comments about the Holy City of American Music, Memphis, Tennessee) and the enigmatic "Strange Boy." The poet is not a happy person on this record. The Memphis portrait aside, this record is *focused* on affairs of the heart. For example, the relational struggles portrayed in "Coyote" (more playful than serious) and "Blue Motel" (more serious than playful) explore the battle to keep love alive. "Coyote" seems to jump back an album or two in its sonic and lyrical style as it uses hitchhiker metaphors to portray a relational struggle. The song uses a scene involving a hawk and a coyote to communicate the relational strife and, once again, demonstrates Mitchell's use of dualities to illustrate a point. The torch standard sound of "Blue Motel" elevates the conflict through its clever application of a Cold War metaphor to capture a battle of substantial wills (yet another duality). Again, the fact that Mitchell refers to herself by name sharpens the point in no uncertain terms. *Blue* never comes so overtly close to home.

The personal complaints lodged in "Black Crow" and "Refuge" offer a wider view of the anxieties facing their narrators. In "Crow," Mitchell uses a road trip observation in which a black crow is seen diving for objects to file a specific life complaint. Like the bird, Mitchell reports, she has spent her life soaring from the skies for glittery earthbound objects, but she has apparently come up empty. The news here is that Mitchell seems tired of trying; the optimism of her youth is fading more and more. The road diary entries of "Refuge" communicate how she has traveled far and wide, attempting to cope with her emotional state. At times, we are told, her melancholy frightens those around her, but she keeps traveling, and thinking. The determination of a child polio victim continues to shine through even though there are moments when her fatigue is evident.

Those highway thoughts are no doubt zooming in on the *real* problem confronting our road warrior, her relational woes. The relational complaints represent this record's centerpiece. We begin with aviation imagery and Amelia Earhart references that are used to portray the narrator's disappointment over another bad day at the love office ("Amelia"). Our narrator is hurt and on the road, gazing at the skies, coping. Like Earhart, she is a woman with a dream—perhaps a life-threatening aspiration to soar where others fear to venture. She is sad, lonely, and hurt. The final stanza's use of the "Cactus Tree" reference invokes a flash from the thematic past, as the narrator is certainly out there with her freedom, yet she just does not seem very happy about that situation. The on-the-road-with-the-blues routine continues with the title cut and its wonderful descriptions and observations that drift quite close to a testimonial. Mitchell continues to struggle with dualities as she observes pieces of herself in those around her and pretends to be pleased with her new freedom. But you know she is pretending when she wrestles with notions of hope and hopelessness, depth and superficiality, escape and surrender. These emotional conflicts reach their apex in the epistle to Sharon, "Song for Sharon." This lengthy, focused, autobiographical piece offers a lifelong look back at romantic failure and contrasts that experience with Sharon's domestic stability. The song bounces from scenes of North Dakota to New York to Mitchell's native Maidstone as it traces a child's infatuation with love, a teen's adventures with love, and a mature woman's disappointment with love. The narrator took one road, Sharon another. Now, Earth Mother is clearly wondering if it is all worth the hassle. "Sharon" is a watershed song. From a writer claiming to steer clear of autobiography, it strikes mighty close to home—it is one extended "dark soliloquy." There are no songs like these on *Blue*.

The relational road trip pauses for the two portraits. "Strange Boy" offers a weird account of a skateboarding post-adolescent who refuses to surrender his youth and, as a result, intrigues the narrator. Apparently the narrator develops a relationship with the strange boy and submits to his powers, and we are left to contemplate their union. Finally, the road trip passes through the Home of the Blues and the Birthplace of Rock and Roll as Mitchell's travelogue enters Memphis by way of "Furry Sings the Blues." Scenes of pre-renovation Beale Street, comments about the city's music history, and asides about a visit with bluesman Furry Lewis are portrayed as only Mitchell can—and there is no relationship in sight! Perhaps the song communicates the Bluff City's potential to offer comfort for the disgruntled traveler seeking musical shelter from life's varied storms.

Critics seem delightfully puzzled by *Hejira*. *Creem*'s Ken Tucker claims the music's pacing suggests that Mitchell could not "traverse the living room in less than a week," while "the preciseness of her imagery is extraordinary and unobtrusive." Larry Rohter opens his review with history and Mohammed's flight before turning to Mitchell: "She is rich, famous and honored, a pop 'prophet' who has profited greatly from her utterances. Snug and protected in her mansion in the hills above Los Angeles, what does she have to fear?" From there, the *Washington Post* review describes the album as "Chapter Nine in the ongoing tale of Mitchell's search for happiness and self-fulfillment." Sam Sutherland discusses the commercial risks associated with the project: "This album reaffirms Mitchell's commitment to a more intimately conveyed and humanly scaled approach to her psychic and emotional odysseys, an approach that here yields poetic and lyrical depth worth the risky commercial odds." And Ariel Swartley offers this compelling observation: "It is the tug of war between the symbolist and the siren that makes Joni Mitchell's albums alternately alluring and forbidding. On the one hand she is the most ruthlessly analytical member of the music-as-therapy songwriting school, and often her songs seem intent only on making private sense of her own experience. On the other hand, as a public performer, Mitchell wants to be heard and even enjoyed." Swartley praises Mitchell's return to her sonic "roots" (via the album's emphasis on her guitar) and admires the philosophical lesson ("It is not the answers that are most important but the search itself") as the review seems to stress an artist in transition, searching for the proper creative balance.

So just when you thought Mitchell was about to take off on a musical flight of fancy, she reveals the extent to which old habits die hard. Just when you think she is about to evolve into Miles Davis, she pauses for personal reflection via the tried and true "love lost" genre with occasional asides about society or the music industry. But *Hissing*'s impressionism and *Hejira*'s introspection actually represent stepping-stones down the Earth Mother's metaphysical path. Refusing to pander to music industry stereotypes or audience demands, wrestling with the incongruities between her Earth Mother manifesto's ideals and the clearly observable realties of her situation, and coping with the ebb and flow of a highly publicized love life, Mitchell now plays her escape card. Just as *Hissing* announced her confusion and *Hejira* embellished her disappointment, the next two albums provide her escape. In jazz, Mitchell discovered a musical world that accepts aging artists, musical innovation, and liberated personalities. In jazz, Mitchell could continue her symbolic quest without acquiescing to pop music platitudes. In jazz, Mitchell could become Miles Davis—or at least Art Nouveau.

Mitchell's transformation into a Black jazz musician is evident on the cover of *Don Juan's Reckless Daughter*. There she appears as the character who debuted at a Los Angeles Halloween party ("Art Nouveau"), complete with blackface and funky attire. Of course, this is all a big joke; nevertheless, it symbolizes the auteur's desire to shake off old identities and their constricting expectations, rebel, and return with a fresh new persona. Since few people would accept her in her Roy Rogers outfit, the portrayal suited her rebellious instincts quite nicely. Joni Mitchell has had enough, and Earth Mother is about to explain why; but first, we pause for personal reflection and musical innovation.

No wonder Mitchell gets upset with critics, fans, and the music industry. They label her music pretentious and inaccessible when it is anything but—unless, that is, one wants *everything* to sound like a Monkees record. *Don Juan's Reckless Daughter* is an ambitious, revealing work that touches all the symbolic bases before it is finished. The Mitchell–Henry Lewy production team (assisted by Steve Katz) once again rendered a ten-track work (running 59:51) that opens with a classic life celebration ("Cotton Avenue") in which we are encouraged, once more, to get up and cut loose. From there, we have a couple of good old-fashioned love challenges ("Talk to Me" and "Jericho") that are presented in good humor. In fact, "Talk" relates what it would be like to go on a date with the girl from "Twisted." We also have two standard portraits—one of senior citizens in Miami ("Otis and Marlena"), the other involving African bliss (the scenic portrait "Dreamland")—that blend Mitchell's short story sensibilities and rhythmic impressionism. We also have two relational struggles ("Off Night Backstreet" and "The Silky Veils of Ardor"), a lengthy tribute ("Paprika Plains"—with orchestral arrangements by English composer Michael Gibbs), an example

of narrative impressionism (the title cut, "Don Juan's Reckless Daughter"),
and an instrumental, "The Tenth World" (written by Mitchell, Alias, Badrena,
Acuna, Airto, and Pastorius). Throughout the piece, musicians such as Airto,
Don Alias, Larry Carlton, John Guerin, Jaco Pastorius, Wayne Shorter, and
more join guest voices (e.g., Chaka Kahn, J. D. Souther, Glenn Frey) to create
layers of sound that conjure images of faraway lands, mystical adventures,
and relational resolve.

The sonic adventure begins with an "Overture" that establishes the tone
for the songs that follow. As we segue into "Cotton Avenue," we witness the
synthesis of a tried-and-true Mitchell song structure (the life celebration)
with the world music rhythms that dominate the project. The swinging good
time initiated in "Cotton" flows smoothly into the frenetic "Talk to Me." Here
the narrator is truly intrigued by her love interest's silence as she rattles
on in her effort to open the guy up in some way (a good strategy would be
for this character to take a deep breath and allow the poor bugger to speak!).
With "Jericho" the love challenge theme continues as the narrator uses the
famed walls of Jericho as a means of characterizing her need to tear down
her relational barriers and allow love back inside. There is no acrimony or
any sign of negativity or fear, just a commitment to lower her defenses and
allow love back into her life. These songs articulate one of the auteur's trademark scenarios: Be happy, dance, and let love into your life. There is a
measure of acceptance communicated through these songs.

The portraits offer strong examples of Mitchell's strategic application of
this songwriting structure. The character portrait "Otis and Marlena" seems
to build on "Edith and the Kingpin" as it portrays a couple in a specific
setting; in this case, we observe an older couple on holiday in Miami. Much
of the imagery is quite negative and Mitchell's obscure comments about
Muslims robbing Washington contribute to the song's uneven qualities. It
is, all in all, an aimless little story with several digs at the hated conspicuous consumption scenario. The scenic portrait, "Dreamland," uses African
rhythms and scenes to present a series of vignettes that blend travelogue
observations with personal revelations. Historical names, tourists, locales,
references to Mitchell's mother, and more crowd this scenic portrait in a way
that obfuscates any message that might be presented within the waves of
relentless images. The layers of sounds communicate the busy qualities of
this aural painting.

That the album closes with two relational struggles indicates Mitchell's
preoccupation with affairs of the heart is alive and well. What the opening
love challenges introduce, these songs embellish further. In "Off Night" we
have a loving relationship threatened by jealousy. The narrator loves her
partner, but her lack of trust is apparently well fed (e.g., finding another
woman's hair in the shower). The couple struggles to play fair and the outcome appears pretty bleak. Yet the struggle continues. The closing track,
"The Silky Veils of Ardor," revisits *Hejira* in its reflective tone. What begins

with a sermonic warning of love's dangers eases into a closing statement of relational resolve. This character has been rode hard and put up wet, nevertheless; she remains game. She is not giving up on love; no matter how much it beats her up. Mitchell's characters display a compelling sense of relational resilience in these songs which relate that the Earth Mother's troubles with society are just not going to separate her from her personal romantic ambitions. This painting gains clarity with each thematic layer.

The two pillars upon which this project rests also delve into the Earth Mother's anxieties and her internal conflict involving her dreams and her perceived realities. The sonic adventure that is the tribute "Paprika" and the impressionistic self portrait "Don Juan's Reckless Daughter" offer a reflective look back on the auteur's life and a candid assessment of her metaphysical present, respectively. The cinematic sounds of "Paprika" involve a 16-minute tour of Mitchell's youth and its implications for her present. What begins and ends with a dance hall scene drifts off into a dream sequence that traces Mitchell's youth, her recollections about local Indians, and her poignant memories about her native environment. As the character drifts off into her dream world, the song features an aural tour of the vast Canadian plains while the dream's contents are presented parenthetically in the liner notes. Earth Mother is in her primal element here; her philosophy—grounded in the Indian mysticism that is so friendly to '60s' utopian ideals involving the environment and individual spirituality—is displayed in unequivocal terms. At song's end, the dream ceases, the dance floor scene returns, and the narrator faces another relational situation. The dream-reality duality is established in a fashion that may, in fact, resolve the Earth Mother's metaphysical dilemma. That is, "Paprika" may represent that moment in which the auteur accepts the failed connection between the dream and the reality and prepares herself accordingly. It is a moment of recognition.

It would be an insult to the mystical jaunt that is "Reckless Daughter" to add some sort of structure to its internal chaos. In this impressionistic powerhouse, the images come in droves. With autobiography sprinkled here and there, the song chronicles an internal struggle between a metaphorical eagle and snake: heavenly ambitions vs. base desires. The eagle and the snake are two sides of the same coin, battling for control of a spirit in turmoil. The pace is furious. Each line applies the internal struggle to a different facet of the narrator's life. Should the narrator indulge herself or deny herself? Should she give in to the earthly snake or soar with the heavenly eagle? During the debate, the narrator seems to address a love interest that also personifies the struggle in terms of man and woman. The imagery grows more complicated as this dark soliloquy unfolds into the ultimate choice that is never made. The debate ends; nothing is overtly resolved. No life prescription is forthcoming. No resolution is articulated.

Yet you just know that is not the case. *Don Juan's Reckless Daughter* is *the* turning point in Joni Mitchell's career. When viewed as a composite, these stories harmoniously chronicle the acceptance of love's difficulties, a commitment to enjoy life to its fullest, and a recognition of the metaphysical dualities that exist in nature. There is no resolution to this inherent conflict. There is a bit of the eagle and the snake in everything; only the proportions vary. To endeavor to reconcile one without acknowledging the other is useless. Acceptance—a key element in the Earth Mother's manifesto—is the key. Remember, there was a snake in The Garden as well. From now on, the Earth Mother's manifesto is laid down, the idealism is replaced by a pragmatism, and Mitchell now focuses on scenarios in which the snake unfairly abuses or directly challenges the eagle with an occasional eagle victory. "Paprika Plains" revisits the dream's origins, "Reckless Daughter" wrestles with the dream's contradictions, and *Reckless Daughter* accepts the incongruity.

Critics did not notice this turning point. Instead, reviews consistently ridiculed Mitchell's songwriting for the very attributes that once harvested critical praise. The *Washington Post* simply concludes that "Joni Mitchell is not happy" and that her new record is "easily the most acidic and strident of [her] works." *Creem* states: "The album isn't any kind of step forward—it's a flawed consolidation of Joni Mitchell's lyric and musical abilities." *Crawdaddy*'s Jon Pareles is more specific: "Somewhere along the way, Mitchell's reverent audiences convinced her that her every thought is profound. Having concentrated on herself for so long, Mitchell's discrimination has eroded; she can't separate out the trivia anymore. Her intimacy has become exhaustive—she tells all, every flicker of ambivalence, every last rationalization, seemingly anything that pops into her head. You feel like you're drowning in her stream of consciousness." *Rolling Stone* maintains that Mitchell "has gambled and lost" with a record that can best be viewed as "an instructive failure." Janet Maslin argues: "It's sapped of emotion and full of ideas that should have remained whims, melodies that should have been riffs, songs that should have been fragments." Last, Don Heckman admits that he finds Mitchell's "frequent need to use her work as a purgative for sundry love affairs a bit tawdry" and that he is "equally put off by the relentless impressionism of her imagery"; yet he insists that the writer "is a first-class storyteller and the creator of superb characters." His *High Fidelity* review closes: "A record with the size, scope, and ambitiousness of 'Reckless Daughter' obviously can't be written off with the praise of a simple bravo or the damnation of an easy expletive. Much of what Mitchell has tried here doesn't work at all. A lot more works very well indeed. Credit her, at least, with aiming for the sun, even if she only managed to wind up in an eccentric solar orbit. That's still higher than most of us will ever get."

Herein lies Joni Mitchell's creative dilemma. The lack of understanding that envelops her work both stifles and inspires her writing. The very songwriting attributes that once garnered so much praise are now ridiculed as self-indulgent. Her efforts to expand the sonic scope of her records is considered to be pretentious, experimental, and a failure. Is there anything Joni Mitchell could do that would please anyone? Just as she noted in her comments to Cameron Crowe that she would be "crucified" whether she stayed the same or changed, she appears to be unable to satisfy her audience, journalists, or her industry. So if you are going to catch it one way or the other, you might as well do what you want—and that is precisely what the auteur does.

For those who view Joni Mitchell's art as self-indulgent, pretentious, and overreaching, this is submitted for your approval: *Mingus*. The June 1979 release was produced by the Mitchell-Lewy team (with assistance from Steve Katz and Jerry Solomon) and features musicians Don Alias, Peter Erskine, Herbie Hancock, Jaco Pastorius, Emil Richards, and Wayne Shorter. Of the album's 11 tracks (running 37:28), five segments feature conversation with the late jazz bassist Charles Mingus or simple spoken comments by the pioneering genius. Four songs contain Mitchell lyrics set to Mingus music; two others are all Mitchell creations ("God Must Be a Boogie Man" and "The Wolf That Lives in Lindsey"). The record presents three portraits that, one way or the other, are associated with Mingus ("God Must Be a Boogie Man," "A Chair in the Sky," and "Goodbye Pork Pie Hat"—originally Mingus's tribute to Lester Young), one scenic portrait ("The Dry Cleaner from Des Moines"), one love treatise ("Sweet Suck Dance"), and one piece of impressionism, "The Wolf That Lives in Lindsey" (complete with wolf sound effects). The album is—in every respect—a tribute.

Charles Mingus was seriously ill with the dreaded Lou Gehrig's disease when he was persuaded to contact Mitchell about a possible collaboration. Knowing that death was awaiting, he was anxious to find the proper lyricist to accompany his final compositions. Mitchell captured Mingus's attention through two related acts: The photograph of Art Nouveau that graces the *Reckless Daughter* cover (Mingus admired her courage by allowing such a shot on the cover), and the piano tuning on the extended "Paprika" cut (the song was assembled over an extended period and the piano tuning changed from one recording session to the other; Mingus noticed the difference and was moved by Mitchell's willingness to include the mistake). Karen O'Brien describes the situation:

> For his part, Charles's interest had already been raised by *Don Juan's Reckless Daughter* and his record company was encouraging him to work with Joni, thinking that the highly regarded Mitchell would help bring his music to a different audience in the rock and pop world. A friend of a friend told Joni that Mingus wanted to meet her; she phoned him and he invited her to come to

New York. Joni agreed but her plans got changed and instead she sent a tape of her music to Charles. He listened to the songs on it and remarked to his friend, the musician and arranger Paul Jeffrey, "She's trying to copy Billie Holiday a little, so maybe she can do something with me."

Originally, Mingus wanted Mitchell to adapt T. S. Eliot's *Four Quartets* (a four-part piece on Christianity) into some form of street lingo that would then be paired with Eliot's work in a call and response fashion; one voice would read Eliot, Mitchell would respond with her words. Mitchell described her ambitions to Cameron Crowe: "My goals have been to constantly remain interested in the music. I see myself as a musical student. That's why this project with Charles was such a great opportunity. Here was a chance to learn, from a legitimately great artist, about a brand new idiom that I had only been flirting with before. . . . This was a unique position. I've never worked for somebody else before." Negotiations ensued. Mingus brought music to Mitchell and the auteur would give it a go (at one point, Mingus presented a piece with *five* melodies, wanting Mitchell to write *five* sets of lyrics). Mitchell described the situation to the *Chicago Tribune*:

> The first meeting was so much fun that I knew I had to do it. In fact, Charles gave me a deadline. He told me I had three weeks to get words to all the melodies he had written for me. Not having a background in jazz, I didn't see how I could. You've got to understand that I just don't crank out songs. I have to wait until something happens for me to depict and transcribe into my medium. But Charles' magnetism made me say yes.

Mitchell used a host of jazz musicians in her efforts to unlock, yet remain true to, Mingus's original material (e.g., John Guerin, Gerry Mulligan, Tony Williams, John McLaughlin, Jan Hammer, and Stanley Clarke). Eventually, Mingus and his wife left New York for Mexico (seeking alternative medical treatment), Mitchell assembled her own band, and the project inched forward. Sue Mingus provided valuable tapes for Mitchell's use as our musical painter moved the sounds about on her sonic canvas. As the project moved forward, Mingus's health deteriorated. Upon his death, he had heard all but one track from the project ("Boogie Man"). Mitchell's liner notes offer her views on this historic—and extremely generous—project:

> The first time I saw his face it shone up at me with a joyous mischief. I liked him immediately. I had come to New York to hear six new songs he had written for me. I was honored! I was curious! It was as if I had been standing by a river—one toe in the water—feeling it out—and Charlie came by and pushed me in—"sink or swim"—him laughing at me dog paddling around in the currents of black classical music. . . . This was a difficult but challenging project. I was trying to please Charlie and still be true to myself. I cut each song three

or four times. I was after something personal—something mutual—something indescribable. . . . These versions satisfy me. They are audio paintings.

Mingus died on January 5, 1979, at age 56. The album was released the following summer. It represents one of Earth Mother's most nurturing acts.

The resulting album is, well, an odd one. At times, you get the feeling that things have been forced just a bit. Assuredly, the work is a tribute. Mitchell's words, lots of Mingus's music, and loads of love shine through here. This record works hard to please. Thematically, the spirit of Mingus dominates the proceedings. Three portraits and five brief statements from Mingus are the central ingredients of this particular jazz stew. The portraits either emphasize Mitchell's impressionism or wander about in a sketchy manner. "Boogie Man" (based on the opening passages of Mingus's auto-biography, *Beneath the Underdog*) presents the many sides of Mingus through lyrics that at first seem cryptic before you realize they are merely sketchy—maybe a little forced. "A Chair in the Sky" is slow, plodding, and full of in-side information about Mingus, his life, the things he will miss upon his passing, and how—if given a chance—he would do it all again. Finally, "Pork Pie Hat" is a hybrid that synthesizes a Mitchell vignette, her impression-ism, and a character portrait all in one track. Throughout these songs, you know where Mitchell is attempting to go, even though her path is occasion-ally hard to follow.

The impressionistic "Wolf" is a private party, with the wolf sound effects providing the most concrete statement within the song (reading interpreta-tions of this song in record reviews is a genuine treat; nobody agrees on anything—and I understand why!). The long philosophical exposition "Sweet Sucker" advances a "love as dance" theory in a slow, again, plodding fash-ion. Mitchell shares seasoned observations on the perils of the love dance in a manner that is cautious, not negative; wise, not cynical. I mean, after all, it *is* just a dance, right? Last, "The Dry Cleaner" uses trademark Mitchell sounds (clear reiterations of "Twisted" may be heard—even though this is a Mingus tune) to frame a really cute song about a very lucky tourist (placed, by the way, immediately after a Mingus comment on his life's good fortune). The words and music are quite busy and a fun time is there to be had. In many respects, this song is a genuine blessing in that it offers a badly needed dose of levity to a serious tribute to an equally serious artist.

The reviews for this record are really quite interesting. There is a quiet respect for this project. For instance, *Creem*'s Joe Goldberg seems to want to have a go at Mitchell, but he pulls back at the last second, and concludes: "I don't think she was anything but well-intentioned. I just think she was fighting out of her weight." Sam Sutherland demonstrates his respect at the outset: "Although unlikely to find wide acceptance among her older fans, 'Mingus' will strike a responsive chord among mainstream jazz fans and more adventurous pop listeners, for despite its flaws, the project marks a

striking collaboration between two relentlessly inquisitive musical maver-
icks." As usual, *Rolling Stone* works so very, very hard to be cute: "She's the
babe in bopperland, the novice at the slot machines, the tourist, the hitcher.
She's someone who has to ask. Which doesn't mean she follows orders or
even listens to directions. But when you're lost in the mystery and the maps
don't mean a thing, it's nice to be with someone who rolls down the win-
dows and hollers." (The whole review reads this way.) Noel Coppage closes:
"Where jazz is concerned, though, I like to think Joni Mitchell is still working on it, diligently if not always efficiently, and she's by no means finished."
Finally, Larry Kart goes straight to the heart of the matter: "A complex man
of great turbulence and tenderness, Mingus always must have been searching for someone who could truly understand him while still remaining at
arms' length. In Joni Mitchell, he found that person. And she, in Mingus,
found the deepest soul she had yet encountered and treated him with just
the right mixture of respect, insight, and independence."

Critics refrained from cheap shots on *Mingus* because the album warrants
respect. Some records are just not intended for mass audiences, and this is
one of those records. Still, as Sutherland argues, it does strike a balance
that *invites* a large audience, and in so doing, falls directly in line with the
other projects from the sonic explorer phase of Mitchell's lifework. Ed Ward's
review of *Mingus* is actually a fine overview of this four-album set:

> Considering how many things could have gone wrong with this record, I'm
> very happy to see it succeed as well as it does. I could surely have done with-
> out the little snips of conversation sprinkled throughout, which gets very an-
> noying very fast, and I wish the air of sanctity that hovers over the album as
> a result was thinned out a little. Nevertheless, though Mingus fans may sniff
> and Mitchell fans likewise, people who don't let labels trap them can have a
> very good time exploring what's here to hear.

To be sure, the same could be said of *Hissing, Hejira,* and *Reckless Daughter.*
A snip here, a lowering of expectation there; a pop hook here, and pop plati-
tude there—any work of art that provokes any type of response whatso-
ever will certainly incur this kind of criticism. You should read the early
reviews of Pete Townshend's *Tommy.* However, it is the last line of Ward's
review that conveys the key observation: "People who don't let labels trap
them can have a very good time exploring what's here to hear."

The musical world offers rebellious artists to those "people" who "let
labels trap them." While Bob Dylan somehow managed to resist the urge
to become Art Nouveau, he did respond to his environment in a similar manner as Joni and Art. When all the publicity labeling Dylan the "voice of his
generation" and a "protest" singer closed in on his agenda, the Minnesota
bard dropped it all. Cold. No looking back, no concerns for his audience,
no cares for his record company, only a firm belief in his talent and its

agenda. Dylan could write whatever he wanted, probably, whenever he wanted. Yet he was not going to succumb to an audience that, in actuality, meant *nothing* to him. Corner a rebel like Dylan, and he will reject you. Joni Mitchell—in her own distinctive way—is that kind of artist.

Joining *Miles of Aisles* as the bookend pieces surrounding the sonic explorer period is the September 1980 live double album, *Shadows and Light*. With musicians Jaco Pastorius, Don Alias, Pat Metheny, Lyle Mays, and Michael Brecker, and backing vocals by The Persuasions, Mitchell takes the material from this phase of her work on the road and issues a sample show from Santa Barbara (recorded in September 1979). Live versions of "In France They Kiss on Main Street," "Goodbye Pork Pie Hat," "Hejira," and "Dreamland" demonstrate Mitchell's commitment to the sonic explorer material, with only "Free Man in Paris" and "Woodstock" coming from earlier works (the album also contains a "Why Do Fools Fall in Love?" cover). Featuring sound from video clips, extended instrumental solos, and waves of vocals floating throughout the piece, *Shadows* represents a compelling example of the sonic layering that dominates Mitchell's productions from this era. Like *Aisles*, the recording captures a relaxed, confident auteur. Stephen Holden offers this view in *Rolling Stone*: "The extraordinary power of *Shadows and Light*, one of a handful of great live rock albums, took me by surprise . . . [Mitchell has] created a brooding instrumental sound that's unique in popular music: a perfect sonic counterpart to her flowing, painterly imagery." Holden describes the ensemble as a "dream band" that directly complements Mitchell's "exhilarating vocals" in a fashion that makes "the current versions . . . better than the originals." He closes with this insightful observation: "Constructing seemingly conflicting images of darkness and light, benefactors and parasites, law abiders and lawbreakers, the singer states her belief in the absolute relativity of moral standards and the ultimate indivisibility of good and evil."

The sonic explorer period unveils Mitchell's musical intuition in one of its most playful moments. She surrounded herself with talented players, placed them in open-ended situations, and arranged their work to suit her creative visions. This musical exploration pioneered sonic strategies that would soon dominate the music industry. Throughout this musical adventure, the auteur's Earth Mother manifesto suffers through a transition in which highly prized ideals succumb to much-hated realities—just as Holden observed. Earth Mother looks inward, reacquaints herself with her first principles, accepts life's dualities, and resolves her metaphysical dilemma during this crucial period. From now on, she will focus her patented nurturing observations on certain interpersonal and societal issues, and render statements regarding their perceived conditions. Our participant commentator has evolved into a seasoned observer whose wit, wisdom, cynicism, and anger will generate powerful—and signature—takes on love, life, the entertainment industry, and house pets.

THE SEASONED COMMENTATOR PERIOD

The personal resolutions Joni Mitchell achieved in *Don Juan's Reckless Daughter* established a context for a series of seasoned commentaries on life, relationships, and business. Here she turns to a steady stream of songwriting strategies that enable her to praise, damn, describe, and interpret her subject matter for herself and her audience. At times, Earth Mother's bitterness over the failed utopian dream drifts toward a distrustful cynicism or a righteous, feisty anger. She has reason to suspect specific sources that not only threatened the dream's emergence, but prohibited its development and contaminated society. Big business, greedy entrepreneurs, corrupt government, and ruthless individuals of all stripes subvert the system for personal, group, or institutional gain. Rest assured, Joni Mitchell is out to expose and condemn such activities. The dream's failure to appear is never taken lightly; it was truly a heartfelt ambition, and Mitchell's indignation provides considerable motivation for her pen.

In this final phase we witness albums with a purpose. From *Wild Things Run Fast* and its portrayals of relational bliss, to *Dog Eat Dog* and its intense societal commentary, to *Chalk Mark in a Rain Storm* and its blend of grievances, to the nostalgia of *Night Ride Home*, to yet another sampler of complaint in *Turbulent Indigo*, to the capstone statement, *Taming the Tiger*, our seasoned commentator sharpens her pencil and pursues her agenda in her own inevitable style. After the personal sacrifices associated with her Earth Mother role and the personal resolutions achieved during her sonic explorer period, Mitchell discovered a creative equilibrium that facilitated her commentary on subjects that have always been near to her heart—and muse. At this point, however, the auteur's emotional detachment produces art that informs—and, occasionally, prescribes—but rarely bleeds openly for its point.

From the airy artiness of *Mingus*, Mitchell returns to a standard pop venue with a message for us all: Keep Love Alive! She explained her sonic strategy for *Mingus* and her new approach on *Wild Things Run Fast* to Vic Garbarini in 1983: "[With *Mingus*] I was trying to become the Jackson Pollock of music . . . I just wanted all the notes, everybody's part, to tangle. I wanted all the desks pushed out of rows, I wanted the military abolished, anything linear had to go. Then at a certain point I began to crave that order again. So doing this album was a natural reentry into it." When Kristine McKenna inquired if her new record was a step back to pop, the auteur replied: "[I don't see it] as a step 'back' toward pop, but rather as a synthesis of a lot of things I've done. There is a return to rock steady rhythms, which I'd abandoned for awhile simply because I was sick of the backbeat, but there's still a lot of jazz phrasing in the vocals." Perhaps Garbarini sums up *Wild Things* best: "You could call it the Concorde version of *Court and Spark*: supersonic production values, razor-edged guitars, streamlined hooks

and melodies—all the nuances of vocal phrasing and rhythmic sophistication she picked up on her jazz pilgrimage applied to good ol' rock 'n'
roll. . . . *Wild Things* also signals a shift back to the first-person confessional
style of her earlier work."

Released in October 1982, *Wild Things Run Fast* contains 11 tracks (running 36:44) that include a sample of Hy Zaret's "Unchained" and Leiber and
Stoller's classic "(You're So Square) Baby, I Don't Care." Produced by
Mitchell with trusted engineer Henry Lewy at the controls, the project features Larry Carlton, John Guerin, Larry Klein, Lionel Richie, Wayne Shorter,
James Taylor, and a host of musicians and singers. This is the record the
biographers denote as the "Joni Loves Larry" project (Mitchell married
bassist/producer Larry Klein); however, my interpretation differs somewhat.
I view this record as a "Joni Wants to Love Larry" venture. Throughout this
album, threat is in the air and songs work to muster the resources necessary to combat those hazards and allow love to flourish. To that end, five
of the album's songs address the love challenge story line ("Wild Things
Run Fast," "Ladies' Man," "Be Cool," "You Dream Flat Tires," and "Man to
Man") in which characters surely have that feeling, yet there are obstacles
to be negotiated. Two songs ("Solid Love" and "Underneath the Streetlight")
follow the love celebration narrative (the Leiber and Stoller cover also en-
acts this theme), and Mitchell's adaptation of Scripture (I Corinthians, Chapter 13) in the love treatise, "Love," leaves no doubt about the auteur's
attitude toward her most persistent songwriting theme.

The album opens with a serious personal complaint about aging
("Chinese Café" with the "Unchained" sample). The song goes *way* beyond
the hints within "Little Green" as Mitchell makes a direct reference to her
child. Since the song continues with more autobiographical references, it
is an awfully revealing comment. A new character, Carol, joins Joni (and
probably Sharon) for a simple, coherent complaint regarding the passing
of time in the old hometown. Once more, we note Mitchell's use of a parenthetical comment that captures the song's essence. From the town's new
construction, to the ever-present love fantasy (via "Unchained"), to the
women and their growing resemblance to their mothers, this song charts
the "Women from the Day" and their nostalgic recollections. Even with
everyone and everything aging and changing, love still rules the roost.

From that opening personal complaint we turn to affairs of the heart. Our
second "love treatise" ("Love") is a capstone statement that uses Scripture
to reiterate the moral of the story from the songs that preceded it and dominate this record. After songs of challenge, celebration, and cautious optimism, "Love" puts it all in perspective. Earth Mother is more than a little
bit prescriptive in her portrayal of love's innocence, purity, and cleansing
powers. Love, we are told, is the be-all and end-all of life. Love makes life
heroic, and, in its absence, tragic. When love is present, a celebration is in
order and Mitchell is happy to comply. These songs of celebration are, in a

word, cute. One feels the need for a parade after "Solid Love" and its "hooray for love" party in which the narrator just cannot get over the fact that somehow, someway, there is a chance for a meaningful relationship. No more romantic thievery, no more overnight flings, no more stifling partners. No sir, by golly, a "Solid Love" is in the house—let us all celebrate. Of course, one way to celebrate is to stroll down to your local streetlight and scream out "I Love You" to all who will listen. And that is exactly what Mitchell does in "Underneath the Streetlight." Joy abounds. The Leiber and Stoller cover seals the blissful deal.

The record's lone romantic complaint ("Moon at the Window") reminds us why love's presence warrants a party, as well as why that precious emotional state presents such a challenge. Love's thieves will rob you blind, the song reports, as it uses symbolic dualities to established the two sides of the love coin. Mitchell's use of an on-off analogy (i.e., a water faucet and light-switch metaphor) communicates the emotion's haphazard state as the narrator longs for a caring love in which an ability to not care is a central part. Love is a challenge, and this record uses this complaint to reinforce that sentiment.

The five love challenges take certain facets of the relational game and contemplate those happenings. The chase is on in "Wild Things Run Fast" (the "Sweet Suck Dance" has evolved into a hunt, and the narrator is on the trail); the nature of the beast is explored in "Ladies' Man" (the narrator is wise to his game and seeks intervention on her terms—her aim is true, but the challenge remains); the game plan is discussed in the highly prescriptive "Be Cool" (the love manual is on display with its rundown of the tools necessary to do an effective job: Keep the situation even, don't over- or under-react, seek balance—dualities abound); cautious optimism is entertained in "You Dream Flat Tires" (memories are long *and* informative; beware); and "Man to Man" looks back on it all as a means of mustering the resources necessary to reenter the hunt. "Man" certainly contains a significant amount of complaint because the narrator is *very* tired of losing; still, never does she rail against former lovers (she actually praises them), and she is doing everything she can to overcome her fear and chase those "wild things" once more. Again, "Joni Wants to Love Larry" is the message here. You may want to run down to the streetlight and scream or count the blessings of your newfound "Solid Love," but you had better be aware that the hunt is demanding; the target is savvy; the game has rules and is risky; and never, ever forget what you have learned from previous experiences. Failure is acceptable here; just understand *why* you failed, incorporate that knowledge into your game plan, and get back on that horse. A seasoned Earth Mother is at her nurturing best in these songs of hopeful experience.

Reviews were generally mixed. *Trouser Press* observes: "*Wild Things Run Fast* isn't a radical departure, or the definitive hard-rockin' statement we always knew Mitchell had in her but was too coy to deliver. Rather, it coalesces the various styles she's pursued over the last 10 years or so in tightly and tastefully arranged songs." Also positing the record's relationship to previous entries, *Stereo Review* questions the musical strategy: "The sound here is electronic, with synthesizers doing something akin to what Tom Scott used to do for her with reeds. . . . But it seems to me the songs have to adjust to it more than it adjusts to them. Consciously or not, Mitchell seems to be fooling around with the style-is-content concept. A good learning experience for her, perhaps, but not that terrific an album for the rest of us." *Rolling Stone* maintains that the album's sound "alternates rhythmically scratchy rock with cocktail jazz" while the lyrics communicate "thoughts on love" that "dart through these songs like foxes in the underbrush, seeming at once to build toward answers, then tripping over contradictions." After *Musician* claims the record "is a return to plain, simple speech, sly autobiography and well-placed gossip" it concludes: "No one is ever likely to cover these songs, anymore than someone is likely to repaint one of Paul Klee's pictures. The songs, the performances, are finished, full and strong!" Finally, *Creem* argues: "Having given up her tortured self-doubting and destructive attempts to analyze love's ineluctably mysterious nature, Mitchell displays the mature composure to distance herself from the past right at the start . . . and to acknowledge, albeit wistfully, that [nothing is permanent]. This isn't an expression of defeat, though; Mitchell simply realizes that naive belief won't make anyone's dreams come true."

Wild Things is a focused work of art, as Henry Lewy told Steve Pond: "The records are always reflections of her mental attitude, and she really found the groove for this record about halfway through, when she got a new boyfriend and everything in her life solidified." "Everything" may have "solidified" in the manner her love celebrations indicate, but those emotions are not the crux of the matter on this project. The lessons of "Man to Man" are genuine. Love is a "challenge," and the outcome is *always* uncertain; therefore, prepare yourself, cleanse your heart, stay in touch with your First Principles, and have at it. If, somehow, those thieves rob you blind or you simply lose, regroup, understand what happened, file that knowledge away, and return to the fray. Love is, after all, worth the effort. It is our lifeblood. It is our redemption. It is our reason for living. These are Joni Mitchell's First Principles, and she has fulfilled her duty to share them with us all. It is, in every respect, a reiteration of "I Think I Understand" from *Clouds*. Now, having reestablished that, Earth Mother has other business on her mind.

Dog Eat Dog is an angry work. Earth Mother's disappointment with her failed manifesto now focuses on those who assassinated the dream. She explained her thematic shift to *Musician* in 1985: "The last album was so dominantly about love, I guess for a while I just exhausted the field. You know, you plant wheat one year and maybe flax the next. I don't like to repeat myself too much." Later, she described the album thus: "Some of it's personal and some of it is general. . . . I just noticed an increase in my *out-*

rage at the general direction of things. . . . It's an angry album." In a *Stereo Review* interview she noted how litigation over a new California tax on musicians who maintain creative control over their work joined her new marital status, and the time she had to watch television news fueled her anger and inspired her pen (there she reports she originally planned to title the project *Songs of a Couch Potato*). After again explaining how her marriage settled her work, she elaborated on the new record's themes to *New Music Express*:

> So with that [marriage] taken care of, you begin to look around you. It's a natural sociological phenomenon, you know. . . . Although I see it in America because I'm here, it's more of a global point of view. We are so inter-related with the news being the way it is . . . world incidents broadcast into your living room . . . the Western world has all the symptoms of downfall if you study it and compare it with all the other civilisations which have gone under. There are the youth cult obsessions, a greater openness regarding homosexuality, the decadent theatre reflecting the repressed savageness of a culture.

Later, she added that the Parents Music Resource Center's "censorship" movement was also an inspiration: "One of the reasons this album is so outspoken in the context of my work is that I think it's a case of use it or lose it. If I don't start speaking out, taking a chance and addressing things that are important to me in this way, we might not have this outlet very long."

And speak out she does. The October 1985 release contains ten tracks (running 43:31) and represents the first Joni Mitchell album without a major Henry Lewy credit (he recorded one track); instead, the auteur is joined by Larry Klein, Mike Shipley, and Thomas Dolby in the producer's role. The crowded producer's chair made for some rough sledding, as she explained to *Stereo Review*:

> This was one of the most difficult albums I ever had to make . . . I had never done any kind of work with a committee where, instead of just going with my natural enthusiasm for something, there were four strong opinions to consider—and a lot of opposition. But frequently, because of the delay and irritation, just like sand in an oyster, a pearl was born.

That pearl features musicians such as Dolby, Klein, Mike Landau, Vinnie Colaiuta, Michael Fisher, Wayne Shorter, and others, along with guest vocalists (in order of appearance) Michael McDonald, Dolby, Klein, Joe Smith, Rod Steiger, Don Henley, James Taylor, and Amy Holland. At this point in the oeuvre, Mitchell employs the proverbial cast of thousands as the production strategy that extends as far back as "Night in the City" and "The Pirate of Penance" assumes control over the proceedings. That is, Mitchell deploys layers and layers of voices, instruments, and sound efforts as she creates sonic paintings of increasing complexity. At times, a call-and-response method is evident; at others, the effects just pile upon each other in a wall of sound. Mitchell's newfound interest in computer technologies is evident in Dolby's presence and *Dog*'s subsequent sound. A new sonic era emerges with this project.

Thematically, *Dog* is a focused enterprise. With two tributes to friendship providing the bookends to this piece, the seven songs in between provide quite a contrast. Mitchell opens with "Good Friends" (with guest vocalist McDonald) and its cloudy account of life between friends. They visit, frolic, argue, and face an unpredictable world together. Could this be the beginning of something more? That is left to our imagination. What is not left to our imagination is the unbridled joy communicated through the love celebration, "Lucky Girl." Amongst the darkness and addictions presented throughout *Dog* is that ray of sunshine that accompanies the discovery of one's soul mate. The narrator counts her lucky stars in this celebratory tribute to her trustworthy special man. In this song, the auteur seems happy and secure.

Yet she is also damned angry. Although we pause just a moment for addiction via the sound effects moment that is "Smokin' (Empty Try Another)" (a Lewy recording of a rhythmic but empty cigarette machine), the seven songs of societal complaint bowl you over. With smooth jazz and pop textures supporting her, Earth Mother explodes against the media and its simplifications that just confuse people ("Fiction"), offers a litany of worldly complaints ("The Three Great Stimulants"), attacks the politically inclined evangelists who profitably pollute the airwaves ("Tax Free"), expands her net for an inclusive attack on All Things Evil ("Dog Eat Dog"), submits an anti-materialism rant ("Shiny Toys"), uses Ethiopia's problems as a case in point ("Ethiopia"), and implores us not to try and wish away world problems with idealistic dreams ("Impossible Dreamer"). Mitchell is loaded for unjust, irresponsible, deceitful bear in these sharp, focused diatribes. The Earth Mother and her nurturing optimism have left the building.

"Fiction" establishes the album's pace and sonic strategy. The song is a pop powerhouse that bops as much as it complains. Mitchell hammers home the confusion that accompanies exposure to all the media that occupy contemporary life. Initially, she seems to concentrate on advertising, yet she loosens up and includes all sorts of media. The layers of voices (featuring music executive Joe Smith) and sounds actually seem to replicate her point: More is actually less. The wall of negativity gains momentum with "Stimulants" and its direct references to abortion, war, needless litigation, threats to personal freedom, the environment, and big business. Earth Mother knows where the devil resides because that snake has slithered out of The Garden and out onto Main Street. Speaking of the devil, if you were a shape-shifter looking for a strategic form from which to preach the evil doctrine of the dark side, where would you hide? Mitchell points out a fine location in "Tax Free" as she presents Rod Steiger as a television evangelist with a wicked agenda. Layers and layers of sound communicate that the moneychangers are in the temple preaching a politically motivated doctrine of self-indulgence. Her argument is crystal clear: They practice politics and they should pay taxes. Earth Mother is on the case.

Since the sound-effects piece "Smokin'" is followed by "Dog Eat Dog," I can only assume that her unsatisfied habit inspired a symbolic fit. "Dog" is an inclusive attack; everybody suffers Earth Mother's wrath. She goes after evangelists, financiers, and, most of all, people in this all-encompassing complaint that addresses the crux of the matter: People cause their own problems. The lawyers, preachers, and wicked financiers get their greedy way because people allow it to happen. These institutional oppressors are merely reflections of the people they intend to abuse—if you could be a profiteering thug, you would do it, too. Why? Well, "Shiny Toys" serves up the answer as quickly as the question is posed. Your materialism is your false god. This is a simple but fascinating song. Earth Mother damns the world's materialism, pauses to recall the simple joys associated with The Garden, and closes with the understanding that life is, after all, choices— and everyone seems to have made theirs.

The fact that Mitchell includes "Impossible Dreamer" on this record is instructive. The song points to environmental problems, famine, painful love, and evil people and how the dream once entertained a genuine alternative. The Garden was a compelling option. But greed won. Thus, to dream the dream is utter folly. The key here, however, is the narrator's nostalgia. Earth Mother truly *loves* that dream, and it will never, ever go away; no matter how angry she gets. She may rant and rave, but her worldview is such a part of her personality that it never goes away. She may pause to praise love, yet her duty requires her to use her observational powers for the greater good. Her conviction is impressive.

That conviction was also noted by music critics. Mark Rowland, for example, writes: "The sound is still Joni Mitchell, but the sentiments are pure Joan of Arc. . . . *Dog Eat Dog* is really a record about social Darwinism, and how that philosophy poisons hearts, our nation, and planet." The *Musician* review concludes the project "is thoroughly modern music, and it's also a throwback to a time when pop stars sang about the world as if they—and it—mattered." Stephen Holden claims the record's "topicality" indicates "a dramatic return by Miss Mitchell to the activist folk-music tradition" while the music is "miles away from anything that could be called folk." Holden continues: "The most futuristic-sounding record of Miss Mitchell's career, it presents her pronouncements within the context of richly layered soundscapes that bear some comparison to Neo-Expressionist painting." Peter Smith declares the auteur "has made her best album since *Court and Spark*," and concludes: "Joni Mitchell . . . has widened her horizons musically, while taking note of the narrowing of potential for most of the rest of the world. It's a risky dance she's chosen; but if the dance wasn't risky, it would just be walking." *Rolling Stone* roundly condemns the work by calling Mitchell's "social criticisms" the "sort of bloodless liberal homilies you would expect from Rush" and criticizing her attack on TV evangelists as "ironic" in that "there's as much sanctimony in this record as in the smuggest Falwell sermon." Finally, the *San Jose Mercury News* puts it all together: "Sharp-edged images have their own significance, but, at times, it is reassuring to know that some artists can be many things, feelings and sounds at the same time, that they have doubts and questions of themselves and others, that, in short, their image is their art and not the reverse. Joni Mitchell is such an artist."

Dog Eat Dog is a powerful record. Although the layers of sound are an occasional distraction, Mitchell's pen chronicles a world in danger of imploding. The evil before us is aided and abetted by a willing populace who gladly exchange their freedom for a fine German automobile. To cope with our materialistic sins, we finance politically motivated ecclesiastics who preach their doctrine of hate all the way to the bank. We give lip service to serious situations such as the Ethiopian horror, but actually that dreadful scenario is merely a fund-raising ploy. Evil abounds. That Mitchell opens and closes this damning editorial with portrayals of friendship and relational bliss suggests that one escape from this hellish situation remains. According to this record, we would be wise to focus on love, turn our greedy ways around, and undertake steps to repair the damage inflicted by our own hand.

Those and other dark sentiments return via the sampler of negativity that is *Chalk Mark in a Rain Storm*. The layers and layers of sounds and voices that characterized the *Dog* project now extend further as Mitchell's exploration of computer-assisted sound design competes for sonic space with her words—words that are piled on top of each other—*and* the studio musicians. That she also wanted more live playing on the album produced a busy production, as she explained to Iain Blair:

> Well, it's true I couldn't face making another record without seeing some real-live musicians on the other side of the glass. So this time I specifically set out to get a much more live rhythm section and mix real instruments with electronic sounds, instead of going all the way with programming synthesizers and drum machines. . . . Perhaps "Chalk" is back to the basics in some ways, but the truth is that it wasn't so much that I felt I'd gotten away from my roots as that employing all the electronic hardware now available is so bloody tedious! [Later she adds] But here we are in 1988, and I just cannot resist playing with all these hi-tech toys. This is an era of amazing gadgetry, and any composer would be half-dead not to want to experiment and be involved.

Produced by Mitchell and Klein (with a host of engineers and assistants; including Henry Lewy), this ten-track work (running 46:25) uses a variety of celebrity voices (Peter Gabriel, Benjamin Orr, Don Henley, Billy Idol, Tom Petty, Willie Nelson, and more) and the usual musical cast (e.g., Klein, Landau, Shorter, and others) to advance the auteur's commentaries on contemporary issues. Mitchell offered this rationale for the additional singers to Steve Pond: "It's an idea I've had for a long time, to sing the narrative and cast my characters. 'Cause the songs have a lot of 'he said' and 'she said' in them. So I thought, 'Who would be the perfect Old Dan in 'Cool Water'? Who would be the perfect bully in 'Dancin' Clown'? Then it became fun, and I just started calling people when I would think of them." There she expressed the attitude that supported the venture: "I feel these times are just pathetic. When I wrote this album, I was just hurting for the culture." A 1988 *Los Angeles Times* interview elaborated on the relationship between her personal situation and her art: "I can't think of any theme that's expired for me except the search for love. I found someone with the values I was looking for in a man and I'm happily married now. I've discovered that with your focus no longer on finding a mate, you get a heightened sense of community, and I've become a bit more political—not too political, though." These are the musical and editorial positions that inspired *Chalk Mark in a Rain Storm*.

Chalk Mark exchanges emotional depth for sonic complexity as it sounds rich yet offers little lyrical yield. The record contains four societal complaints ("Number One," "Lakota," "The Tea Leaf Prophecy," and "The Recurring Dream"), a love challenge ("My Secret Place"), a scenic vignette ("Cool Water"), a portrait ("The Beat of Black Wings"), and three relational complaints: "Dancin' Clown," "Snakes and Ladders," and "A Bird That Whistles" (an adaptation of the traditional "Corrina, Corrina"). Again, the layers of sound and piles of voices make for extremely busy listening that often buries any message that might be offered; in fact, there are moments when I sense that Mitchell is offering the idea of a message, without any message itself.

Occasionally, as in the tracks "Cool Water" (with Nelson), "Dancin' Clown" (with Idol and Petty), "My Secret Place" (with Gabriel), and portions of "Number One" (with Orr), it is really difficult to discern just what all the commotion is communicating. As the record unfolds, there are moments when you cease caring. For example, the love challenge "My Secret Place" is a highly repetitive, evasive account of a special invitation to a special place where only special people are allowed. Things get twisted around, though they never lose their special qualities. The song is, well, special. The vignette with Nelson ("Cool Water") is beyond me; I just wish someone would give these people a beverage. The original song by Bob Nolan has been revised, and Mitchell loads it with her trademark descriptions, but nothing ever happens. Ever.

The relational complaints also share this quality. "Dancin'" dances around its point as much as anything, yet with time, we see that love is a bully that threatens us all. The use of Idol's aggressive vocals to play the bully role works in this evasive, rocking complaint. The drum machine must have overheated during the recording of "Snakes and Ladders," in which layers and layers of voices and drums provide a platform for an extremely negative portrayal of a relational life cycle. Harsh views on materialism, society, and contemporary male-female roles provide strategic contrasts in this sonic bombast that revisits "The Arrangement" and its inherent difficulties. The symbolism is unequivocal: Climbing that relational ladder only prepares you to slide back down and start over again. Love is a vicious cycle that goes nowhere. Now *that* is cynical. Finally, the closing cut's reiteration of "Corrina" ("A Bird That Whistles") simply moans "woe is me" and leaves us to contemplate that sad state. We are certainly walking an extremely beaten path here.

Turning to the societal complaints, "Tea Leaf" talks about one thing (Mitchell's family and the wonderful story predicting her family's unlikely emergence) while it appears to want to talk about another (an antiwar sentiment). Mitchell's parents' story is delightful, yet the connection to the war is more than fast and loose. Although her father fought in World War II, the connection is simply not made—at least overtly. The other societal complaints are more focused, but they just do not have the personality that accompanies most of Mitchell's work. They complain from the head, not from the heart. "Number One" (a denunciation of the win-at-all-costs mentality) and "Reoccurring Dream" (a relentless anti-advertising attack) almost reduce their points to meaninglessness with their very heavy-handed cynicism. Surely, the "Number One" mentality and unrestrained materialism threaten our moral fiber, yet these tracks just fail to arouse any emotions. They simply offer layer upon layer of ranting. "Lakota" is inviting as it denounces how the Indians have been used and abused; however, the sonic traffic is so heavy that it prohibits any focus. You *know* where the song is going while you just do not care how it gets there. These songs are musical tributes to attention deficit disorder.

Such is not the case with Killer Kyle's story in the "Beat of Black Wings." Mitchell paints a dark portrait of the soldier-turned-misanthrope who uses the album's title to summarize his worldly status. His country, his woman, everybody except the bartender has betrayed this poor soul who is searching for a role in Bruce Springsteen's *Nebraska* film. What makes the song so vivid is the fact that society does this to young men without a second thought. In an album so full of fast and loose imagery, "Black Wings" is a striking exception.

Record reviews seem to *want* this to be a good record; at times, reviewers seem to pull for the seasoned songwriter. For instance, the *Washington Post* opines: "Mitchell seems to have tired of talking about herself and her romantic obsessions. . . . Mitchell has evolved from the confessional poet of 'Blue' to the cocktail crooner of 'Court and Spark' to the be-bop dabbler of 'Mingus,' and now she positions herself as pop's oracle, declaiming about mistreatment of Indians and Viet vets and the insidiousness of commercial culture." The *New York Tribune* reports: "Despite her fame and popularity, Joni Mitchell has always been an artist who follows her instincts, even when they lead her far from her audience's expectations. On her new album, she sticks to those instincts, but still manages to meet her listeners halfway. The result is her best and most accessible album in a long time." The *Keene Sentinel* argues *Chalk Mark* is "her latest act of inscrutability" in a series of works that "are always challenging and dignified, not for every taste, always just out of reach." Finally, the *Austin American-Statesman* strikes that middle ground and concludes: "Mitchell's new release is certainly not a masterpiece when compared to her best work, but since it's essentially a transition vehicle it works quite well."

Transition vehicle or not, this is one of those albums in which the title says it all. *Chalk Mark* is not a memorable record. Mitchell's fascination with sonic toys is crowding her songs, robbing them of their lyrical vitality, and diluting their potential messages. Furthermore, her anger has grown so cynical that it is diluting its impact. The combination of *Dog* and *Chalk Mark* laid her complaint out for all to consider. To continue in this fashion is to invite the kind of emotional beating she endured toward the end of her lifework's initial phase. Unlike her exploration of jazz, the programmed sounds of synthesized drums, strings, and what have you are overwhelming—not supporting—her lyrical inclinations. Those lyrics are not impressionistic, they are just unfocused, cloudy, and tired. The key term here is "overproduction." Just where is David Crosby when you need him?

These observations were not lost on anyone. The artist, her audience, and her record company understood the declining state of Mitchell's sales, as she explained to David Wild in 1991: "All the records that I've made with Geffen have cost a lot of money, and they haven't recouped, which is dangerous, because you're maintaining the integrity of your product, but you're becoming indebted to the company store." That delicate balance between "maintaining the integrity of your product" and generating sales is a demanding one, that is certain. The fact that the auteur refers to her work as "product" signals an understanding of the corporate side of her business. Subsequently, Mitchell responds to her dilemma with a middle-of-the-road piece of pleasant nostalgia, 1991's *Night Ride Home*.

In an *Entertainment Weekly* interview Mitchell described *Night Ride* as a "collection of middle-aged love songs." Perhaps. The record (released in February 1991) is a soft, flowing piece that uses layers and layers of voices to present songs of youth, youthful ambitions, and those wonderful days of yore. "Love" may be in the air, but none of the album's ten songs (running 51:43) focuses on that haphazard condition. Instead, the Mitchell-Klein production offers a life celebration (the loving "Night Ride Home"), four portraits ("Cherokee Louise," "Come in from the Cold," "The Only Joy in Town," and "Ray's Dad's Cadillac"), two personal complaints ("Nothing Can Be Done" and "Two Grey Rooms"), one societal complaint ("The Windfall [Everything for Nothing]"), and one piece of narrative impressionism, "Passion Play (When All the Slaves Are Free)." Sonically, the record is tame when compared to previous entries. The musicians (Alex Acuna, Vinnie Colaiuta, Bill Dillon, Klein, Michael Landau, and Wayne Shorter) and backing vocals (David Baerwald, Karen Peris, and Brenda Russell) may layer their efforts in a traditional, painterly fashion, yet the sounds work harmoniously in support of the tune and, in turn, allow Mitchell's nostalgia to shine through in a fashion absent on *Chalk Mark* or *Dog*.

At times, the songs are bittersweet. The kid games and scenes of Mitchell's Canadian youth on "Cherokee" are tainted by the parental abuse Louise endures. It is a simple, sad portrait that is rich in nostalgia (kids swinging in trees, teenagers fighting with parents, kids placing pennies on railroad tracks). Kid games quickly turn to kid abuse (a foster parent rapes Louise, it appears) as the song rotates between youthful scenes and the search for a hiding Louise. Mitchell paints a fine scenic portrait that is as rich in detail as it is in compassion. "Two Grey Rooms" does not really do that much, yet there is a sense of intense sadness for what could have been conveyed by the narrator's nostalgic stalking (the song's emotional qualities are enhanced by Jeremy Lubbock's fine string orchestrations). The personal complaint focuses on the narrator's secret efforts to gain a daily glimpse of a former lover or love interest. She sits, patiently awaiting him to simply walk beneath her window, dreading those days when he walks elsewhere. Again, not much happens, but the emotional quality of Mitchell's descriptions is impressive. Her explanation of the song's origins is intriguing. She told Robert Hilburn that it took seven years to find the story that she felt "fit the music." She continued:

> It's a story of obsession . . . about this German aristocrat who had a lover in his youth that he never got over. He later finds this man working on a dock and notices the path that the man takes every day to and from work. So the aristocrat gives up his fancy digs and moves to these two shabby gray rooms overlooking this street, just to watch this man walk to and from work. That's a song that shows my songs aren't all self-portraits.

An *extremely* close reading of the lyrics would in no way reveal the song's homosexual orientation. The first-person narrative offers no suggestion of a dimension that truly thickens the plot. The moral of the story: Beware of autobiographical assertions!

Speaking of autobiography, "Come in from the Cold" is a pretty song with soft harmonies and nostalgic references that conjure feelings of failure—those youthful ambitions have never materialized. This self-portrait seems to return to Mitchell's "Urge for Going" as it describes a teenage dance and its close supervision by suspicious adults, her dreams of freedom and subsequent enslavement, her rejection of her iconic status, her distrust of men, and her fear of loneliness, and it closes by second-guessing certain life decisions. Here again, Mitchell uses layers of voices to create the impression of an internal conversation in which one dark soliloquy is answered by another. Ultimately, the song chronicles the narrator's sadness—an emotional state that one just has to attribute to Mitchell since the autobiographical detail is so rich, so poignant, so sincere. Earth Mother's disappointment is disheartening and the personal complaint "Nothing Can Be Done" drives that disillusionment home. "Nothing" is a woeful tune that uses layers of sounds to communicate how the narrator must surrender to aging, accept her nostalgia for her youth, and develop coping strategies for it all. From "Cherokee" and its dreamy memories, to "Two Grey" and its regret, to "Come In" and its disappointment, to "Nothing" and its acceptance we gain an understanding of the bittersweet qualities of one person's maturation throughout her personal life cycle.

The auteur pauses for a spot of chrome worship through the life celebration "Night Ride" and the self-portrait "Ray's Dad's Cadillac." In the former, we experience a simple, sweet ditty about a ride home on the night of the Fourth of July. With crickets in the background, the narrator announces her love for her man, their love of the road, and the serene qualities of a quiet drive. In the latter, Mitchell presents a joyful account of her youthful escapades in her boyfriend's dad's car. Ray's dad is also her math teacher, so we are treated to the fact that success in one context (the car) does not necessarily lead to success in another (the classroom). The song is funny, insightful, and terribly nostalgic—especially in light of the other songs of bitter regret. Once again, we learn there is nothing as touching as a few poignant moments in a fine automobile. Earth Mother is, after all, an American.

Pulling *Night Ride* in another direction is its return to *Dog Eat Dog* through "The Windfall." This classic Mitchell diatribe rails against those seeking something for nothing. The auteur is grinding her axe on a topic near and dear (supposedly, a former housekeeper sued Mitchell over her firing) as she lambastes lawyers, the legal system, and everyone who desires those "Shiny Toys" that somebody else pays for. Mitchell's anger is as righteous as it ever gets at any time on this song. She is mad as hell and one gains the impression that she is not going to take this anymore. In fact, she is *so* upset that she contemplates the end times *immediately* after "Windfall" via her adaptation of W. B. Yeats's "The Second Coming" titled "Slouching Toward Bethlehem." Could it be she wants those lawyers to go to hell so badly that she fantasizes the Second Coming as a means of expediting their fate? When this sermon is considered in light of the previously discussed songs, our aging artist seems to be preparing us for the harvest that will eventually accompany our failure to return to The Garden. Mitchell's fantasy failed to materialize, and her reality suggests that all this evil is leading to something big—for instance, the end of the world.

Night Ride also features two songs that reach back to the songwriting past. In "Passion Play" we observe Mitchell's impressionism at work. This pleasant-sounding, floating piece is extremely repetitive and extraordinarily cryptic. Clear, simple language is used to frame a series of impressions that appear to address spiritual matters (e.g., sin, redemption, and some form of slavery). This is a private party, that is certain. However, when taken in the context of this project's songs, it, too, seems suggestive of some sort of judgment or reckoning that is ultimately decisive. Not so exclusive is the travelogue portrait, "The Only Joy." This cute account of a tourist's interest in painting a local young man who captures her fancy is full of vivid street scenes and travelogue vitality. She describes the busy daytime street and its empty evening counterpart, the flowers in the young man's hair, and his attractive qualities (were she younger, she claims, she would have chased this wild thing down; regardless of his speed). Both songs return to songwriting strategies that have all but disappeared during this intense period of serious commentary.

That blend of the old and the new captured the attention of music critics. For example, Tom Moon writes: "For the first time in years, Joni Mitchell isn't harping or chiding or whining or lecturing. She is simply doing what she does best. She is observing. . . . With this record Mitchell continues her evolution without alienating anybody." Moon's insightful review continues: "But for Mitchell, middle age is less a barrier than a vantage point. She is still grappling with the emotions and observations that worm into her songs, and her wise, dispassionate treatment of this conflicting information gives her work perspective." Geoffrey Himes concurs: "Her 16th album . . . pares away the techno-rock experiments of her previous two albums to put the emphasis back on her frail soprano and her hollow-body jazz guitar strumming. The lyrics dominate the foreground, and the 10 songs are unified by the author's middle-aged perspective on her youth and her current milieu." Jay Cocks maintains it is Mitchell's best work in ten years: "It's easy to like and hard to forget, and it shows that Mitchell—for all her restless musical experimentation—has an undiminished skill in navigating some of the deeper estuaries of the mainstream." After Tom Sinclair complains about the album's tendency toward "overproduction," he closes: "Old-time Mitchell fans may well prefer the incandescence of her *Blue* period or even the abstract expressionism of *Mingus* or *Shadows and Light*. Still, *Night Ride Home*, if not the masterpiece some might have hoped for, is a convincing demonstration of her continuing validity as an artist."

Night Ride is tranquil by recent Mitchell standards, but it is nevertheless pretty doggone blue. Aging is horrible, youthful dreams yield only nostalgia now (at times, pitiful nostalgia), lawyers and moneychangers are destroying what is left of justice, and nobody can be trusted in any way. Earth Mother is pining for her youth, that is for certain. But she does more than that. She is very much in touch with her youthful ambitions and equally aware of exactly what interfered with those dreams' ability to reach fruition. Joni Mitchell knows why the dream failed, and that makes her observations more than blue; her resentment, her bitterness, her anger, her inner turbulence—all of her intensely held emotions are evolving into a darker shade of blue. Maybe a shade more indigo than blue.

Thematically, individually, and professionally, Joni Mitchell was in a state of flux after *Night Ride*. Her debts to the "company store" were mounting. Her songwriting conveyed a disbelief that transcended her art; *she* was in a state of dismay. Mitchell described her situation in this lengthy 1994 commentary to *Mojo*:

> I had the choice to give this record to Geffen and call it my swansong, to head up into the Canadian backbush and get on with my painting. But because Geffen hadn't done much with me in the time I was with them—I was just kind of hired and forgotten, on a lot of levels—the feedback from everyone around was that that would be a shame. And Mo Ostin at Warner's was very enthusiastic about having me back. See, in my entire career there hasn't been a lot of excitement about my albums coming out. There is excitement about this one, for some reason. People are ready to listen, they're more ready to take something a little more to heart and to mind than they have in the past. And unlike some of my peers I haven't hit a writer's block: when I hit a block I just paint, which is an old crop rotation trick. So since I haven't lost my voice, and since I'm over the middle-age hump and at peace with becoming an elder . . . although, of course, I did ask myself whether a woman of my age could continue in this youth-oriented genre. As a painter you're just beginning to ripen at 50, but as a musician there's a lot of scrutiny as to how you look and so forth. It's such a shallow and fickle business.

Mitchell reinforced these comments in a 1995 *Musician* interview when she revealed that *Swan Song* was, in fact, the working title for her next record. That was averted by a change in labels as she returned to her original record company and Warner's Reprise label.

Instead of experiencing some form of block, Mitchell was far more interested in tackling those who corrupt justice, abuse women, or promote divisiveness within society. She recounted her motives for what would become *Turbulent Indigo* for Robert Hilburn: "The album isn't about justice. It's about a quest for justice . . . understanding what justice is. I pulled up behind a Cadillac while I was waiting for the traffic light and the license plate said, 'Just Ice,' and I started thinking about that." And think she did. Those deliberations yielded an artist so transfixed by her observations that she contemplated self-mutilation. At least metaphorically. The cover of *Indigo* features a tribute to Van Gogh's famed *Self-Portrait with Bandaged Ear* (Van Gogh severed his left ear and gave it to a prostitute as a gift, then he painted the portrait) with Mitchell in the same pose, ear bandaged and all. That she wanted to include "little tin ears" (according to a *Vogue* interview) in the package demonstrates that her anger was yet to rob her of her sense of humor (she canned the idea due to costs).

Turbulent Indigo (released in October 1994) was produced by the Mitchell and Klein team and features ten songs (running 43:05). During media interviews on behalf of the project, Mitchell revealed that her marriage of ten years to Larry Klein ended the day before the sessions began. Mitchell told Jim Farber: "It wouldn't affect our art, but it did affect how we felt toward one another. . . . There was tension." She continued: "I was bullying him out of the nest. . . . For him, the 'Mr. Mitchell' aspect of things came into play." On another occasion, she related to Fred Shuster that the record "was made under an unusually difficult situation," but she and Klein "emerged as friends." It is hard to imagine that such conditions failed to impact the project's tone.

The record includes a cover of Hartman and Midnight's "How Do You Stop" as well as a coauthored portrait, "Yvette In English" (written with David Crosby). *Indigo* also contains a rich personal complaint, the Old Testament tale that is "The Sire of Sorrow (Job's Sad Song)," along with three societal complaints ("Sex Kills," "Not To Blame," and "Borderline"), a relational complaint ("Last Chance Lost"), and four portraits: "Sunny Sunday," "Turbulent Indigo," "The Magdalene Laundries," and the aforementioned "Yvette." It is a special moment when one song captures the essence of an extended work of art the way "The Sire of Sorrow" does this album. Mitchell is, indeed, a darker shade of blue here, and "Sire" portrays her torment via its biblical rhetoric. Using layers of voices to communicate her stance by way of a call-and-response exchange with some unidentified disputant, the song is a harsh look back on life, its frustrations, and its perceived punishments. She attacks doctors, describes her personal torments, and expresses her disgust through this morality play that begs more questions than it resolves. This is, assuredly, one dark soliloquy that probes the essential question, "What happened to it all, and why?"

This record may not reveal the "why," but it surely does portray the "what." Sex appeals cheapen life and kill people ("Sex Kills"), institutions enslave the innocent and berate them ("Magdalene"), divisiveness prohibits unity ("Borderline"), men pound their women and get away with it ("Not to Blame"), and love has evolved into a contest with no winners ("Last Chance"). Even the great artist is cheapened and misunderstood ("Turbulent") in a world that is so harsh that people want to isolate themselves, shut out the light of day, and embellish the darkness ("Sunny"). These songs transcend shades of blue as Mitchell thrusts us into a black hole of negativity where no light penetrates and only evil antimatter exists—a nonhuman form that defiles the Earth Mother's manifesto and its treasured doctrine of peace and love.

In "Sex Kills," Mitchell attacks doctors, lawyers, environmental hazards, kids with guns—everything that upsets the prescribed balance of life. When she uses a reference to the Indians and their violated wisdom, she once again takes us to "Paprika Plains" and the foundation of her Earth Mother manifesto. Though the song never directly speaks to the AIDS epidemic, it lurks in the background as yet another example of the devastation. Mitchell's "Magdalene Laundries" is a powerful portrait of a monastery where "fallen women" are sent to repent their sins over dirty laundry. Girls are impregnated by their fathers and priests and sent away—ignored by everyone while they rot in perpetual slavery. Those women lucky enough to marry are blessed with the joys of relational pugilism, as "Not to Blame" chronicles wife-beaters, their oh-so-handy excuses, and the system that allows it all to happen. Mitchell explained the stance that supported these songs to Nicholas Jennings: "It isn't that I set out to suddenly become a feminist, but the things that upset me the most, or that stimulated thought, all seemed to be atrocities against women. The album is really symptomatic of the times." She elaborated on her stance to *Goldmine*: "I saw so much injustice levied at women this time. I always hung with men all my life, and I've always felt that the better way than the feminist stance, which is pointing outward and saying 'them' and 'us,' was a dialogue between a man and woman, like, 'What's wrong here?' Working closer, working with rather than pointing at would be more effective. Let's come to a greater understanding. Are we really that different or is it sociologically imposed?" Mitchell uses *Indigo* to take aim at *people* who abuse *people*; regardless of their gender.

In essence, Mitchell discusses why she never accepted the feminist worldview in "Borderline." As her remarks to *Goldmine* indicate, the division of people by gender is just another means of separating people from each other. She interpreted the song in an interview with *Rolling Stone*'s Janice Dunn: "Borderlines—roads, fences, they're like cholesterol in the arteries. In terms of the psyche, my country is in a state of division. Every province wants to be its own country. . . . Everybody seems to love to draw these lines. So, as we come to this millennium, everyone's a divisionist in some way. So it was a contemplation of that." So, what kept us all from uniting in a blissful Garden of Eden? Division. Division that propagates greed, promotes abuses by the supposedly strong, allows the hypocritical to hide their hypocrisy through institutional action, and, in the most damning characteristic of all, separates us from our natural environment. Mitchell's negativity is overwhelming, yet her argument is cogent and compelling. Earth Mother remains on the case.

The album's title cut also attacks a basic misconception about another of Mitchell's treasured ideals, her beloved spouse, Art. She explained the song's origins to Robert Hilburn: "The title song . . . comes from a conference of the Canadian Council of the Arts that I spoke at in the early '90s. The name of the conference was 'Making van Goghs,' and they said they wanted to focus on indigenous peoples, ethnic groups, and women. I opened my talk by saying you cannot make van Goghs, and that artists can be encouraged or even groomed but not manufactured. Art is the result of experience, and van Gogh's despair and suicide are not what you'd want to duplicate." To reinforce her opinion, the auteur wrote a song to nail down her point and painted a cover portrait to communicate her stance.

Though the Hartman-Midnight cover is not as dark, and "Yvette" soothes like the summer rain on this vast, dry plain of remorse (it is another travelogue portrait of a charming French woman), these are but brief respites from this powerful editorial. There is no optimism, no nurturing, no utopian fantasies on *Turbulent Indigo*; just deeper and deeper shades of blue. As I have said before, Mitchell often refers to herself as a person who is many ages, all at once. Her constant references to her "creative child" indicate the essential qualities of that portion of her personality to her work. Like an abused child, Earth Mother was damaged by her worldview's failure, and her distrust is gaining momentum. As she ages, her perspective gains greater clarity. The enemies come into clearer focus. Her heroes grow in stature. And the incongruities between the two explode in song. Interestingly, there are no resolutions offered. No concert on Max Yasgur's farm is going to resolve this quandary.

The Grammy Award–winning record enjoyed the praise of a not-always-so-friendly music press. *Rolling Stone* reports: "Plenty has been written about the rockers of the '60s hitting their 50s, but Mitchell is virtually the only female pop star to pass that mark with her artistry undiminished. *Turbulent Indigo* is Mitchell's best album since the mid-'70s and a work that is highly musical, poetic and very, very sad." *Musician* concurs: "In *Turbulent Indigo*, the triumphant veteran of the sensitive songsmith wars has concocted her most compelling album in years, just in time for a return to Reprise, her old label. . . . The vision Mitchell paints here is not a pretty picture, by and large. But, inescapably, *Turbulent Indigo* is a thing of deep, dark beauty." The *Winston-Salem Journal* observes: "By carefully combining beautiful words and cutting turns of phrase, Mitchell expresses complex emotions in a manner that stirs and stings with poetic grace. At a time when many of her contemporaries are wrestling with advancing age and fading creativity, Mitchell has crafted a work of dark wisdom and beauty."

Joni Mitchell's career takes a serious—and last—turn after *Indigo*. Having lodged perhaps her strongest complaint regarding 30 years of systematic observation, she pauses for a series of well-deserved awards, assembles her first "greatest hits" package, records her final album of original material, and concludes with the first two installments of a three-part resolution to her career. A 1996 *Los Angeles Times* interview about her greatest hits package reveals Mitchell's response to the wave of awards that accompanied the two-album release. In September 1996, she received Canada's Governor General's Performing Arts Award; that December she received a lifetime achievement award from the National Academy of Songwriters; and in the spring of 1997, she was inducted into the Rock and Roll Hall of Fame (in her *fourth* year of eligibility). Mitchell related her views on the Rock Hall induction to Robert Hilburn: "Well, it's a boys' club isn't it. And it's kind of a joke. . . . There are so many people in it. It's like a hockey hall of fame where they let in anyone who has ever scored a goal. But then, I never considered myself a rock artist or a folk artist. People just saw a girl with an acoustic guitar and said, 'Folk singer.' But to me, my roots were in classical music." *That* is the attitude Mitchell holds toward any recognition of a career that she is certain is widely misunderstood. *They* took her, *they* marketed her, and they never, ever cared about *her.*

That attitude fueled the production of the auteur's first "greatest hits" package. Now this is unusual—rare is the artist with Mitchell's longevity who has but *one* "greatest hits" release. She never allowed any of her record labels to release any form of "greatest hits" work. When she did, it was done in her unique, rebellious fashion. *Hits* and *Misses* were issued in October 1996. The former contains 15 accomplished songs, such as the first album release of "Urge for Going," along with standards such as "Chelsea Morning," "Woodstock," "California," "Raised on Robbery," "River," "Both Sides, Now," and more. The latter offers 14 songs near and dear to the artist that did not receive the recognition she felt they deserved, such as "Passion Play," "The Beat of Black Wings," "The Magdalene Laundries," "Sex Kills," "The Arrangement," "Hejira," and more. There are no detailed liner notes included, just photos of Mitchell (suggesting not-too-inside jokes about her feelings toward the songs), lyrics, and a simple statement of thanks to those who worked on the project. She offered this assessment to Hilburn: "I tend to be dismissive of my early songs in favor of championing my underdog children . . . I think the songs after 'Court and Spark' show a lot of growth and I worry that much of it is destined for obscurity." I feel this package says so much about Mitchell's work. Instead of building a multidisc boxed set or just placing the two albums in one package, she separated the two, allowing consumers a choice and restricting her record company's ability to capitalize on the older material. Ever the artist, Mitchell was weary of taking the songs out of their original contexts, fearing that they would lose their symbolic strength. Her respect for the "album" concept restricted her ability to pick and choose cuts and reassemble them in any order other than their original presentation. No amount of money or industry encouragement could inspire her to chop up her lifework. The only reason she relented was to support her "underdog children." Earth Mother may be many things, but she is not a capitalist—and she is loyal to those children.

It is not hard for me to imagine young Joan Anderson out in the middle of some field, kicking up the dust with her treasured "Ocean's 11" in front of glaring headlights while Chuck Berry's "Sweet Little 16" is blaring away from the assembled car radios. I can see it as clearly as I can see the Memphis skyline. A group of teenagers involved in an act of unadulterated, unbridled joy. With that imagery in mind, I conclude this discussion of

Mitchell's original studio material with her sixteenth release, 1998's capstone statement *Taming the Tiger*. Not only does Earth Mother return with a classic sampler of her trademark sounds and sentiments, she says goodbye and good luck once she has finished her labors. As if that were not enough, she serenades us with one of those wonderfully funky guitar tunings via the concluding instrumental track, "Tiger Bones." A career of joy, turmoil, idealism, disappointment, fright, and fight closes with *Taming the Tiger* (the liner notes offer a "special thanks" to her daughter, Kilauren, and grandson, Marlin, as well as a series of paintings).

Produced by Mitchell (with accompaniment by Brian Blade, Mark Isham, Larry Klein, Greg Leisz, and Wayne Shorter), the album's 11 tracks (running 44:17) feature one cover (the goodbye toast that is Willadsen and Jones's "My Best to You"), the instrumental, coauthored love celebration ("The Crazy Cries of Love") and two additional love celebrations ("Love Puts on a New Face" and "Face Lift"), a love challenge ("Stay in Touch"), a societal complaint ("No Apologies"), two relational complaints ("Man from Mars" and "Lead Balloon"), a scenic portrait ("Harlem in Havana"), and the damning professional complaint, "Taming the Tiger." The record is, as you can see, a thematic sampler that includes standard Mitchell story structures that are systematically bound together before the auteur wraps up the album and her career with the cover song/instrumental goodbye toast. *Taming the Tiger* is a statement from a master spokesperson.

An album that displays a host of creative signatures opens with one of the oeuvre's most consistent characteristics, a scenic portrait. "Harlem in Havana" uses industrial jazz sounds to convey a light, lively portrait of a night out on the town where everyone is dancing, happy, perhaps a bit risqué, and totally intrigued by the band. The song is full of colorful descriptions as the sheer joy of "Chelsea" or "Morgantown" floats through the lyrics, but nothing ever happens; just more and more scenic description. The innovative sounds, colorful imagery, and joyful tone make this a classic Mitchell life celebration/scenic portrait and, therefore, a fitting opening for this capstone record.

From there, we receive a touch of the tried-and-true relational complaint—this time, with a much lighter touch. "Man from Mars" finds our narrator pining for her lost cat with an intensity previously reserved for wayward lovers. The pain associated with a missing pet is much too intense to discuss here, but it is nevertheless a beautiful example of the torch strategy: soft, melodramatic, oh so intense. (To ease your mind, the cat eventually returned home!) "Lead Balloon" certainly conveys relational conflict, but the details are omitted. Layers of voices and sounds lodge what appears to be a business complaint as the narrator endures problems with an industry operative of some sort. Still, nothing really happens; the story merely communicates that the narrator's tirade went over like a, well, lead balloon.

The scent of show biz angst builds and bowls you over with the powerful title cut. Here the auteur renders a state-of-the-art professional complaint as she bites the hand that feeds her by way of a direct, coherent, unequivocal attack on the mentally challenged fools that she perceives run her industry. You have to admire the strength of the songwriter's convictions as she describes industry product as cheap interludes and juvenile junk food. After absorbing this intense diatribe, you know the narrator would much rather be with Mars and the other cats—away from the spotlights, the glamour, the moneychangers, and much, much closer to The Garden.

Such strength of conviction reappears via the classic Mitchell societal complaint "No Apologies." Earth Mother's parting shot against society's evils is thorough and carefully executed. Rapists, drug dealers, environmental abusers, lawyers, and cheesy financiers are just ruining what is left of The Garden, and Earth Mother has a go at them as only she can. She is angry as hell. Tired of the institutional cheapness that ruins everything for everybody. You get the impression that Earth Mother is just going to go out and blow up a law school.

Having attacked the record business and the social system that greases its greedy wheels, Mitchell turns to affairs of the heart. The love songs make this record special. "Stay in Touch," with its mature, seasoned love challenge, complements the blissful accounts registered in "Love Puts on a New Face," Don Freed's "Crazy Cries," and the autobiographical "Face Lift." "Touch" is a swan song. It features a veteran of love who understands what has gone well and what has gone poorly. Now, she wants to apply that knowledge with the joy of a new love in her heart. The narrator's life experiences have taught her well that she has been burned, but this character applies the knowledge from "I Think I Understand" in a mature manner. To surrender to love is an admirable trait. To surrender to love with the wrong person is a tragedy, and to give up on love is an even greater catastrophe. The polio survivor who composed this song is, in every respect, the consummate fighter. There is no quit in Joni Mitchell.

The Freed-Mitchell composition "Crazy Cries" uses the sounds of yesteryear and compelling imagery to paint a love picture of simple, all-consuming adoration. The couple is so caught up in one another that nothing else matters. That tone permeates "New Face" and "Face Lift" as well. Both songs relate how love is the ultimate answer. In "Lift" the autobiography is strong as the auteur communicates that relational joy yields the best surgical repair available. It is a poignant, touching song that demonstrates how infatuation is not the unique province of the young. Older couples, too, may fall over one another in happy-go-lucky, occasionally silly, ways. This song's placement before the goodbye toast that is the "My Best to You" cover and the "Tiger Bones" instrumental clearly indicates that though Earth Mother may not have had the pleasure of witnessing her utopian worldview's manifestation, she nonetheless has discovered her own personal Garden, full of mature, but youthful, love. With that, the curtain falls with sweet number sixteen. Age and experience bring more than cynicism and distrust, and *Taming the Tiger* happily projects that lesson as it says "goodbye" and, perhaps most important, "good luck."

Critics praised the project. Robert Hilburn writes: "Backed by superbly tailored, jazz-accented arrangements that are at once aggressive and soothing. . . . Mitchell reflects on love, tempering her optimism with the caution (and wit) of someone who never forgets the accompanying struggle." George Varga claims, "Each listening reveals a wealth of nuances and a finely honed sense of logic, form and melody, much like a challenging film or book that creates and occupies a world of its own." R. S. Murthi offers this insightful analysis: "The songs here, despite brimming with scholarly allusions, are more straightforward than many of the things she's done before. And the narratives in them convey a sense of resignation to the evils of existence that mirrors her current mindset as a seasoned and somewhat weary commentator on the joys and sorrows of life." After discussing "New Face" and "Stay in Touch," J. D. Considine concludes: "Mitchell not only conveys the passion and pace of grown-up romance, but suggests—musically and lyrically—that love does indeed get better with age. Moreover, because she's focused on personal concerns instead of social issues, Mitchell engages the listener at an emotional level, drawing us in and letting us feel as if we have something deep in common. That may not be the stuff of which hits are made, but it's far more satisfying in the long run."

With her swan song warmly received, a stack of international awards stashed away in the cupboard, her new love and family by her side, and Mars safe at home, Joni Mitchell retires Earth Mother. And Earth Mother deserves a rest, for it has been a long, arduous career full of every conceivable emotion and experience. When Edna Gundersen inquired about Mitchell's future, the auteur replied:

> I want to record standards, where I'm just a singer and there's only one mood to sustain. My songs tend to entail more acting than singing. Instead of having so much nuanced drama to do, I'd like to sing some pretty notes and lighten up. It's the way I feel right now. I did most of my heavy worrying between 27 and 33. It made me strong but it nearly flattened me. I thought so deep and so hard, it scared the wee out of me and I entered into a long depression. I like my life better now.

If this book says anything to you about Joan Anderson, you should dust off your Cole Porter songbook and start looking for selections. When this artists says "I want to _____" it is time to make plans and prepare yourself, because she will either achieve her goal or die trying. Earth Mother may have failed in her attempt to bring The Garden to the world, but Joni Mitchell never failed to carry the message in her own, adventurous way.

Sure enough, the auteur recorded her standards, and in so doing, initiated a three-part exploration of orchestral music with the March 2000 release *Both Sides Now*. The Mitchell–Larry Klein production features the 70-piece London Symphony Orchestra (arranged and conducted by Vince Mendoza) with special appearances by Herbie Hancock, Mark Isham, and Wayne Shorter. The album contains 12 tracks (running 51:37) of classic torch songs that include two Mitchell compositions ("Both Sides Now" and "A Case of You") as well as (in order) 1933's "You're My Thrill" (by Clare and Gorney), 1942's "At Last" (Gordon/Warren), 1939's "Comes Love" (Brown/ Stept/Tobias), 1968's "You've Changed" (Carey/Fischer), 1953's "Answer Me, My Love" (Winkler/Rauch, and English lyrics by Carl Sigman), "A Case of You," 1954's "Don't Go to Strangers" (Evans/Kent/Mann), 1925's "Sometimes I'm Happy" (Caesar/Grey/Youmans), 1939's "Don't Worry 'Bout Me" (Bloom/Koehler), 1933's "Stormy Weather" (Koehler/Arlen), 1937's "I Wish I Were in Love Again" (Hart/Rodgers), and "Both Sides Now." For insight into the strategy behind the songs' arrangement, we turn to producer Larry Klein's liner notes:

> As we began the process of selecting the songs for this record, Joni came up with the idea of having the record trace the arc of a modern romantic relationship. I thought that this idea was innovative, exciting and especially appropriate considering that the focal point of her work has been an inquiry into the nature of modern love. The album would be a programmatic suite documenting a relationship from initial flirtation through optimistic consummation, metamorphosing into disillusionment, ironic despair, and finally resolving in the philosophical overview of acceptance and the probability of the cycle repeating itself.

The results are a testament to the torch tradition's rich history as the Mitchell-Klein team achieves a synthesis of the old standards' depth and Mitchell's seasoned articulation of those emotions. Massaging sentiments that are essential elements of her lifework, Mitchell broadens her scope by reaching across generations of song and embracing eternal emotions as seen through the eyes of professional songwriters who have never stood before an audience and represented their words. Here the celebrity-singer-songwriter-turned-diva takes her "acting" career into an established realm in which she sings "some pretty notes" that may "lighten up" personally while probing deep into the relational angst so prevalent in her own songwriting. Perhaps Mitchell would have been wise to do this earlier—as Elvis Costello did with *Almost Blue*—and allow herself an opportunity to embrace her emotions through the words of other writers. But Mitchell would never accept that strategy. Her perceived duty was just too strong. Her acting career came much too late for that strategy to work.

Critics, by and large, applauded the effort. David Brinn observes: "Mitchell's voice has over the years gathered a husky tone, attesting to the decades of use and inevitabilities of age. But rather than hinder, it provides quirky character to these late-night ballads. You can picture her with a half-drunk martini in one hand, and nubby cigarette in the other." Michale Clark concurs: "Mitchell's ease with the musical layers makes it clear that she could have had a career vastly different than the folksy path she chose." Richard Harrington also focuses on Mitchell's vocals: "Like any canny veteran, she covers encroaching vocal limitations with richer interpretive nuances—you can feel these songs as much as hear them. She also seems relieved to be away from autobiography: These songs address aspects of love in universal terms that may seem quaint in today's era of clumsy explicitness, but resonate in a timeless manner." Finally, Stephen Holden has mixed views. He opens, "Few contemporary voices have aged more shockingly than Joni Mitchell's" although "that very huskiness lends her torch singing the battered authenticity we expect of middle-aged jazz singers with their years of after-hours living and accompanying voices." For Holden, Mitchell's "[Billie] Holiday-like phrasing, smoke-charred timbre and anguished intensity take you to the core of songs describing states of emotional torture." As these comments suggest, the aging auteur and the ageless material were a match made in torch heaven—rarely would these songs ever sound any better.

Both Sides Now was the perfect musical outlet for a songwriter who has said what she has to say. With that accomplished, the auteur turned to the emotions behind a large portion of her lifework, stepped outside the stories themselves, and embellished the songs' sentiments with the attitude, vocal style, and creative presence of the seasoned warrior that she was. Her brief 11-city tour in support of the record also featured the full orchestra and guest appearances. Reviews were mixed. Joel Selvin questioned Mitchell's approach: "She toyed with time, spitting out phrases like trumpet runs behind the beat. She practically smothered the songs with technique." Joan Anderman disagreed: "So with her fingers fluttering and wrapped head-to-toe in resplendent hues of apricot and red, Mitchell simply sang the songs in the deep, knowing tones of a seasoned romantic." And Rob Lowman put it all in perspective: "Like all artists, Mitchell has gone through different phases, exploring different forms of music. Some more successful than others. In this one she seems to have freed herself from her past in order to examine it. Look at the self-portrait on the cover of 'Both Sides Now,' it's not the Mitchell of 'Big Yellow Taxi.' We now have another side of Joni Mitchell, and Friday's show was an intriguing taste of it."

Part two of this three-part excursion into orchestral music involved November 2002's double disc release, *Travelogue*. This Klein–Mitchell production advanced the sonic strategy from *Both Sides* (once again, Vince Mendoza leads the London Symphony Orchestra); except this time they recast material from Mitchell's oeuvre. Handsomely packaged with many photographs of Mitchell's paintings (including several references to the September 11, 2001, horror via paintings of George Bush and Osama bin Laden) along with a lyric booklet, the set seems to wave goodbye with every visual and aural offering. That she dedicated the work to her parents suggests that as well ("This album is dedicated to my parents, Bill and Myrtle Anderson, who sent me off on this journey"). Lush arrangements, a veteran voice (with an occasional backing choir), and timeless songs transformed in, at times, significant ways make *Travelogue* an intriguing listening experience. Once more, Mitchell seems to step outside of her own songs, peering in at their inner workings and revising her commentary to suit the new musical surrounding. She floats across the oeuvre; selecting songs from different eras and bringing them to fresh contexts. Songs such as "Otis and Marlena," "You Dream Flat Tires," "Trouble Child," "Sex Kills," "The Dawntreader," "The Last Time I Saw Richard," and "Borderline" assume new identities through the new arrangements and vocal presentations. Although virtually every review decried the treatment, "Woodstock" is finally unveiled to be the serious social critique that it is. No longer hiding behind pop or folk sensibilities or suffering the audience misinterpretations that plagued Bruce Springsteen's "Born in the U.S.A.," the song conveys the sense of failure Earth Mother endured as her military aircraft never metamorphosed in the manner she predicted. The song is a slow, sad look back at a dead dream— and few things are sadder than dead dreams. *This* is Joni Mitchell's "swan song, revisited."

Travelogue's reviews are mixed. John Rockwell claims that "Joni Mitchell's new 'Travelogue' isn't billed as a farewell, but it's hard to see it any other way." Rockwell expresses difficulty with many of the revisions, yet he understands Mitchell's situation: "Any artist must constantly question his or her past accomplishments; to repeat oneself risks becoming a hack. . . . That said, restless experimentation also suggests a quality of unwelcome self-indulgence that has always marked [Mitchell's] music and her personality." The auteur was right: They will crucify you either way. Richard Harrington also struggles with the piece: "Like Bob Dylan riffling through his back pages, Mitchell and Mendoza rearrange her songs in such a way that few replicate the originals. While some gain emotive and interpretive depth from their reworkings, several are clumsily re-imagined." VH1 senses that Earth Mother may once again be pulling for some of her "underdog children": "Though there are a couple of Mitchell's staples included here, one of the most striking achievements of TRAVELOGUE may be the way it renovates the reputation of some of the tunes from Mitchell's less well-regarded '80s efforts. Okay, Joni, you've pulled it off; now will you give us another batch of new songs?" Finally, the love-hate relationship between *Rolling Stone* and Joni Mitchell continues: "The arrangements treat Mitchell's tunes as precious artifacts, making little attempt to seduce the listener; only on 'The

Circle Game,' for example, do the strings provide the kind of romantic sonic brocades associated with great orchestral rock." So *that* is what *Travelogue* is—"orchestral rock." (And I'm a geologist.)

Once the album appeared, controversy quickly followed. The aforementioned *W* interview, Mitchell's announcement "These are my last two records," and her subsequent explanation to the *Toronto Star* indicated, once more, the volatile qualities of Mitchell's relationship with her industry (see the biography section). Or perhaps her attitude extended further, as these comments from a 2000 interview with Alan Jackson indicate:

> You ask how I feel about America as she is these days. Well, one of the reasons I'm not writing is that I'd rather not say. I can be a very harsh critic, so I've decided to take a sabbatical until I can be nice again! I don't want to be a prophet of doom. I don't even want to get started on it all in conversation here and now. But I admit I feel impotent in the face of much of what we've allowed ourselves to become. It's a crass and corrupt world. The sediment has risen to the top. No, I am not without optimism, but that optimism is more of a blind faith than any kind of intellectual certainty.

Remember when Kris Kristofferson first heard *Blue*? Do you recall what he said to Mitchell? "Save a little for yourself, Joni" is what he said, and this is what he meant by that comment. Mitchell gave so much of herself—and received so little that *she* valued in return—that it permanently scarred her. That she claims she had something like a nervous breakdown after completing that record (which required her exodus to Canada) indicates the depth of Kristofferson's observation ("I thought so deep and so hard, it scared the wee out of me" says it all, doesn't it?). Although she paused for reorientation during the sonic explorer period, once she achieved a personal equilibrium with *Don Juan's Reckless Daughter*, Mitchell sharpened her axe and mowed through the forest of evil that surrounds The Garden. She could afford a chainsaw, but no, she wanted to physically have at those responsible for her dream's demise. The lawyers, the moneychangers, the entertainment industry—rapists and thieves of all sorts—represented evil barriers that just had to be identified and attacked. Earth Mother donned her Roy Rogers outfit and chopped away with the determination of a ten-year-old polio survivor except now it involved more than *her* future. She wanted to keep the *world* from becoming a "cripple." It cost her dearly. You have to admire her tenacity.

I conclude this treatment of Joni Mitchell's lifework with personal tradition. In my previous study of Bob Dylan's and Bruce Springsteen's work, I borrowed an idea from Greil Marcus's book *Invisible Republic*, in which that writer characterized Dylan's "basement tapes" from 1967 as a small American town, "Smithville." Marcus used that metaphor to demonstrate his interpretation of the characters, values, and story lines that control Dylan's work with The Band in the informal musical period that was his respite in

Woodstock, New York, after his 1966 motorcycle accident. He describes the songs as the town and the song characters as its populace and their everyday activities. Now, if we transform Mitchell's oeuvre into Smithville, what would that town and its occupants be like? I think I know. Joni Mitchell's Smithville is in Mesopotamia. It is the Garden of Eden—a place where every morning is a butterscotch morning; every afternoon is full of bright blues, gorgeous greens, and radiating reds; and every night is peaceful, comfortable, and horribly romantic. There is no electricity in Smithville, so candlelight is the chief means of lighting. Smithville is an art colony where everyone paints, draws, sings, writes, and dances—and all the art is given away, "for free." Health foods, nature walks, skinny-dipping, and other wonderful, natural treats are readily available—and you may smoke in public, if you like. There are no marriages in Smithville. People date for a while and move on to other lovers as they wish; however, there is never, ever any acrimony and nobody ever speaks ill of a former lover. In fact, there are no institutions in Smithville. Lawyers are not allowed to enter the town, so there is no need for courts (a handshake is binding in Smithville), governments, banks, or even schools. People cooperate with each other, share responsibilities and duties, and pass along life's wisdom in informal settings. There is only one taboo in Joni Mitchell's Smithville: You never ask someone how they are doing. Confessions have been banned by unanimous vote.

CHAPTER 4

The Exemplars

Having established the ebb and flow of Joni Mitchell's lifework, we now turn to specific exemplars that capture the internal workings of her various songwriting strategies. Our auteur may float here and there with her sonic urges—picking and choosing different sound designs to support her Earth Mother observations; however, when we consider the narrative strategies used to convey those views, we notice that a steady staple of storytelling structures is used to organize her thoughts. There is, then, a clear focus to the work from a narrative point of view. Instead of a random sampling of epics, comedies, tragedies, or other narrative forms, we witness a consistent framework that is systematically applied to suit Mitchell's preconceived ends. While she may anxiously await some miraculous intervention in the recording studio, the auteur enters that situation with a narrative blueprint firmly in mind. Albums are preconceived projects with specific objectives; only their articulation is cast to the creative winds in the hope of unimagined innovation. Mitchell may seek to restrain her "critic" as she records her ideas, but the narrative architect who supervises the venture relies on storytelling tools that have been specifically honed for the purposes at hand. Those structures provided the playground for Mitchell's creative child and, therefore, established certain parameters for the proposed project. As usual, there is method to the inventive madness—sounds and their arrangements may frolic in the studio playground, but the words flow from a more systematic process. Joni Mitchell always has a narrative agenda.

Before we begin, we should pause for an important observation: Joni Mitchell *is* her art. This is not in any way to suggest that all of her work is autobiographical. On the contrary, from the very outset, the auteur used people, places, and things that she had seen, heard about, or imagined to illustrate a specific point. For instance, the heartfelt sentiments of "Two Grey Rooms" have all the markings of autobiography—the rooms' description, her feelings for the character who merely walks by each day, the depth of her recollections, virtually everything about the piece suggests the level of intimacy one associates with personal experience. But that certainly is not the case. Had she not told Robert Hilburn that the song is a portrait of a homosexual relationship that stresses a personal complaint about love long lost, we would never have known. *That* is nowhere in the song. Structurally, the song portrays one person's feelings toward another. It is sad, nostalgic, just plain pitiful. The emotional qualities of that imagined situation are so deep, so representative of Mitchell's public personality, and so detailed that she *becomes* the song. And she accepts it. Though this type of intimate writing "scared the wee" out of her, she continued to bear the responsibility that accompanied it. Not only did Earth Mother refuse to hide, she accepted her characters' sins—and, vicariously, her audience's as well. If she is a diarist, then all the world is her diary. Joni Mitchell is her art.

To be sure, the Earth Mother Manifesto is the lifework's heart and mind. It is nothing less than a peace and love prescription for living. Through it, the auteur argues a simple doctrine: By honoring certain basic principles, we may all reenter the Garden of Eden—a utopia where individual freedom is guaranteed, relationships are nurturing, and social institutions practice the golden rule. That manifesto stresses personal freedom, relational acceptance, and simplicity; it is protective of the environment (in fact, the Earth is worshiped); it is anti-capitalistic and anti-institutional; and it is inclusive. By definition, there are no strangers in Earth Mother's world. Everyone is a brother or a sister. Everyone deserves love. Everyone deserves honesty. It is idealistic beyond belief. Joni Mitchell believed it and practiced it, and when it became overwhelmingly clear that her idealism had little relationship to her reality, she used that worldview as a yardstick to measure the reality that betrayed her so severely. Not only did she use her yardstick to measure, she bludgeoned her perceived oppressors with it—lashing her targets with painful blows that hurt like the scalding compresses once applied to her polio-stricken legs. Earth Mother became madder than the proverbial hornet, and she never exorcised those feelings through her work; she just accepted them a little bit better. Finally, when she could no longer write something "nice," she simply quit writing. Joni Mitchell is her art.

The musical portion of her art is fascinating in that capstone wisdoms appear very early in her career, their morals are massaged through subsequent reiterations, and once all the dust has settled, they are recast in alternative forms. How could any writer in her early twenties write "Both Sides, Now"? It is as seasoned an observation as any expression ever gets. The recognition that your views on clouds, love, and life may all be an illusion is a pretty strong conclusion. The same holds for "I Think I Understand" and "That Song About the Midway." Mitchell articulates the need to face and accept your fears, to deal with your potential oppressors, and to recognize your illusions *on her second album*. Moreover, "The Cactus Tree"—her eternal love prescription—appears on her *first album*. During Mitchell's participant-commentator phase, she systematically shapes her manifesto. Her guiding principles are introduced, honed, and exemplified throughout her first six albums. Then it all crashed in. Her pleas not only were unanswered, they were heckled. The media that made her used her shamelessly. From there, a dazed and confused Earth Mother regrouped, reoriented, and rebounded through a sonic world tour. She fell in love again; this time, with what she admiringly called "Black classical music." Since Earth Mother could not become Miles Davis, she became Art Nouveau. Through Art and his musical friends, Mitchell reconciled discrepancies between her ideals and her realities. All it cost the auteur was her audience and her standing in the music industry—and she really did not care about either one of them. Both had betrayed her. Besides, she still had her manifesto. Subsequently, she reentered the pop music world, armed with her manifesto yardstick, and proceeded to pound her oppressors through Earth Mother commentaries that took no prisoners. When she finished, she went home to Mars and her paints—confident of her victory.

What a story.

With thanks to Mr. Townshend, throughout this amazing journey we note the consistent use of a small number of narrative structures. Mitchell uses just seven narrative strategies throughout her lifework. There are but two exceptions to this rule. She presents the many shades of her Earth Mother manifesto through portraits, complaints, celebrations, challenges, struggles, testimonials, and narrative impressionism. In each case, we see one form or another of the trademark Earth Mother comment: the nurturing observation. She may cry with us, cry for us, scold us, suffer for us, encourage us to play with somebody else, attack our oppressors, whatever. Throughout Mitchell's lifework, songs hang on a single observation that is embellished in some fashion for our personal edification. Her nurturing observations labor to enlighten, to encourage, to understand, or, when necessary, to protect. When Mitchell speaks of her "duty" as a celebrity-singer-songwriter, she references her perceived obligation to generate her lyrical trademark, the nurturing observation.

Mitchell's portraits are her lifework's centerpiece as they depict individuals and locations, offer tributes, and articulate sermonic self-disclosures. At times, we note narrative blends such as a synthesis of a scenic portrait and a tribute (e.g., "California") or a character and a location (e.g., Mitchell/Crosby's "Yvette in English"). Our second approach, the complaints, are quite diverse. Across the oeuvre, Mitchell complains about loving, and personal, professional, relational, and societal matters with considerable consistency. Often, the intensity of her complaint is indicative of the work's perceived function at that point in time. "Woodstock," for example, may sound more celebratory in its original incarnation and evolve into a dirge years later, but it was a societal complaint the whole time. Her celebrations focus on two topics: life and love. The joyous life celebrations (that occasionally appear in her scenic portraits as well) are a signature Mitchell story line and a fundamental element of Earth Mother's worldview. The joy of life is *the* essential nurturing observation of her Return to the Garden life prescription. Mitchell's challenges focus squarely on affairs of the heart. Therein lies the ultimate aspiration, the universal goal. Since interpersonal relations are almost always problematic, we have a number of stories that portray relational struggles and the ever-present battle to keep love alive (these struggles occasionally involve professional conflicts as well). For those moments in which everything crystallizes into a compelling insight, Mitchell deploys the testimonial narrative strategy. Life's lessons are on display in these heartfelt treatises. Finally, the oeuvre offers multiple examples of the technique I call narrative impressionism. Here Mitchell offers rich descriptions, powerful observations, and the occasional chaotic soliloquy that never goes anywhere. There is no plot progression; therefore, no story. Still, the technique can be used to convey a moral or Earth Mother lesson that exists free of a narrative anchor, floating in its own nurturing observation. The fact that only *two* songs fall outside these categories indicates the degree of focus associated with Mitchell's lifework. The relational plea, "The Same Situation" (from *Court and Spark*), and the "nothing song" that is "Smokin' (Empty, Try Another)" (from *Dog Eat Dog*) are the lone exceptions to the framework that systematically emerged as Mitchell's lifework unfolded. (Cover songs or adaptations of poems and Scripture are omitted from this analysis.) Let us begin with the cornerstone of the auteur's career, and the signature portraits.

The portrait narrative strategy appears on the very first album with "Michael from Mountains," "Marcie," and "The Dawntreader." Each character portrait has a specific point to make about the nurturing soul from the mountains, the struggling lover, and the adventurous sailor. In *Clouds* we see but one example, the informative character portrait "Roses Blue," in which Earth Mother warns against quick fixes such as palm readings, tarot cards, and the like; instead, she urges you to get in touch with your laughter and return to nature. Herein lies the strategy's significance, in that the portrait paints a picture of an individual who personifies a specific trait from the emerging manifesto; hence the nurturing observation. Michael's kindness, Marcie's desperation, the sailor's wanderlust, and Rose's misconceptions are all crucial elements of a credo that stresses nurturing, empathy, adventure, and genuineness. The trend continues with *Ladies of the Canyon* and "For Free," the title cut, and "The Circle Game." *Blue* introduces two new spins on the strategy with the tribute to her daughter ("Little Green"), the scenic portrait ("Carey"), and the hybrid scenic tribute "California." The innovative trend advances with *For the Roses* and the first self-portrait, "Let the Wind Carry Me." There the auteur recalls her youthful struggles with her mother, her father's loving intervention, and the formidable conflict between two sets of instincts, one maternal and one adventuresome. *Court and Spark* deploys the portrait strategy with some regularity. The character sketch "Free Man in Paris" is joined by narrative vignettes such as the title track, "People's Parties," and the delightful "Raised on Robbery." With *The Hissing of Summer Lawns* the tactic focuses on relationships as Mitchell portrays a drug dealer and his moll in "Edith and the Kingpin" and an unhappy materialistic marriage in "Harry's House." Earth Mother holds these two scenarios up for our inspection as she warns her flock of the consequences of certain actions (two compelling nurturing observations). Things lighten quite a bit with *Hejira*'s character portrait "Strange Boy" and the hybrid scenic-character portrayal, "Furry Sings the Blues." *Don Juan's Reckless Daughter* offers a smart sampling of the portrait strategy with "Otis and Marlena" (character), "Dreamland" (scenic), and the epic "Paprika Plains" (tribute).

The approach gets a bit sketchy with the *Mingus* project as Mitchell uses "God Must Be a Boogie Man," "A Chair in the Sky," and "Goodbye Pork Pie Hat" to say various things about Charles Mingus—the nurturing observation briefly evolves into the nurturing tribute. True to Mingus's work, these character sketches are cloudy, impulsive, and evasive—quite unlike the other installment, the playful "The Dry Cleaner from Des Moines." There is a pause in the steady flow of portraits at this point because *Wild Things Run Fast* and *Dog Eat Dog* omit the strategy through their focus on relational and societal happenings, respectively. The portrait returns with *Chalk Mark in a Rain Storm* as we witness two extremes by way of the cryptic "Cool Water" (a scenic vignette for the thirsty) and the pointed characterization that is "The Beat of Black Wings." *Night Ride Home* offers what appears to be a major dose of autobiography through the hometown recollections that are "Cherokee Louise" (character), "Ray's Dad's Cadillac" (self-portrait), "Come in from the Cold," and the travelogue entry, "The Only Joy in Town" (scenic-character). The nostalgia is powerful in these rich recollections of Canadian days gone by. In *Turbulent Indigo* we once more observe Mitchell's use of this narrative strategy to make specific points on certain topics. "Sunny Sunday" (character), the title track (character), "The Magdalene Laundries" (scenic-character), and "Yvette in English" (character-scenic) all speak to issues of concern to Earth Mother as she portrays the social withdrawal, the creative turmoil, the victimization, and the glamour associated with her characters. Finally, we conclude the lifework with an energetic scenic portrait, the happy-go-lucky "Harlem in Havana."

This is, by far, the most thoroughly mined of Mitchell's narrative veins. Her portraits with a point, her scenic portrayals, her relational portraits, and her painterly self-portraits weave and bend their way throughout thirty years of songwriting. For more insight into the strategy, let us turn to one of the oeuvre's most compelling self-portraits, *Night Ride Home*'s "Come in from the Cold":

> Way back in 1957
> We had to dance a foot apart
> And they hawk-eyed us
> From the sidelines
> Holding their rulers without a heart
> And so with just a touch of our fingers
> We could make our circuitry explode
> Oh all we ever wanted
> Was to come in from the cold
>   Come in
>   Come in from the cold
>   (we were so young)
>   Oh come in
>   Come in from the cold
> We really thought we had a purpose
> We were so anxious to achieve
> We had hope
> The world held promise
> For a slave
> To liberty
> Freely I slaved away for something better
> And I was bought and sold
> And all I ever wanted
> Was to come in from the cold
>   Come in
>   Come in from the cold
>   (we were so sure)
>   Please come in
>   Come in from the cold
> I feel your legs under the table
> Leaning into mine
> I feel renewed
> I feel disabled
> By these bonfires in my spine
> I don't know who the arsonist was
> Which incendiary soul
> But all I ever wanted
> Was to come in from the cold
>   Come in
>   Come in from the cold
>   (you were so warm)
>   Oh come in come in
>   Come in from the cold
> I am not some stone commission
> Like some statue in a park

I am flesh and blood and vision
I am howling in the dark
Long blue shadows of the jackals
Are falling on a pay phone
By the road
Oh all we ever wanted
Was to come in from the cold
    Come in
    Come in from the cold
    (i was so low)
    Oh come in
    Come in from the cold
Is this just vulgar electricity
Is this the edifying fire
(it was so pure)
Does your smile covert complicity
Debase as it admires
(just a flu with a temperature)
Are you checking out your mojo
(oohoo)
Or am I just fighting off growing old
(just a high fever)
All I ever wanted
Was just to come in from the cold
    Come in
    Oh come in from the cold
    (it was so pure)
    Please come in
    Come in from the cold
I know we never will be perfect
Never entirely clear
(when the moon shines)
We get hurt and we just panic
And we strike out
Out of fear
(you were only being kind)
I fear the sentence of this solitude
200 years on hold
(for my loving crime)
Oh and all we ever wanted
Was to come in from the cold
    Come in
    Oh come in from the cold
    (when the moon shines)
    Oh come in
    Come in from the cold
When I thought life had some meaning
Then I thought I had some choice

(i was running blind)
And I made some value judgments
In a self-important voice
(i was outta line)
But then absurdity came over me
And I longed to lose control
(into no mind)
Oh all I ever wanted
Was to come in from the cold
    Come in
    Come in from the cold
    (you were so kind)
    Please come in
    (so kind)
    Come in from the cold
    Come in come in
    Come in from the cold.

"Come In" is one of the oeuvre's longer songs that takes the time to embellish its point and the emotions that surround the nurturing observation regarding how "simplicity" has been violated. The song also demonstrates the "layered" method of call-and-response dialogue that appears throughout the lifework (the use of parenthetical comments that highlight or respond to the previous statement). The song follows the narrator's life cycle as she moves through the anxious moments of her youth into the even more anxious conditions of adulthood. Throughout the journey, she concentrates on simplicity—all she wants is warmth: physical, interpersonal, professional, and societal warmth. To stand alone or drift away from your guiding principles is to remain in the "cold." As you read these lines, notice how Earth Mother is everywhere: the character's youthful innocence, her aspirations, her wide-eyed optimism, her sincere belief in *everybody's* potential. These are the founding principles of a worldview that guided Earth Mother's pen for 30 years. Suddenly, however, things turn. She was "bought and sold," and her innocence was threatened by unwanted complications. Next we consider a relationship and, I believe, her physical situation (the "bonfire"-polio connection seems strong to me) before a bold statement of defiance ("I am flesh and blood and vision / I am howling in the dark"). Now, distrust enters a more complex picture as the narrator questions what she observes, calling upon her experience to make sense of another's motives. The simple thrill of touching someone else has evolved into a potentially diabolical game. The song turns reflective as she acknowledges that perfection is evasive, questions her decisions and her attitudes, and aspires to escape from it all. It is a fascinating account of how an individual emerged from a group, the values that group held, and how that person struggled with a world that did not exactly share that perspective. Wide-eyed optimism evolves into distrustful reflection; youthful promise turns into mature acceptance. More important, responsibilities are acknowledged and, in some respects, decisions are regretted. Nevertheless, all this character ever truly desired was the simple warmth that accompanies shelter from the metaphorical cold. The song never attacks or blames, it merely accepts what has happened and perpetuates a lifelong desire.

Mitchell's portraits are rarely superficial. Her ability to present a character or scene that exemplifies a specific point or principle is one of her work's landmarks. From the beginning, she used characters such as Michael, Marcie, the boy from "The Circle Game," Harry from "Harry's House," Killer Kyle from "The Beat of Black Wings," or the girls in "Magdalene Laundries" to illustrate a love of nature, the perils of love, the loss of youth, the failures of materialism, the victimization of innocents, or societal hypocrisy—simple, straightforward, nurturing observations. Moreover, her scenic accounts of the "California" lifestyle, outrageous bar activities ("Raised on Robbery"), travelogues, and the philosophical treatise that is "Paprika Plains" take those descriptions as a means of demonstrating principles associated with the Earth Mother manifesto. The portrait strategy is one of Mitchell's most compelling narrative tools, and she has used it wisely across the years.

Our second category, the topical complaint, is a narrative strategy that appears in many forms. Throughout her lifework Mitchell complains about life issues, professional matters, love (for one song), relationships, and societal happenings with considerable regularity. Her personal or life complaint story structure first appears in *Clouds* with "That Song About the Midway" (a blend of personal and professional complaint) and returns with *Blue*'s "River" and "The Last Time I Saw Richard." From there, the personal complaint ducks in and out of the work by way of "Trouble Child" (from *Court*), "Black Crow" and "Refuge of the Road" (*Hejira*), "Chinese Café" (*Wild Things*), "Nothing Can Be Done" and "Two Grey Rooms" (*Night Ride*), and "The Sire of Sorrow" (*Indigo*). These songs focus on *personal* matters such as escape from undesirable situations (e.g., "River"), perceived injustices (e.g., "Trouble"), aging (e.g., "Chinese"), or nostalgia ("Rooms"). That narrative logic appears in the brief list of professional complaints as well. While many songs make reference to show business and its lifestyle, these songs *concentrate* on that topic and embellish emotional responses that are directly associated with the music industry. The strategy first appears in *For the Roses* ("For the Roses" and "Blonde in the Bleachers") and returns in the title cut of *Taming the Tiger*. The same could be said for the oeuvre's lone "love complaint," "Moon at the Window" (from *Wild Things*), in that many songs refer to love issues or professional matters in one way or another, but this brief list of compositions focuses on their topics in telling ways. "Moon," in particular, deals with the notion of "love" more than any individual "lover" or situation as it propagates the nurturing observation that there are, indeed, romantic thieves in this world.

The relational and societal complaints are more extensive. The relational complaint first appears on the debut album by way of "I Had a King" and the cloudy, layered "The Pirate of Penance." It returns in *Roses* ("Lessons in Survival"), *Court* ("Just like This Train"), *Hejira* ("Amelia," "Hejira," and "Song for Sharon"), *Chalk Mark* ("Dancin' Clown," "Snakes and Ladders," and "A Bird That Whistles"), *Indigo* ("Last Chance Lost"), and *Tiger* ("Man from Mars" and "Lead Balloon"). Throughout these stories, Earth Mother rarely attacks an individual or lashes out at a specific situation; she laments the passing of a relationship, wishes everybody well, and, on occasion, wallows in her pain. For example, she lost her king because they were from different eras ("I Had a King"), a relationship fizzled out because the participants moved in different social circles ("Lessons"), she identifies with another strong woman who experienced failure ("Amelia"), she regrets the loss of her main man (the feline angst of "Mars"), and she speaks her mind to a business associate ("Balloon"). The complaint is surely lodged, but in a more benign or understanding fashion.

That cannot be said for the expressions of Earth Mother's wrath that are the societal complaints. Though early on, Mitchell tempers these attacks with peace and love attitudes, later she pulls no punches as she pounds away on the enemy, blasting the target for the evil it perpetuates. Things begin to simmer in *Seagull* as our hippie princess identifies her future enemy in "Nathan La Franeer" and "Song to a Seagull." The concrete jungle and its materialistic ways are identified as a threat to The Garden at the very outset as Mitchell senses the evil money-hungry ways of cab drivers, airport attendants, and urban utilities. Afterward, she pauses for a direct, incisive complaint via "The Fiddle and the Drum" (*Clouds*), in which Earth Mother laments the sad conditions that bring war and *wants to help* those who suffer from those afflictions. In *Ladies* the story sharpens as Mitchell identifies the materialistic enemy in "The Arrangement," laments environmental abuses ("Big Yellow Taxi" and its dose of relational complaint as well), and ponders a generation's future as well as the conditions that threaten that future ("Woodstock"). After a considerable pause, the narrative strategy returns with a vengeance in *Dog Eat Dog* and its seven songs of societal complaint: "Fiction," "The Three Great Stimulants," "Tax Free," "Dog Eat Dog," "Shiny Toys," "Ethiopia," and "Impossible Dreamer." Remember, this is the auteur's "angry" album in which she blasts the media (e.g., "Fiction"), television evangelists (e.g., "Tax Free"), materialism (e.g., "Shiny Toys"), those who abuse situations for personal or political gain (e.g., "Ethiopia"), and the useless daydreams of the uninformed (e.g., "Impossible"). The fire returns in *Chalk Mark* ("Number One," "Lakota," "The Tea Leaf Prophecy," and "The Reoccurring Dream"), *Night Ride* ("The Windfall"), *Indigo* ("Sex Kills," "Not to Blame," and "Borderline"), and *Tiger* ("No Apologies"). These songs feature frontal attacks on specific subjects (e.g., "Dream," "Windfall," "Sex Kills"), philosophical lamentations (e.g.,

"Borderline" and "Lakota"), and the negative consequences of particular worldviews (e.g., "Number One"). For insight into the strategy and the strength of Earth Mother's emotions, we turn to an example that demonstrates her wrath as we consider the powerful societal complaint "Sex Kills":

I pulled up behind a Cadillac;
We were waiting for the light;
And I took a look at his license plate—
It said, "Just Ice."
Is justice just ice?
Governed by greed and lust?
Just the strong doing what they can
And the weak suffering what they must?
    And the gas leaks
    And the oil spills
    And sex sells everything,
    And sex kills . . .
Sex kills . . .
Doctors' pills give you brand new ills,
And the bills bury you like an avalanche,
And lawyers haven't been this popular
Since Robespierre slaughtered half of France!
And Indian chiefs with their old beliefs know
The balance is undone—crazy ions—
You can feel it out in traffic;
Everyone hates everyone!
    And the gas leaks,
    And the oil spills,
    And sex sells everything,
    Sex kills . . .
    Sex kills . . .
All these jackoffs at the office
The rapist in the pool
Oh and the tragedies in the nurseries—
Little kids packin' guns to school
The ulcerated ozone
These tumors of the skin—
This hostile sun beatin' down on
This massive mess we're in!
    And the gas leaks,
    And the oil spills,
    And sex sells everything,
    And sex kills
    Sex kills . . .
    Sex kills . . .
    Sex kills . . .
    Sex kills . . .

Earth Mother lays it on the line here with a simple, unpleasant nurturing observation: Evil abounds. The song contemplates the social Darwinism that is the evil alternative to Earth Mother's Garden of Eden rhetoric. The Earth is threatened by environmental disasters, the strong feed on the weak, the privileged abuse the masses, hatred abounds—threat is ubiquitous. The world is full of incompetents, rapists, and gun-carrying children; the environment is crumbling; and the sun is no longer our friend. What a "massive mess," indeed. This is a classic complaint. No solutions are proposed, no remedies offered; instead, we are presented with the nurturing observation that evil abounds, and are left to consider the consequences.

These types of stories slowly begin to dominate the oeuvre during the seasoned commentator phase. Once Earth Mother resolves her personal take on the situation in *Don Juan's Reckless Daughter*, she concentrates on "the moral of the story" for her audience. Occasionally, things strike pretty close to home as the auteur blasts something or someone that is near and dear to her—and, of course, a threat to us all. But it would be wrong if I were to omit an example of the heartfelt personal complaint that, in many respects, launched the auteur's career. In these stories, Mitchell lays out a personal situation for our consideration, and leaves us to contemplate her sadness. One compelling example of that narrative strategy appears on the album that so many claim changed songwriting, *Blue*. As an example of probing the universal through the personal, we cannot do any better than "River":

> It's coming on Christmas
> They're cutting down trees
> They're putting up reindeer
> And singing songs of joy and peace
> Oh I wish I had a river
> I could skate away on
> But it don't snow here
> It stays pretty green
> I'm going to make a lot of money
> Then I'm going to quit this crazy scene
> Oh I wish I had a river
> I could skate away on
> Oh I wish I had a river so long
> I would teach my feet to fly
> Oh I wish I had a river
> I could skate away on
> I made my baby cry
> He tried hard to help me
> He put me at ease
> Lord, he loved me so naughty
> Made me weak in the knees

I wish I had a river
I could skate away on
I'm so hard to handle
I'm selfish and I'm sad
Now I've gone and lost the best baby
That I ever had
I wish I had a river
I could skate away on
Oh I wish I had a river so long
I would teach my feet to fly
Oh I wish I had a river
I made my baby say goodbye

It's coming on Christmas
They're cutting down trees
They're putting up reindeer
And singing songs of joy and peace
I wish I had a river
I could skate away on.

Here we have the state of the art of the confessional songwriting strategy. The song complains, that is for sure. But it does so in an intimate,
self-disclosing manner that propagates the nurturing observation that personal pain is a natural condition and the desire for escape a natural response. With Christmas as a backdrop, the auteur desperately desires a
change: a change in profession, a change in location, and a change in personality that would enable her romantic ambitions to materialize. The
complaint is *not* with him. *He* was wonderful. The complaint is about *herself*
and the personality traits that pushed her lover away. If she were not so
"hard to handle" and so "selfish," she would not have these problems, she
seems to believe. The song is simple, clear, and innovative. Earth Mother
probes her sadness in public, for all to experience. Who knows, maybe
you, too, have looked for a river, a road, or some path of escape. And if
you have, this song suggests, it is not difficult to understand why. "Flight"
is a natural response.

But so is joy. "Happiness" is such an important part of the Earth Mother
manifesto that it is hard to imagine why audiences seem to overlook this
portion of Mitchell's songwriting. As early as "Roses Blue" the auteur advocates laughter as a remedy for life's ills. The fun-loving travelogues, the
hippie-go-lucky urban street scenes, the bouncy, bubbly suburban portraits
all portray the happy side of the narrative coin, and in so doing, illustrate
an important element of the Garden of Eden rhetoric: Joy is free. The life
celebration genre appears on the debut album with "Night in the City" and
"Sisotowbell Lane." The strategy reappears via the landmark work "Chelsea
Morning" (from *Clouds*) and returns with "Morning Morgantown" (*Ladies*),

"In France They Kiss on Main Street" (*Hissing*), "Cotton Avenue" (*Reckless Daughter*), and "Night Ride Home." These songs feature colorful descriptions of everyday events and items; happy, nurturing characters; and glimpses of The Garden that are not available elsewhere. In fact, "Sisotowbell Lane" may *be* The Garden.

The love celebration strategy is, more often than not, not as complex. That is, it seems to focus on the love interest and his personal situation more than on scenic descriptions or group activities. Ironically, the genre first appears on *Blue* ("My Old Man") and takes a long respite before reappearing on the "Joni Loves Larry" album, *Wild Things Run Fast* ("Solid Love" and "Underneath The Streetlight"), continues as the bright spots on *Dog Eat Dog* ("Lucky Girl" and the friendship celebration, "Good Friends"), and provides the foundation for the capstone statement that is *Taming the Tiger* ("Love Puts on a New Face," "Crazy Cries of Love" [with Freed], and "Face Lift"). The unadulterated joy that typifies the life celebration genre is sharpened and pointed in these songs of unabashed relational bliss. Relationships, these songs communicate, are essential to the spiritual equilibrium that accompanies entry into The Garden. For insight into the celebration narrative strategy, we turn to the landmark work "Chelsea Morning":

> Woke up, it was a Chelsea morning, and the first thing that I heard
> Was a song outside my window, and the traffic wrote the words
> It came ringing up like Christmas bells, and rapping up like pipes and drums
>> Oh, won't you stay
>> We'll put on the day
>> And we'll wear it till the night comes
> Woke up, it was a Chelsea morning, and the first thing that I saw
> Was the sun through yellow curtains, and a rainbow on the wall
> Blue, red, green and gold to welcome you, crimson crystal beads to beckon
>> Oh, won't you stay
>> We'll put on the day
>> There's a sun show every second
> Now the curtain opens on a portrait of today
> And the streets are paved with passersby
> And pigeons fly
> And papers lie
> Waiting to blow away
> Woke up, it was a Chelsea morning, and the first thing that I knew
> There was milk and toast and honey and a bowl of oranges, too
> And the sun poured in like butterscotch and stuck to all my senses
>> Oh, won't you stay
>> We'll put on the day
>> And we'll talk in present tenses

When the curtain closes and the rainbow runs away
I will bring you incense owls by night
By candlelight
By jewel-light
If only you will stay
Pretty baby, won't you
Wake up, it is a Chelsea morning

Here Earth Mother offers the nurturing observation that "the best joys in life are free." It is, my friends, all a question of *attitude*. You may awaken in the morning to the cacophony of street sounds and either complain of the relentless noise or hear a magical symphony. You may pull back the curtains and witness a threatening urban jungle or a delightful urban dance. The bright light of the day may signal another segment of life's drudgery or another invitation to the magic of life's simple delights as signified by colors bouncing off the walls, fruit arranged on the table, and the loving aroma of life. It is, my friends, all a question of *attitude*—and this song conveys the simple love of life that is the cornerstone of The Garden philosophy. Simplicity, acceptance, loving desire. These are the uncomplicated virtues that enable a life perspective based on nurturing love for your fellow human—a world without greed, possessiveness, or manipulation. Without sounding too cynical, it is, most assuredly, a *fantasy*.

Not all of Mitchell's celebrations are as fantastic as "Chelsea." The sheer joy in love celebrations such as "Solid Love" and "Underneath the Streetlight," or the poignant simplicity of a pleasant ride home with the one you love (e.g., "Night Ride Home"), do not entail any radical fantasy or unrealistic ambition as they portray the simple, liberating emotions that accompany loving relationships or societal acceptance. But most important, these celebrations provide a meaningful *contrast* to the conditions that threaten The Garden. Without these joyous accounts of life's simple pleasures, "The Arrangement" would not represent the threat that it harbors. Had we never left The Garden, we would not need to return. Hence, these narrative contrasts provide more than an escape; they offer a vision of what could be—if only the materialistic urge could be subdued.

Those materialistic, socially subversive urges provide a context for the love challenge, relational struggle, relational plea, and testimonial narrative strategies that are also vital parts of Earth Mother's nurturing prescriptions for living. The love challenge strategy emerged with the first album through the pivotal composition "The Cactus Tree." From there, it floats in and out of the oeuvre with "Tin Angel," "I Don't Know Where I Stand," and "The Gallery" (from *Clouds*); "Conversation," "Willy," "Rainy Night House," "The Priest," and "Blue Boy" (*Ladies*); "Help Me" (*Court*); "Talk to Me" and "Jericho" (*Reckless Daughter*); "Wild Things Run Fast," "Ladies' Man," "Be Cool," "You Dream Flat Tires," and "Man to Man" (*Wild Things*); "My Secret

Place" (*Chalk Mark*); and "Stay in Touch" from *Taming the Tiger*. These songs range from direct, coherent expressions of loving ambition (e.g., "Help Me"), to cloudy, unfocused accounts of love's apparent demands (e.g., "Blue Boy"), to prescriptive commentary on how to play the game (e.g., "Be Cool"). On one occasion, the challenge has worn the narrator down because the demands of building a solid relationship seem too strong; thus the oeuvre's lone relational plea, "The Same Situation." As I noted earlier, Mitchell claims this song is about a Hollywood bachelor who victimizes his all-too-willing prey and leaves a wake of broken hearts. The song is pitiful. When the narrator pleads for Divine Intervention in the form of just *one* honest, sincere man, the depth of her emotion is compelling.

There are occasions on which the challenge has been accepted, but the situation is either in some state of turmoil or just fails. Regarding the former, Mitchell deploys the relational struggle narrative to articulate how people cope with difficult interpersonal situations. Concerning the latter, Mitchell turns to the aforementioned relational complaint or the more encompassing testimonial to convey her observations. The struggles are limited, yet essential. They first appear in *Blue* ("All I Want," "This Flight Tonight," and "A Case of You") and *For the Roses* ("See You Sometime," "You Turn Me On, I'm a Radio," and "Woman of Heart and Soul"), and return briefly via "Car on a Hill" (*Court*), "Coyote" and "Blue Motel Room" (*Hejira*), and "Off Night Backstreet" and "The Silky Veils of Ardor" from *Reckless Daughter*. The testimonials are also few, yet powerful. The first appear on *Clouds* ("I Think I Understand" and "Both Sides, Now") and return in three songs: "Down to You" (*Court*), "Sweet Suck Dance" (*Mingus*), and "Love" (*Wild Things*). Here seasoned observations are used to paint pictures that instruct. We are told to accept our fears (e.g., "I Think"), to embrace our illusions (e.g., "Both Sides"), to better our situations (e.g., "Down to You"), and to keep things in perspective (e.g., "Sweet Suck Dance"). These lessons are important to relational success in that the delicate balances necessary to see love through require the personal understanding, interpersonal acceptance, and unadulterated sincerity these songs convey. Remarkably, the essence of all of these strategies was presented on Mitchell's *first* album through the foundational song that provides our exemplar, "The Cactus Tree":

> There's a man who's been out sailing
> In a decade full of dreams
> And he takes her to a schooner
> And he treats her like a queen
> Bearing beads from California
> With their amber stones and green
> He has called her from the harbor
> He has kissed her with his freedom
> He has heard her off to starboard
> In the breaking and the breathing

Of the water weeds
While she's so busy being free

There's a man who's climbed a mountain
And he's calling out her name
And he hopes her heart can hear three thousand miles
He calls again
He can think her there beside him
He can miss her just the same
He has missed her in the forest
While he showed her all the flowers
And the branches sang the chorus
As he climbed the scaly towers
Of a forest tree
While she was somewhere being free

There's a man who's sent a letter
And he's waiting for reply
He has asked her of her travels
Since the day they said goodbye
He writes "Wish you were beside me
We can make it if we try"
He has seen her at the office
With her name on all his papers
Through the sharing of the profits
He will find it hard to shake her
From his memory
And she's so busy being free

There's a lady in the city
And she thinks she loves them all
There's the one who's thinking of her
There's the one who sometimes calls
There's the one who writes her letters
With his facts and figures scrawl
She has brought them to her senses
They have laughed inside her laughter
Now she rallies her defenses
For she fears that one will ask her
For eternity
And she's so busy being free

There's a man who sends her medals
He is bleeding from the war
There's a jouster and a jester and a man who owns a store
There's a drummer and a dreamer
And you know there may be more
She will love them when she sees them

They will lose her if they follow
And she only means to please them
And her heart is full and hollow
Like a cactus tree
While she's so busy being free.

This song uses five vignettes to communicate the nurturing observation that "freedom is essential" to relational success. First, we are taken on board "The Dawntreader" for another freedom sail before hearing from "Michael," who returned to his "mountain" only to look back and miss what he had left behind. Next, we seem to have a prequel of "The Arrangement" before it all goes so wrong. Finally, we witness what appears to be Earth Mother's stance on the subject as the song's last stanzas present the wandering flower child with many suitors—all of whom are destined for failure should they encroach on her freedom. The sailor is so sweet, the mountain man is so earnest, and the businessman seems so dedicated; nevertheless, they are involved in some serious competition. This song is the musical accompaniment to the ubiquitous '60s slogan "If you love something, set it free." It is simple, direct, and an essential element of the Earth Mother manifesto.

The love challenges, celebrations, struggles, testimonies, and the lone relational plea occupy a crucial place in the oeuvre. On occasion, these sentiments represent vital parts of scenic or individual portraits, such as in the "Dawntreader" and "Michael from Mountains" examples cited above, or in the "Come in from the Cold" self-portrait or the "For Free" characterization. They also play a central role in many complaints as Mitchell uses these sentiments to articulate a contrast (e.g., "Snakes and Ladders") or describe a failed situation that warrants the complaint (e.g., "River"). In all cases, they represent the bright side of Earth Mother's worldview: "Sex" does not kill on "Sisotowbell Lane," they do not pave over gardens in "Morgantown," and children forget their troubles with each bright, sunny "Chelsea Morning."

Our last songwriting strategy involves the technique Bob Dylan pioneered, narrative impressionism. Here recurring tag lines, choruses, or musical punctuation is used to shape a series of statements void of plot progression. The song may feature wordplay, but it is not an example of it. These songs actually *sound* like stories as they stroke sentiments, raise images, or engage in various forms of symbolic folly, but they never tell a story in any explicit way. Instead, they propagate imagery or manipulate scenes that drive home points in more crafty fashions. Their subtlety is often their strength, in that the parade of images and symbols that float through these occasionally busy songs may distract you from—or camouflage—an underlying theme or point. That message just is not presented in terms of a story. It is an approach to songwriting that may render as much brilliance as it does embarrassment. The narrative impressionism songwriting strategy is a difficult method to master.

Mitchell's lifework features the technique in a concentrated manner. That is, she offers an impressionistic song here and there, but showcases her version of that approach in *For the Roses* and *Hissing of Summer Lawns*. We first see her impressionism in *Clouds* via "Songs to Aging Children Come" and in *Blue* with the title track. It is in *For the Roses* that it blossoms by way of "Banquet," "Cold Blue Steel and Sweet Fire," "Barangrill," "Electricity," and "Judgement of the Moon and Stars." After pausing for her pop master-piece *Court* and its live colleague (*Miles of Aisles*), she returns to the impressionistic style with *Hissing*'s "The Jungle Line," "Don't Interrupt the Sorrow," "Shades of Scarlet Conquering," "The Hissing of Summer Lawns," "The Boho Dance," "Sweet Bird," and the enigmatic hymn "Shadows and Light." In fact, of *Hissing*'s ten songs, seven involve the narrative impressionistic method. That style returns with the pivotal title cut from *Reckless Daughter*, "The Wolf That Lives in Lindsey" (from *Mingus*), and "Passion Play" (*Night Ride Home*). Never does Mitchell indulge in wordplay for wordplay's sake; instead, she consistently provides some form of structure that organizes the expression (often this is achieved through repetition). As an example, let us turn to the oeuvre's turning point, the impressionistic self-portrait "Don Juan's Reckless Daughter":

> I'm Don Juan's reckless daughter
> I came out two days on your tail
> Those two bald-headed days in November
> Before the first snow flakes sail
> Out on the vast and subtle plains of mystery
> A split tongue spirit talks
> Noble as a nickel chief
> Striking up an old juke box
> And he says:
> "Snakes along the railroad tracks."
> He says, "Eagles in jet trails . . .
> Coils around feathers and talons on scales . . .
> Gravel under the belly plates . . ."
> He says, "Wind in the Wings . . ."
> He says, "Big bird dragging its tail in the dust . . .
> Snake kite flying on a string."
>
> I come from open prairie
> Given some wisdom and a lot of jive!
> Last night the ghosts of my old ideals
> Reran on channel five
> And it howled so spooky for its eagle soul
> I nearly broke down and cried
> But the split tongued spirit laughed at me

He says, "Your serpent cannot be denied"
Our serpents love the whisky bars
They love the romance of the crime
But didn't I see a neon sign
Fester on your hotel blind
And a country road come off the wall
And swoop down at the crowd at the bar
And put me at the top of your danger list
Just for being so much like you are!

You're a coward against the altitude—
You're a coward against the flesh—
Coward—caught between yes and no
Reckless on the line this time for yes, yes, yes!
Reckless brazen in the play
Of your changing traffic lights
Coward—slinking down the hall
To another restless night
As we center behind the eight ball
As we rock between the sheets
As we siphon the colored language
Off the farms and the streets
Here in Good-Old-God-Save-America
The home of the brave and the free
We are all hopelessly oppressed cowards
Of some duality
Of restless multiplicity
(Oh say can you see)

Restless for streets and honky tonks
Restless for home and routine
Restless for country-safety-and-her
Restless for the lights of reckless needs
Restless sweeps like fire and rain
Over virgin wilderness
It prowls like hookers and thieves
Through bolt locked tenements
Behind my bolt locked door
The eagle and the serpent are at war in me
The serpent fighting for blind desire
The eagle for clarity
What strange prizes these battles bring
These hectic joys—these weary blues
Puffed up and strutting when I think I win
Down and shaken when I think I lose
There are rivets up here in this eagle
There are box cars down there on your snake
And we are twins of spirit

No matter which route home we take
Or what we forsake

We're going to come up to the eyes of clarity
And we'll go down to the beads of guile
There is danger and education
In living out such a reckless life style
I touched you on the central plains
It was plane to train my twin
It was just plane shadow to train shadow
But it felt like skin to skin
The spirit talks in spectrums
He talks to mother earth to father sky
Self indulgence to self denial
Man to woman
Scales to feathers
You and I
Eagles in the sky
You and I
Snakes in the grass
You and I
Crawling and flying
You and I
(By the dawn's early light)
You and I

Here we have what may be Joni Mitchell's most complex—and most re-vealing—single composition. The nurturing observation involves a personal acceptance of life's contrasts. The logic of "I Think I Understand" returns in this exploration of dualities as it encourages acceptance as an avenue of hope. The war within the narrator may well represent the war within ourselves. From that general observation, we move to the specifics of Mitchell's case as she probes deeper and deeper into her Indian roots, their spiritual logic, and her personal battle. *Her* battle renders something she treasures. It generates her art. She may quarrel with herself about her nightlife urges and her domestic ambitions; she may want to crawl with her snake every bit as much as she wants to soar with her eagle; but the struggle supports the art—and *that* is what matters. So she resolves to cope with her dangerous education; accepting her lot in life, as it were. By accepting her dualities, she acknowledges their significance within her Earth Mother manifesto. Her ideals (our eagle) coexist with her realities (our snake) as "twins of spirit" whose interplay renders that most precious of all entities, her art. This personal resolution paved the way for the seasoned Earth Mother commentaries that follow. Once the auteur reconciled *her* ideals with her realities, she moved into a position to attack those responsible for the dream's failure. Eagles and snakes may coexist in The Garden with little to no difficulty unless one attempts to overtake the other and, in turn, upset their natural equilibrium. Armed with such an understanding, Earth Mother now sets out to point to where such incongruities operate and to damn their evil ways.

The focus that makes Joni Mitchell's lifework so poignant and so compelling is the same force that made it so demanding for the auteur. It is a relentlessly probing body of art in which there is no rest for the weary. The True Believer shared what she truly believed, and when that clashed with what she truly saw, she became truly confused. To the rescue came Art Nouveau and his classical soul brothers. Through this sonic vacation the auteur resolved several pivotal issues and became able to return to the pop music world revitalized and refocused. But that was no party, either. The True Believer became truly angry, dutifully reported that anger, and wore herself out once again. Joni Mitchell's inability to "save something for" herself proved to be debilitating. Little wonder professional recognition has meant so little to an artist who truly left her blood all over the studio floor or public stage. To the extent that Bob Dylan was detached from his audience, Joni Mitchell was attached. Perhaps if she had changed her name to the world's most famous musical personality, pretended to be someone that she is not, and exorcised her anger through song, her career would not have endured the pain it did. And since Joni Mitchell *is* her Art, any pain her symbolic spouse incurs, she incurs. Although I cannot speak to that personal pain, I can report that its public manifestation changed songwriting forever.

PART II

Elvis Costello

INTRODUCTION

Television's "morning show" genre is a fundamental part of the programming day—striving for that magical blend of news, entertainment, and styl-
ish commentary. Some syndicated shows forsake news segments and
emphasize entertainment-oriented interviews and performances. One such
program—the highly successful *Live! Regis and Kathie Lee*—deployed the
tried-and-true dual host strategy to positive results, using humor, probity,
and charming curiosity in clever combinations that relaxed the pressures
of a live production. On the morning of September 29, 1998, Regis and
Kathie Lee welcomed Fran Drescher, D. L. Hughley, and one of the musical
world's fascinating creative alliances to their program. When Burt Bacharach
and Elvis Costello graced the airwaves that morning, a genuine cool cat appeared alongside an authentic rebel. As the group gathered around
Bacharach's piano, the hosts asked about the union, its origins, and the
songs that emerged from their collaboration. In response to Kathie Lee's
inquiry about the songs' themes of love and love lost, Elvis Costello replied:

> It's early in the day for talking about these things, isn't it? [laughs] . . . we took
> the cue from the first song, "God Give Me Strength" . . . a song of lost love,
> but a very powerful feeling, not a beaten-down feeling, you know. And we
> said maybe we could look at that subject. I mean, it's the reason why we're
> all here: desire and love and infidelity and all of the problems that we create
> [with] one another. And [we] just wanted to sing some stuff that came from
> inside here . . . and I think people will recognize themselves in the songs. I hope
> they will, anyway.

It's early in the day for talking about these things?? This from the guy who carried a bent nail in his pocket in case of trouble? *This* from the guy who started bar fights by shouting the most outrageous statement he could imagine? *This* from the guy who publicly wished the United Kingdom's prime minister dead so he could stomp on her grave? *This* guy is concerned about a conversation's relationship to the time of day?

What a mysterious person this "Elvis Costello" is. Critics love him, they say, because he looks like them. Critics damn him because he refuses to rest in one musical mode. Critics hail him as the rebirth of George Gershwin and Cole Porter. Critics deride him for his idiosyncratic lyrics—even though the record they just praised as signaling the new Gershwin was far more enigmatic than the piece under consideration. Critics just cannot get a grip on this Elvis Costello fellow. Assisting all this confusion is the artist's insistence on changing names, shifting industry affiliations, confronting journalists, and revising his sonic strategies with each project. There are times when the guy seems to change personalities as well as his name, record company, or musical orientation. I mean, who carries a bent nail one day, wishes the prime minister dead the next week, and questions television topical etiquette the following year? Clearly, one thing is certain. These personalities involve *complete* reinventions. The "Costello" with the bent nail is just as genuine as the "Costello" who questions the unsavory qualities of that morning's conversation. As Declan McManus once noted to a teenage friend, the music business is "all acting" anyway, so why not reinvent yourself if it suits your creative agenda? Throughout all of his different "roles," the lifework systematically evolves. The music that flows from this individual rests on a creative foundation that involves nothing less than his destiny. The man was born to his job.

When we turn to the published or broadcast work on Costello, we discover that Planet Costello is, of course, nowhere near as developed as the industry benchmark, Dylanology. To my knowledge, fans and "experts" have refrained from raiding his trash, developing computer programs to chart and interpret his word choices, and attempting to clone him from the DNA obtained from a used cigarette butt. Yet citizens of Planet Costello have erected impressive web sites, developed detailed "bio-bibliographies," and formulated idiosyncratic schemes for chronicling his work and varied activities. Academics, journalists, and dedicated fans chart his every move—often over thinking the simplest act—as they look to Costello for theoretical insight, newsworthy commentary, spiritual guidance, personal comfort, and, on some occasions, entertainment.

Like Bob Dylan, Costello is not interested in any of this. There was a time when he even refused to acknowledge the praise offered by his industry colleagues, arguing that the deification of musical personalities was more than a little bit warped. With time, however, such opinions have relaxed and Costello gracefully accepts the recognition he receives from the Grammy

Awards, the Ivor Novello Award, the Edison Award, and, most recently, the Rock and Roll Hall of Fame and the ASCAP Founder's Award. His is an accomplished career, and Costello has mellowed to the point of acquiescence on such celebrity honors. But his art has in no way mellowed. Again, like Dylan, this is a rebel who refuses to settle down, who insists on pushing his creative agenda, who accepts the challenge of advancing his career into new musical frontiers. His informed rebellion keeps his art alive; even though it confuses and, occasionally, confounds everybody else. Elvis Costello is an English Bob Dylan: an irrepressible rebel who will reject you because you praise him, who feels artistic recognition is the harbinger of creative stagnation, and who—more than likely—battles with himself. The result is one impressive body of work.

Elvis Costello has taken the torch tradition to new venues, that is certain. This troubadour has visited so many courts of love that he has become a permanent sojourner. He is a troubadour without a home, refusing to rest in one musical habitat for more than a single project. He has successfully entered such diverse courts of love as the classical chamber, the lounge manor, the punk cave, the rock-and-roll castle, the techno-dance palace, the folk chateau, the roots shack, the country mansion, and even the songwriters' dormitory, in which he wrote for others what could come only from him. In every case, he brings a decidedly punk attitude—a melodramatic, irreverent, aggressive perspective—to his art. It is that attitude and its diversity of expression that make his contribution to the torch tradition so unique. So relax, sit back, clutch your bent nail, and enjoy a merry jaunt through the fires of relational hell as Declan McManus, Elvis Costello, and Citizen Elvis take us on a musical exploration of human relationships and the conditions that make them so difficult.

CHAPTER 5

The Artist

When Bob Zimmerman invented "Bob Dylan," he devised elaborate accounts of Dylan's life. The imaginative youngster concocted wild tales about his character's parents (he was, often, an orphan), his travels (with carnivals, rodeos, whatever worked), and his musical influences, experiences, and famous affiliations. He once demonstrated his mastery of Indian sign language for a doubting party audience (he was, at that particular moment, a Sioux). "Dylan" knew no boundaries as he shared his inventions with friends, lovers, and, of course, journalists. When he received a crucial break with a *New York Times* story, Dylan spent much of his "interview" propagating his "history" for a dismayed Robert Shelton. National newsmagazines (e.g., *Time*), music historians (e.g., David Ewen), and more took the fictional bait and ran with it, turning young Dylan into an effective, one-person public relations operation. When Declan McManus (and Jake Riviera) invented "Elvis Costello," McManus not only refused to devise a personal history, he aggressively resented any inquiries into anything. "Costello" briskly resisted any discussion of musical influence, deftly avoided any talk of his youth, and fiercely attacked interviewers whenever possible—that is, when he bothered to talk to reporters. We have, then, two invented celebrity characters deploying two distinct publicity strategies: the charming folkie from Americana and the spiteful punk from Her Majesty's United Kingdom. Fortunately for everyone, both were short-lived.

Declan Patrick McManus was born on August 25, 1954, to Lillian and Ross McManus at St. Mary's Hospital in the Paddington area of London. Declan was born into an Irish-Catholic musical family. His grandfather was a professional musician, his father was a singer and trumpet player, and his mother worked in the record section of a department store. These musical influences shaped the young man's life; for example, his father—a member of the popular Joe Loss Orchestra—brought home advance pressings of contemporary pop records in order to practice the songs (making them available for his son), and his mother played jazz records and passed along the knowledge gleaned from her job at Selfridge's department store. Sources claim young McManus learned to operate the record player before he could walk. Brian Hinton reports that Lillian and Ross calmed their child "not with toys, but with the music of Frank Sinatra." Everywhere, it seems, Declan McManus was immersed in music of one form or another. He explained this facet of his youth to ASCAP's Erik Philbrook:

> To be honest, and I'm not saying this to be cute, but this is the truth. My mother tells me that one of the first words that I uttered as a child was "skin" in reference to "I've Got You Under My Skin." And I used to request it before I could form proper sentences. So I suppose that's a pretty young appreciation of Cole Porter. I grew up in a musical household, but I didn't have a formal musical education. So I wasn't subjected to music the way that a lot of people are subjected to it and are given a fright of it. I had a generous, open-minded musical education and the availability of a broad-range of music in my parents' house and through my own curiosity.

As life progressed, these influences molded a broad, comprehensive musical knowledge that systematically supported an eclectic approach to his eventual profession. Consider Joyce Maynard's comments for *Life*:

> There will have to be invented, soon, a term comparable to "well-read" to describe those children of the record-boom generation who are knowledgeable about popular music the way some people are with bodies of literature. Elvis Costello has that kind of nearly encyclopedic knowledge of recorded sound, and he moves easily from the Beatles to early Motown, '60s psychedelic, Burt Bacharach, George Jones. He'll speak of a song Dolly Parton recorded on Monument Records 16 years ago, the drum track on a particular single, the backup singers on a commercial.

To that end, the interview disc that accompanies his 1995 reissue of 1986's *Blood and Chocolate* conveys Costello's view that his musical knowledge is "very natural . . . kind of ingrained . . . brainwashed, I think."

There appear to be few (if any) interviews with childhood friends, schoolmates, or teachers about Declan McManus's formative years. Maynard notes that McManus was raised "in a blue-collar section of London" and that he was "a pretty straight kid" who, as "an altar boy," was able to recite "the entire plainsong mass in Latin." Our altar boy was consumed by music, as David Sheppard observes: "The precocious nine-year-old jazz buff was always racing home from the playground to indulge an early predilection for the records of Mel Torme and Ella Fitzgerald, an implausibly mature taste

for one so young. As a result, he remained something of a loner throughout his school years." Sheppard maintains that "school held little interest
for Declan" because his life revolved around "his phonograph." With time,
his interest in music making expanded from the record player to a variety
of instruments, as *People*'s Eric Levin writes: "At Catholic schools he underwent trial by violin lesson and sampled other instruments as well. 'They
were boring,' he says. 'They made screechy, horrible sounds, and it took
too long.' Deliverance came in the form of a guitar he picked up at 15. 'It
was magic. I couldn't believe it was so easy, because everything at school
was hard work for no reward.'" (Sheppard contends McManus received a
guitar from his father for his twelfth birthday; Costello told *Musicians'* David
Wild he started playing at 13—as always, sources differ.) All indications are
that McManus grew up in a private world of music. In 1990, he told Timothy
White he had few friends and that his life had always been that way. Later
in life, after he left his native England for Ireland, he articulated his rationale for the move—and this aspect of his youth—to Mark Rowland:

I think it's being more overtly anti-English than pro-Irish! I am quite anti-
English, always have been, and it sounds paradoxical because—I am English.
I was born here and I'm a third generation removed from Ireland and I don't
have any of that "old sod" bullshit mentality. I really hate that kind of sentimentality. It's bogus. . . . I've never been part of any strong community, never
lived anywhere where there was that feeling, based around a school or a
church. Maybe a little bit, but not enough to define that sort of clan identity a
lot of people take through life. I just never fit in here. The whole empire and
the Queen bit, it rolls me up the wrong way. There's an almost masochistic
instinct in English people. My grandmother used to refer to the "higher-ups";
she literally believed the people she worked for were better than her. It seemed
incredible to me. I couldn't persuade her otherwise.

Though he never felt comfortable with English society or part of any
specific "community," it appears that McManus appreciated his parents' way
of life. Lillian and Ross were open-minded, liberal-thinking, progressive
people who detested racial barriers, elitism, and conformism. Ross, it seems,
embarrassed his son with his youthful, hippie demeanor and musical taste
(Maynard, for example, quotes her subject's teenage fears that his father
would show up at school wearing a "caftan"). Once more, we turn to
Rowland's interview for insight:

But my parents were different. My friends always thought my folks were great,
because they were hip to the music and had more contemporary attitudes.
They were like liberal socialists. My mother used to sell records, from the '50s
through the '60s, and my Dad was a trumpet player who was very into the
modern jazz and bop eras, before he became a dance-band singer. And it
seemed like a glamorous thing, to have your Dad on the TV or radio every

Friday and he makes the odd record and Mom buys records and I got loads of records off my Dad because he had to learn the songs of the day and so there were records going in the house all the time. And they liked other kinds of music. My Dad liked Charlie Parker and Dizzy Gillespie and Irish music and Paraguayan music, and that stuff.

His father's show business career did more than spawn an interest; it *educated* Declan. Friday afternoons featured the radio broadcast the *Joe Loss Show*, and young McManus often accompanied his father to the station for rehearsals and the show. Sheppard explains: "A great treat for the pre-adolescent . . . was to sit in on these Friday afternoon performances and rub shoulders with the likes of The Hollies, The Merseybeats, Engelbert Humperdinck and even The Beatles, the latter of whom were steadily monopolizing his attentions." Tony Clayton-Lea notes that young Declan accompanied his father during summer concert tours (meeting "jazz stars such as Ronnie Scott, Phil Seaman, Bill McGuffie, and Tubby Hayes"), and that Lillian took her son to the Liverpool Philharmonic when she worked as a "part-time usherette." She also took him to see Tony Bennett when the boy was eight years old. With exposure to a variety of musical forms, direct experience with musical personalities, concrete involvement in the music profession, and constant exposure to the ever-expanding music media of his day, Declan McManus was systematically educated for a career in commercial music. He understood the need to cultivate his talent; the operational practices of broadcasters, record companies, and journalists; and the fickleness of audiences from observing his father, his father's colleagues, and their environs firsthand.

Hinton reports that McManus "concentrated" on pop music and its "changing trends" from ages 11 to 16 and that he wrote songs as early as 12. That biography also notes that McManus failed his exams for grammar school, attended a secondary modern in Hounslow, and completed his schooling in Liverpool (moving there with his mother at age 16 after his parents separated). McManus, it appears, operated on his instincts, as he related to *Musician*: "I'd convinced myself that my inability to get qualifications to get to the university was the same thing as not wanting to go. I had no idea how I was going to do what I wanted to do. I wanted to play music but it was all very vague." Yet he seems to have been *groomed* for his profession. His biographers note that his first recording experience involved playing the guitar in support of his father's vocals for one of England's most popular television ads, for R White's Lemonade. Although McManus may question his decisions about college—even discussing them in song—his path in life seems so direct, so clear—almost beyond his control.

Early in his musical maturation, McManus understood style and image as they relate to artistic presentation. He would feign interest in his peers' (and father's) musical affiliations while privately cultivating his own tastes.

When singing, he used either an American or a Liverpudlian accent, which-ever was deemed appropriate—announcing, as Hinton conveys, that "it's all acting." Clearly, the young man understood the business and its nuances. One formidable learning experience involved his first public appearance in 1969. In 1989, Costello discussed that debut with *Folk Roots*:

> It was funny because the very first time I played in public I was a floor singer and Ewan MacColl was the main singer. I got up with my little guitar and I was 15 or something, and he sat in the front looking exactly the same as he does now and he sat there, head bowed all the way through my set, and I'm sure he just nodded off! That was the Crypt at St. Elizabeth's in Richmond, which was a well-established folk club. I used to go every week whether or not I played. . . . So I had a traumatic first appearance with this old bloke falling asleep, or *pretending* to fall asleep during my song—as you can imagine, that was pretty crushing. But apart from that I was fortunate because I got to see some really good people.

From the R White's Lemonade ad to his debut before Ewan MacColl to his experiences at the Richmond venue, McManus's various associations continued to feed his musical education. By the time he graduated from high school, his was not a question of *what* but of *how*. He recounted the period surrounding his high school graduation to Greil Marcus and *Rolling Stone*:

> I graduated from secondary school in 1973. It was the first year of 1 million unemployed in England in recent times—in Liverpool, anywhere up north, it was worse. I was very lucky to get a job. I had no ambition to go into further education; I just went out and got the first job I could get. I went along to be a chart corrector, tea boy, clerk—because I wasn't really qualified for any-thing. I got a job as a computer operator, which happened to be compara-tively well paid: about twenty pounds a week. I'd just put tapes on the machines and feed cards in, line up printing machines—all the manual work the computer itself doesn't have arms to do. I had something of an ambition to be a professional musician. I was already playing guitar in high school—playing in folk clubs on my own. I was writing my own songs—dreadful songs, performing them more or less religiously. I didn't think the songs were worth recording—but the only way you get better is to play what you write. Then you have the humiliation of being *crushed*—if they're obviously insubstantial. If you don't put them over you quickly learn from experience.

His computer job afforded more than a source of income; it offered an op-portunity for reading and writing, as he told the *Guardian* in 2002: "I was in an air-conditioned office, with all the time in the world needed to just sit and think." His one side effect, Sheppard explains, was that the "con-stant exposure to flickering screens and brutal strip-lighting" gave him head-aches, resulting in an eyewear prescription that contributed to his eventual image.

McManus's friendship with Allan Mayes, their participation in the band Rusty, and his association with Nick Lowe's band, Brinsley Schwarz, were pivotal happenings. Mayes told Hinton of McManus's interest in American acts such as the Flying Burrito Brothers, Gram Parsons, the Nitty Gritty Dirt Band, and The Band—bands that favored musicality over celebrity pretension. While McManus and Mayes evolved though a host of bands and sounds, the Brinsley Schwarz/Nick Lowe affiliation was a steady influence on the young performer's quest for a professional career. Sources indicate that Brinsley Schwarz played short songs, without long solos, and defied current fashion—rejecting the sights and sounds of the day just like McManus's heroes Parsons and The Band. On April 18, 1973, McManus appeared solo under the name Declan Costello (a family name) and honed his act still further.

In 1974 McManus moved back to London, married Mary Burgoyne, and fathered a son, Matthew, in January 1975. Suddenly his day job gained importance, his duties expanded dramatically, and his musical aspirations grew more complex. To meet his responsibilities, McManus accepted another computer operator position, this time at the Elizabeth Arden facility in Acton. With a new family, job, and musical setting, it was only fitting that he joined a new band, Flip City (the name was inspired by Burgoyne's love of Joni Mitchell's cover, "Twisted"). Flip City was an active participant in London's pub rock scene, modeling themselves after The Band and influenced by Hank Williams and Bruce Springsteen. Borrowing a page from The Band's history, the group shared a house and bonded around a firm rejection of current musical trends and their perceived commercialism. Flip City received a substantial break when Charlie Gillett plugged the act on his radio show, *Honky Tonk*. Although Flip City disbanded in November 1975, the artistic attitude it fostered directly complemented the eclecticism McManus's parents nurtured, the anti-commercialism of his musical heroes, and the love of *music* that emanated from both sources. As Costello succinctly explained to David Wild on Bravo's *Musicians*, "it was all part of the process of learning how to write songs."

McManus adopted the stage name DP Costello after Flip City's demise ("DP" in honor of Gram Parsons' album, *GP*). With the new name came the new commercial strategy of personally confronting record executives by appearing in their offices to hawk his wares. He discussed his approach on *Musicians*: "I had this idea. I think I'd watched a few too many Hollywood films about songwriters . . . there was a fictional history of Rodgers and Hart, a fictional history of Jerome Kern, a fictional history of Cole Porter and it had a really unnatural affect [sic] on me. I really thought you went into offices and I'd go 'OK, I've got a song for you' and I'd play really, really loud." He supported that strategy when he borrowed a Revox reel-to-reel and produced a demo tape that, according to Sheppard, featured two songs that appear on his first album. He was quite enterprising—sending tapes, making appointments, pushing his original compositions. On August 15, 1976, he performed on Gillett's radio show. The act was distinctive. Hinton describes Costello's intimate vocals on original songs that explored dark situations: "There is something almost too personal in their delivery, a sense of someone you just don't want in your life invading your brain." One early composition, "Wave a White Flag," portrays domestic violence through unsavory images that foreshadow future songwriting themes. His singing style, his songs' thematic content, his evolving artistic-commercial philosophy, and his growing contempt for the music industry were all merging to create an artist with the willpower to see *his* ambitions through.

Sheppard claims that both Charlie Gillett's Oval label and Virgin Records extended recording offers to DP Costello that were declined. Again, the Brinsley Schwarz connection emerges. Schwarz's manager, Dave Robinson, and enterprising entrepreneur Andrew Jakeman (soon to be Jake Riviera) consolidated to form a new record label, Stiff (a term with many connotations), to produce their new solo act, Nick Lowe. Riviera worked with the band Chilli Willi and, like Costello, promoted his product aggressively by personally carrying records to shops. On the very day Stiff released its debut single, DP Costello responded to a music press ad and delivered one of his four-song reel-to-reel demos to the label's office. After dropping off the tape, Costello ran into his old friend Nick Lowe in the subway, they talked, and Lowe recommend Stiff as Costello acknowledged that he had, in fact, just left their office. How interesting that Costello's relentless efforts to push his music would come full circle to a group of people he had known for years—a group that featured the one person (outside of his family) who could be considered Declan McManus's mentor, Nick Lowe.

Though Lowe and Stiff would resolve Costello's search for a musical home, the scars resulting from sitting in record executives' offices and enduring the humiliation of personally pushing his music were deep. Once Stiff released their new artist's first records, they arranged for a few interviews with the British music press. In all cases, these scars surfaced. Consider these June 1977 remarks to Allan Jones for *Melody Maker*:

> But I never lost faith. I'm convinced in my own talent, yeah. Like I said, I wasn't going up to these people meekly and saying, "Look, with your help and a bit of polishing up, and with all your expertise and knowledge of the world of music we might have a moderate success on our hands." I was going in thinking: "You're a bunch of f___ idiots who don't know what you're doing. I'm bringing you a lot of good songs, why don't you go ahead and f___ well record them." They didn't seem to understand that kind of approach. No, it didn't make me bitter. I was *already* bitter. I knew what it would be like. I had no illusions. I have no illusions at all about the music business. It was no sudden shock to be confronted by these idiots. I didn't ever think that I was going to walk into a record company to meet all these fat guys smoking big cigars who'd say something like, "Stick with me son, I'll make you a STAR." I'm not

starry-eyed in the slightest. You can tell what all these people are like instinctively. You just have to look at them to tell that they're f___ idiots. But, I don't want to come off sounding like I'm obsessed with the music business. I couldn't give a s___ about the music business. They just don't know anything. That's all you've got to remember. They're irrelevant. I don't give any thought to any of those people. They're not worth my time.

With a music professional as a father, years of personal experience observing the difficulties of the entertainment industry, an artistic philosophy that rejected pretension from the outset, and the humiliation of personally hawking his music, Declan McManus—as these remarks indicate—harbored resentments that would remain an essential part of his professional decision-making for the rest of his career. As he told Charlie Rose in 2002, "I see music as distinct from the record business." These opinions were products of *years* of systematic observation. They will, as the Rose comment indicates, never die.

Stiff was another matter. Costello knew the people associated with the new label, which had to play some role in the unfolding events. Remember, Costello had turned down offers, so his hunger was not so consuming that it rushed his judgment. Jake Riviera recalled receiving Costello's demo for Nick Kent:

Elvis's tape was actually the very first tape we received at Stiff. It was so weird because I immediately put it on and thought, "God, this is fuckin' good"—but at the same time I was hesitating because after all it was the first tape and I wanted to get a better perspective. So I phoned Elvis and said, "Listen, I've listened to your tape, it sounds really good and I'm interested, but could you give me a week in which to check out a bunch of other tapes and I'll get back to you?" Elvis said "Fine" and so I waited a week, received a load of real dross in the mail and immediately got back in touch.

Stiff originally wanted to sign Costello as a writer, but the Riviera/Robinson/Lowe team reconsidered and signed him as a recording artist.

Now our story takes a *serious* turn. A fascinating convergence of entrepreneurial assertiveness and artistic aggression rendered another name change for DP Costello that would bring as much sorrow as it would anything else. Riviera decided to rename his act Elvis Costello in order to command the musical world's attention; moreover, he instructed his charge to, according to Sheppard, wear "outsized spectacle frames" and "one-size-too-small thrift-store suits" in order to "accentuate his myopic and somewhat scrawny appearance." To complement this look, Costello was encouraged to "play up the angrier and more vitriolic elements that shot through his recent songwriting." The anger and vitriol would extend far beyond the music. From his stage performances to his media encounters to his relationship with his audience, Elvis Costello took the angry young man theme to new realms, synthesizing his lifelong contempt for English society, his deep-seated distrust of the entertainment industry, his ever-present rejection of popular trends, and his relentless drive for musical innovation into one formidable presence. The artistic philosophy, "it's all acting," would now receive its greatest test.

At this juncture, we must pause to embrace the complexities of this situation. From this point onward, we are required to distinguish the auteur, "Elvis Costello," from the artist and his personal history. Remember, the *art* yields the *auteur*, and *this* auteur is a three-headed entity with different aspects of that character controlling different factors at distinct points in time. First is "Declan McManus" with his encyclopedic knowledge of music drawn from youthful experiences with various artists and situations. This aspect of the auteur's persona will consistently inspire a musical restlessness that fuels a relentless effort to expand the oeuvre's creative reach. Next is "Elvis Costello" with his aggressive ambitions that provide the commercial veracity to support McManus's unbridled creativity—at times, that aggression borders on recklessness. Moreover, Elvis Costello's voice, and overall performance style, contribute an emotional quality that directly reinforces that character's combative disposition. As Jim Miller observes in *Newsweek*: "The vinegar of Costello's voice makes the sweetest lines turn sour, and that's only fitting: the lyrics are a barbed valentine." Finally, a third entity emerges as the lifework unfolds, "Citizen Elvis." Citizen Elvis is his namesake's photo negative. Unlike Citizen Kane, Citizen Elvis refuses to co-opt a corrupt industry to his personal ends (literally forsaking money for creative freedom); instead, he stands alone—railing against English society, the useless diversions it fosters, its impact on women, its entertainment industry (often presented as an extension of the state's agenda), and the consequences of it all for everyday people and their varied relationships. This "Citizen" is not going to die alone, pining for a lost childhood toy; rather, he will die, no doubt, of exhaustion—angry, *punk* exhaustion. Citizen Elvis is a product of an internal fire that cannot be extinguished by money, fame, or success. As we shall observe, it will take years to form his editorial policies, but once they are in place, Declan McManus's musical restlessness and Elvis Costello's pugnacity will provide creative platforms for Citizen Elvis's "barbed valentines." "Elvis Costello" is a complex artistic persona whose attributes synthesize his biography, artistic agenda, and personality.

Stiff originally planned to split Costello's debut album, with one side featuring Elvis and the other the Stiff act Wreckless Eric (the idea modeled a Chuck Berry/Bo Didley album, *Chuck Meets Bo*). That plan was shelved, and Costello was joined in the studio by an American band, Clover (later to be Huey Lewis and the News), for the sessions that rendered *My Aim Is True*. Sources reveal that the sessions required about 24 hours of studio time and cost about 2000 pounds, and that Costello used sick days and holidays throughout the process in order to maintain his Elizabeth Arden job. Things take off at this point. The first single, "Less Than Zero," was issued on March 25, 1977. "Elvis Costello" made his first public appearance on May 27 at London's Nashville Rooms. And a new backing band was quickly recruited because Clover had its own contractual obligations. Pete Thomas (the drummer from Riviera's Chilli Willi), bassist Bruce Thomas, and music student Steve Nason (a keyboard player soon to be known as Steve Nieve) formed The Attractions. The group made its first appearance on July 14, 1977; according to David Sheppard, "In their shiny suits and skinny ties the band may have looked like a pilled-up version of the Merseybeats, but the sound they made was something else entirely." That "sound"—a blend of the Thomas and Thomas (no relation) rhythm section, Nieve's fluid keyboards, and Costello's rhythm guitar—provided forceful, nervy, aggressive support for Costello's melodramatic vocals.

James Perone describes the musical world's initial exposure to that "sound" when he recalls the creation of the single "Watching the Detectives." He claims that "after observing his wife watch a detective program on television," Costello "telephoned Nick Lowe late at night and insisted that the producer immediately set up an 'emergency' recording session so that Costello could get exactly the sound he wanted." With Clover unavailable, The Rumours' drummer and bassist were rounded up, and Steve Nieve overdubbed the keyboard parts later. It is Nieve's keyboard that generates a sound quite distinct from the other *My Aim* tracks. Clover's more traditional guitar breaks, rhythms, and backing vocals disappeared as quickly as they were recorded, making *My Aim* a genuine anomaly in the Costello canon. Though The Attractions' personalities clashed throughout their career, their music deploys a rhythmic counterpoint that merges punk attitude with established musical orientations in an effective, innovative fashion.

Much has been made of Elvis Costello and The Attractions' role in the 1977 "summer of hate" that fostered the punk/new wave musical movement. Though the era may have featured a return to basics musically, it also unveiled a new age of marketing. Leading the way in both categories were the Sex Pistols with their raw, cacophonous sounds and shrewd, enterprising marketing. The Sex Pistols seemed spontaneous, yet they may have been more contrived than The Monkees. The *real* punks may have been Stiff's acts, as Costello told David Wild: "What I wanted to do was approach the music with the same attitude, the same attack as punk, without sacrificing all of the things I liked about music—like, say, *tunes*. As a result we had a goody-goody image to a lot of people." After Wild deems the act the "Herman's Hermits" of punk, Costello offered his take; they were really the only *true* punks of that era:

> I recorded my first album for a couple of thousand dollars, while a lot of those punk bands were really well produced in expensive studios. The Sex Pistols recorded in Air, a fancy studio, with Chris Thomas, a real producer. So the

idea that the Pistols were some kind of up-against-the-wall, rebellious thing is a lot of nonsense. We *were* the real punks—the folks who recorded for Stiff Records. But like all really good things that are spontaneous, Stiff only really lasted for three months. And then the label exploded, or *im*ploded, I should say.

Sociologically, Costello was never a part of the punk scene, as he related on a Time-Life video: "I was never part of any punk rock thing. I mean, I used to read about it, but it was some sort of elitist thing to me. I lived in the suburbs. I couldn't afford to go to nightclubs at night. I had a wife and kid and I had to go to work." Musically, however, Costello not only emerged a punk, but he would never resign his station. Once more, we turn to Time-Life's *History of Rock 'n' Roll* video:

> The music was going to pay my way. It had to pay my way to the same extent as my job. I've had a strange career in the sense that I started out on an independent label . . . I was signed within six months to a very big corporation in America. I was a pop star—there's no other word for it. I found it really at odds with what I believed in being a musician for the long term was. From there on, I just did whatever the hell I wanted to. And left it to the record company to sort out. That's their job. Mine is to make music; theirs is to sell it. . . . It never said in my contract that I had to make the same record over and over again. I think it's harder for people to change the rules in rock 'n' roll. It's such a very, very limited form musically that it comes down to somebody's imagination, what they have in their heart.

Just as these comments reveal, things unfolded quickly. Robinson and Riviera split, leaving Riviera, Lowe, and Costello to form the Radar label. After a strategic street stunt in which Costello performed on the sidewalk in front of the hotel housing a Columbia Records convention in London, he was signed to that international music giant (and arrested for his trouble). With a major label distributing his music in the United States, several singles climbing up the English music charts, and a new band prepared to enter the studio for its first album project, Elvis Costello was, assuredly, a budding "pop star."

Central to it all was that image. Though he looked like a shrink-wrapped Buddy Holly, his attitude was anything but that of jovial rockabilly. Interviews with noted English music journalists such as Allan Jones and Nick Kent were manipulated to reinforce an image that extended well beyond the cartoon qualities of the punk movement. Costello told Kent how he maintained a "little black book" in which he registered the names of those who hindered his ascent (most punks, it was assumed, were *unable* to write, much less organize anything). There he uttered the infamous line that he knew nothing of love; rather, his lyrical motivations were elsewhere. He declared: "The only two things that matter to me, the only motivation points for me writing all these songs . . . are *revenge* and *guilt*. Those are the only emotions I know about, that I know I can feel. Love? I dunno what it means, really, and it doesn't exist in my songs." While that interview continued, Costello and Kent were interrupted by a group of music executives arriving for lunch, prompting a brief conversation with a female member of that entourage. Upon her departure, Costello assured Kent they were safe because he had brandished a bent nail that he carried in case of trouble (a *bent nail?!?*). As Costello and Riviera restricted media access, these comments gained momentum (reprinted, it seems, in *every* article), growing out of all proportion and ensuring the doomed qualities of a seemingly clever publicity strategy.

The most formidable test of a band's commercial viability is the U.S. market, the scene of many an English musical victory. For a band to be successful in the United States, odds are that it must dilute itself, strive for some musical middle ground, and charm the ubiquitous American media. The Jake Riviera/Elvis Costello and The Attractions act did none of this as it went out of its way to ignore these long-standing prescriptions. Initially, the American press focused on the obvious: the "Elvis" moniker, the Buddy Holly look, the "punk/new wave" sociology, the "revenge and guilt" rhetoric. Let us consider several examples of Costello's 1977–78 coverage. *Rolling Stone* focuses on Costello's "horn-rimmed glasses, business suit and slim-Jim tie"; the *Washington Post* stresses that he "seems to be a genuine anarchist" who is "mad at the world, a desperado with a guitar instead of a gun"; and *Time* concludes, "The British-born Costello may look a bit like Woody Allen with a guitar, but there is nothing timid about his music." After a November 16, 1977, San Francisco show, Greil Marcus reports: "The coldness of his demeanor—Costello never cracked a sneer, let alone a smile—made the humor of his lyrics inaccessible, or irrelevant . . . all at once, he communicates the arrogance of the next big thing, and the fear of the imposter." Similarly, the *Chicago Tribune*'s Lynn Van Matre questions the show's "novelty" while praising its "undeniably energetic and distinctive" style—an "energy" that "seems almost self-contained, remote." *Crawdaddy* printed this fine description of the new Elvis: "an absurdist portrait of a Chaplinesque tough guy: clunky shoes, rolled-up dungarees, horse-blanket overcoat snatched from a thrift shop bin, rumpled trilby hat over horn-rimmed glasses." There Costello defined himself, no doubt attempting to stoke the fires at bit: "I'm not an artist. . . . Even the word musician I kind of balk at. I'm a songwriter, and I'm a singer. But no hyphen, see? Don't make that mistake. Even a simple mistake like that can be costly in terms of misinformation."

These initial impressions were reinforced by Dave Marsh's 1978 piece in which he discusses why music critics were enamored with Britain's latest import: "I like him, but how could I help it? He is so much the perfect rock critic hero that he even looks and acts like one of us: scrawny, bespec-

tacled and neurasthenic, doesn't know when to shut up, bone-dull onstage."
("Bone-dull onstage"?!?) Marsh's opinion would be challenged in a *very* short
time. For their first American tour Riviera booked major cities. As they traveled to San Francisco, Los Angeles, New Orleans, Atlanta, Chicago, Philadelphia, Boston, New York, and other metropolises, Costello and The
Attractions countered the prevailing performance style with short, intense
punk *shows* as opposed to the more conventional, extended *concert*. Often
the act refused encores, leaving audiences angry and resentful. The short,
45-minute outbursts were musical attacks full of Marcus's "sneers" and "arrogance." The act barely paused between songs. It was a full-out musical
assault. Backstage, a self-absorbed Costello refused interviews, avoided
photographers, and annoyed an already isolated press. Our "perfect rock
critic hero" tested his admirers' patience.

That was not the only thing being tested by Riviera's calculated assault
on America. Subbing for the Sex Pistols, Costello and The Attractions appeared on the popular television show *Saturday Night Live* on December 17,
1977. There the band imitated a performance by Jimi Hendrix on British
television by starting a rehearsed song, only to cut it off in favor of another
number. When Costello waved off "Less Than Zero" and roared into
"Radio, Radio," he angered network officials to a point where he was reportedly banned for an extended time. The stunt received just the kind of
publicity that furthered Costello's rebellious, angry reputation while it also
afforded a personal sense of satisfaction for an artist who rejected the self-
congratulatory attitudes he witnessed from the *SNL* cast. The act gained so
much notoriety that it was re-created during the program's twenty-fifth anniversary special.

What was initially construed as new wave/punk rebellion rapidly evolved
into a widely reported arrogance. A publicity strategy that restricted photographers and refused interviews frustrated—and eventually angered—the
American media. In the absence of direct commentary, rumor flourished.
Costello addressed the mounting negativity in a May 30, 1978, interview
with Robert Hilburn:

> I never think of what I do as being negative. I don't understand reviewers who
> call it that. Just because you say you don't like something doesn't mean you're
> negative. If you don't like things that are negative, that's a positive statement.
> That's how I see my music. Some people tell me I should calm down, be pa-
> tient and hope for the best. But I'm not prepared to play the game *their* way.
> Everything they do is designed to make you conform and fit in. That's not what
> I want to do. I never want to be routine. I'm not interested in just being an-
> other tame circus act they trot out on "Saturday Night Live."

Through it all, Costello released music at a furious pace. His first recording with The Attractions, *This Year's Model*, appeared in March 1978. Costello
described his new record's approach for *New Music Express*: "It's a new

interest of mine, y'know—people owning people, people playing with other people like pawns. Not like a 'pawn of society' or even a 'pawn of the corporation'. Just one-to-one. So that's one new thing that's still just as emotional as before." *Model*'s aggressive sounds fit nicely in the musical blitzkrieg that was a Costello show.

While traveling across America promoting the new record, Costello absorbed the sights and sounds of the tour and synthesized them into the songs that constitute the January 1979 release *Armed Forces*. He told Bill Flanagan that *Armed Forces* had lyrics based on "out the window" observations and tunes that "reflected the monotonous, rootless music we were listening to: Abba, Kraftwerk, David Bowie." He explained: "If you take the songs apart they don't actually make any sense. They don't say very much. . . . That was my *moment* record. Probably the only one I will have because that was my pop star record. . . . The record inevitably doesn't make any sense because we were all completely mad. After making three records you realize you've sort of created your own tradition. Then the process becomes a little more difficult."

That tradition featured short, pulsating, aggressive songs that not only advanced the "revenge and guilt" angry-young-man rhetoric but also directly fed a confrontational stage act and its uncooperative publicity campaign. Not so slowly, but surely, it all began to unravel. Reports about a photographer who was beaten up in Milwaukee by Costello's entourage, about a tantrum in Santa Monica in which Costello stormed offstage, about fans attacked by Costello's crew, and about threats hurled and punches thrown by Riviera complemented shows that, again, refused encores and pumped shrieking feedback through the sound system to empty the venues. On March 6, 1979, Costello appeared on a radio broadcast sponsored by St. Louis station KSHE in which he derided the host station and lauded a competitor (that he believed played more of his music than KSHE). Costello did more than break the rules; he was rude, arrogant, and a little more than likely to be the kind of guy who carried around a bent nail. Just over a week later, the ticking bomb exploded.

On March 15, 1979, Costello played Columbus, Ohio. After the show, the band returned to their Holiday Inn for drinks at the bar. There they encountered Stephen Stills's band, also performing in Columbus that evening. Drinks flowed. Insults flew. A fight ensued. A key element in the fracas was Costello's use of several racial slurs directed at James Brown and Ray Charles in an effort to anger one of Stills's band mates, Bonnie Bramlett. Costello's use of absurd, mean-spirited, shock statements was a steady staple in a verbal arsenal that was an essential part of the "Elvis Costello" *punk* character. His attacks on American bands, popular celebrities, motherhood, and babies were commonplace from day one. That evening it all turned bad. The fight was brief, the damage was considerable, and a new oratorical genre emerged: the punk apology.

A 1997 *Uncut* piece by Allan Jones chronicles the madness for posterity. What began with trendy punk aggression turned into outright hostility. That the *Armed Forces* tour staff wore military clothing and rode in a bus featuring a "Camp Lejeune" destination sign fueled an artist-media battle that was, to say the least, self-defeating. When musical-pugilist-turned-public-relations-operative Bonnie Bramlett spread word of the "fight" to anyone who would listen, it all crashed down on Camp Costello. The post-Columbus media frenzy was unmanageable. An extremely hostile music press counterattacked at every opportunity. A New York press conference proved useless. Riviera had also angered Columbia Records by sending a load of shovels to the corporate office in response to their refusal to secure Shea Stadium for a show (offering, it seems, a tool appropriate for the label's efforts to, in Riviera's view, *bury* his act). Everywhere there was hostility—much of it richly deserved. A 1982 interview with the *Los Angeles Times* reveals that Riviera and Costello searched for a publicity tactic to turn the tide—as Costello told Hilburn: "Even without the incident in Columbus, I think we would have come off the road for a while. Things were pretty intense. Jake Riviera and I used to even talk about it being time for a motorcycle accident." Costello's reference to Bob Dylan's 1966 motorcycle accident that resulted in a seven-year hiatus indicates both his views about Dylan's mishap and his sense of desperation—a despair that was a product of his own publicity strategy. Costello's reflections on this period are instructive, as these remarks to *Rolling Stone*'s David Wild reveal:

> You have to understand that I had never made my living with music. . . . Suddenly I had all these ludicrous sort of things to live up to. And I reacted badly to it. That made good copy—not just the Columbus thing, but other punch-ups that we had with various photographers that wouldn't take no for an answer. We were all moving very, very fast. And there's a tremendous amount of fun to be had in terrorizing people that are so thick-skinned. So we kept going along like some sort of bizarre episode of *The Monkees*, running around, drinking lots of vodka and turning up in these places where things were so comical that we'd just push 'em right up into the absurd rather than even try to rationalize them.

The events of 1977–79 set the tone for an entire career. Although their intensity would wane, they would forever haunt the auteur—proving, once again, celebrity publicity's capacity to overshadow celebrity art.

The Costello troupe dealt with matters by returning home, touring England and Europe, and recording music. The soulful *Get Happy!!* appeared in February/March 1980, an outtake compilation was released in October/November 1980 (*Taking Liberties* in the U.S.; *Ten Bloody Marys and Ten How's Your Fathers* in the U.K.), and *Trust* was issued in January 1981. Throughout, the Nick Lowe–Attractions production team generated musically diverse, always aggressive, sonic platforms for Citizen Elvis's emerging editorials—

commentaries that were systematically evolving across time. Costello's remarks to Bill Flanagan about the *Get Happy!!* project capture the tenor of the times:

> That album was demented, and the way it was recorded was crazy. We did it in Holland. We'd go to the café and see a beautiful waitress and say as a joke, "I want to possess her." "'Possession.' That's a good one!" I'd write a song about it on the way back to the studio, just to see if I could do it, then we'd record it. It got to be a game. It ran away with itself. Which is probably why a lot of those songs aren't very good. When you push yourself that hard, the songs come out overwrought. Yet sometimes when you're throwing things away like that, you'll write something really true to your secret feelings in spite of yourself.

The auteur actually admitted that he wreaked havoc in his personal life in order to generate material for songs. The pace, the publicity (good *and* bad), the music—everything—was a mirror image of a Costello show: wild, frenetic, short-lived. Like Dylan's 1966 or Springsteen's 1984, the madness had to end.

In May 1981 another page was turned when Elvis Costello and The Attractions brought punk attitude and an English film crew to Nashville, Tennessee, to record *Almost Blue* under the guidance of Music City veteran Billy Sherrill. The October 1981 release covers country songs from such famed writers as Hank Williams, Merle Haggard, and Declan McManus's hero, Gram Parsons. The record created quite a stir, sold few copies in the United States (but did well in the U.K.), and offered a respite for an artist reeling from his own act. The mayhem surrounding the band simply moved to Nashville, but the relief gained by singing covers rested a pen in need of a respite. Typical of Costello's explanations was the one printed in *Folk Roots*: "That was just indulging something that I wanted to do. To sing songs of a certain emotional stamp without having to write them myself."

Everything changes at this point. Gone are the short, no-encore confrontational shows of the past. Gone are the media hostilities and unnecessary restrictions. Gone is the shock-oriented, ridiculously provocative rhetoric. Even Nick Lowe goes away; taking the spirited Costello/Attractions studio sound with him. Although Costello may downplay the artistic qualities of his work or denounce assertions that label him, he never disavows his aspiration to be a lifelong musician. To achieve that end, these changes were made. From this point onward, "Elvis Costello" assumes a kinder, gentler public persona that is reasonably accessible, strategically informative, and systematically cooperative. Ultimately, Costello replaced one public relations campaign with another. It was "all acting," after all. Still, while those facets of his career may change, the volatile love–hate relationship with the music industry continues to shift with the economic weather; this war between the punk and the establishment never, ever ceases. The auteur's battles with the music industry involve little acting.

Costello's 1981 return to American stages featured two-and-a-half-hour shows which received strong reviews that, more often than not, compared his new and old styles. For example, the *New York Times*'s Robert Palmer observes: "When Mr. Costello was touring this country two years ago, some critics and fans found him remote and arrogant. At the Palladium he was neither." Another interview with the *Los Angeles Times* discussed the new strategy: "I think I was definitely beginning to lose control of things. . . . It's too personal to go into all of it, but I will say I made several wrong turns in succession around the time of the 'Armed Forces' album. I found myself getting farther and farther from what I started out to be and moving toward all the things I hated."

The change in public persona accompanied a shift in musical styles. Costello entered a "punk tunesmith" era featuring highly produced, musically polished productions which reached for that pop middle ground that so often yields commercial success. The three albums from this period—1982's *Imperial Bedroom*, 1983's *Punch the Clock*, and 1984's *Goodbye Cruel World*—use accomplished producers to layer instruments, sound effects, and vocals in a systematic fashion. The songwriting on *Bedroom* inspired critics to deem Costello the next George Gershwin or Cole Porter (prompting him to tell Robert Hilburn: "I'm not trying to be Cole Porter. I don't live in a penthouse and walk around in a dinner jacket, waving a cigarette holder."), and Columbia's weird promotional strategy (a one-word campaign, "Masterpiece?") raised more questions than it resolved. Matters worsened with the strained, often evasive, *Punch the Clock* and *Goodbye Cruel World*. The albums' wall of sound production strategies occasionally buried a strong Citizen Elvis editorial or, even worse, elevated a vacuous pop sentiment. In any event, *Punch* provided a needed commercial push. Costello explained his new situation in another interview with Robert Hilburn:

> I have no plans to go in the studio again. . . . I think it might be a mistake to race in and make another record to sort of capitalize on this slight [upward] bleep in my commercial standing in this country. I'd hate to be overeager to jump on a bandwagon that's painted the wrong color. Then I really would end up compromising myself. I've no more intention making "Punch the Clock—Part II" than I had of making "Imperial Bedroom—Part II." The important thing is to avoid formulas so that you always keep your alternatives open.

Costello described *Punch*'s production strategy in a 1986 *Musician* interview: "*Punch the Clock* was the first time the band did backing tracks and over-dubs. I don't think there were any live vocals on the record. It contradicted everything I'd believed about going in and playing your songs and getting performances." And yet, after all these comments, he repeated the process with *Goodbye Cruel World*. The wall of sound bombast dissipates somewhat, but the uneven songwriting exacerbates Costello's artistic dilemma. He described *Goodbye* to *Melody Maker* in 1986: "So really it was just a mistake. Everybody makes mistakes from time to time. Unfortunately, they're preserved on vinyl in this case."

The 1985 *Best of Elvis Costello—The Man* release (a project with multiple titles, depending upon its location), like the 1980s outtake compilations, signaled Costello's record company's recognition of the uncertainty surrounding its artist. A personal and professional era was coming to a close. Costello's domestic life faced the issue of divorce, and his professional relationship with The Attractions was rapidly deteriorating. A 1989 *Rolling Stone* interview cites an informed Nick Lowe's views on the Costello-Attractions musical team: "That lot had a very strange relationship. . . . It was very abrasive. There was never any real warmth between them. But you don't have to be in love with the bass player to make great records. They certainly respected each other. But they were never really pals." Public recriminations would flow for the next ten years as that "abrasive" relationship intensified and eventually dissolved. Finally, Costello was quite public with his dissatisfaction over Columbia Records' handling of *Imperial Bedroom*. To turn the tide on these crucial issues, Costello relied on his music. A worldwide, solo acoustic tour with T-Bone Burnett facilitated a series of decisions that ended the punk tunesmith era and initiated a final, decisive career turn.

The back-to-basics, acoustic tour featured Burnett and Costello separately, and to close the evening, they appeared together as the "Coward Brothers." In the middle of that tour, Costello produced the Irish band The Pogues (*Rum, Sodomy and the Lash*), and became involved with the group's bass player, Cait O'Riordan (they eventually married). During a second leg of the Coward Brothers' tour (deemed their "second comeback tour") Costello plotted his next move with Burnett—a strategy that would back off from "Elvis Costello's" punk attitude, relax "Citizen Elvis'" caustic pen, and, in turn, allow Declan McManus's encyclopedic musical knowledge to flourish. The project, 1986's *King of America*, contained one song with The Attractions, thereby signaling the end of an increasingly tumultuous relationship. He explained his new style to the *New York Daily News*:

On my last two albums, the keyboards were almost overpowering. . . . So I wanted a record where there wasn't a single extra note or word. In musical construction, this is my simplest record since the first. It's also, to me, a punk album—in the sense that it's anti-success and doesn't aspire to fit any current format. . . . The important thing . . . is balance. I took one pure pop-radio hit *off* this album because I wasn't happy with it. A song like "Big Light," about hangovers, gives relief from the emotionally intense songs. I'm not Leonard Cohen, where you only play the record if you're in one mood.

King of America represents a significant shift in Costello's professional orientation. He legally changed his name to Declan Patrick Aloysius MacManus, accepted Burnett's collegiality (he co-produced the record), and ushered in his career's final phase. Remember, from the outset, Costello consistently discussed his desire to bring punk attitude to *tunes* that deployed that aggressive irreverence without totally forsaking musicality.

Our final songwriting phase presents a "punk composer" who systematically issues a punk roots record (1986's *King of America*), two punk pop albums (1989's *Spike* and 1991's *Mighty Like a Rose*), a punk chamber music record (1993's *The Juliet Letters* with the Brodsky Quartet), a punk lounge album (1998's *Painted from Memory* with Burt Bacharach), and a punk techno project (2002's *When I Was Cruel* and *Cruel Smile*). In each case, we witness the punk style that stresses irreverent, melodramatic, rebellious treatments of its subject matter and supporting musical genre. At various intervals, this phase features The Attractions with 1986's *Blood and Chocolate* (Costello's last studio recording for Columbia), 1994's *Brutal Youth*, and 1996's *All This Useless Beauty*. Band dynamics—like the songwriting—vary with each project as bit by bit, the group disintegrates. Intermixed throughout are "greatest hits" records (e.g., 1989's *Girls, Girls, Girls*; 1994's *The Very Best of Elvis Costello and The Attractions 1977–1986*; 1997's *Extreme Honey: The Very Best of the Warner Bros Years*), cover albums (1995's *Kojak Variety*), television show sound tracks (1991's *GBH-Soundtrack* and 1995's *Jake's Progress*), a movie sound track (1988's *The Courier*), a "mini album" project with Bill Frisell (1995's *Deep Dead Blue*), catalog reissues (twice!), another outtake compilation (1987's *Out of Our Idiot*), a five-disc live compilation with Steve Nieve (1996's *Costello & Nieve*), and songs on movie sound tracks, tributes, and charity projects. Our punk composer has written pieces with Burnett, Aimee Mann, Paul McCartney, O'Riordan (and more); served as the artistic director for the 1995 London Meltdown Festival; and worked in various capacities with a long list of musicians (writing an entire album for Wendy James, 1993's *Now Ain't the Time for Your Tears*). He has also written orchestral pieces (e.g., 1995's *Edge of Ugly*); composed what George Varga describes as a score for a "dance production based on Shakespeare's 'A Midsummer Night's Dream'" (the 200-page *Il Sogno*); composed the piece *Three Distracted Women* for the Brodskys and Anne Sofie von Otter; produced von Otter's *For the Stars: Anne Sofie von Otter Meets Elvis Costello* (a 2001 release on which Costello also performs); composed "Put Away Forbidden Things" for the tercentenary Henry Purcell celebration; performed on John Harle's *Terror and Magnificence*; and appeared in a variety of television programs and movies. Erik Philbrook reports that more music is in the making by way of a recording of the Shakespeare piece (featuring the London Symphony Orchestra) and a collaboration with Bill Frisell in which they honor songs from the twentieth century (*A Century of Song*). Finally, as this book entered production, Costello enjoyed an active late-2003. In September, he issued a new record, *North*. In December, he married Canadian jazz singer Diana Krall. *Rolling Stone* describes the new recording as a "lavishly arranged" work featuring a "twenty-eight piece string section" conducted by Costello. The album's content and the artist's comments indicate that *North* extends Costello's experience with the torch genre through his singing, arrangements, and thematic orientation.

Everywhere we witness some manifestation of Declan McManus's musical restlessness, Elvis Costello's punk aggression, and Citizen Elvis's pointed editorials. The ratio is project-dependent. McManus and Costello may join Burt Bacharach to generate torch songs with an edge (i.e., *aggressive* melodrama but without Citizen Elvis's acidity); McManus and Citizen Elvis may temper Costello's pugnacity and create songs written for other voices (e.g., *All This Useless Beauty*); McManus may work solo and explore tunes of personal interest (e.g., *Kojak Variety*); or the three may just fight it out by way of crazed impressionism driven by techno beats and slashing guitars (e.g., *When I Was Cruel*). The combinations are endless, as Costello related in an October 10, 1999, interview with WXRT-Chicago: "I'm not in the world of rock, I'm in the world of music." The auteur explained his musical diversity: "I sing all sorts of different songs. The whole world and the whole range of human emotions can be in an evening if you let yourself . . . when you go to a play, you don't want to see a play that's all in one note or a film that's all in one note. You certainly don't want to see a music show that's in one note." That Elvis Costello's musical career has steadfastly avoided any preoccupation with any single "note" is perhaps its most dominant characteristic. Just look at his 1990s chamber music, lounge tunes, orchestral pieces, rock albums, sound tracks, pop records, and a host of creative activities that must make Elvis Costello's decade as diverse as any artist's at any time—and his creative fire still burns.

Across this chaotic, unpredictable era of musical genre-hopping, two attributes remain relatively stable: his insistence on innovative performance strategies (more on that later) and his combative relationship with the music industry. Costello is passionate about his contractual relationships with record companies. Perhaps his difficulties began in that baby crib, crawling out to change the record on his parents' player, deeply believing that each record should feature a different label with its own unique sound. Whether it was the backstage talk about record or broadcasting executives that he overheard during his dad's rehearsals, or the humiliation he endured singing an original song to an executive who interrupts the session to take a telephone call from his hairdresser, or his inability to comprehend an industry unwilling to stick to obvious divisions of labor (*artists* make records, *companies* sell them), Costello, it seems, has never reached a comfortable compromise with the industry that supports him. Perhaps he simply suffers at his own hand, as these 1989 remarks to *Rolling Stone* indicate:

But I don't lose sleep over record sales. I once tried to explain to a lawyer why I run my career like I do. He was completely perplexed, because it runs against all logic with the lawyers and accountants and all the record-company people when you tell them that you deliberately try to lose money. I do things to keep interest in my career, bold things like a gig with the Royal Philharmonic, an eighty-six-piece orchestra. It was a disaster, but it was interesting. Like doing the last tour with the Spinning Wheel and two different bands while playing thousand-seat theaters. Do you know how much money I lost on that? But it was worthwhile because people damn well talked about it. That's the good side of show business—doing something interesting. Doing something that matters to you and to the people who come to see you. Playing 11,000-seat open-air theaters in Chicago with corporate sponsorship is *not* interesting. . . . The truth is, I would rather do it my way and lose money.

Lose money he did. As he roams from Columbia to Warner Brothers to Rykodisc to PolyGram to Island's Def Jam label (to name but a few of his affiliations), Costello avoids standard commercial prescriptions, ignores the tried-and-true industry formulas, and stretches the ever-present artistic-commercial tensions. His hostilities are outright and his opinions are straightforward. Consider these comments to Greg Kot in the *Chicago Tribune*:

I've always been fed up with the music business. It's crass, ugly and demeaning. . . . There's a tremendous amount of aggrandizing of very small ideas from the executive level, from the artists themselves and particularly from the journalists. But unfortunately what I do for a living is write songs and the way I avoid becoming a martyred poet who lives like a beachcomber is to make records, and therefore I have to subject myself to some of these indignities, like appearing on television and doing things that have nothing to do with what I do.

The operative phrase here is "always been fed up," in that—unlike his shifting public relations strategies or other aspects of his "acting" career—Costello has consistently, and publicly, waged war with his employers. It seems as though it is the one facet of his career that resists negotiation—although, of course, it does not.

From DP Costello to Elvis Costello to Declan MacManus to Napoleon Dynamite (his *Blood and Chocolate* moniker) and more (e.g., The Emotional Toothpaste, Little Hands of Concrete), our auteur has deployed a variety of labels designed to meet the needs of the moment. They are nothing more than brand names, as he related to David Fricke:

I was tired of the way people saw Elvis Costello: they saw this funny pair of glasses and a load of mannerisms, and they had all these preconceived ideas of what I was and who I was . . . I started to think of it as a bit of a curse. I started to wonder if there were people who were not listening to my records simply because they associated me with 1978 or '79. Elvis Costello was becoming a brand name, kind of like Durex. [Durex is a popular English prophylactic.]

On another occasion, he explained to Bill Flanagan the rationale behind the new "MacManus" surname: "I mean, it's a simple thing. I want my life back. This Elvis Costello thing is a bit of a joke really. He doesn't exist. Except in the imaginations of people who've got the records and come to the concerts and wait for me to throw some stupid tantrum. It came out of insecurity. Some of it was real and some of it was playing with reality and some of it was *playful*." Whether based on insecurity, publicity, or playfulness, Elvis Costello's work is always an *adventure*. After he completed *Painted from Memory* with Burt Bacharach, he announced to *GQ*: "My aim is to write no words in the distant future. I would like to become a good enough musician to not use words. Maybe I'll never get there, but it's better than having no ambition. To have an ambition that you maybe never fulfill makes you try harder." After writing *Il Sogno* and achieving that ambition, he explained to *Time Out* that he wanted to compose a concept piece such as Willie Nelson's *Red Headed Stranger* as a follow-up to *When I Was Cruel* (a major innovation in and of itself). Perhaps this statement about *Il Sogno* to the *San Diego Union*'s George Varga sums the auteur's creative worldview best:

I'm doing this because I want to write something, and not to write some new language, which so many composers see as their sole responsibility. It's amazing if you can do that, but I don't believe every composition can strike new ground. It takes time to figure out what's valid and what is cul-de-sac. The artists I'm most attracted to, like Duke Ellington and Charles Mingus, always moved their music forward. You get that same sense of Dylan as well. Most of the great musicians I pay any mind to have that quality, and if I can't maintain that in my own work, I fail.

Failure, of course, is in the eye of the beholder. The musical world is so complex, with so many competing perspectives, that artists are wise to anchor their work as close to home as possible. Otherwise, "success" and "failure" are judged for them through criteria that may have very little to do with their creative agenda.

Musicians from the rock era face obstacles unique to that genre. For instance, every "rock" artist has—at one time or another—to deal with questions of age. For some performers, the question is irrelevant; for others, the concern is genuine. Apparently, Costello crossed the age bridge right after recording *All This Useless Beauty* and the record's closing track, "I Want to Vanish." He explained that situation to Alan DiPerma and *Pulse* in an article about 2002's *When I Was Cruel*:

Even though that was originally written for June Tabor, ["I Want to Vanish"] was about the most personal song I'd ever sung. Essentially, it was saying "the game is up." But of course the game isn't up. I felt older when I was making that record than I do now. I felt like I was detached from the rhythmic motor of music, because I felt that was totally the product of youth. Now I don't think that way anymore. And I think I mainly got that from older artists in the world who are inspiring. Bob Dylan's last couple of years give you reason to believe that an artist can carry on making great work. Age is not important. It's how sharp you are and how true you are to what you believe in.

As this biography reveals, Declan McManus has—from day one—maintained an artistic philosophy that provides the creative foundation for his work. That worldview emerged from a musical education that flowed naturally within his environment. He was raised by music professionals, and what he "believes in" is evident in his early role models (e.g., The Band, Gram Parsons), his affiliation with Brinsley Schwarz, the courage of his convictions in his confrontations with record executives, his ceaseless genre-hopping, his inventive tours, and—perhaps most important—his Citizen Elvis editorials. He may shift roles as part of a changing publicity strategy or modify his attitude toward the mechanisms that compose his industry, but Elvis Costello has never wavered with regard to his *musical* ambitions. Those ambitions provide his personal criteria for judging the success or failure of a given project. Furthermore, they are the essence of our next topic, the creative impulse that sustains his work.

CHAPTER 6

The Impulse

That Elvis Costello was thoroughly *educated* for his life's profession is beyond all doubt. His musical lineage, his personal experiences, his professional maturation—virtually everything about his life—worked in some sort of cosmic harmony to produce one of the musical world's most innovative citizens. As that biography indicates, the product of this systematic schooling maintains several strong opinions about his chosen vocation. Listen closely and you can hear Judge Elvis pronounce, Hear ye, hear ye: Artists are here to make music; companies are here to market it; diversification in performance is the spice of artistic life; the musical world's various genres represent tools to be used in service of creative needs, not barriers raised to restrict entry or restrain usage. *These* are the guiding principles that enable our auteur to shape the subject matter before him into musical statements that serve *his* creative agenda. Oppose him, and he will fight you. Inhibit his activities, and he will dismiss you. "Elvis Costello" is fearless, and one only hopes that he does not end up destitute because of it. This chapter presents the artistic philosophy, the creative influences, the songwriting principles, and the compositional processes through which Costello applies his talent (i.e., his impulse) in service of his craft (i.e., his art). As with most "auteurs," there is genuine method to the inventive process—and that, my friends, is what made him an *auteur* in the first place.

The foundation of Costello's artistic philosophy involves his positions regarding industry roles, performance standards, and creative co-optation. Once he has an idea, he deploys musical structures that serve that inspiration in a strategic fashion. He readily models existing musical, literary, or cinematic techniques in service of his songs, and in so doing, enhances his lifework's sonic diversity. When we pull back to examine his motivations, it appears as though this approach is a response to the dogmatic programming that dominates the music industry. Costello explained his stance to Tony Lioce and the *Providence Journal* in 1983:

> As far as switching styles from album to album is concerned, well, different kinds of music should be available to people, don't you think? Music belongs to everybody, after all. These musical ghettos the radio stations have created don't allow people to have a completely open interest in music. Radio's a bit better than it was a few years ago, perhaps, but it still isn't exposing people to enough different kinds of music that they have a choice between one style and another. It's all just marketing. The record companies and radio stations say they're labeling things to provide an element of convenience to the consumer, to help you keep from buying a record you're not going to like. But in fact, all they're doing is making certain kinds of music unavailable to you, so you can't tell whether you like them or not.

From this we gather that Costello endeavors to educate "the public" as he was educated, opening consumers' ears to a variety of aural possibilities. Yet these ambitions extend beyond such institutional exigencies to more personal aspirations. On an individual level, this artist insists on shifting musical gears as a means of avoiding conformity, as these 1989 comments to the *Chicago Sun Times* reveal: "I think the uniformity of everybody else's career shows an amazing amount of artistic cowardice, maybe because they don't have any ideas . . . . I refuse to think myself abnormal because I get bored easily, and I would be bored to keep repeating myself. I think everybody else is out of step." This need for musical diversity transcends an avoidance of professional conformity or a rejection of industry marketing in that it is also a response to a specific creative imperative. Consider these remarks to *Folk Roots*:

> I hear sounds that I think are entirely appropriate not only to the context but to the subject and the emotion of the song so I'll use them. . . . It's not like a series of overcoats that I'm wearing. It's not like "Look at me, haven't I got a big wardrobe?" That's not what it's about. What it's about is telling the stories as well as you possibly can. . . . You go very far afield and you find the most outlandish things. When you start going to West Africa and finding that guy who wants to be Jimmie Rodgers . . . I think that's great—let's mix it all up. Like Miles Davis in the '60s. He could have been the king of jazz forever and he wanted to be Sly Stone. I think that's really cool. Cool and brave. It's all there. It's not so much world music, it's a world *of* music.

In every respect, the *song* is Costello's creative currency; consequently, he cruises the "world of music," borrowing, revising, extending what he discovers in service of his song ideas. Such tactics avoid unwanted (commercially inspired) repetition, open a host of musical doors for his audi ence, and provide diverse aural possibilities that stimulate his muse. With Steve Nieve and The Attractions, Costello elevated the practice to a science—using different styles, feels, and traditions either to inspire the compositional process or to unpack an existing project. In fact, they became masters of musical camouflage. He described the process on the 1995 interview disc that accompanied *Blood and Chocolate*'s reissue:

> We never made any bones about the fact that we just modeled things on other things. Sometimes very consciously altogether; sometimes with me thinking about it and not telling the rest of the band. . . . I was quite a long way in before I ever did anything that was overtly . . . obvious. . . . A lot of the things that we borrowed from, in one way or another, were things that I'd been passionate about some time before, so I wasn't overwhelmed by them. I could look back at them affectionately . . . like I knew all the Small Faces records backwards when I was thirteen. But I didn't have any occasion—or any ability—or any platform to use any of that information until I was twenty-three, so it was ten years later.

He elaborated on the practice for Bill Flanagan's book, *Written in My Soul*:

> The process of writing wasn't such an artistic endeavor as some of the more pompous critics would like to believe. Every record wasn't the bloody tablets of stone. In the construction it was a lot more of a hack job. But hopefully in the *heart* of the thing, in the good songs, was the true bit. There's a little bit of Tin Pan Alley in it. I don't have any purist tradition to lean on. Every pop musician is a thief and a magpie. I have an emotional affinity for certain styles, but none of them belong to me. Though I'd lift musical ideas from anywhere, I don't want to make it seem like the *content* of the thing was done with the same reckless abandon. There was a lot more feeling behind it, even if it wasn't pondered over. I never considered writing songs just a craft. It was like if you sat down at a desk and scrambled for a pencil and couldn't find one, you'd write in lipstick. The same thing happens with musical things. If I couldn't find a rhythm I'd borrow one and then change it.

We are talking about commitment here. This individual is driven by a specific charge that requires him to do whatever is necessary to flush out the impulse's creative directive. On occasion, Costello reached out to those songwriters who traveled before him, seeking advice, direction, or inspiration. For example, he sent the song "The Long Honeymoon" to Sammy Cahn in order "to make connections with a previous era of songwriting rather than limiting your thinking to a world defined by rock & roll or by beat group music." Costello is unrelenting in his pursuit of musical knowledge. It is the guiding beacon of his artistic philosophy.

As he searches the sonic landscape for diverse ideas, his lyrics follow a more disciplined regimen. Costello consciously avoids overly prescriptive or unnecessarily revealing commentaries. Just as he may borrow a melodic phrase to suit a specific end, he may lift a personal experience and use it to enliven a story. Never, however, is an experience used in the manner encouraged by the "songwriting as therapy" school. That the auteur detests that approach is evident in these 1998 remarks to Larry Katz and the *Boston Herald*:

> Unlike a lot of current rock writers, I don't believe there is superior authenticity in setting your diary to music. There's this bogus notion that it's somehow more real if you cut yourself and bleed on the page. I think that's lazy. There is as much self-revelation in "What Is This Thing Called Love" by Cole Porter as there is in any song by Kurt Cobain. One is not superior to the other. My job is to create stories with music and words and invite people to identify themselves with those songs, not with me personally. These new songs [from *Painted from Memory*] are loaded with emotional details, but they're not inviting contemplation of my personal circumstances. They're inviting contemplation of the listeners' circumstances and how the songs touch them.

Costello is unequivocal. He may borrow or transform a specific piece of music, he may interject a personal observation or experience, he may subscribe to a particular school of songwriting; nevertheless, all activities are in service of the song. His "job" is to "create stories" through songs that audiences "identify" with in some fashion—not share his life, hopes, fears, or culinary techniques. Moreover, these tactics serve an intense desire to avoid mainstream musical prescriptions and their commercial objectives.

With such a philosophy guiding the work, one is not surprised that the auteur's creative influences range far and wide. Initially, "Elvis Costello" refused to discuss musical influences, telling Alan Jones and *Melody Maker*, "This influence stuff . . . is really irritating, 'cos people are always trying to pin you down to sounding like somebody else." Over time, he lowered his guard and shared perhaps the most accurate response to the "influence question" with *Folk Roots*. When asked what he modeled himself after, Costello replied: "Everything! You'd get one record one week and try and sound like that and the next week it would be something different." A pivotal part of that development was, of course, his parents. The guy could operate a record player before he could walk, and his parents supplied the platters for rotation. Ross and Lillian McManus raised a living musical encyclopedia—a well-trained, well-rounded thief and magpie. Still, something had to anchor this unrestrained passion, lest he become a useless dilettante who is great at cocktail parties and on game shows. *That* influence involved none other than the Fab Four and that group's pursuit of strong *songs*—many of which, unfortunately, were diluted by the pure steam of celebrity. In 1981, Costello conveyed this point to *Melody Maker*'s Paulo Hewitt: "I think the biggest influence all along was Lennon and McCartney. . . . And I always had a thing about *songs* and it was only later when I started to write songs myself that I realised how obsessed I was with songwriters and less with groups and images." Remember, Costello aspired to bring that punk attitude to *tunes* that conveyed his melodramatic aggression.

Costello's influences extend from his cradle to his own private classroom. His mother's jazz, his father's eclecticism, The Beatles' songwriting—and later, T-Bone Burnett's dedication, Paul McCartney's and Burt Bacharach's discipline, the Brodskys' technical knowledge, and little beat boxes with funny knobs influenced the content and form of his musical renderings. Costello's education, however, is a continuing one. He explained that facet of his art in a discussion with Lisa Traxler concerning his emergence as "the next" Cole Porter after *Imperial Bedroom*:

> Without making too much of a fuss of it, I was just trying to find some new musical ideas. So I did start listening to a lot of pre-rock 'n' roll music—a lot of jazz ballads and the sort of songs of that era—and I even wrote a couple of songs which were after the fashion. The song structure of "Almost Blue" from *Imperial Bedroom*, for example. But obviously I'm not from that era. I can't really just make myself turn into that kind of thing. And also the world has changed as well, so it would be inappropriate and a bit of a sham, really. You end up being some show-business re-creation of it, like Manhattan Transfer: technically correct, but they always seemed to be devoid of any feeling. So this was the challenge in doing that—trying to employ some musical ideas which were exciting and fresh to me, ones I hadn't used before—incorporate them into my own sound and try to mold them into something new.

That sums up Elvis Costello's career in a single statement—a career predicated on a specific philosophy that requires his impulse to operate in a freestyle but systematic fashion. His "job" is to tell stories through musical structures that serve those accounts in a manner that facilitates an identification with that narrative. His "job" is *not* to share his innermost thoughts, conform to contemporary commercial styles, adhere to industry marketing strategies, or respond to audience whims. Elvis Costello's "job" is to use *songs* to satisfy his creative impulse; therefore, we would be wise to pause and consider his philosophy of a "song."

There have been times when Costello resisted any discussion of songwriting principles. Once he declared to Timothy White: "The songs are lyrics, not speeches, and they're tunes, not paintings. Writing about music is like dancing about architecture—it's a really stupid thing to want to do." On another occasion he told Allan Jones: "I've never really known *what* you're supposed to expect from songs. . . . And I think there's a danger in the very talking about it, it makes it seem like you've achieved more than you have." And on the 1995 *Blood and Chocolate* interview disc he explained why he rarely discussed a song's content:

> I didn't try to explain what any of the songs meant or anything like that. I've never really bothered about that sorta stuff 'cause I think it interferes with people's enjoyment of the music; their own particular personal view, their personal interpretation . . . very subjective views of songs which make them unique. The songs then become their own. . . . I've never been terribly comfortable with this thing of these little poems, you know, on the sleeve. I think it makes great claims for the words . . . I didn't think the words stood up to being read that way. I intended them to be heard rather than read.

It appears that all of the talk about his wordplay and semantic gamesmanship inspired a relaxation of that attitude and prompted Costello to talk about his writings. Those "little poems" appeared in more and more liner notes, and essays describing a project's objectives and development became the norm, especially with the systematic reissue of his catalog. That his official web site features audio descriptions of current song histories testifies to his acquiescence in this matter.

Most of Costello's comments are instructive and offer further proof of his guiding artistic philosophy. As early as 1977 the budding auteur demonstrated his firm grip on his songwriting objectives, as these remarks to Dave Schulps indicate:

> I suppose you try to make people think a little bit . . . you intend to have people identify with what you're writing. Not to be crass about it and say, "How will I write a song which will go to the heart of every kid in the land?" or, on the other hand, be like Cat Stevens and write these terribly introspective songs that only have meaning to yourself. That's it, really. I don't really plan these things. I just write them and they come out as they are.

In 1978, he extended his point in an interview with *Crawdaddy*'s James Willwerth:

> What I do is a matter of life and death to me . . . I don't choose to explain it, of course. I'm doing it, and I'll keep doing it until somebody stops me forcibly. . . . My songs have to do with situations. . . . They aren't philosophical treatises. I didn't name the songs "guilt," "revenge," or "sarcasm." The journalists did that. . . . I'm more interested in people dancing than thinking. . . . I don't like concepts. Individual things are more important. Being stood up on a date hurts more than a Big Concept. . . . I write singles-length songs. . . . If you can't get it down in three minutes, you ought to give it up. It's not mock anger that I express.

His argument sharpened in a 1982 *Rolling Stone* interview. When Greil Marcus inquired if Costello's songs aspired to affect how people "respond to the world," he replied: "Well, that's the initial intention of writing the songs to begin with, isn't it. That's the view that you put into that *one song*—whether it be about something extremely large, or not at all."

Since songs are designed to impact how people respond to the world, Costello contends certain songwriting principles should govern the process. For Costello, his task is straightforward: "I like to be truthful about things, some of which are quite painful, but only because they happen to other people as well, and that's the job of songwriting." In other words, Costello strives for universal perspectives that may build on personal experiences without the self-indulgence of the more confessional songwriting techniques. Early in his career, audiences presumed Costello's songs portrayed auto-biographical stances because they were so intense, so angry, so spiteful. When Allan Jones asked if Costello went too far with that style, the song-writer offered this detailed response:

> Maybe in retrospect . . . I can recognise sometimes where I maybe went over the line. But then again, I was never really that specific. I mean, people who really do pay too much attention for their own good have tried to peg certain songs to certain people. It's like a game, isn't it, that started in the early Sev-enties with people like Joni Mitchell. People always wanted to know who those songs were about. And people have tried that with me, and it's always been wrong. The fact is, those songs were never merely *confessional*. . . . Even if you're satisfying your own selfish desire to put somebody down in a song or praise them, it isn't important that everybody knows who you're writing about or the specific emotional situation that provoked it. The song should have a universal appeal, otherwise it doesn't serve any purpose. It becomes merely self-indulgent. Like, "Let me tell you some more secrets about myself. . . ." It's all me me me. And that just gets really f***in' painful after a while. But then you get people saying, "Well at least it's honest." But *is* it? Is it honest to go around going, "Look at my open sores." I don't think it is. I think it's just f***in' indulgent.

Costello is remarkably consistent with this argument. He may probe a per-sonal sentiment, examine a historical event, or denounce a public trend, but he restrains his individual interpretation of that happening and aspires to a more universal perspective. Sometimes it works, sometimes not. Often, the auteur deploys "Citizen Elvis" in a fashion that sharpens a given song's editorial qualities, heightens its universal appeal, and avoids personal as-criptions. Unfortunately, popular audiences and professional critics fail to acknowledge Citizen Elvis's presence, and therefore presume that these highly emotional narratives involve autobiographical sentiments. Citizen Elvis is yet another tool to be applied in this creative process; he operates from a particular stance, not from Declan McManus's diary.

Evidence of that songwriting philosophy exists in Costello's insistence on topical distance. His comments to *Musician*'s Mark Rowland state his case:

> I don't see people whose music I like in terms of an hour-long documentary. It's a much more raw kind of feeling that's inside you. And if I started to explain

it, I wouldn't get it out right. A lot of the time you have nice conversation and fun talking about things and slagging people that are beneath contempt; it's easy and it's sitting around fencing with words and being terribly smart and smug. Everybody does it. But when it comes down to the stuff I really care about, I hardly talk about it at all. Because it really goes beyond words.

If, for some reason, Costello indulges a deeply held personal sentiment, he camouflages it via a systematic personal code. There is a delicate balance involved in his songwriting, and he articulated that stance to Greg Kot in 1991:

Every song I've written is taken at least somewhat from personal experience. I think the mistake is to imagine that you're somehow a prisoner of these uncontrollable lusts and desires which torment you through the songs. It's nonsense. There's a theatrical element in there, some distance. It doesn't mean I don't feel any less, but a little more ability is involved than just a knee-jerk response to personal experience. There have been times when I've done that, but more often the deepest personal lines have been put in a coded form because that's how I first awakened to them. If you sing everything you feel, it's like you're asking for sympathy. Instead, I try to portray certain things, hopefully in a sympathetic way.

In his pursuit of "sympathy," in his aspiration to "universal" appeal, Elvis Costello uses Citizen Elvis to generate a "theatrical" aura that promotes personal distance. Why? Because that is how he was *educated*. Declan McManus sat backstage at his father's shows, read the music papers, listened to experienced musicians, and formulated a professional strategy to guide his career. Much of this involved conscious decisions; some of it is clearly intuitive; nevertheless, all of it is systematic. It appears as though he formulated a "songwriting spectrum" that enabled him to position himself in a comfortable position. Consider these 1986 comments to Bill Flanagan that explain his early works and their relationship to that period's musical scene:

On the first two albums there's a lot of what people took to be the "wimp" and "loser" thing. Because I was really anti the posturing of rock & roll, the crotch-thrusting element of it. I tried to write the opposite of that. I am really grossly offended by Led Zeppelin, not only because they're total charlatans and thieves, but because it actually embarrasses me. . . . That was uppermost in my mind when I wrote "Miracle Man" and some of the other songs that seemed to be me making some sort of myth out of the wimp. It wasn't a conscious thing of me trying to make a myth out of what people took me to be; it was more an attempt to redress the balance against the weight of tasteless songs. There were two types of rock & roll that had become bankrupt to me. One was "Look at me, I've got a big hairy chest and a big willy!" and the other was the "Fuck me, I'm sensitive" Jackson Browne school of seduction. They're both offensive and mawkish and neither has any real pride or confidence. But those songs on the first couple of records helped mold my *persona*. But to me there was a lot of *humor* in it. I was laughing at the alternatives. It was wanting to have another set of clichés because the old clichés were all worn out.

Clearly, this is not a man who learned the guitar, jotted down a few songs that would appeal to a contemporary audience, and allowed the chips to fall where they might. Costello conveys considered opinions; statements that reveal the extent of his musical education. That systematic schooling provided the key to his songwriting philosophy: Maintain perspective on your work. His 1994 interview with Flanagan summed up his orientation in no uncertain terms:

> This is the dilemma in writing songs. You can write about a totally unique experience, so unique to yourself that it is almost meaningless to other people. But you still have some distant admiration for the song, because it conjures up a mood which you have not necessarily experienced. I've written songs like that and in retrospect realized that they don't communicate a universal experience. They don't even pretend to. . . . Joni Mitchell's talking about fairly rarefied things on *Court and Spark* and particularly *Hissing of Summer Lawns* . . . I still think they're her two best records, not the earlier ones that people love so much or the later ones where it just becomes either too self-conscious or, probably, just *too* rarefied. That can happen. It happens to most. . . . I've been lucky to not be so famous . . . I can still move around. I discussed this once with Dylan: the difficulty of maintaining some perspective. That was the thing I was most curious about. You can have the most fantastic imagination but you've still got to have some substance to draw from. You can draw from other people's experiences and piece it together with other things, but it won't always ring true. I also don't think you can live an experimental life just so you can have subject matter. I know—I've done it.

This "Elvis Costello" is quite a creation. The blend of Declan McManus, Elvis Costello, and Citizen Elvis renders a highly considered artistic entity that displays a firm grip on his guiding philosophy—a perspective that draws upon his musical influences, his personal experiences, and his systematic self-education to formulate a concrete professional strategy. What strikes me as unusual is the fact that he appears to have formulated this perspective before recording the first note. This is not a seasoned professional looking back on his career; rather, his earliest interviews delineate these views in very precise terms.

A major element in this creative process is the artist's mental construction of his audience and how that outlook informs his work. From the outset, Costello was unequivocal, as these 1977 remarks to *Melody Maker* reveal: "But, please remember, I don't sit around wondering how people see the world, or how *they* feel about things. I don't attempt to express *their* feelings.

I only write about the way I feel. I mean, I'm not arbitrator of public taste or opinion. I don't have a following of people who are waiting for my next word. I hope I *never* have that kind of following. People should be waiting for their *own* next word. Not *mine.*" He reinforced that argument to Timothy White in 1990:

> I don't see myself as a champion of anybody. I've never stressed it enough that I write from my own point of view. I'm not writing for *anybody* else. What people identify with in the songs is their business. That's what *use* they make of the songs, the same way they make use of something they've read in a book or see in a film. I don't make any demands on the audience in terms of them seeing me as a spokesperson or a champion. I don't cast myself in any roles like those. I'm just an individual.

Without question, Costello shares Bob Dylan's view on audiences. Since individuals do what they will with a given work, it is foolish to subjugate yourself to any particular perspective. Write for yourself and maintain your freedom, this perspective argues. To write for others is to abdicate that freedom and imprison your pen; just ask Pete Townshend, Bruce Springsteen, or Joni Mitchell. Costello summed up his view on his audience and its impact on his writing for Erik Philbrook in 2003:

> I write for myself. The idea of self-indulgence in art is completely obscure to me. You should only please yourself. Nothing else matters. Because people are trusting you to have your own idea and if you're patronizing the audience, talking down to them, trying to guess what they would like to hear, then you should be writing advertising jingles. It has nothing to do with creative songwriting. You have to listen to your own voice and not give a damn about anyone else.

With that, we come full circle. Look at the consistency of Costello's commentary. From the initial remarks about the music industry's stifling dogmatism, to his insistence on genre-hopping in service of his songwriting (and fighting industry constrictions), to his reliance on his musical education to flush out or frame song ideas, to his rejection of confessional platitudes and the corresponding aspiration to elevate universal emotions (even if it requires camouflaging a personal experience), to his commitment to his craft over his perceived or designated audience, Elvis Costello maintains a firm understanding of his professional orientation—an outlook that guides his creative impulse's drive to weave stories about situations of consequence for diverse audiences. For further insight into his creative operation, let us consider Costello's compositional process.

After reviewing Costello's commentary on the compositional process, it appears as though he is not from the methodical-rhyming dictionary-thesaurus school of songwriting. Nor is he from the Bruce Springsteen-perfectionist school. If anything, he writes like Bob Dylan—catching ideas, riding them as far as he wants, and walking away once he has exhausted that inspiration to *his* satisfaction. Again, like Dylan, the words lead the way. There appear to be two strategies guiding his music-word interplay. On one hand, the music supports the words, as he explained to Christopher Scapelliti; the instrumental portions of a song serve the idea's "mood." Specifically, he argued: "So I figured, well, that's what you're trying to do when you make records—it's not necessarily to do the most dazzling thing [instrumentally] but something that has the right kind of mood, the right kind of fire to accompany the thoughts in that song." On the other hand, he deliberately deploys the music as a strategic counterpoint to the song's sentiments, as he revealed to Lisa Traxler in 1985: "And I've always worked with the idea of having a contrast, a juxtaposition of quite evil lyrics against a very sweet tune. We did that with 'Oliver's Army.' And there's quite a lot of that on *Imperial Bedroom*, and therefore by the end of it, I was quite convinced that it in some way counterbalanced the darker things in the lyrics." Either way, the lyrics dictate the strategy as they guide the song's eventual sound. To that end, Costello's 1995 interview disc reports that he never bothered to "master" the guitar because he wanted the music to "fit the rhythm of the words" that supports the "lyrical impulse" guiding the enterprise. He may learn to read music to communicate his ideas (e.g., *The Juliet Letters*) or turn to professional engineers from a totally different musical orientation (e.g., *When I Was Cruel*), but he never loses sight of that "lyrical impulse" and its required "mood."

Assembling lyrics is apparently a blend of tactical maneuvering and inspirational subservience. Costello is forthright in his discussions of his songwriting practices. For instance, his comments to *Musician* reveal a steady use of literary ambiguity as a means of deflecting personal attribution and enhancing a song's thematic power. He explained that he tries to "avoid mawkish first-person revelation" by using "ambiguity" to "reinforce meaning way beyond what you'd get by saying something straight out." He continued: "I was conscious of a certain amount of lyrical technique, and one was the use of ambiguity to make a thing more potent than it would have been if I'd just said, 'Look at me with all my wounds.'" Later in that interview, he discussed other, similar, techniques:

> Once I discovered ambiguity and irony could be strong techniques, I started thinking that *obscurity* was as well. You start kidding yourself that a song is really evocative, and in fact it isn't. It's just muddled. If the music isn't clear it *isn't* evocative. I never thought of it like, "This is my quest! I must be clearer!" But that's the way it came out and maybe it's time to stop messing about and hiding behind things. . . . Sometimes I deliberately leave the ending of a song ambiguous so that listeners can have it any way they want. It might sound like a cop-out, but that's the way it happens in real life.

Feeding such practices is the auteur's natural penchant for puns and wordplay—a talent that has caused him as much grief as joy. He discusses this facet of his writing on the *Blood and Chocolate* interview disc:

> I don't even notice it. I got kind of tired of reading about it in articles about what I do 'cause I don't see it as a dominant thing at all. I think it was more obvious, maybe, on *Armed Forces*, there were some like really terrible puns . . . . It wasn't the main reason. I mean all good pop lyrics—unless they really, re-ally, really . . . don't try to use any words that they won't understand in Taiwan . . . you know, "I will always love you," any idiot can understand that. You could play that to a Martian, you know, songs like "I second that emo-tion" . . . they're based on wordplay . . . I took my key from Smokey Robinson with all those things.

With his intuitive grasp of wordplay came a spontaneous style of writing. As early as 1978 he told *Crawdaddy,* "Each song is how I felt when it was written, the spur of the moment."

That approach has produced some humorous anecdotes. Brian Hinton cites a Q interview in which Costello reported buying a Dictaphone in order to get down a tune that came to him, and he claims the songwriter once stood in an "open phone box, singing to his own answer-phone." From there, Hinton describes how the auteur initiates the songwriting process: "Elvis starts a new song by writing phrases from his notebooks and rough jottings onto a large sketch pad, to see what pattern emerges." Sounding very Dylanesque, Costello supported Hinton's description in these comments for Flanagan's book: "Usually I collect fragments of songs—verses, title, lines—over a period of time. I might write a song in ten minutes, I might write it over two weeks. It's like a water tank fill-ing up; enough time goes by collecting phrases and fragments and at some point songs start coming out." His 1986 interview with Allan Jones builds on this notion by adding a mathematical metaphor to the creative equation:

> Isn't it possible that a song can be like a series of fractions to which the cho-rus is the common denominator and each of the verses is a separate scene, you know? That happens in "Brilliant Mistake," it's a larger scale observa-tion with some personal note at the end of it. The same occurs in "American Without Tears." It's a straightforward narrative story with a little personal conclusion.

At times, Costello collects "fragments" and "phrases" (his "fractions") and searches for patterns (his "common denominator") that enable him build a narrative that closes with "a little personal conclusion." At other times, as he related to Timothy White, he deploys a slightly different strategy:

I sometimes like to make an impression rather than a statement. . . . Almost unconsciously, they give off the feeling of an event without describing it. . . . I occasionally get visions in my head that I just write down, and there's no experience of having worked upon them. . . . I go into a trance when I'm writing, and can remember very little, like, except sitting down once with the newspaper. It can just be a mass of print, or at other times a mass of one-liners that stick out as possible parts of songs. With "Pills and Soap," I had written the title down as something that had come off the TV, and it suggested all these ideas. The substance of the later verses came from reading a newspaper, and these other things leaped out at me. It was as mundane as that.

All of this reveals that Costello's compositional practices adhere to his stated artistic philosophy. The lyrics drive the song and everything else serves that "mood." Our Machiavellian magpie/thief does what is necessary to achieve his songwriting ends. Once his lyrical impulse initiates the inventive process, either a direct/concrete or an indirect/abstract response—or some combination—may follow; either way, Costello maintains the narrative tools and the musical knowledge to complete the job.

Central to that songwriting strategy is Costello's use of language. The auteur described his relationship with words to the New York Times's John Leland: "But you know Monet? I look at his paintings without my glasses and they're in focus and 3-D. I think that about words. Sometimes you're trying to make a 3-D picture and not really saying exactly what you mean. But sometimes no one has any idea what you're talking about. And you realize, I don't even have any idea what I'm talking about." That description is not entirely accurate, however. There are moments when Costello's language use is his most precise songwriting tool—creating concrete images of thematic abstractions in an exact fashion (e.g., he dressed the song "Any King's Shilling" with language from that historical period). Quite simply, the musical world is a huge playpen for our auteur, and he grabs something from here, something else from there, and assembles it all in service of the song idea in question. That may involve a personal experience camouflaged by some obscure metaphor, a historical reference applied in a precise manner, or some general observation articulated in a playful, humorous fashion. Costello's flexibility is one of his principal attributes. His is a malleable muse that serves a host of professional and personal functions.

I close this discussion of the compositional process with this marvelous commentary that was obtained by Dimitri Ehrlich in 2002. When asked to characterize his songwriting practices and their relationship to his audience and industry, Costello responded:

I care what people think once the thing is created. But as I'm trying to write, usually it comes to me in a very odd way. Most of the time, it comes quite quickly; or if I write part of a song, and then ages later I write the rest of it, I certainly haven't been thinking all the time, well, how is this gonna sit with those people out there? That might be one small percentage that is the show biz bit of your brain that kicks in from time to time. Bear in mind that I'm not this pure folk artist; I'm not this pure anything artist. There's a favorite film of mine that has a character who's a clerk in an office, and he gives it all up to go and be a modern artist. It's like a satire of England's middle-class modern art in the '50s. He becomes a very celebrated artist, and at the end of it he's asked how he creates his paints, and he says, "In a bucket with a big stick." It's such a brilliant line, because it's the way I feel about what I do. How do I write these songs? In a bucket with a big stick.

Ahhh, back to the water tank/bucket again. What a telling metaphor. That bucket may yield a clear, concise Citizen Elvis editorial or it may spill over with lyrical fractions with or without a common denominator to hold it all together. It is, most assuredly, not your standard bucket. First, it has a trick handle that can be quite problematic for those hoping to control it. Second, it is a remarkably flexible bucket; able to cast its contents across a variety of surfaces. Third, it is a strong, sturdy bucket; able to withstand physical abuse and neglect. Nevertheless, in all cases, it functions systematically. This tool was honed, modified, and specifically built for its job. And, as we are about to discover, the lifework that flows from that bucket is as diverse and innovative as any in the history of popular music.

CHAPTER 7

The Oeuvre

McManus, Costello, MacManus. Just who *is* this guy? An artist may change names, physical appearance, musical orientation, creative medium, industry affiliations, professional management, and much more so frequently that discussions of these personal and professional matters bend and weave with the artistic wind. This week's country star is next month's movie star; a pop poet becomes a punk screamer; a rock sex symbol evolves into a refined lounge act; a painter turns to architecture. The combinations, the possibilities, are endless. Creative people follow instincts that respond to impulses that may, or may not, be consciously shaped by an acknowledged artistic or commercial agenda—a program that, by rule, must also negotiate with a diverse, occasionally fickle, entertainment industry. Remember, an "artist" may revise everything, but the lifework—the oeuvre—unveils the "auteur." When we consider "the auteur," we examine the convergence of biography, artistic philosophy, creative impulse, and stylistic tendency as it manifests in that individual's lifework. We must, therefore, always respect the distinction between the person and the art, and acknowledge the proverbial wisdom "Trust the art, not the artist." Whether the artist goes by a name, a phrase, or a symbol, the *art* reveals the *auteur*.

Elvis Costello's lifework is divided into three developmental stages: (1) the "making of Citizen Elvis" period, (2) the "punk tunesmith" era, and (3) the "punk composer" phase. Our first installment begins with Costello's debut album, 1977's *My Aim Is True*, and includes 1978's *This Year's Model*, 1979's *Armed Forces*, 1980's *Get Happy!!*, 1981's *Trust*, and concludes with the 1981 country music cover album, *Almost Blue*. The brief but important punk tunesmith period opens with 1982's *Imperial Bedroom* and extends through 1983's *Punch the Clock* and 1984's *Goodbye Cruel World*. Our most extensive—

and diverse—phase, the punk composer era, opens with 1986's *King of America* and continues with 1986's *Blood and Chocolate*, 1989's *Spike*, 1991's *Mighty Like a Rose*, 1993's *The Juliet Letters*, 1994's *Brutal Youth*, 1995's cover album *Kojak Variety*, 1996's *All This Useless Beauty*, 1998's *Painted from Memory*, and closes with 2002's *When I Was Cruel* and *Cruel Smile*. (Costello's Fall 2003 release, *North*, appeared as this book entered production. Although not featured in this study, the project represents a direct extension of the arguments advanced here. *North* is, in every way, a testament to the torch song tradition.) Contributing to the respective categories are Costello's systematic reissues of his catalog containing outtakes, B sides, and live performances, as well as his various "greatest hits" and compilation projects such as 1980's *Taking Liberties* (U.S. release) and *Ten Bloody Marys and Ten How's Your Fathers* (U.K.), 1987's *Out of Our Idiot*, and more. Finally, the auteur's participation in projects such as John Harle's *Terror and Magnificence*, 2001's *For the Stars: Anne Sofie von Otter Meets Elvis Costello*, and appearances on other albums, movie sound tracks, and thematic compilations are considered as necessary.

By focusing on the McManus, Costello, and Citizen Elvis triumvirate as the auteur "Elvis Costello," we may transcend some of the complications raised by name changes, genre shifts, management reorientation, or corporate transitions. As the art speaks, hopefully, we listen. Throughout our adventure, notice the consistent application of the auteur's guiding philosophy. His mission has been steady—and, dare I say, his aim remains true. Notice, now, *his* aim—not his record company's, not his manager's, certainly not mine—*his* aim remains focused. In one of his earliest interviews, the 1978 encounter with Nick Kent, young Costello declared his vocational ambition: "I'm in it to disrupt people's lives . . . my ultimate vocation in life is to be an 'irritant'! Not something actively destructive, just someone who irritates, who disorientates. Someone who disrupts the daily drag of life just enough to leave the victim thinking there's maybe more to it all than the mere hum-drum quality of existence." Building upon that starting point, a 1989 interview with Mark Rowland probed Costello's early music and its "obsessive" treatment of male-female relationships:

> It didn't seem obsessive at the time and I still don't think it is. I think it's perfectly natural for anybody my age, suddenly let off the leash like that. If there was anything self-conscious about the way I wrote it was the idea to grab hold of a person, to not make a song wishy-washy. In other words, an inspiration from the punk thing. But I never thought, "Well, here's a subject." I just wrote songs and I was quite shocked when people turned around and said, "He's a misogynist!" No, I'm not! I love women! Honestly. Take my word.

The "punk thing" extended beyond male-female relations. When *Folk Roots* inquired as to Costello's opinion concerning political songs, he replied:

"The main thing you should do with any song that's about anything you can call political is start a fight with it. That should be the main aim. It's not going to change anything. . . . The best you might do is start up some sort of punch-up which might get people talking about it . . . that's the very best you can ask for. The least you can ask for is to be completely ignored and for it not to be played." For many, this outlook seems embedded in the negative; however, Costello qualifies that view in these 1990 remarks to Timothy White:

> Well, even if the emotions in my songs are negative, they are *definite* emotions. That's the main thing about them. To some extent I'm satisfied with the songs that give only an impression of an emotion instead of adamantly saying, "This-is-the-way-I-feel," but they're the ones that are the least memorable. They're passive songs—you have to come to *them*. The other songs, whether negative, positive, angry, or glad about something, come at *you*.

Names, record companies, band mates, musical genres—virtually everything around Elvis Costello—may change, but his artistic worldview remains constant. Whether writing about male-female relations, English politics, or gardening, Costello aspires to "come at" the hearer, to stimulate—even irritate—the listener through aggressive portrayals of his subject matter. In other words, at the heart of the auteur is a driving *punk* attitude—an aggressive, irreverent, melodramatic artistic worldview that provides the foundation for the art that we now examine.

THE MAKING OF CITIZEN ELVIS

If ever a recording artist's first album foreshadowed his or her musical career in any way, this is the one. Elvis Costello's initial entry is the functional equivalent of a college music appreciation class, "Genre Dancing 101." *My Aim Is True*'s (released in July/August 1977) 13 tracks roam from classic Brill Building pop to old-time rockabilly to contemporary rock to traditional country sounds to create the musical platforms upon which the emerging wordsmith plies his trade. While the Nick Lowe–produced soundscape introduces a restless musical mind, the words convey the caustically clever bite that characterizes Costello's songwriting talent. To be sure, a creative philosophy guides this trek across the American musical spectrum as the auteur deploys a pop musicality through a punk attitude: The music is accessible, the lyrics are inviting but aggressively evasive. That is, we may not always know what he says, but we certainly know how he feels.

The album's 13 tracks complain in a relentless manner. Nine songs address relational matters and role issues with varying degrees of negativity. "Miracle Man," "No Dancing," "Alison," "Sneaky Feelings," "(The Angels Wanna Wear My) Red Shoes," "Mystery Dance," "Pay It Back," "I'm Not

Angry," and "Watching the Detectives" use a host of metaphors and word games to convey feelings of anger, resentment, revenge, and, occasionally, dismay about that haphazard emotional state that is a romantic relationship—real or fantasized. The record's four songs of societal complaint occasionally turn to relational matters as symptoms of the greater ill as well. "Welcome to the Working Week" warns of the perils of city work life, "Blame It on Cain" provides the escape clause for those seeking to avoid personal responsibilities, "Less Than Zero" sums up Costello's views on bigoted politics, and "Waiting for the End of the World" anxiously awaits His return so that He may clean up His mess (as exemplified by corrupt ecclesiastics). Costello's biting, sneering delivery throws symbolic tantrum after symbolic tantrum, often at the expense of the author's subtle humor. Clever lines and playful images get buried in this blitzkrieg of aggression.

The strategic juxtaposition of sound and lyrics that typifies Costello's work with The Attractions is absent on this record (the postproduction addition, "Watching the Detectives," is an exception). The music—again played by the San Francisco–area band Clover—is tied directly to the songs' sentiments. "No Dancing" uses "The Leader of the Pack" musical snippets and the infamous dance-sex metaphor to relate the sexual subjugation associated with emotional slavery; "Miracle Man" uses rockabilly sounds to articulate the relational abyss that accompanies life with a greedy, insensitive bitch; "Red Shoes" revisits a Robert Johnson–type deal involving a podiatric fountain of youth (although the angels may covet his shoes, his date still dumps him); "Mystery Dance" involves little to no mystery in its portrayal of a hapless but devoted lover lacking in basic skills; "Pay It Back" contemplates revenge for self-inflicted wounds as Costello explains that in order to pull the wool over his audience's eyes, he must first deceive himself; and "I'm Not Angry" screams just that, as the narrator battles with his own emotions. The songs deploy personal and public metaphors through a consistent musical strategy: Each song rails away for around two minutes (or less) and closes with long, repetitive fades. For example, "I'm Not Angry" spends over a third of the song with its closing, repeating the title over and over. From "Alison" and its poignant sentiments to "Watching the Detectives" and its potential metaphors to the music's evocation of diverse but established structures, *My Aim Is True* reflects the songwriting strategies that will control the budding auteur's pen for the next 25 years.

When *Trouser Press* inquired why the songs were so "bitter," Costello replied: "Because I'm an extraordinarily bitter person. I don't like to sound as if I'm too obsessed and can't feel any other way, but it just happens that those songs evince that kind of feeling and, therefore, the album is like that. . . . People have noticed that a lot of the album is about being rejected, but I don't like the idea of getting too analytical about it. It's just what the songs are about, I don't think about them too hard." He continued his commentary with *Crawdaddy*: "My album has no love songs. Not in the sense that I choose them. Quite a few of my reviews have tended to picture me as an emotional masochist. Well, many of the songs *are* involved with revenge and guilt. Some are about being tricked. These are the stronger feelings, the ones you are left with at night." There can be little doubt that *My Aim* introduces a rage of negativity that, at this point, involves underdeveloped impressions—literally, a series of initial responses to situations of consequence. At times defiant, at times submissive, always aggressively melodramatic, the record represents the birth of Citizen Elvis: an irreverent but thoughtful social critic with a sharp eye for hypocrisy (e.g., evil ecclesiastics, thieving politicians, conniving lovers). Songs such as "Red Shoes" may reveal emotional confusion; nevertheless, Citizen Elvis is *intensely* affected by what he sees, and this album creates the baseline from which his lifework interprets those observations.

What seems to dominate the record, however, is its overbearing commitment to *image*. At this point, critics have not been fully contaminated by the image that soon engulfs the artist. Consequently, critical responses focus on the *art* as well as the *artist*. *Creem*'s Mitch Cohen claims, "In his preoccupation with frustration and mental revenge, his cynicism stemming from a realization that life's guarantees are worthless, and his imperturbable buoyancy in the face of it all, Elvis Costello is a contender." The *Washington Post*'s Joseph Sasfy is enamored of the young writer's lyrical style: "If Costello has fallen back on archetypal rock rhapsodies, he has also invested them with idiosyncrasy and attached them to sardonic and occasionally surreal dissections of the modern relationship." *Rolling Stone*'s Greil Marcus concentrates on style as he describes Costello as "an underfed, misanthropic Buddy Holly" who demonstrates "that not only are things quite strange in England today, they are capable of getting a lot stranger." Marcus briefly departs from his sociological treatise for an aside about the music, which he claims "tends toward the neurotic" as the artist "sings as if there's a gun at his back." While instant commentary on his musical samplings and lyrical prowess advances as the lifework progresses, it would be years before anyone realized that two of *My Aim*'s strongest songs were left in the racks because they were *country* tunes. "Radio Sweetheart" and "Stranger in the House" convey a musical range that eventually dominates this artist's career. Yet the image controls the work at this point. The Stiff Operation refused to chance a loss of control over their marketing strategy by releasing songs that could possibly counter their plans—even if they revealed a range of talent totally absent from the 1977 musical world.

My Aim Is True's sequel appeared in July 1978. This second Nick Lowe production is certainly an extension of the debut offering in that *My Aim*'s characters and scenes reappear—with a significant plot twist. Although several of *This Year's Model*'s songs were supposedly written during the *My Aim* period (or before), the innocence that underpins many of *My Aim*'s tracks now gives way to a state of emotional war. The character who passionately desired insights into the "Mystery Dance," who withstood the abuses associated with his inability to achieve "Miracle Man" status, and who denounced both his anger ("I'm Not Angry") and his responsibilities ("Blame It on Cain") has evolved into a confrontational figure who now understands that "the girl" is just as hung-up as he is (e.g., "This Year's Girl" and "Pump It Up") and deserves in-kind retribution (e.g., "Lip Service" and "Hand in Hand"). And although he is certainly no "Miracle Man," he can see through her "Lipstick Vogue" pretensions. The innocence has been replaced by some form of Clint Eastwood machismo through which Costello confronts the emotional fascists who threaten his life with a "go ahead, make my day" bravado. Costello's characters are not only up for the fight, they are beginning to relish it.

In this sea of negativity, many ships sail in many directions. Some courses are easy to chart; others are more obscure; and still others overtake and collide with one another. The intensity and urgency of the sound demand your attention, but your ability to focus is prevented. Just as you manage some sort of grip on one expression, the wind changes and another course emerges. Why all the mania? Because this is a record with an attitude—a *punk* attitude. Elvis Costello and The Attractions' first album contains 13 tracks that transcend the Sex Pistols' incoherent noise or the New York punk scene's inaccessible metaphors by way of clear, biting lyrics that leave little doubt that this is a full frontal attack. Two songs—"Night Rally" and "Radio, Radio"—rail against political fascism through portrayals of dark patriotism/fascist segregation ("Night") and emotional mind control through the mass media ("Radio"). "Night" communicates how mundane forms of political affiliation (e.g., party symbols, pledges, anthems, gatherings) may inspire evil patriotism; moreover, when it is joined with "Radio," we observe an extension of the political mobilization process through the media. In other words, you may not choose to attend their rally or sing their anthem in the shower, but your range of potential influences is *still* under their management. For Costello, the people who program the radio may be foolish, yet they could be fools with a plan. "Citizen Elvis" is coming to grips with his subject matter.

This Year's remaining tracks draw relational battle lines through songs that either directly address the interpersonal war or describe the various battlegrounds in which such confrontations occur. Regarding the latter, "(I Don't Want to Go to) Chelsea" is a highly repetitive complaint about prissy girls, relational revenge, and geographical avoidance; "Living in Paradise" is a muddy account of jealousy, more revenge, and a self-fulfilling prophecy (i.e., love is nice only for a while, then the hell emerges); and "Pump It Up" is an inclusive statement. Here negativity abounds as Costello attacks bad music, cheap club talk, horrific women, and cheesy fashion all in one compelling narrative stroke. The song's driving beat adds to the experience's intensity as The Attractions hammer home the point: Club life not only takes you nowhere, it is merely another "Night Rally" sponsored by the same mental programmers who invade your life on all fronts. Club life is the domain of the damned.

The pleasantries continue with songs that confront the relational war that love—or the thought of love—brings. "No Action" is a jealous tirade. "This Year's Girl" relates that "she" is just as hung-up as "he" is, and how "she" manages to take all the boredom in stride: Cheap idolization and ineffective lovers are just part of the show. "The Beat" is a thinly veiled account of the lonely man's sexual alternative. "Little Triggers" describes how one lover pushes her partner's emotional buttons as a recreational alternative. "You Belong to Me" conveys that an ounce of romantic prevention is worth a pound of relational cure. And the trilogy, if you will, that is "Lipstick Vogue," "Lip Service," and "Hand in Hand" communicates the essence of it all. Costello's war of the sexes hinges on these three songs that unequivocally relate (1) that "love" is the functional equivalent of a sick organ in need of extraction to the point that, if left untreated, it will cause its victim to question his humanity (the theatrical musical presentation that is "Lipstick"); (2) that such conditions create a need for promises to the point that promises are all the narrator can muster the energy to offer ("Lip"); and (3) that if the two combatants want to give a relationship a try, well, the narrator is not going to suffer by himself. The last entry is the key to unlocking the passion that consumes *This Year's Model*: Misery demands company. Our narrator may be a jerk, but he is an *experienced* jerk; so if there is going to be a price to be paid, he is not going to pay it by himself. The victimage of *My Aim* is over in *This Year's*.

The intensity of these expressions seemed to frighten critics. *Rolling Stone*'s Kit Rachlis opens with this analogy: "Listening to Elvis Costello is like walking down a dark, empty street and hearing another set of heels. His music doesn't make you dance, it makes you jump." Rachlis argues, "I don't think there's been a rock & roller who's made fear so palpable or so attractive. . . . Costello is brutal toward everyone, but what saves him is that he's just as brutal toward himself." *Crawdaddy*'s Jon Pareles wonders where Costello "gets so much venom" and claims that the writer is "continuously savage" on his "tough and committed" record; nevertheless: "It is also so wrongheaded, so full of hatred, and so convinced of its moral superiority that it makes me uneasy. . . . Costello distrusts his entire universe, particularly its female side, and I get the feeling negativity won't pull him through." (As an aside, several of Pareles's observations are weird. "Pump It Up" is about masturbation? "You Belong to Me" is about a pedophile? "The Beat" contains verses "that resemble Bacharach/David tunes"?) Years later, *Rolling Stone* places the record in a historical context by describing how it "served notice to the world that the oddly named, anemic-looking, bespectacled Englishman was a literate and angry rocker to be reckoned with" and that his second album made his initial entry "look tame in comparison."

This was the musical world into which Elvis Costello plunged. With an audience consumed with style, an industry dominated by accountants, and many critics draped in self-importance, the "bespectacled Englishman" set the tone for a career that would involve a series of creative challenges that would prove difficult to negotiate. Loving relationships may involve as much pain as joy, and Costello dared to explore the agony through a melodramatic lens that adhered to a specific attitude. For the music industry, punk was a fashion or marketing ploy. For Elvis Costello, punk was an artistic attitude that he would take to pop, rock, soul, and country music; consequently, *This Year's* is nothing less than a punk manifesto that outlines the terms of engagement.

Punk image overtakes punk art in a big way with Elvis Costello's third album, *Armed Forces* (released in February 1979). Nick Lowe's third production takes a back seat to Jake Riveria's publicity machine as the wit, wisdom, and sarcasm of the recordings fall prey to a public relations plan gone wrong. What initially seemed clever turns acrimonious and debilitating. Jokes about "it's time for a motorcycle accident" shake their humor in favor of their strategic utility. A rapid-fire, relentless, and rebellious performance style that was reinforced by a mean-spirited, aloof, and uncompromising method of media management now backfires. Of course, the principal victim of it all would be the music—supposedly the source of the artist's motivation.

Costello was never one to write with the clarity of a Hank Williams or a folk-era Bob Dylan, and his third album takes a serious songwriting turn as his lyrics grow rather dense. More and more images or lines are packed into several songs while others subscribe to his established style. Clearly, then, *Armed Forces* is a transitional piece. Nevertheless, there is not a positive song on this record. Costello's stance moves from that of the victim (*My Aim*) or combatant (*The Year's*) to that of participant-observer. The observations are sometimes direct, sometimes indirect, and always negative. Happy, cheery pop sounds provide springboards for dark rumblings and shadowy suggestions. That the project's working title was *Emotional Fascism* indicates the extent to which the "Night Rally" rhetoric pervades this record.

Interestingly, the album's thematic centerpiece is *not* a Costello composition. The lost idealism and corresponding pain over that loss are conveyed via Nick Lowe's "(What's So Funny 'Bout) Peace, Love and Understanding." The song laments the passing of heartfelt ideals about love, trust, and empathy as it questions the cynicism that permeates a dark, impervious, discordant society. Although Costello often states that Lowe's song was motivated by "sarcasm," his vocals betray that sentiment. From there, we witness a wave of negativity that includes six complaints about personal, relational, vocational, and societal matters; five examples of Costello's narrative impressionism; and two instances of wordplay. Throughout the work, the writing grows cloudy, with fewer and fewer coherent statements. Subsequently, a continuum of clarity emerges with songs such as Lowe's on one end and tunes such as the symbolic frolic presented in "Green Shirt" on the other.

The two relational complaints—"Big Boys" and "Party Girl"—drive home their respective points in a fairly uneven manner. "Big Boys" features a dramatic musical setting that relates how lovers struggle to get close to their romantic targets, only to fear failure once they achieve intimacy. The song—a classic role issue complaint—rotates perspectives (shifting pronouns) as it turns from testimonial to tutorial. "Party Girl" is a bit more direct in its account of romantic ambition and predestined failure. Although both parties want love—indeed, covet love—the pessimism is prohibitive. Loving relationships seem to be engulfed in a cynical cheapness that reaches its peak in the vocational and romantic diatribe "Busy Bodies." This track sharply delineates the vacuous qualities of sex-on-the-job as it posits the notion that such afternoon delights may offer little yield. Costello's clever lines indicate the prohibitive qualities of sleep-yourself-to-the-top career strategies. Job complaints continue with the delightful "Senior Service," in which the narrator—a junior employee—longs for his senior colleague's demise. He wants everything his target has: his desk, his paycheck, his seat at the pub, his lover, his company automobile. Hey, he wishes the guy would drop dead! "Service" is a wonderfully vicious pop tune. Finally, the negativity paints with broader strokes as the author takes another shot at English imperialism via "Oliver's Army." This anti-establishment ditty rails against international imperialism as a vocational alternative as Costello seems to massage the pervasive view: "Nothing happening this afternoon? Why not join the Royal Cause and kick a little butt?" Throughout these songs we experience Costello's wit, cynicism, apprehension, and disdain with varying degrees of clarity. Citizen Elvis's emergence is almost complete.

Costello's observations take a cryptic turn with his narrative impressionism. Remember, this songwriting strategy involves the use of recurring tag lines, choruses, or musical punctuation to create the illusion of narrative coherence (i.e., the "common denominators" that hold his "fractions" together). The song sounds like a story when, in actuality, the recurring traits provide a context for various forms of wordplay. The progenitor of the approach, Bob Dylan, used the technique to revolutionize songwriting, and Costello's invocation falls directly in that tradition, albeit in his own unique style. Armed Forces contains five examples of the strategy: "Accidents Will Happen," "Goon Squad," "Moods for Moderns," "Chemistry Class," and "Two Little Hitlers." Although the song features several strong lines, "Accidents" shifts perspectives (via pronoun use) and employs image fragments and clichés in an irregular fashion. The strategy holds for "Moods" and its impressionistic account of a dying relationship that uses a swinging instrumental track for lyrics that go nowhere (mostly repeating the song title over and over); "Goon" revisits "Night Rally" and "Oliver's Army" through its cloudy account of social conformity and its consequences; "Chemistry" is a sketchy—but overwhelmingly negative—take on relationships in which the metaphors are dangerously intriguing (Beware!); and "Two Little Hitlers" uses pop sounds to explore a serious battle of wills in which two fascist tyrants have at each other. The metaphors in "Hitlers" are difficult to unpack individually, but when taken together with the recurring tag lines, they paint a classic Costello relational portrait. Once more, the song appears to be a compelling example of the auteur's "fraction–common denominator–personal conclusion" songwriting strategy.

Armed Forces' final songwriting style involves Costello's unbridled wordplay. "Green Shirt" and "Sunday's Best" use pop song and circus sounds, respectively, to frame negative images and fragments about something. In "Green" we have people, colors, suspicions, investigations and their targets—everything but any semblance of coherence. Still, somebody is going to get in trouble—*that* is for sure. This attribute also holds for "Sunday's" as the hint of nationalism cloaks a series of fractured images that just happen to rhyme. The two tracks' sing-along style provides a rhythm for expressions that might as well be in another language.

Armed Forces takes the anger and resentment of *My Aim* and *This Year's* and obfuscates it through a growing impressionism that may be the result of Costello's role as a *participant*-observer—and a feisty participant at that. Although the instrumental track may suggest a merry walk in the pop park, Costello's lyrics and delivery raise the negative ante by subverting the record's communicative power. Again, we may not know what the narrator is saying, but we most assuredly know how he feels: His humiliation is over, his combativeness is waning, and his perspicuity is sharpening—an observational power focused through a punk critical lens. These songs feature *aggressive* responses to the events they chronicle. There were critics who shared this take as well. Janet Maslin's insights are compelling:

> He sings about violence with a vibrant romanticism, and about love with murder in his heart. He writes short, blunt compositions that don't pretend to be artful, though they are, and don't demand to be taken seriously, even though they're more stunning and substantial than anything rock has produced in a good long while. He doubles back on himself at every turn, and you're forced to take it or leave it. . . . No Elvis Costello love song is without its axe to grind or its hatchet to bury, but at least the emotion, however strangled, comes through. Costello never sounds exactly willing to give himself over to sentiment, yet he works hard to make himself more than marginally accessible: a gangster with a heart.

Maslin astutely notes the similarity of Costello's and Bob Dylan's writing, and the two artists' "faith that if this line doesn't get you, the next one

will"—a writing style that lends itself "to endless rediscovery" for their audiences. In other words, an artistic philosophy that encourages the artist
to write for himself opens the door to endless revelation, avoids audience-
driven platitudes, and elevates idiosyncrasy as an art form. While both
writers maintain their own versions of the melodramatically aggressive punk
attitude, Costello's work is a far more focused enterprise. You see, for Bob
Dylan, *Blood on the Tracks* was an album. For Elvis Costello, *Blood on the
Tracks* would become a career.

The auteur's fourth album advances his idiosyncratic attack on human
relations in no uncertain terms; however, the punk attitude that supports
this orientation now turns to an adaptation of an established musical genre
to achieve its ends. *Get Happy!!* (released March 1980) is widely noted as
Costello and The Attractions' "soul record" as the band turns to Memphis/
Motown traditions for inspiration. The subsequent album takes soul music
into a new realm: punk soul. Fast songs with lightning paces may borrow
licks from their musical soul brothers, but it is all presented with a distinctive twist. Such tendencies make *Get Happy!!* unique in the history of popular
music. Costello describes the project's sonic origins on his 1995 *Blood and
Chocolate* interview disc:

> It happened to be that I'd started listening to a lot of the music that I'd lis-
> tened to when I was about fifteen . . . a lot of the Motown and Atlantic and
> Stax stuff again. And digging out lots of singles and trying to find like odd
> singles that had funny sounds on, just for inspiration really. We literally made
> the decision over a couple of pints of beer. . . . Why don't we just try playing
> some of these songs slower and put sort of like more rhythmic accompany-
> ing parts rather than these tricky, nervy kind of accompaniments that we'd
> been used to doing? And it just fell into place.

Get Happy!! is a full-out assault on an idea and the musical genre that supports it. No musical genre invokes the torch tradition with the grace and
depth of soul music—not pop standards (often too cute) or country (often
too pedestrian). Although Costello talks around his subject more than anything else, his voice and aggressive instrumental interpretations of soul
music drive home his point. Occasionally, the lines that serve as song anchors are unable to hold the piece in place; the language drifts off, the
message floats away. On the other hand, *Happy!!* features several classic
Costello complaints. Although fragmented, uneven, and—again—held together by that strong line or two, these pivotal phrases lift the account from
impressionism or wordplay and deliver their respective points through
Costello's singing and The Attractions' musicality.

Happy!! contains five songwriting strategies. There are three love "warnings" that feature some sort of relational decision (the "him or me" rhetoric of "Love for Tender" [a variation of Cole Porter's "Love for Sale"?], "The

Imposter," and "Secondary Modern"), three societal complaints ("Opportunity," "Human Touch," and "King Horse"), three instances of narrative impressionism ("Clowntime Is Over," "5ive Gears in Reverse," and "Beaten to The Punch"), one example of free-form wordplay ("Temptation"), and eight relational complaints that stress different facets of that volatile condition. Without question, this fourth Nick Lowe production hammers home views on romantic issues through "Possession" and its sketchy views on love (it is for sale, ultimately boring, and bound to end in acrimony—a self-fulfilling prophecy in the making); the swinging instrumentals of "Men Called Uncle" and its take on the lusty ambitions of older men; the classic "New Amsterdam" with its subtle digs at the social conditions that make relationships so difficult; "High Fidelity" and its hypocritical views on infidelity; the youthful nostalgia of "Black & White World" and the narrator's longing for the days of yore when everything was so simple and imagination was everything; "B Movie" and its aggressive complaint in which the narrator's retaliation may be more than his partner wants (the hint of violence is strong); "Motel Matches" and its splendid metaphor for cheap love; and the resplendent relational assault "Riot Act." In many respects, Elvis Costello's first four albums reach a thematic climax via "Riot Act." Society's promises—such as one's wedding vows—have lost their meaning and the narrator's pain is evident in Costello's slow, emotive singing. Yet the character remains strong in the face of betrayal, responding much like Monty Python's "Black Knight" who lies on the ground—legless and armless, totally defeated with no possible means of fighting, yet his resolve remains unshaken. This is the spirit that dominates *Get Happy!!*

Once more, Costello's covers of "I Can't Stand Up (for Falling Down)" (by Banks and Jones) and "I Stand Accused" (by Colton and Smith) provide the thematic foundation for the album. What's interesting is why Costello's characters cannot seem to maintain any sense of relational equilibrium. Throughout *My Aim*, *This Year's*, and *Forces*, the budding auteur has complained about English society in one fashion or another. That complaint recurs in "Opportunity" with its "Night Rally"/"Goon Squad" imagery that attacks corporate society by way of another "Senior Service" pitch to preside over the enemy's demise. Just as in "Human Touch," the story features a brief taste of a relational complaint that is a product of society's disintegrating institutions. That is, a society built on lies, deceit, corporate imperialism, and the maintenance of an undeserving aristocracy eventually crumbles under the strain of its own deceptions. This results in a citizenry who cannot trust themselves, understand their roles, or engage in the types of relationships that hold a society together; hence, "King Horse" and its bar scene mating rituals and cartoon behaviors. Elvis Costello's work chronicles this situation. Deteriorating relationships are a symptom of a greater ill. While Citizen Elvis's punk venom seems to focus on the male-female battleground, it intuitively understands the *real* culprit and, as the work advances, the societal-relational connection unfolds with greater clarity.

As in *Armed Forces*, as the participant-observer's sociological opinions advance, he turns away from direct expressions to convey his views and deploys various combinations of narrative impressionism and wordplay. Emotions are offered through snippets and fragments that are open to interpretation. "Clowntime" features blackmail, the ubiquitous people-in-the-shadows imagery, and unsafe love through a "clowntime" metaphor that is either obvious or oblique (*you* decide). "Beaten to the Punch" suggests a relational complaint in which the narrator flails about, niggling on some target through a line here and an image there—all of which is held together through the song title's heavy repetition. "5ive Gears" falls somewhere between impressionism and wordplay through angst-ridden expressions that would lead to suicide except that the narrator is so down that he cannot muster the resources to breathe the exhaust fumes necessary to kill himself (now *that's* down). Last, "Temptation" uses a wonderful soul groove as a context for pure wordplay—nothing happens as the song jumps from image to image with an occasional pun or clever line. These songs are rich in feeling as Costello's vocals communicate the aggressive despair that underpins the cloudy, enigmatic expressions therein. In other words, Citizen Elvis turns not to *logic* to argue his case, but relies on *emotions* that capture his points and embellish their consequences.

Critics ignore this unfolding story line and focus on the interplay of private lyrics and public music. For instance, Tom Carson relates that the record is "so private that you don't listen to the songs so much as eavesdrop on them." The key is the author's singing: "Costello's vocals have an emotional accuracy and a sensuous immediacy that are nothing short of astounding. This is the singing of a man who's so depressed that his bitterness is the one thing that keeps him sane. And the melodies, his most romantically baroque yet, offer a wicked, brittle, ironic counterpoint." Jeff Nesin concentrates on the lyric-music interplay as well: "The songs turn on clever verbal hooks and twists mounted on a straightforward and accessible melodic structure, punctuated by subtle and often unexpected touches and cemented by fierce sincerity in the vocals." *Rolling Stone* reflects on the record in its "decade in review" piece that takes us from the sublime to the ridiculous by suggesting that *Get Happy!!* may "be the most listenable *mea culpa* in rock history." Somehow, someway, the magazine concludes that Costello's use of soul sounds was an apology for his remarks about Ray Charles and other Black musicians in the ridiculous 1979 Columbus, Ohio, bar fight. Remarkable.

From this vantage point, *Happy!!* constitutes a thematic sampler wrapped in punk interpretations of soul sounds. The victim from *My Aim*, the combatant from *This Year's*, and the participant observer from *Forces* all converge in the aggressive portrayals of *Get Happy!!* Costello's characters need the "Human Touch" that is so difficult in a world of social deception and relational intrigue. No longer able to muster the naiveté to "Blame It on Cain" or attempt to cut Robert Johnson–type deals with angels, no longer capable of chalking it all up to cheap club life or false promises, and unwilling to accept the accidental consequences of an intense battle of tyrannical wills, Costello's characters now refuse to sell their love, force their partners to make choices, and seem willing to confront the evil forces behind it all. Consequently, the album is essentially uneven; like guerrilla warfare, coming at you from all sides in unpredictable—and sometimes ineffective—ways. Yet when the attacks score, they are hurtful beyond their scope, resulting in disproportionate damage. No doubt just as the musical warlord intended.

With the fifth album of original material, *Trust* (released February 1981), we observe Costello's not-too-subtle use of irony as a literary device. There is nothing to "trust" in this Nick Lowe–produced diatribe on human relations. Here the victim-turned-combatant-turned-observer evolves into a "commentator" who uses the victim's (i.e., *My Aim*'s) penchant for genre dancing to communicate a burning distrust of manhood, women, relationships, club life, news media, and British society as a whole. The only thing this record "trusts" is that life—if given a chance—will destroy you. You may even get taken out by your own weapon. Elvis Costello and The Attractions' music never sounded better, and life's prospects never appeared bleaker.

This project features some absolutely sterling songwriting. There are moments when the practice of songwriting does not get any better than this—regardless of its thematic orientation. With a penetrating country tune, a Cole Porter list song, an empty theatrical number (Broadway at its best), a brutal pop song about domestic violence, and a constant litany of love-is-hell songs with biting, incisive lyrics, *Trust* is a dark masterpiece.

The album's 14 songs fall into four categories. There are four societal complaints ("Clubland," "New Lace Sleeves," "From a Whisper to a Scream," and "Fish 'n' Chip Paper"), two role complaints ("You'll Never Be a Man" and "Watch Your Step"), a piece of narrative impressionism ("Shot with His Own Gun"), and seven relational complaints featuring various blends of lament, assault, and warning. With regard to the latter, *Trust* features a Cole Porter–style list song ("Lover's Walk") that screams BEWARE of love's varied pitfalls and pratfalls; a cryptic expression of "love kills" imagery that relates how relationships ensnare more than they enlighten ("Pretty Words"); a rich example of The Attractions' rhythm-piano interplay that supports a compelling account of how relationships foster a Cold War or witch-hunt mentality ("Strict Time"); an inclusive complaint about society, club life, and the types of relationships they yield ("Luxembourg"); a quintessential country music rendition about the cheating game and how a guilty participant can overcome his anxieties by merely moving his partner's rings from one hand to the other ("Different Finger"); a vicious (and theatrical) account of domestic violence in which Costello sides with the victim as he chronicles how she foolishly ignores repeated warnings and gets pounded for it (the unsavory assault "White Knuckles"); and a simple, yet somewhat evasive, treatment of growing up and suffering the relational indignities that accompany adulthood ("Big Sister's Clothes"). Throughout these relational complaints, Costello hammers home the cheap, abusive, physically dangerous qualities of romance in a world void of any form of trust through clever lines, playful puns, and idiosyncratic metaphors.

Trust's societal complaints detail the conditions that render this relational hell. Leading the way is "New Lace Sleeves" and its layered, musically complicated account of the Big Lie. Here English society is attacked through scenes that portray how social graces and refined attire are symbols of British Imperialism and its corrupt dedication to its aristocracy (retribution is forthcoming, we are assured). With the Big Lie sucking the life out of society, citizens turn to cheap, vacuous venues to vent their frustrations and massage their anxieties. "Clubland" reports that these escape traps are not a refuge, but a sentence, while "From a Whisper" chronicles how temptation abounds among the drunken vacuity of bar talk. Nevertheless, the dancing dead from both songs are hungry for action and blind to the consequences. In many respects, this is the English parallel to Bruce Springsteen's portrayal of the lost American's reliance on chrome worship—one relies on dance clubs while the other cruises the strip in his hot rod. Both sets of characters are luckless and locked out by a social system beyond their comprehension. Finally, the media complaint lodged in "Fish 'n' Chip Paper" notes the intrusive, sensational nature of the news media and how today's thrills are tomorrow's waste.

But Costello's interpretation of British society extends beyond ruined relationships; it takes aim at individualism as well. The role complaints "You'll Never Be a Man" and "Watch Your Step" demonstrate how these conditions affect men. In "You'll Never," the narrator describes how men choose to fight instead of talk even though it just adds to their frustrations, questions whether men are strong or are just fakes, and ponders why men reject their emotional—or feminine—side. These men are thoughtless, violent brutes incapable of coping with their situations (interestingly, Costello claims the song was written for a *woman*). "Watch Your Step" reinforces that complaint with its portrayal of a world constantly threatened by "Goon Squad" antics in which men just may not be as tough as they appear. With these personality traits, Costello seems to say, little wonder men have such problems with relationships—regardless of their context. All of this leads to the highly theatrical-sounding but lyrically empty piece of impressionism that is "Shot with His Own Gun." The music builds and weaves while negative, but evasive, imagery paints a picture of a character who seems to suffer at his own hand. Costello's commentary is unequivocal. The victim's heartfelt but aggressive lamentations, the combatant's punk bravado, and the participant-observer's punk impressions give way to the punk commentator's insight. And that Citizen Elvis editorial is decidedly anti-English.

Critics, it appears, did not make this connection. Instead, they focus on the technical aspects of the songwriting, the musical flexibility of the songs, or his apparent shift in tone. Ken Tucker maintains *Trust* is Costello's "biggest tease"; it "indicates that the artist is now feeling constrained by the love-'em-and-lacerate-'em image" to the point of changing his writing style. *Newsweek*'s Jim Miller discusses Costello's past as a preface to a consideration of his present: "By disciplining this quick wit and applying it to his work, Elvis Costello has fashioned his own emblematic stance—an acid moodiness conveyed through music of blunt economy and pleasing nuance . . . [on *Trust*]. But beneath the caustic wordplay and customary spite, he betrays some vulnerability. For the first time, [he] sounds more hurt than angry." Robert Hilburn uses the same strategy as he observes that Costello traditionally "speaks in the feverish language of someone engaged in emotional combat, not someone simply reflecting on it"; however, *Trust* "is softer and more consoling." Tucker, Miller, and Hilburn have a point: Both the writing style and its content are changing—a creative phase is coming to a close.

Costello's work has evolved from the raw, intense revelations that characterized *My Aim* into a more refined, intense commentary on the conditions around him. Instead of the violent outbursts of *This Year*'s man-in-the-ring, we receive the seasoned warnings of the wise but incensed commentator. The enigmatic impressions of *Armed Forces*' participant-observer have been replaced by the systematic editorials of one capable of grasping the big picture—and sharing it as well. Costello does more than complain that "You'll Never Be a Man"; he explains why. He does more than describe the frivolity of pretty "New Lace Sleeves"; he considers what they symbolize. His articulation of the assorted self-fulfilling prophecies that dominate *Trust* communicates his understanding of the social conditions that foster those outcomes. *Trust* is dark and ominous; moreover, it is the resolution to a five-album exploration of English urban life. Unlike Pete Townshend's brilliant *Quadrophenia* and its exposition of fashionable violence in British youth culture, Costello's work dares to explore the *cause* of his sociological calamity (as does Townshend's *White City*). As Costello's work progressed and Citizen Elvis's pen matured, his view expanded. Little wonder he eventually moved to Ireland.

After his recuperation from his highly publicized motorcycle accident, Bob Dylan reentered the musical world by way of a country album recorded in Nashville, Tennessee. In an era of psychedelic concept albums and art rock pretensions, Dylan selected their musical opposite as the vehicle for his much-anticipated return. It was a new beginning for the accomplished auteur, a transition from one artistic orientation to another. With his shift in creative mission came a corresponding change in musical style. Nashville is many different things for many different people, but for Bob Dylan—and Elvis Costello—it provided a creative respite, an opportunity for personal and artistic revitalization.

Elvis Costello's renewal begins with closure as his career's "the making of Citizen Elvis" phase ends in Music City with an album of covers, *Almost Blue*. An era of victimage, confrontation, idiosyncratic observation, and systematic commentary concludes with a series of "reflections" offered through the words of Gram Parsons, Don Gibson, Charlie Rich, Merle Haggard, Hank Williams, and other country music veterans. In so doing, the auteur disassociates *his* image from *his* reflections by relying on established songs—compositions that capture the tenor and the tone of a classic Citizen Elvis editorial. The queen may *seem* to be nowhere in sight, but the emotions that flow from Her Majesty's United Kingdom weave in and out of every one of these songs.

Released in November 1981, *Almost Blue* was produced by the legendary Billy Sherrill. Sherrill—credited with introducing Phil Spector's "wall of sound" production style to Nashville—produced an impressive number of successful records in the '60s and '70s with such artists as George Jones, Tammy Wynette, Charlie Rich, Johnny Paycheck, Barbara Mandrell, and young Tanya Tucker. Here the "punk" truly met the "godfather" as the brash Citizen Elvis encountered the complacent, comfortable musical aristocrat. How this worked is anyone's guess, especially when you consider that the two-week whirlwind production process was filmed for a *South Bank Show* television documentary. Costello described his motivation to Lisa Traxler: "I think that was a very punk thing to do, to go to Nashville and make a record with Billy Sherrill." Later, he adds: "Even Billy Sherrill was completely confused as to why we wanted to cover all these very old, well-worn songs. Most of the songs had been recorded at least two or three times, sometimes by the same artist. So he was rather confused."

The original work contains 12 tracks, opening with a revved-up version of Hank Williams's "Why Don't You Love Me (Like You Used to Do)?," moves to Don Gibson's "Sweet Dreams" and Johnny Mullins's "Success," and continues with songs by Gram Parsons/Chris Ethridge ("I'm Your Toy"), Merle Haggard ("Tonight the Bottle Let Me Down"), George Jones/Virginia Franks ("Brown to Blue"), Jerry Chestnut ("Good Year for the Roses"), Charlie Rich ("Sittin' and Thinkin'"), Lawton Williams/George Jones ("Color of the Blues"), producer Sherrill ("Too Far Gone"), Lou Willie Turner ("Honey Hush"), and Gram Parsons/Pam Rifkin ("How Much I Lied"). The Rykodisc reissue features several live songs, such as Johnny Cash's "Cry, Cry, Cry," Lee Ross/Bob Wills's "My Shoes Keep Walking Back to You," and a song Leon Payne must have written with Costello in mind, the incredibly dark "Psycho." Throughout, Costello trades English clubs for Nashville honky-tonks, diabolical British women for their conniving Southern counterparts, and Royal despair for Delta despondence. These songs are reflections on the psychological consequences of human relations that feature victims, confrontations, jaded observations, and resigned commentaries. They are, then, extensions of Elvis Costello's lifework.

How critics missed this is beyond me. Rare is any attempt at any form of thematic interpretation; instead, critics focus on Costello's singing, The Attractions' playing, or simply the fact that they all showed up in Music City. Robert Hilburn opens his *Los Angeles Times* review: "Elvis Costello's new country album . . . is a major disappointment." For Hilburn, "Costello has allowed his affection for country music to blur his artistic judgment"; his performance "lacks the purity and range to compete effectively with the original versions of these mainstream country tunes." After saying he is not surprised that Costello would attempt a country record, the *Washington Post*'s Geoffrey Himes writes: "It is surprising that Costello would make such a middle-of-the-road country album. . . . 'Almost Blue' is not revealing the way Bob Dylan's 'Nashville Skyline' was, but is indulgent the way Dylan's 'Self-Portrait' was." *Creem*'s Craig Zeller probably got his name etched in Costello's little black book with these remarks: "Time after time he comes off like some hack lounge singer coming to fingertip grips with heartbreak." Last, *Rolling Stone*'s Martha Hume assumes a more reasonable stance. She argues that "a truly great country singer" not only controls his or her voice, but also gives life to the song's characters in a fashion that projects "some idea of the performer's personality." Hume feels Costello achieves that standard on several of *Blue*'s tracks, and concludes: "I'm sure that Costello isn't going to abandon rock & roll for the Grand Ole Opry, but his performance on *Almost Blue* is no joke, and the Attractions do a decent job as a country band. There is, by the way, a special bonus: *Almost Blue* is the first Elvis Costello album on which the listener can understand all the words."

These responses seem to indicate most critics' inability to see the forest for the trees (Hume is, of course, the exception). That Costello selected "mainstream" songs over idiosyncratic preferences yields not a "middle-of-the-road" production but a systematic statement. These widely known songs contain sentiments that are clearly consistent with Citizen Elvis's expositions. Although the Royal Family is absent in these numbers, the *consequences* of the social system that fosters such an aristocracy are present. The characters in these songs question their self-worth, wonder about fundamental life roles, seek frivolous escapes, and wallow in their conditions. In every respect, they constitute a series of "reflections" on the emotional states that have dominated Costello's work, as he told *Creem*: "The most confessional record is *Almost Blue*, ironically enough, which I didn't write any of. That's perhaps the most unhappy record I ever made—I was the most unhappy when I made that record, which is why it was called *Almost Blue*. . . . I got myself in that melancholic mood, a self-fulfilling prophecy, I suppose. I sing these songs, therefore I am."

With these "confessional" reflections, "the making of Citizen Elvis" phase concludes. From this point forward, Elvis Costello will apply his Citizen Elvis critical lens to a variety of life situations through a host of musical genres. Whether he employs the sounds of chamber music, pop standards, rock and roll, or roots music, the auteur brings a punk attitude to his subject matter. The aggressive, irreverent worldview that renders Citizen Elvis now evolves into a musical acrobat willing to accept creative challenges that require him to operate without a net—risking artistic standing, industry support, and audience loyalty. I guess all this proves a simple, yet compelling, point: You can take the auteur out of the punk genre, but you cannot take the punk out of the auteur.

THE PUNK TUNESMITH

The second stage of Elvis Costello's lifework features a "punk tunesmith" who applies his unique approach to songwriting within the ever-changing world of popular music. The raw, driving sounds that typified most of Nick Lowe's productions now yield to layered, textured works that marry Citizen Elvis and George Martin. That is, the playful sophistication of Costello's writing style weds the inventive sophistication of Martin's production approach (as implemented by Martin's colleague Geoff Emerick, and later by popmeisters Clive Langer and Alan Winstanley). Rest assured, Citizen Elvis remains active; however, his editorials takes a serious three-album turn. *Imperial Bedroom*, *Punch the Clock*, and *Goodbye Cruel World* are marked departures from the lifework's initial phase.

Imperial Bedroom (released in July 1982) is, in a word, startling. With *Imperial Bedroom*, Citizen Elvis shelves his quest for sociological accountability in favor of a deeply introspective examination of "the self" and "relationships." Instead of denouncing aristocratic society, attacking romantic partners, or assaulting specific situations, *Bedroom* probes the self, accepts personal responsibility for relational problems, pleads for help (that's right, *pleads*), and offers advice to those who aspire to love. True to form, the introspection is aggressive. Costello's characters unveil a compelling sense of guilt for their substance abuse problems, their tyrannical attitudes, their acid tongues, their philandering ways, and their lost loves. Through it all is a sense of celebrity angst that hangs just off center stage, lurking in the shadows. These characters are embattled, self-destructive, and resigned to their fates as they turn to relationships as their last avenue of hope. Citizen Elvis needs therapy.

Just as *Armed Forces* uses impressionistic tactics to frame Citizen Elvis's observations on societal and relational matters, *Imperial Bedroom* deploys the strategy as a means of introspective self-examination. Characters are wrestling with the bottle and other self-destructive tendencies as they probe their situations through cryptic complaints. The melodrama is rich in these penetrating glimpses into the characters' rapidly deteriorating situations. The thrill is gone.

A major shift occurs in the relational complaints as well. Narrators now accept a measure of responsibility for their predicaments. Fierce attack yields to exhausted acknowledgment as characters are tired of sleeping with clinched fists, resorting to cheap escapes, and succumbing to domestic violence. They are, in fact, *so* tired that they plead with their partners to have patience, to believe in them, and not to joke around about their love. These characters are on the brink, and their plea for help is sincere and chock-full of vulnerability. That they see hope in their relationships demonstrates the extent of this change in characterization.

This dramatic thematic turn features 15 songs that vary in their instrumental-production complexity. Most of the tracks involve the layered sounds featured on *Trust* except for one major change: They use signature sounds. Throughout *Bedroom* one hears snippets of "Penny Lane," "All You Need Is Love," "A Day in the Life," and other famed Beatles compositions. Sometimes Emerick's use of these signature sounds is discreet; other times they bowl you over (e.g., ". . . And in Every Home" and "Pidgin English"). Costello reports in the reissued album's liner notes: "To some extent *Imperial Bedroom* was the record on which The Attractions and I granted ourselves the sort of scope that we imagined The Beatles had enjoyed in the mid-'60s. We had engaged the engineering skills of the sonic, and somewhat unsung, genius behind many of those productions." Consequently, they booked the studio for "an unprecedented 12 weeks" and pursued their Beatles Moment. Beatles Moment or not, the lyrical-instrumental counterpoint recurs throughout the piece and often camouflages the songs' introspection.

Thematically, *Bedroom* contains four narrative strategies. The record presents a relational warning ("You Little Fool"), two relational pleas ("Human Hands" and "Kid About It"), five instances of narrative impressionism ("Beyond Belief," "Man Out of Time," "The Loved Ones," "Little Savage," and "Pidgin English"), and seven relational complaints: "Tears Before Bedtime," "Shabby Doll," "Long Honeymoon," "Almost Blue," ". . . And in Every Home," "Boy with a Problem" (written with Chris Difford), and "Town Cryer." The relational fun begins with the Brian Wilson–*Pet Sounds* (read: cluttered) production "Tears Before Bedtime," in which Costello issues a classic love complaint with a new twist: As the character laments his situation through clever lines and phrases, he accepts responsibility for his role in the situation. She is suspicious while he is vicious. When you sleep with your fists clinched, well, you have problems. The trend continues with "Shabby Doll" and its evasive account of how the old tricks just fail to work anymore. The character's pretenses are exposed, his old remedies are useless, the jig is up (dare I say the emperor has no clothes?). In "Honeymoon" Costello explores the woman's feelings about her husband's possible infidelity; "Almost Blue" uses lounge music sounds (you can practically smell the smoke) to present a mournfully rich portrayal of love lost; "And in" offers a cloudy view of that unfortunate relational interlude that accompanies one partner's incarceration; "Boy with a Problem" features a central character who accepts full responsibility for the havoc his drinking has wreaked on his relationship—his contrition is acute; and "Town Cryer" sums up the situation completely. This highly theatrical track revisits that old self-fulfilling prophecy that there is no escaping the personal hell the narrator is destined to endure. No matter who the partner, this character is predestined to cry. He is more than pitiful.

Such sentiments fuel the relational warning, "You Little Fool," in which daddy's little girl is about to venture away from home and into the inferno of relationships. "Big Sister's Clothes" fit this character nicely, thank you. Furthermore, her parents' failure to prepare her makes her ripe for the abuse that is sure to follow. While there seems to be little optimism for our "Little Fool," the relational pleas communicate a striking new theme in the Costello songbook: hope. The theatrical "Human Hands" charts how the characters from "Clubland" have grown older and now need each other. Most of the song involves the narrator's efforts to reassure his mate of his dedication—he may say the wrong things, but he loves her dearly. Bitterness remains, however; his dedication is complete (he says). Age has brought commitment and, as "Kid About It" indicates, nostalgia. Here Costello uses one of his signature homonymic puns to plead with his partner to not joke around about their love, all the while pondering his lost youth (a reiteration of "Black & White World" and its days-of-yore sentimentality). For these characters, youthful dreams have passed unfulfilled, and they now need each other—even though they remain distrustful.

Why all of this relational anxiety? What happened to the confrontational bravado?

Costello answers those queries by way of his impressionistic accounts of "men in trouble." "Pidgin English" is a cryptic relational plea for adherence to love's basic principles (as communicated through a Ten Commandments analogy), while the remaining songs embellish heavy personal complaints. Costello's punning wordplay and opaque metaphors delineate the drunk and disorderly natures of characters on the edge of ruin. One character is so far gone he is "Beyond Belief" as he battles drink, Wonderland fantasies, celebrity images, and the ubiquitous idyllic woman. But nothing ever happens, and we are left to contemplate these uneven images. "Man Out of Time" emerges from a wall of sound that effectively communicates the intense inner struggle portrayed by the song's central character (whose life is also a drunken mess), while "The Loved Ones" uses snappy rhymes and dark images to present a character presiding over his own demise. When he leaves, he will be remembered—and instantly replaced (the stench of celebrity angst is strong). Finally, "Little Savage" advances this impressionistic self-loathing with a striking twist: She transforms him (and he *needs* it) and inspires him to be more than the spiteful punk that he is. In other words, she offers *hope*.

Imperial Bedroom is a genuine surprise among Citizen Elvis's full-bore attacks on his perceived enemies. On this record, the enemy is clearly within. Instead of lashing out at the women—including Her Majesty—or the despised bully boys who have populated his editorials to date, the auteur aggressively attacks his narrators (to suggest that all of this is autobiographical represents an inferential leap that I am unwilling to take). They are their own worst enemies. What a thematic innovation! Punk introspection.

The critics were impressed as well. In its four-and-a-half-star rating (out of a possible five), *Rolling Stone* describes the thematic shift evident in the album: "Costello has become an expert storyteller; he now knows that the accusing finger can often be pointed in both directions, and this has given him a newfound generosity of viewpoint." Responding to Columbia's "Masterpiece?" ad campaign, *Creem* takes issue with that assertion (although Walls enjoyed the album) and concludes with a state-of-the-artist statement that is pretty darned prescient:

> It's fascinating to listen to, uh, Elvis (I predict a name change within the next five years, probably back to Declan as various restricting aspects of the original EC image continue to be discarded) as he expands the emotional content of his music, slowly, surely, inevitably. Still, I hold back on the ultimate praise, not too perversely I feel, thinking "masterpiece?", no, this is too open-ended, too still-alive to be embalmed by such a pickling word—the opposing forces of EC's new-found compassion and his old hatred haven't really reached any kind of synthesis yet. But they will. Then . . . ?

The *Washington Post* also notes the thematic change: "For the first time, Costello's lyrics do not attack romance as a broad form of 'emotional fascism,' but examine his own specific relationships, prompting surprising admissions from this master of misanthropy." Finally, the *Atlantic Monthly* offers a thoughtful, state-of-the-artist essay that opens with autobiographical claims: "Autobiographical in ways its lyrics do not hide, the record portrays domestic life as an unstable balance of power in which conflict both threatens love and restores it." Winner's praise is unrestrained: "The album takes the enormous promise of his earlier songwriting and develops it in ingenious new dimensions. . . . The posture of angry young man he had proudly cultivated has evolved into a stance more sympathetic to human failings. When he focuses on marriage on the rocks, he no longer jests at scars, but tries to communicate the pain." Still, Winner rejects all this as "the new Cole Porter" talk because Costello's "double-dealing, raw sexuality" is nothing like Porter's "urbane manners, refined sentiments, and polite sociability."

Despite claims from the *New York Times* and others, Costello is no Porter, Gershwin, Kern, or Hart, even though he changed his songwriting style on

Imperial Bedroom. While the language is void of "urbane, refined, or polite" sentiments, the stories and impressions offered here indicate an expanded emotional scope. Again, charges of autobiography seem quite risky because writers are certainly allowed to fondle emotions beyond their direct experience; on the other hand, the detail and depth of Costello's writing is so intimate that one wonders. As always, the true test is that of time—only time will reveal whether *Imperial Bedroom* was a chapter from an unfolding story or an excerpt from an unfocused diary.

With *Punch the Clock* Costello's oeuvre moves from George Martin's "Penny Lane" to overwrought interpretations of Memphis horns through a Motown commercial mentality. Any trace of the Tin Pan Alley sentimentality that permeates *Imperial Bedroom* vanishes. Clive Langer and Alan Winstanley's wall of sound productions erect huge, foreboding, opaque edifices that are impenetrable—preventing any view of what is going on inside the songs. The key term here is "inaccessible." Only Citizen Elvis's triumphant return to sociological criticism saves this record from a narrative/ songwriting point of view.

Some of the musical world's finest smoke and mirrors are deployed here in an attempt to make something public out of private idiosyncrasy. Things occasionally get strange when such elaborate, layered, dense pop music is used to frame such cryptic utterances. Tightly sequenced sounds support a word machine that is often stuck on Shuffle. Any sense of the heartfelt observations from *Bedroom* go flying right out the imperial window. In many ways, these songs make the crazed mania of *Get Happy!!* seem introspective. The bright light that shines through this emptiness involves the return of Citizen Elvis's editorials—the artful "Shipbuilding," the intriguing "Invisible Man," the angry "Pills and Soap," and the dysfunctional "The World and His Wife." In quintessential Citizen Elvis rhetoric, these songs scream, "Look what you're doing to us!" These flashes from the past give pause and inspire curiosity about the album's remaining adventures.

Punch the Clock (released August 1983) features the TKO Horns and backing vocals by Afrodiziak. The album's 13 songs involve the aforementioned four societal complaints, a relational complaint ("Charm School"), a personal complaint ("Mouth Almighty"), an example of enigmatic wordplay ("Let Them All Talk"), and six installments of narrative impressionism: "Everyday I Write the Book," "The Greatest Thing," "The Element Within Her," "Love Went Mad," "TKO (Boxing Day)," and "King of Thieves." Although the relational complaint and personal complaint take us back to *This Year's* and *Bedroom*, respectively, seven of these tracks manage to take us nowhere. From the opening salvo, "Let Them All Talk," we are bowled over by a sonic tidal wave that supports cryptic wordplay. Suggestions about sex, aging, and radio programming fly by on a musical magic carpet that effectively uses volume to kill the senses. Things calm down with the pop veneer of "Everyday," in which book puns are used to frame a series of remarks about a love interest—but nothing happens, it just spins around. Varied comments about male-female relations (marriage? infidelity? baking?) whirl through overlapping voices and sounds on "The Greatest Thing," in which everything gets lost in the noise. More fractured relational impressions appear via "The Element Within Her" and its la la la Moon and June songwriting—a song that solidifies the view "nothing ventured, nothing lost." By the time "Love Went Mad" appears, the wall of sound bombast has induced aural exhaustion (still more impressions about bad relationships, manhood, and old-time family music making). After a brief interlude for the beautiful "Shipbuilding," the pain returns through "TKO," in which the production feeds on itself with asides for silly word games and repetitive lines that connote empty impressions of embattled relationships (those boxing metaphors run deep). Finally, "King of Thieves" drives the impressionistic nail in the songwriting coffin through metaphors and puns that are inaccessible or—worse—invite over-reading.

Still, just as you prepare to join the state of Costello's songwriting by jumping off the Mississippi River bridge, along comes Citizen Elvis. The first sign of a reprieve appears via "Shipbuilding" and its elegant portrayal of war's double-edged sword (it creates jobs and takes lives). Chet Baker's horn work certainly stands in stark contrast to the TKO bombast. With "The Invisible Man" Citizen Elvis contemplates a character wasting away in the suburbs. The song uses hints from "Night Rally," "New Lace Sleeves," and "Radio, Radio" to suggest that while the "Invisible Man" rots in front of movies, somebody is up to something sinister; the radio programmers may have switched to film as their weapon of choice. "The World" offers a splendid sampling of pedophiles, incest, infidelity, abandonment, and the glue that holds this lovely mess together: patriotism. It is a classic editorial in which the narrator points to one of modern society's more unsavory yields: the dysfunctional family. But the dysfunction does not end there. "Pills and Soap" attacks the news media for its sensational coverage and the hypocritical aristocracy that is behind it all, and closes with a warning: Your patriotism could be the death of you, and then *you* will be in the news (Costello released this controversial song as "The Imposter," dodging BBC inquiries regarding its political slant by assuring them it was about animal abuse, a partial truth). These songs—when combined with "Charm School" (an attack on fake, superficial club dates) and "Mouth Almighty" (a loud statement about a character who cannot keep his mouth shut and alienates his lovers)—lift *Punch the Clock* from the pop doldrums of Costello's enigmatic impressionism and Langer/Winstanley's overproduction.

Such an uneven recording inspired diverse responses from music critics. Jock Baird complains: "Elvis has turned his highly charged confessional into a damn Stax/Volt revue, complete with fat horn section and two black female singers. . . . We're talking *airplay* here, folks." Christopher Connelly

writes that the "old themes are back: fighting, beauty and the greed of na-
tions," and concludes that the project is a "satisfying, if unstartling, opus."
Laura Fissinger reports: "*Punch the Clock* is a (fairly) simple case of reach
exceeding grasp. . . . Elvis seems a little bored with certain emotional cul
de sacs, a little fed up with his own word games." Richard Cromelin reasons: "The man who brilliantly dissected life in terms of 'Armed Forces'
appears to have declared neutrality. It doesn't suit him, and the sooner he
rejoins the fray the better." Last, the *New York Times* offers praise for a work
that uses old sounds that are "familiar" and recasts them by "compacting
and juxtaposing these allusions with a dazzling sleight of hand." After describing Costello's angry youth and his recent move toward "warmth" and
"sincerity," Stephen Holden quotes Costello: "It's easy to bluster. . . . It's not
so easy to do something quietly, from the heart."

It is hard to imagine that Costello thinks *Punch* is "quiet" or "from the
heart." Citizen Elvis's editorials are certainly evocative, but the idiosyncratic
impressionism and overwhelming productions are so loud, so insistent, so
obtuse that they stonewall the listener—forcing us to respect the musical
moat that restricts entry into Costello's musings. *Punch* takes the wall of
sound descriptor from the realm of metaphor and uses it to barricade
Costello's words. The accessibility that characterized much of *Imperial Bedroom* has been replaced by its photo negative. All of which raises questions
about where the auteur would turn next.

The second installment of Langer/Winstanley's work with Elvis Costello
represents a marked departure from the initial edition. The wall of sound
bombast dissipates, the enigmatic wordplay recedes, and a conventional pop
record emerges. Although music critics argued that *Goodbye Cruel World* was
less accessible than its predecessor, my analysis differs. *Goodbye*'s songs
achieve an improved sonic balance, allowing the vocals and instruments to
work *with* one another as opposed to *against* each other. Not only does this
result in a more palatable listening experience, but it allows Costello's, The
Attractions', and Langer/Winstanley's craftsmanship to shine through.

The two albums' opening cuts set the standard for comparison. *Punch*
attacks you with "Let Them All Talk" and its musical barrage of enigmatic
wordplay. *Goodbye* greets you with a full-fledged pop song, "The Only Flame
in Town" (sung with Daryl Hall—a richly symbolic act in and of itself).
Whereas "Flame" may sacrifice depth for pop accessibility, it does so with
the charm and grace of a Brill Building standard. To the extent that "Let
Them" uses a wall of noise strategy to overwhelm the listener, "Flame" uses
direct images and tightly controlled instrumentals to underwhelm you. We
have, then, an aesthetic choice. Listen, and make *your* decision.

Both records feature uneven songwriting. On *Goodbye*, fewer songs drift
into obscurity as Costello uses his trademark imagery and puns in a more
organized fashion. That writing is also uneventful. The occasional caustic

line may bite or conjure an image from days gone by, but when compared to the rest of the lifework, the songs come off tired and stale. These songs are exactly what they seem: standard, accessible pop tunes.

The album's 13 tracks fall into four categories. We have five relational complaints ("The Only Flame in Town," "Home Truth," "Inch by Inch," "The Comedians," and "Sour Milk-Cow Blues"), four life or moral complaints ("Room with No Number," "I Wanna Be Loved" [by Farnell Jenkins], "The Deportees Club," and the Citizen Elvis editorial "Peace in Our Time"), three examples of narrative impressionism ("Love Field," "Joe Porterhouse," and "The Great Unknown"), and one instance of wordplay, "Worthless Thing." "Worthless" and "Great Unknown" demonstrate that fine line between free-form wordplay and its more structured counterpart. Both songs present a series of vignettes tied together by a recurring tag line or a vague story structure. The difference is a matter of degree. In "Worthless," we witness what appears to be a relational complaint: two verses about Memphis, Tennessee, and Elvis Presley (that seem to involve statements against idolatry), and a final verse about a female television personality (I think). They all are deemed to be of limited value by the chorus. In "Great Unknown," a wedding is turned into a wake due to the groom's unfortunate passing. The song opens with a coherent vignette about a mob murder (our groom), followed by muddy descriptions of the bride and unattributed social banter held together by a chorus that reinforces the confusion. All of these characters are sailing into uncharted waters, we are told. "Great Unknown" is slightly more coherent than "Worthless," but this may well involve a distinction without a difference. In contrast, "Joe Porterhouse" is held together by the narrator's insistence that the characters withhold their emotions throughout the various lines that seem to lament Joe's absence (is he dead? asleep? on tour?). Whatever is going on here, it goes beyond wordplay in that there is clearly a logic holding the thing together—even though that logic evades me. Finally, we have the state-of-the-art of the narrative impressionism strategy in "Love Fields." Steady, repetitive refrains frame a series of impressions about sexual encounters in various locations. Costello's soft, tender vocal heightens the song's romance, but nothing ever happens as impression after impression rolls by. None of these songs features the wry wit or cryptic cynicism that we associate with Elvis Costello's writing; they appear to be songs without much purpose.

The relational complaints follow tried-and-true formulas. "The Only Flame" contains little mystery—the narrator uses incendiary metaphors to communicate that he has options; "Home Truth" is a straightforward tale about a couple facing the end—the lies are out of control, domestic life is stifling, everything is so far gone that the narrator has no idea how to rebuild the relationship; "Inch by Inch" is a cloudy account of a conflict in which the partners seem to enjoy toying with one another to deleterious effect; "The Comedians" uses clever lines and inviting metaphors to convey a basic love complaint (his heart hurts, he's up all night, and there's deceit in the air); and the rocking "Sour Milk-Cow Blues" deploys classic Costello lines to relate how the narrator is way down on his partner's list of pleasures, how she has lost her magic, and how both of them are trapped in relational hell. Unlike *Goodbye*'s impressionism, these relational tales feature coherent examples of Costello's patented puns, ironic symbolism, and aggressive cynicism.

Goodbye Cruel World offers a thematic shift by way of the four life (or moral) complaints. These are not the societal editorials that usually flow from Citizen Elvis's pen; rather, they select specific situations and explore them with an eye toward their larger implications. "Room with No Number" returns to "Busy Bodies" with its clever account of the varied activities at the local no-tell motel (everybody sneaks around, everybody is discreet, everybody is woefully unhappy); the cover "I Wanna Be Loved" embraces that sentiment as the lonely narrator seeks romantic bliss; and "The Deportees Club" offers the mixed emotions of a narrator who loves his liquor and hates bar life. These songs do not attack individuals or specific situations; rather, they merely lament the conditions they portray. "Peace in Our Time" heralds the return of Citizen Elvis with its sarcastic treatment of Neville Chamberlain's bonehead agreement with the Nazis, the activities of the ever-present "Goon Squad," and Ronald Reagan's invasion of Grenada. Citizen Elvis usually focuses his editorials, but this statement—like the other life or moral complaints—is more general as it suggests that regardless of where you turn, the ruse continues. (Perhaps by casting a wider net, Citizen Elvis dilutes his catch.)

Critical responses were generally mixed, in that writers seemed to have difficulty castigating the artist who had heretofore been deemed the "critics' darling." Don Shewey reports that *Goodbye* is "as murky an album, musically and lyrically, as Costello has ever made." Fred Schruers concurs: "Though this LP is bristly with subtle invention, he's not making major changes in style. There's no reason the magpie, working this close to the top of his form, has to turn into a chameleon." Mitchell Cohen argues that *Goodbye* offers "some exemplary demonstrations of his passionate dedication to craft (or crafty dedication to passion, either will do)," however: "Like *Punch the Clock*, *Goodbye Cruel World* is a jumble, lacking the focus of his best works . . . and much of it goes kablooey. My advice is to disregard the sideshow and concentrate on what's going on in the center ring." The *Los Angeles Times* offers two opinions that basically agree. Kristine McKenna opines: "The Picasso of Pop, Costello spews music forth at an alarming rate, and though there's been much brilliance in his torrential outpouring, his body of work could use a trim and a haircut." Robert Hilburn agrees when he says, "I still believe that his aim is true," as he urges Costello to take a vacation.

These remarks indicate that Costello's work has grown tired for these writers. Whether the creative fatigue was the result of his mad rush into the music industry, the intensity of his artistic orientation, the conflicts associated with celebrity life and its inherent abuses, the absence of Nick Lowe's leadership, or some combination of these and other issues, Costello's tenure as a punk tunesmith now seemed to be threatening his professional future. Cohen's advice seems worth considering: "disregard the side show and concentrate on what's going on in the center ring." The punk tunesmith era may have sacrificed the "center ring" for the various sideshows teasing the auteur. Or maybe the center ring was empty, and the sideshows were all Costello had. After *Almost Blue*, the fire abated. To my ears, even *Imperial Bedroom* seems tired. Its introspection was so uncharacteristic of this artist that it raised questions about his creative direction. While *Almost Blue's* reflections achieved closure for Citizen Elvis's bold initiation into identity issues, relational conflicts, vacuous club life, and disingenuous social structures, *Bedroom* presented a listless punk wallowing in the aftermath of his aggressive, irreverent assault on the perceived evil before him. I mean, *punk* introspection? From there, matters worsen as the auteur turned to pop-meisters Langer and Winstanley to frame these diluted takes on those same subjects. There were flashes, but no fires—and Elvis Costello plays with *fire*. I disagree with Schruers; a chameleon merely changes colors, not hearts or souls. The creature remains the same, regardless of color. And this musical chameleon needed a rest, maybe a new producer, and an industry that understands that changing musical genres—like shifting colors—does not indicate a loss of creative heart or artistic soul. Oh, well, as we are about to discover, two out of three ain't bad.

THE PUNK COMPOSER

When I was a kid, my dad—the consummate meat eater—used to say that a little T-bone is much more nourishing than a lot of rump. I never thought that I would use this wisdom in any way. But he was, of course, right on. John Henry "T-Bone" Burnett grew up in musically diverse Fort Worth, Texas. Throughout his career as a performer, songwriter, and producer, that sense of diversity has remained ever present. Prior to winning the Grammy Award for the American roots music classic, the *O Brother, Where Art Thou?* sound track, Burnett worked with such varied artists as Gene Clark, Delbert McClinton, Roy Orbison, Counting Crows, The Wallflowers, and Gillian Welch. One of his many successful production credits involves the work of Christian pop singer Leslie Phillips (she later changed to her nickname, "Sam"). Burnett not only was able to shape beautiful sounds for a talented artist, he also was able to share his born-again Christian values through his work. Burnett's moment of conversion is a personal matter, yet when he toured with Bob Dylan's Rolling Thunder Revue in the mid-'70s, the word is that everyone involved in that experience either underwent a religious revelation or entered some form of infirmary. Burnett supposedly played a significant role in Dylan's conversion to Christianity several years later. As we all know, the born-again Christian's greatest achievement involves facilitating another person's spiritual salvation—what is known as "saving" someone. For that reason, T-Bone Burnett must be quite proud of *King of America*.

T-Bone Burnett did not convert Elvis Costello to Christianity, but he surely played a major role in saving him. Costello's tenure as a punk tunesmith left him creatively listless and artistically lost. The Elvis Costello thing had, indeed, worn thin. The image and its rage, the domestic difficulties that accompany celebrity, the ever-present commercial pressures, and more placed quite a weight on Costello's shoulders. In response, he changed his name to Declan MacManus, ceased his work with The Attractions, conducted an acoustic world tour with Burnett under the name The Coward Brothers, and initiated a musical renaissance. During it all, he produced an album for The Pogues and became romantically involved with Cait O'Riordan. The *King of America* liner notes detail how MacManus used the acoustic tour as an opportunity for songwriting and—with Burnett—planning a production strategy that was not based around The Attractions. The result represents a major musical turn that may well have "saved" the auteur's career.

To describe *King of America*, I rely on a culinary metaphor, since this record represents a fascinating musical stew. Chef Burnett's (the project's producer with MacManus) main ingredients involved a seasoned blend of Citizen Elvis's pen, Declan McManus's encyclopedic musical knowledge, and Elvis Costello's voice. Burnett's stew is an exquisite mix of American musical sounds and English sensibilities (in this case, the heralded punk attitude). That is, traditional American sounds provide stages for aggressive metaphors, melodramatic scenarios, and sarcastic wordplay. Central to this stew's success is its reliance on a variety of domestic spices that flavor the tunes in signature ways. Burnett enlisted members of Elvis Presley's TCB Band (Ron Tutt on drums, guitarist James Burton, and bassist Jerry Scheff), New Orleans drummer Earl Palmer, jazz bassist Ray Brown, keyboard player and future producer Mitchell Froom, drummer Jim Keltner, bassist T-Bone Wolk, and, for one song, The Attractions (Steve Nieve also played on one other track). Other musicians and singers appear as well, for Burnett assembled bands that served the various *songs*. If a song called for a rocking groove, enter the TCB boys; if a track required a more subtle jazz feel, enter Palmer and Brown. The *songs* guided the enterprise—not image, commercial concerns, or celebrity egos—and that orientation yielded one fine musical concoction.

Like any well-prepared stew, each bite offers a different flavor, and *King of America* (released January 1986) is the most thematically diverse entry in the Costello canon to date. The record also features a shocking innovation: the oeuvre's first *positive* song. The record's 15 songs involve six relational complaints ("Brilliant Mistake," "Lovable" [written with Cait O'Riordan], "Our Little Angel," "American Without Tears," "Poisoned Rose," and "Sleep of the Just"), three societal complaints ("Little Palaces," "Eisenhower Blues" [by J.B. Lenoir], and "Glitter Gulch"), two personal complaints (Benjamin, Marcus, and Caldwell's "Don't Let Me Be Misunderstood" and "The Big Light"), two relational pleas ("Indoor Fireworks" and "I'll Wear It Proudly"), one piece of narrative impressionism ("Suit of Lights"), and our striking innovation, a relational celebration, "Jack of All Parades." The album's sonic balance serves Costello's writing by elevating his voice and allowing his singing to carry the songs. Remarkably, there are times when Costello seems to laugh ("Glitter Gulch" and "Eisenhower Blues"), which, in a sense, captures the project's essence. The Coward Brothers—free of that nasty Elvis Costello image—were in their element.

Once again, a cover song reveals the thematic thrust of a Costello album. His version of "Don't Let Me Be Misunderstood" returns to *Imperial Bedroom*'s introspection through the narrator's plea for patience. This character admits his faults, seeks understanding, and declares his love for his partner in one huge personal complaint. Demonstrating the album's sonic flexibility, that narrative strategy continues via the rocking number "The Big Light," in which we witness the downside of a big night on the town. The narrator had *way* too much to drink, and the song chronicles his efforts to recall what he did and who he did it with as the "Big Light" of a new day glares in his eyes (the song offers a nice tip of the hat to honky-tonk champion Merle Haggard).

The complaint narrative strategy also supports the Citizen Elvis editorials. "Little Palaces" advances "The Invisible Man" story as it describes England's decaying public housing (our "palaces"), the domestic violence that abounds there (child beating is the abuse du jour), the inhabitants' continued reliance on cheesy media (a soap opera), and their addiction to the Royal Fantasy (expanded to include the pope). Costello's vocals contribute to the song's piercing intensity. On a lighter note, "Eisenhower Blues" brings Citizen Elvis's socioeconomic criticism Over Here, and "Glitter Gulch" satirizes what "The Invisible Man" watches when he is not being programmed by radio, movies, or soap operas: game shows. This rollicking country swing number lambastes the mindlessness of stupid games shows and their money-hungry contestants. Costello's sarcasm oozes from his voice as he rushes through the song's account of game show idiocy.

The relational complaints vary in their directness and intensity. The bouncy "Lovable" seems so cheerful when, in fact, it offers a harsh take on loving relationships and how they always end in pain, involve evil and foolishness, promote gossip, and are based on lies. It is a penetratingly weird song with its signature juxtaposition of music and lyrics. "Our Little Angel" uses country sounds to depict the mating rituals at the local bar as Citizen

Elvis brings his "Clubland" editorial to an American honky-tonk. Barroom love is the harbinger of romantic failure, since public ambition always spawns personal disaster. It is all a frivolous spectator sport in which bar patrons watch the guys hit on their "Little Angel" to no avail. It is all a waste of time, sort of like taking a power tool to a large book—a useless exercise that yields nothing. The jazz sounds of "Poisoned Rose" relate the bittersweet qualities of romance (everybody tries, everybody fails), and "Sleep of the Just" probes the emotional collateral damage done by soldiers and their one-night stands. For her, it is a nightmare; for him, she is just another photo on the barracks wall. But the plot thickens with "Brilliant Mistake" and "American Without Tears." These songs contain vignettes that are tied together by their respective choruses and tag lines. They are evasive, cryptic, and open for interpretation. "Mistake" rotates through commentary on America, a description of an encounter with a television reporter, and a series of reflections on love. Through it all, it seems to complain about the damage inflicted by relationships; claiming that what was once a good idea has turned sour. Its structure is close to impressionism. "Tears" opens with scenes and sounds of New Orleans, turns to a tale of G.I. brides from World War II, and closes with references to the narrator's escape from England to America. Through it all, the chorus relates the sadness that seems to have been abated by the change in scenery.

Costello's interviews and the album's liner notes indicate the risky nature of interpreting his songs. For example, he told Mikal Gilmore that the song title "Brilliant Mistake" came from a conversation in which someone asked him what he thought about Los Angeles. Costello replied: "I said I thought it was a brilliant mistake, and I came to recognize that as a fairly good description of America as a whole. It's a country with great intentions, founded on noble principles, and it very rarely lives up to it all. But having said that, I also realize that there's a lot about the place that remains great, and there's a lot of ambitions and dreams that America is still made up of." Then Costello admitted, "I think the album offers a very oblique statement about America. In fact, while it isn't exactly a love letter, it *is* an attempt to inject a little love into the situation." Later in that interview, he revealed that "Tears" not only recounts the tale of two "Englishwomen who had come over here a long time ago with complete trust, and were accepted by this country," but also is a statement against the anti-American sentiments that existed in England at that time [!!]. He assured Gilmore that the record contained "no political statements" and—at the end of the interview—Costello explained the project's title. After announcing that his life had taken a turn for the better ("Life's Great: It's Official" would be the newspaper headline for a state-of-the-artist piece, he boasted), Costello concluded: "I mean, if you can't laugh with it all, what's the use? That's *really* why I call this record 'King of America.' I think it's the *funniest* title I've ever come up with." With all the talk about Elvis Presley and the use of his band, Costello's name change, and the music's heritage, the auteur chose the title because of its humor.

Costello's joyous state of mind is evident in his songwriting for *King of America*. The album's two relational pleas communicate emotional growth in that instead of wallowing in the aftermath of yet another failed romance, these characters are prepared to fight for their love. "Indoor Fireworks" issues a heartfelt plea for perseverance. Sparks fly and times are tough; conversely, sparks fly and times are great. Here Costello uses a house metaphor to explain that a house/love can be strong, safe, beautiful, and a symbol of stability; however, it can just as easily burn down and leave you homeless and empty-handed. The narrator is in for the long haul; he will do what it takes. "I'll Wear It Proudly" reinforces that sentiment. If the world thinks him to be a fool for standing by his love, so be it. He has found love, and he is determined to make it work. Such sincere dedication erupts in an unprecedented statement of relational joy, "Jack of All Parades." This character has played the game and suffered the consequences. The lovers' parade has run its empty course. Remarkably, *honesty* wins the day as the narrator mistakenly announces his feelings and reveals his love. That brilliant mistake renders the oeuvre's first relational celebration—a story that revisits the "Clubland" relational mentality through the parade metaphor and bids adieu to those painfully cheap escapades.

Although Costello's penchant for impressionism appears but once (the evasive "Suit of Lights"—supposedly inspired by his father's humiliation while singing before a rude audience), *King of America* represents a hybrid of the songwriting signatures we have witnessed to date. Burnett's production used an all-star musical cast to strike a balance between music and lyrics that allowed everybody's talent to flourish. Citizen Elvis's editorials ring true, the emptiness of bar life echoes on, the relational challenges continue, and the internal conflicts wreak their havoc. However, the record's sound makes these observations more palatable. The wall of pain production strategy in which words and music assault the listener in a manner that inhibits an appreciation of either one ends. Clever sounds that cancel each other out are replaced by clever sounds that have room to breathe. To be sure, the punk attitude remains, but its articulation takes a compelling artistic turn.

Critics praised the results. Tom Moon compares the past and present: "If he occasionally hit the bull's eye with his barbed darts in the past, Costello now is crowding the board. . . . Costello's formerly too-smart wit has been set to music that truly speaks, breathes, questions and feels." Lennox Samuels declares, "If this marks the rebirth of Declan McManus, it is an auspicious return." *Stereo Review* argues that the record suggests "a sort of modernized Sun Records sound that nudges Costello into the most unpredictable and emotive singing of his career." Such praise was joined by critiques that are just tired of Costello's writing. The critics' darling, it appears, has worn out his welcome. The *Los Angeles Times* considers the songwriting to be as "obtuse and cryptic as anything [Costello has] done." Although *Rolling Stone* applauds the change in sounds, Mark Coleman maintains: "The LP is littered with dozens of memorable lines but only a handful of coherent songs . . . choruses sink under the weight of verses." In agreement, Jeff Nesin writes: "Even with careful study of the enclosed lyric sheet, several songs remain opaque at best. I can live with ambiguity better than most, but when a track is written and sung with such precision, such palpable passion, I suspect it's about something specific and I'd like to know what. . . . I don't expect piety, but his terminal suspicion of any and all culturally sanctioned happiness gets tired, too." What happened to all that Cole Porter talk? Just a few records ago playful ambiguity was a sign of sophistication.

The Coward Brothers consolidated their resources and rendered a musical work that captures the songwriter, singer, and the musicians in peak form. Burnett's production strategy—with its emphasis on the song as the project's artistic currency—kept Costello focused on his individual songs, the musicians focused on Costello, and the lyric-music interplay focused, period. That The Coward Brothers' plan *saved* a spiraling career seems certain, for assuredly Costello's writing transcends the pop barrage of the previous three projects. But the threat remains. You see, once an individual has been saved, that person faces an even greater spiritual challenge. The potential for "backsliding" is ever present. Old habits die hard. As a result, the spiritually washed tend to shun the halls of sin: The old environs are avoided, old accomplices are dodged, the old habits are forsaken. A fall from grace may occur as a result of a seemingly innocent act—such as returning to the studio to record with The Attractions.

There is no better place to start our treatment of September 1986's *Blood and Chocolate* than with the auteur's views, offered in the liner notes of the record's 2002 reissue: "The album was a pissed-off 32-year-old divorcé's version of the musical blueprint with which I had begun my recording career with The Attractions. My relationship with the band had now soured almost beyond repair. . . . Having said all of this, the year I made this record was also the year of my marriage to Cait O'Riordan. There were a lot of things that I wouldn't have to do again. Like messing up my life just so I could write stupid little songs about it." The emotional tide that carried feelings about divorce *and* marriage along with a surging negativity with band mates washed over *Blood and Chocolate*. It is hard to fathom that the same artist released *King of America* and *Blood and Chocolate* in the same year.

As Costello suggests and the critics celebrate, this is an album with an attitude. Nevertheless, for a record that is supposedly *so* vengeful and *so* spiteful, it is, in reality, running on empty. The assaults attack and "I Want You" is creepy beyond belief, yet most of these songs do *nothing*. They are exercises in creative nostalgia. The music seems just as uneventful when taken as a whole. Nieve's patented counterpoint is virtually absent in this musically lifeless-but-loud exercise. The record has the feel of a required exercise: a contractual obligation or a nostalgia trip that just flat-out *killed* any sense of inspiration. In many respects, the songs are ripe with a vacuous evil that fosters viciousness for the sake of viciousness.

The album's impressionistic tracks cover the spectrum. On one end is "Tokyo Storm Warning" (written with Cait O'Riordan) and its rich, forceful imagery. Of course, nothing ever happens, but the images are compelling. A driving, steady rock beat takes us around the world with Citizen Elvis. No location, it seems, is spared his wrath in this impressionistic bombast. The chorus drives home what is hammered in the verses: The world is a wild and crazy place. This is the first song in Costello's oeuvre to remind me of Bob Dylan's work. Other songs hint at Dylan's writing through Costello's unique style, but this track deploys the classic feel of the American auteur's signature imagery—the characters seem straight out of *Tarantula*. (Jon Young designates the song as "Elvis' 'Subterranean Homesick Blues.'") On the other end of the impressionistic spectrum is "Crimes of Paris" and its unrelenting gibberish. The chorus and musical structure hold together a song that is rhythmic and uses English, yet beyond that, who knows? Everything is there—spite, envy, jealousy, feigned strength, condescension, violence—everything but a clue as to what is happening. It just seems as though something vital is missing, and that "something" probably holds the key to unlocking what appears to be an inside word game. In the middle of our impressionistic spectrum is "Battered Old Bird." Minimal music accompanies this vivid account of the various occupants of an apartment building or house. The details are sketchy but the descriptions run deep. As always, nothing happens, though Costello's singing leads you to *believe* that *something* is up here.

The Nick Lowe production features eight more tracks that focus on relationships. We have two relational assaults ("Uncomplicated" and "I Hope You're Happy Now"), a relational warning ("Honey, Are You Straight or Are You Blind"), and five relational complaints: "Home Is Anywhere You Hang Your Head," "I Want You," "Blue Chair," "Poor Napoleon," and "Next Time 'Round." Most of these relational complaints fall flat due to an overriding emptiness. The exception, "I Want You," represents the rising tide that lifts all ships. The track opens with a six-line statement of eternal devotion before turning into the school song for Stalking College. Our narrator has it bad; that is for sure. His jealousy is all-consuming and his madness is complete. This song needs a warning sticker—Costello becomes the Vincent Price of torch singers. The other complaints not only pale in comparison, they leave you wondering what happened. Our most direct entry, "Home Is Anywhere," is a sad tale of a man who is at home wherever he is, because his head is *always* down. The complaint is traditional, the scenario is pitiful, and Costello reinforces it all through a character who is drunk on pain and sleeplessness, and is contemplating murder. "Blue Chair" (featuring a love triangle in which we eavesdrop on *part* of a conversation in which competing suitors banter, hurl insults, and declare love), "Poor Napoleon" (a song with "Don't Worry Baby" sounds and scenes of spiteful recrimination—is she a prostitute??), and "Next Time" (a serious complaint with more than a little bit of death imagery—she'll be the death of him) are just what Costello said they were: reiterations of *This Year's Model*. Sometimes an artist may revisit a theme and revive its vigor, and sometimes that exercise falls flat and tired. "I Want You" certainly represents the former, while the remaining tracks suggest the latter.

The relational assaults feature signature spiteful insults. "Uncomplicated" uses powerful, aggressive music to drive home a powerful, aggressive message: It is not over, stupid girl. Unadorned lyrics and a forceful delivery convey the simpleminded qualities of the narrator's target. Just as delightful is "I Hope You're Happy" and its hateful assault on an old flame's lover. Demonstrating that maturity is always an undesirable option, the song concludes with a schoolyard rejoinder, I never loved you anyway (nah nah nah nah nah). We endure more immaturity with the relational warning "Honey, Are You Straight" and its evasive account of a lover who appears to advise his mate to beware of the competition. The warning is straightforward, but the details are tricky—just as the auteur likes them. Shades of *This Year's Model II* abound.

The songs' most striking quality involves Costello's singing. He is so emotive and so passionate that one would like to hear him sing the phone book or, better yet, a dictionary. He gives such compelling urgency and vigor to lines that are, quite often, lifeless. The themes are tired and contain more inside wordplay than metaphor. The band is despondent. But the singing reaches for emotions that pump life into stillborn scenarios. The thematic vigor is gone, but the will to fight remains. Such trends indicate the validity of Costello's opening remarks.

I stand virtually alone in these condemnations. The critics loved *Blood and Chocolate*. *Musician* declares the record to be "essential Elvis Costello" that "'celebrates' the fully recharged Elvis, brimming with vitriol." The *Los Angeles Times*'s Robert Hilburn relates: "In fact, the album revives Costello's artistic glow so commandingly that I checked with his record company to make sure these weren't leftover tracks from the 'Armed Forces' days. . . . Costello's artistic pulse is so alive again that the appropriate subtitle may be 'Welcome Back.'" The *Dallas Morning News* wonders why Costello used the "Napoleon Dynamite" moniker on this "superior" project and concludes: "This singer may be uncertain what name he wants to work under, but while he finds out, music fans continue to benefit from his permutations." *Creem* observes that Costello is "as relentlessly pessimistic as ever— one of his most endearing traits—which is a relief after a year of teeth-cutting optimism." Only *Rolling Stone* expresses any reservations about this return to days gone by. First, the magazine makes fun of the Declan MacManus name change on *King,* saying the "new guise lasted about as long as one of David Bowie's haircuts" before arguing: "For all the signature wit and wordplay of Costello's lyrics, the songs are too frequently glib or sketchy. . . . Like so many of the characters on his new album, Elvis Costello seems to be circling his possibilities, hiding a fear of the future behind an infatuation with the past."

Declan MacManus, Napoleon Dynamite, or Elvis Costello. Just as the auteur struggles with his *nom de disque,* he seems to wrestle with his creative direction. Our artistic backsliding metaphor works perfectly here because the auteur revisited the past in order to—once again—provide his record company with viable product. This conscious attempt to satisfy Columbia Records may have pleased critics and fans who appreciate art that runs in its designated place, but it would serve a higher calling for Costello. With this, we seal the creative deal as the Costello-MacManus-Dynamite character bids farewell to the late '70s, The Attractions, producer Nick Lowe, and the New Wave albatross that strangles his creative impulses. In order to shed an image that constrains you, you must disassociate yourself from those trappings—as per *King of America.* Instead, Costello wallowed in that image, abdicated the progress achieved with T-Bone Burnett, and rendered an album so tired that it purged any inclination to return to this mode of operation for close to ten years. For that reason, *Blood and Chocolate* represents a victory—Costello's backsliding facilitated a renewed commitment to what saved him in the first place: his rebellious, innovative talent.

After the 1986 twin releases, Elvis Costello stood at an artistic crossroads. Deteriorating relationships with The Attractions and Columbia Records joined a growing confusion over his professional direction to produce one wayward auteur. In response, Costello changed record labels and joined Warner Brothers (for the first time, one label controlled worldwide distribution), returned to T-Bone Burnett (and Kevin Killen) for production assistance, and formulated a new studio strategy. To this point, Costello had proven himself to be a master of the live-in-the-studio production style. Though he occasionally brought demos to the studio to guide the process, the final recording featured a live band playing together—a method that directly contributed to the wall of sound recordings that typified his work with The Attractions (punch-ins, etc., occurred as necessary).

With *King of America,* T-Bone Burnett insisted that the *song* serve as the artistic anchor that held the sessions in place. Should difficulties emerge, the song—and its needs—would settle the issue. In order to avoid a record that resembled *King of America II,* the production team of Burnett, Killen, and Costello expanded that approach through the implementation of an ensemble recording strategy. Such techniques involved a mixture of the old and the new. From the old came Declan McManus's penchant for genre dancing; varied musical styles would be deployed as platforms for Citizen Elvis's musings. The new involved the sound-by-sound method of ensemble recording in which various musicians were presented an incomplete track and asked to build upon that starting point. Costello described his approach to the *Chicago Tribune*'s Iain Blair: "There are a lot of different things going on in this album because I basically approached it more like a film project." He explained that his experiences recording his first movie sound track (*The Courier*, starring Cait O'Riordan) served as his inspiration: "I imagined the songs as being like different scenes, which all needed lighting in different ways. But that's not to say there's an overall theme or thread running through the album. On the other hand, there are a lot more third-person stories on 'Spike' than on some of my other albums, so it was very important for me to find the right musicians and special instrumental sounds that'd bring the songs to life and make them more vivid." To that end, Costello states in the album's 2001 reissue liner notes that he began the project with the "blueprint of five albums" in his head and, somehow, "elected to make all five albums at once."

Again, like *King of America*, the list of musicians and singers is most impressive. Drummer Pete Thomas is the lone Attraction in a musical cast that includes (in rough order of appearance) Paul McCartney, Roger McGuinn, Ralph Forbes, Jim Keltner, Michael Blair, O'Riordan, Marc Ribot, Benmont Tench, Jerry Scheff, Jerry Marotta, The Dirty Dozen Brass Band (Gregory Davis, Efrem Towns, Kevin Harris, Roger Lewis, Kirk Joseph, and Charles Joseph), Allen Toussaint, Mitchell Froom, Willie Green, Donal Lunny, Steve Wickham, Davy Spillane, T-Bone Wolk, Ralph Forbes, Chrissie Hynde, Christy Moore, Derek Bell, Buell Niedlinger, Frankie Galvin, and others (including Burnett). The instruments vary as well: We hear guitars, drums, horns, glockenspiel, bells, lunge maracas, Chinese drum, Oldsmobile hubcap, parade drum, tympani, banjo, Indian harmonium, Magic Table, metal pipe, bouzouki, fiddle, vibraphone, Martian dog-bark, bodhran, whiplash, anvil, and snowbells. The album was recorded in Dublin, New Orleans, Hollywood, and London, with the musical cast varying according to location and sound strategy.

After listening to *Spike* (released in January 1989) you feel as though you have been on a long, draining journey. Its rich, poignant social commentary, heartfelt scenes from people's lives, satirical views of life's ironies, varied accounts of romance gone wrong, and biting pieces of impressionism are presented through layers and layers and layers of music, sound effects, and noises. Whew. The sounds rotate from raucous New Orleans–based carnivals to plaintive Irish melodies to overwhelming pop walls of sound to musical vaudeville to simple torch structures. The lyrics are in turn direct, cryptic, elegant, mean-spirited, mournful, and fun-loving. It is as eclectic a piece of art as anyone will find anywhere—I mean, where are you going to find a song containing an alligator guitar, a trigger bass, a drunk adulterous husband, a vengeful wife, and a Martian dog-bark? ("Pads, Paws and Claws" features this unlikely ensemble.)

The album's 15 tracks offer an instrumental ("Stalin Malone"), a satire ("God's Comic"), two life sagas ("Veronica" [written with Paul McCartney] and "Any King's Shilling"), three relational complaints ("Chewing Gum," "Pads, Paws and Claws" [with McCartney], and "Baby Plays Around" [written with O'Riordan]), three pieces of narrative impressionism ("Deep Dark Truthful Mirror," "Miss Macbeth," and "Coal Train Robbery"), and five societal complaints: ". . . This Town . . .," "Let Him Dangle," "Tramp the Dirt Down," "Satellite," and "Last Boat Leaving." Citizen Elvis's commentary is sharp as ever, and more encompassing than previous entries. He wishes the prime minister dead because she has betrayed everybody ("Tramp the Dirt"); he points to a supposedly sophisticated society's blood-thirsty ways ("Let Him Dangle"); he demonstrates the personal pain that accompanies the call to duty or exile ("Last Boat"); he portrays the cheap personalities that occupy tawdry towns (". . . This Town . . ."); and he re-ports the vicarious pains that accompany a programmed life ("Satellite"). Citizen Elvis is in top form on *Spike*.

Several of these editorials feature some of the songwriter's finest work. For example, "Tramp the Dirt Down" is a compelling story that builds on Citizen Elvis's well-established anti-English sentiments. The track opens with traditional Irish folk sounds and a typical public relations scene in which a politician is photographed kissing a baby. Our narrator interprets the subsequent newspaper photograph as the ultimate act of betrayal: Kiss the baby now and kill it later. First, the narrator hopes to outlive Margaret Thatcher (mentioned *by name*) so that he may oversee her burial and stomp down the dirt on her grave. Afterward, we are treated to several tragic scenes—all products of the societal deceit that Citizen Elvis has chronicled throughout his career. The song ends by hoping *you* outlive the regime so that *they* do not bury *you* to a chorus of cruel laughter. Now this is serious stuff, as Costello explained to the *Los Angeles Times*'s Chris Willman: "There's no reasonable argument intended there; it's an *unreasonable* response to very unreasonable events. . . . If you call somebody 'a madam of a whorehouse' as I do, it's a fairly cheap insult. But there are plenty of times that they patronize you and insult your intelligence. So let's trade the language; let's talk at their level." If the prime minister ever wished Costello dead, I am unaware of it; however, the auteur's point is not only well taken, it is a di-rect reiteration of a long-standing editorial position: Aristocratic England abuses its citizenry. Sonic changes may abound on *Spike*, but Citizen Elvis holds steady.

Balancing those editorials are sentimental recollections of days and lives gone by, as well as a fun-filled view of His life Up There. The two "life sagas" introduce a new songwriting strategy in which Costello overviews an older woman's life ("Veronica") as she loses her grip on reality during her sunset years and an important scene in the life of a historical character (in this case, Costello's grandfather in "Any King's Shilling"). "Shilling" is a period piece that focuses on a specific moment, while "Veronica" is a pop wall of sound that looks backward as a means of coping with the present. Both songs are touching portrayals that demonstrate that the songwriter's emotions cut at least two ways. (Interestingly, the *Washington Post*'s Geoffrey Himes interprets "Veronica" to be about "a young woman so confused by adult sexual roles that she's not even sure of her own name.") The satire "God's Comic" introduces humor into the mix by way of vaudeville sounds that communicate more than a little bit of mischief. No heavy moralizing or punishing complaints here, just a lighthearted piece of satire that posits the irony of it all—an irony that is the product of a Divine sense of humor.

Costello's impressionism turns dark on this project—often through caustic lines that drift close to wordplay. For example, the splendid New Orleans musical backdrop that supports "Deep Dark Truthful Mirror" introduces what appears to be a straightforward relational complaint that shifts quickly into an impressionistic powerhouse. The relational complaint remains in the shadows (reiterated by the chorus) as Costello weaves images of a circus(?), a bar scene, and lavish accounts of butterflies, turtles, deceased primates, and Jesus. Much like Bob Dylan's "A Hard Rain's a-Gonna Fall," the imagery is in turn startling, beautiful, and disturbing. In contrast, "Miss Macbeth" and "Coal Train Robberies" are truly chaotic. The theatrical sounds of "Macbeth" lead you to believe the story is more coherent than it is (there appears to be some kind of teacher-student thing going on), just as "Robberies" presents jumbled scenes crammed together by loud, cacophonous "music" that screams at you.

Finally, the relational complaints make their points without the heavy-handedness that characterizes much of Costello's work. "Chewing Gum" uses busy sounds (including a "metal pipe") to relate a mail-order bride's disappointment over her fantasy's failure to materialize. "Pads, Paws" features more musical chaos to chronicle how a worthless drunk damages his wife's life and how she makes him pay for it. The other side of the relational aisle appears via "Baby Plays," as we move from the cheating man to the cheating woman: She cheats, he suffers—plain and simple. Although the sounds vary from track to track, the themes remain relatively constant: Distrust is ubiquitous.

Spike is a special record rich in artistic value with a sprinkling of commercial hooks. Music critics from America's newspapers seem to agree. Geoffrey Himes states that *Spike* "captures the 33-year-old professional Costello . . . as accurately as those early albums captured the 22-year-old misfit he once was." The *Boston Herald* reports that "at its best, 'Spike' is a work of startling, breathtaking genius" through its "stunning display of eclecticism." The *Los Angeles Times* claims the project "bristles with renewed invention, energy and expression," and the *San Francisco Examiner* argues: "As off-putting as the wide scope of styles and instrumentation are initially, 'Spike' may someday be regarded as Costello's most rewarding offering. . . . All this variety gives 'Spike' the feel of a musical drama without a narrative." The *Philadelphia Inquirer* declares, "It's Kurt Weill and Cole Porter trapped in the body of an angry, slightly brainy English punk whose best offensive weapon is a pointed barb, his second best a snarling (but still tuneful) exclamation." Finally, the *Oakland Tribune* concludes: "On first listen, everything seems muddily like just another overdone Costello project. But dig beneath the surface and there's a new world of sound to accompany Costello's lyrics, which don't fall into any easily pigeonholed pattern. Some songs are specific and their details sharply etched. Others are vague and enigmatic. But they work most of the time. If only more pop stars were willing to take chances to do something as creative."

Elvis Costello emerged from the *Spike* project with a new artistic direction. But not everybody appreciated this shift in artistic professional orientations. As he toured the world to promote his project, Costello granted countless interviews with print and broadcast media—often appearing on live radio shows to hawk his new wares. Now this is, indeed, in stark contrast to the old days and the public relations style that focused on combative control. When the *New York Daily News*'s David Browne heard Costello utter the same line on a radio program that he heard during an interview with David Letterman, he balked: "If Costello wants to be seen as a mature, wise tunesmith, fine. But both 'Spike' and his press junket appear to signal the end of one career and the beginning of another, and that's too bad." Why? Costello seems to have anticipated this criticism in his closing comments for the *Boston Herald*: "I could easily have sat back and kept making the same record and been a millionaire by now, if all I wanted was fame. . . . But if fame and money were that important to me, I wouldn't be making albums like 'Spike.'" The auteur takes his argument to the industry level in his liner note essay when he notes that *Spike* was his best seller to date: "When I listen to it now, this seems pretty curious—not because the songs are bad but because they are rather odd, each track being very different from the next. I'm not so sure that anyone would bankroll a record of this kind these days. So I am rather glad that we made *Spike* while I had the chance."

Once more, we revisit the "minstrel's dilemma." The choice between pleasing the audience and satisfying the artistic impulse recurs time and again as artists grapple with longevity. Artists continually wrestle with audiences incapable of grasping the evolutionary qualities of an unfolding professional career. Costello adjusted his promotional style, and in so doing, employed specific responses in certain situations, just like *any other public relations campaign*. What PR campaign invents new answers for old, recurring questions? That is an extremely foolish strategy that brings thematic incoherence to what is designed to be a systematic process. Moreover, by focusing on such trivial matters, critics miss the big picture. The

"Costello" Browne pines for is long since gone, but the work *is* evolving and *Spike* represents an important midpoint in the three-album transition that propels the auteur's musical adventure forward.

When Elvis Costello entered the musical world in 1977, his carefully contrived image fueled his emergence. Ever since his debut, Costello has struggled with that image—wrestling with the music press, battling record companies, coping with band mates; even changing names to facilitate re-invention. The creative impulse that *requires* Costello to strive for artistic innovation continually waged war with those who would have him remain in one musical place by repeating projects and enabling a more concrete understanding of his work. By 1991, these conditions created static re-sponses to dynamic activities. Fans, critics, industry executives, and fellow musicians applied their preconceived notions about Elvis Costello to the situation at hand, often preferring their opinions over any observable real-ity. Consider the *New York Times*'s response to May 1991's release, *Mighty Like a Rose*. Karen Schoemer carefully articulates the consensus opinion about the auteur's songwriting when she reports that Costello is "such a skillful manipulator of words" that people often "overlook the fact that he has almost nothing to say." She continues:

> His songs are virtual piles of words: he stacks them one upon another, shoves them together to create unusual images, then shoves the images together to create abstruse sentences. Mr. Costello's lyrics have complete authority over his music: he writes melodies that rise and tumble oddly to keep pace with his verbal spate, and he sometimes extends a melodic phrase when he wants to tag an extra line into a verse.

From there, Schoemer describes the new record by noting that "for one so obviously in love with words," the writer "is startlingly inarticulate in com-municating his ideas," to the point where the songs' "wordiness drains [their] emotional content." Schoemer concludes, "If he truly has something to say, he's not telling us."

What happened to all that Cole Porter talk?

When the media labeled Costello the next Porter or Gershwin, the songwriter was in the midst of an introspective binge. That was the *Impe-rial Bedroom* era, when Citizen Elvis introduced the world to punk introspec-tion and its aggressive, irreverent thoughtfulness. But *Mighty Like a Rose* is nothing like that. In fact, Schoemer must have reviewed another album, for there is no impressionism on *Rose*, and little wordplay. Of course there is the occasional enigmatic line or idiosyncratic image, but on the whole, *Rose* is not what she suggests. Perhaps she was so moved by *Spike* that she pre-ferred to stay there, confusing "Miss Macbeth" with "The Other Side of Summer."

I may be crazy, but *Mighty Like a Rose* strikes me as an extremely coher-ent work of art. Our commentator from *Trust*—a veteran Citizen Elvis—

returns with a series of editorials that occasionally complain, yet more often than not simply report on life's events. Many times, these "reports" are quite compassionate. The bitterness of *Trust* has been replaced by empathy. Citizen Elvis *shares* his characters' feelings instead of merely denouncing their situations, attacking those responsible for such conditions, or ridiculing their positions.

Produced by Mitchell Froom, Kevin Killen, and "D.P.A. MacManus," the record's 14 tracks represent a reiteration of *Spike*'s artistic strategy. Musically, many of *Spike*'s cast members return for an encore, occasionally bringing another round of crazed instruments that contribute to the layers and layers of music, sound effects, and general noise (e.g., a calliope, a "Hung Upside Down Rickenbacker Tremelo Bass," and the ever-present "Big Stupid Guitar"). Where *Rose* departs from *Spike* is in its thematic coherence. First, Citizen Elvis takes us back to *Trust* with four compelling editorials. We open with three societal complaints—"The Other Side of Summer," "Hurry Down Doomsday (the Bugs Are Taking Over)" (written with Jim Keltner), and "How to Be Dumb"—that communicate how the world is a polluted, sick place populated by dimwits. "The Other Side" is a classic Costello composition that deploys pleasant, layered pop sounds to frame biting, caustic lyrics that attack the Earth's environmental conditions, her inhabitants, and John Lennon's naive perfect-world scenario, "Imagine" (among other things). That the world is one huge deteriorating mess is reinforced by the second track, "Hurry Down," and its end-of-the-world sermon that uses an invasion by giant bugs to lighten the heavy-handed message (sonically, the song is a tidal wave of converging instruments and sound effects). We cap the opening round of societal complaints with a rocking, Attractions-style number, "How to Be Dumb," in which Citizen Elvis zeros in on people and their pitiful ways. People lie, listen to rude bands, adhere to silly fashions, and aspire to their rightful place in a museum where life's mistakes are immortalized. Although individual lyrics are occasionally cryptic, the message shines through as Citizen Elvis paints a dark picture of societal deterioration and those responsible for that condition. In a new twist, however, the complaint's focus is on "people," not aristocratic culture or manipulative governments. Simply, dumb people are ruining the world and facilitating the doomsday that is just over the horizon. (Biographers report that "Dumb" is a response to Bruce Thomas's novel about life on the road with a rock band. Reportedly, the book features several not-too-subtle jabs at Costello.) Later, Citizen Elvis attacks the programmers once more via "Invasion Hit Parade"—a dense song with layered sounds and multiple scenes ranging from what appears to be a personal complaint about the entertainment industry to comments about musical slavery (thanks to those evil programmers) to a concluding warning of ultimate victimization (the "Invisible Man" has no chance).

We revisit the long-standing relational complaint strategy through "So Like Candy" (written with Paul McCartney) and "Sweet Pear." The relational elegies communicate sincerity as "Candy" laments a love lost (the narrator will worship those photographs for the rest of his life) and "Pear" embellishes the terrifying fear that a love lost, and then regained, may once more be lost, this time forever. There is nothing arrogant or aggressive about these torch songs—they are pitifully sad and remorseful.

From there, *Rose* presents songs that neither complain nor celebrate; they commentate. We have two social commentaries ("Harpies Bizarre" and "Couldn't Call It Unexpected No. 4"), three relational commentaries ("After the Fall," "Georgie and Her Rival," and "Playboy to a Man" [written with McCartney]), and a relational testimony, Cait O'Riordan's "Broken." The social editorials use varied sounds—"Bizarre" features a quaint, ballroom musical feel; "Couldn't," a circus/carnival backdrop—as platforms for observations about the mating game ("Bizarre") and life's potential disappointments. In both cases, scenarios are embellished and followed by clear, concise editorials. "Bizarre," for example, describes a man scouting for women and a woman who is intrigued by the man, and closes with a narrator's view of it all (of course, he thinks it is all useless). "Couldn't Call It Unexpected No. 4" presents a woman who seeks a man with her father's virtues and a disappointed mother through fairly sketchy accounts. The key to it all is in the middle verse, in which Costello announces his responsibility to report what he sees. He proclaims that it might seem trite to some, but he is the lucky bloke who has to fight through it all and make sense of what he sees. It is, after all, his *job*.

This narrative strategy recurs via the relational commentaries in which Citizen Elvis chronicles how lovers toy with one another ("Georgie") and work desperately to keep love alive and sensual ("After the Fall"), and the irony of romance, in that today's abusive, conniving playboy may be tomorrow's emotional slave (the "what goes around, comes around" tale, "Playboy to a Man"). In all cases, Costello does not judge as much as he reports that the "Clubland" mating ritual may gain in sophistication as time passes, yet the results remain the same; that unimaginative lovemaking may drive restless spirits elsewhere, only to return reinvigorated and determined to enliven their sex lives; and that love enslaves the staunchest warrior. These observations peak in O'Riordan's haunting account of loving dedication. There our character announces that he or she can and will cope with anything and everything *except* the loss of his or her beloved. In the absence of that love, death is the only option. The song does not complain or celebrate as much as it testifies: Love is everything.

Perhaps the most striking songwriting innovation involves the character-narrator interplay featured in "All Grown Up." Here a young woman announces that maturity has brought her bitterness, hatred, and weakness. In response, the narrator demands that she come to grips with herself, stop blaming others for her difficulties, and get on with her life. It is a remarkable moment. Instead of embellishing the negativity, Costello intervenes with a mature assessment of the situation that offers encouragement. The responsibilities discussed in "Couldn't Call It Unexpected No. 4" manifest themselves in "Grown Up," except that Citizen Elvis is not content to report; he acts. The "Clubland" antidote may have failed, and the world is populated by fools, but that is no reason to resign yourself to your fate, Citizen Elvis compassionately declares. The song's musical theatricality reinforces this sincere prescription for living.

Costello's sharp cynicism returns through *Spike*'s opening societal complaints and quickly mellows into compassionate, occasionally humorous, accounts of life's difficulties. Maturity is demanding. Loving relationships are ironic and all-consuming. Interpersonal gamesmanship is, ultimately, a waste of time and effort. And pain is always just around the corner, lurking, searching for innocent and not-so-innocent victims. These songs are anything but piles of words jammed into idiosyncratic images; they are coherent, seasoned commentaries. Costello's anger is certainly present, but it is accompanied by empathy and—dare I say it?—wisdom.

The critical responses to *Rose* jump all over the place. *Rolling Stone* cutely concludes: "The usual pall of despair hangs over *Mighty Like a Rose*. Alison, that slut, still haunts every song, in various guises, deceitful and elusive as ever." Stephen Holden asks, "Has the 35-year-old post-punk songwriter given up on humanity, or is he just having fun playing devil's advocate?" *Down Beat* provides a technical assessment: "In total, this is complex, well-crafted pop music. And, at his best, Costello is a sponge who surrounds himself with inspiring musicians, soaks up their knowledge and style, then squeezes out material that is uniquely his own." Jim Farber thoughtfully comments: "In the end, though, what's most impressive about Costello's writing is how confidently he nails life's allusions to the wall. . . . Costello understands that in rejecting life's pretty lies there's great freedom. Not to mention enough focus for his rage to last a lifetime." And *Musician* argues: "A dozen spins with lyrics in hand and you'll maybe start picking out the underlying themes. They're doozies: Death, despair, failed lives, broken dreams, fatally flawed relationships, submission and, finally, self-loathing are here in abundance. Faith, hope and redemption are not. . . . *Mighty Like a Rose* [is] one of the most overwhelming albums about sexual politics ever crafted."

Mighty Like a Rose is many things to many people. "A dozen spins" may reveal the record to be an "overwhelming" treatise on "sexual politics" or a "pile of words" that "create abstruse sentences" or chapter 14 of an ongoing novel about "Alison." For a work of art to elicit such a variety of responses demonstrates the extent to which art defies rational logic, scientific scrutiny, or ideological imposition. Nevertheless, from the perspective of auteur theory, this project indicates the evolutionary qualities of the artist's lifework. In some respects, the rebellious punk from *My Aim* remains and his musical genre dancing continues. In other respects, that punk has developed skills that have broadened his sensibilities, instilled compassion, and sharpened his observational powers. As Citizen Elvis's editorials mature, Declan McManus's musical restlessness and Elvis Costello's commercial recklessness advance as well. *Down Beat's* musical "sponge" is about to absorb a totally new set of influences as the punk enters the chamber music room and challenges the musical world once more.

From the layered sounds of Oldsmobile hubcaps, upside-down bass guitars, calliopes, and Magic Tables, we turn to the layered sounds of violins, violas, and violoncellos. With *The Juliet Letters*, Declan McManus's musical restlessness and Elvis Costello's commercial rebellion bask in the soft, candlelit glow of the musical world's most refined, sophisticated genre. When classical musicians Ian Belton, Paul Cassidy, Michael Thomas, and Jacqueline Thomas—known collectively as the Brodsky Quartet—teamed with Cosmopolitan Punk Elvis Costello to write and record the world's first punk chamber score, music history turned yet another page in the continuing saga that is the auteur's oeuvre. To be sure, pop sounds and classical sensibilities have shared the same musical playground before, but rare is the creative synthesis that emerged from *The Juliet Letters* project. This was not Frank Sinatra fronting some symphony or Jeff Lynn orchestrating a classical stroll down rockabilly lane; on the contrary, this was a musical marriage in which both partners shared their strengths, compensated for their weaknesses, and endeavored to create something that transcended both sets of experience. Whether or not one likes *The Juliet Letters*, one *must* admire the artistic process that produced the record.

The record's liner notes reveal how mutual admiration led to the creative curiosity that spawned such a daring project. After attending each other's concerts and discovering musical commonalities, a collective chemistry slowly emerged. Costello described the unlikely union to Chris Willman:

> I suppose some people in the classical world imagine all people in rock 'n' roll are barbarians. And equally we have the misconception that they're all very, very refined people, that they're probably all sons of counts or something. . . . I think a preconceived idea of people who have no knowledge of classical music whatsoever is that the string quartet is some nimsy little thing with people in powdered wigs—sort of playing in the corner in a shopping mall, the way they sometimes do to denote sophistication. Well, play those people Bartok's quartets, and tell me that it isn't as wild and abandoned as any punk music that's ever been made up—yet it's all composed, it's not accidental. You can bring both things to it.

When Cait O'Riordan discovered a newspaper article about a professor's curious writing habits, a project was born. Costello explained the situation to Larry Katz: "It seems there was this professor in Verona . . . who from around 1968–1972 somehow got the letters from the dead-letter office written to Juliet Capulet. It's strange to write a dead imaginary person, but then people write Sherlock Holmes. Anyhow, this professor took it upon himself to write these people back. It was a rather poetic and, I think, very beautiful thing to do." The story inspired the group to pursue that approach, albeit in a songwriting mode, as Michael Thomas told Katz: "It certainly was a new experience for us. None of us had ever written lyrics before. I don't think any of us had even written a letter before. Then it was hard enough to stand there and read them in front of the other members of the quartet, let alone one of the great lyricists of our time. So embarrassing."

Embarrassment aside, a methodology gradually emerged. *Rolling Stone* quotes Costello's recollection: "We worked haltingly at first . . . drawing up a list of the different types of letter. Everyone went home and tried to write a suicide note one night—just like school." As school progressed, obstacles emerged. One hurdle involved Costello's inability to read music and his corresponding difficulty with communicating his ideas to the Brodskys. In response, Costello learned to read music, as Paul Cassidy recounted to Bill Flanagan:

> Elvis. He's a very special guy. He knows more about classical music than I do. He's obviously gone into great depth over the last six or seven years. When we started working together he wasn't able to read or write music, so the initial workings were quite slow because he would put his ideas on tape or play them to us, and we would be busily writing these things down, which is difficult and time-consuming. His ideas were coming thick and fast, but he's not the greatest piano player in the world. Sometimes we'd just look at each other and say, "This guy's off his rocker," 'cause we couldn't hear what he was hearing. It was well-formed in his brain, but it wasn't coming through his fingers. So he just decided to learn how to read music—which he did in about six weeks! Elvis started turning up with his ideas written out in four staves. Absolutely amazing.

Once the team shared a common technical language, the task of writing lyrics yielded further complications. Michael Thomas told *Billboard* how the team insisted on lyrical collaboration: "It would have been easier for Elvis to go away and write a song, and one of us to go away and write another, but we decided early on to make it a five-way collaboration, for better or worse." Costello shared his views about this process with Willman:

> But any time I felt like there might be an obstacle, I kept reminding myself how much more of a jump they were making in terms of the compositional writing process. Because although they're constantly engaged in the making

of music, most of them have not composed since they were in college. . . . And I've always had the firm conviction that everybody has at least one good tale to spin, even if it's over a couple of drinks in the bar. And in this case the impetus was there to go home one night and try and write—particularly as we had a letter form, and everybody can write a letter. Now, not everything that they wrote was brilliant, but neither was everything that I wrote brilliant. But little by little we assembled a text, and I'm sufficiently experienced to recognize a good line when I see one, and I acted as an editor.

Although *Billboard* reports Costello's claim that the results resemble "a good collection of short stories," a narrative reading of *The Juliet Letters*' "text" offers a different conclusion. Any discussion of *Letters* must begin with some recognition of what constitutes a "letter." Is there any expectation of a response, or is it merely a declaration? Is some understanding of context necessary? While musical compositions need not consider such matters, these inquiries establish the starting point for interpreting *The Juliet Letters*. At their best, these songs take us into the fragmentary world of letters, in which people correspond with some recognition of their particular *context*. Unlike short stories, characters need not be established and values are evidenced in the shared understanding that comes from the correspondents' relationship (real or fantasized), not in the text itself. Letters delve into private worlds where people grunt and moan in idiosyncratic ways. To take letters out of their context is to drain their meanings or, even worse, distort their contents. Even though these lyrics use straightforward language with little to no wordplay or enigmatic metaphor, they are terribly evasive due to their reliance on the epistolary mode of expression: We are peeking into someone else's mail with no knowledge of the correspondents, their histories, or the letter's context. Such a creative strategy elicits strong responses—either you will love this work or you will hate it. There is, it seems, no middle ground.

Produced by the Brodskys, Costello, and Kevin Killen, *The Juliet Letters* (released in January 1993) contains 20 tracks, three of which are instrumentals. Several songs directly invoke the epistolary strategy, such as "For Other Eyes" and its account of a paranoid lover who fears her partner is cheating; "I Almost Had a Weakness" and its portrayal of a hateful, mean-spirited old woman who distrusts her relatives (fearing they just want her money); "Taking My Life in Your Hands" and its suggestion that the writer is writing to a ghost or a character from a dream (the letters return unopened, yet he or she keeps writing); "Dear Sweet Filthy World" and its clear, concise suicide note; "The Letter Home" (from the "letter as therapy" branch of the epistolary tree) and its relational nostalgia and remorse; "This Sad Burlesque" and the writer's hope that a deteriorating relationship will rebound; and "I Thought I'd Write to Juliet" with its twisted missive in which the writer writes to a dead Juliet to inform her that he has received a letter from a stranger(!). Some songs supposedly involve letters, yet their contents are more than a little bit evasive and fragmentary (e.g., "Expert Rites," "Why?," and the seemingly accessible "Jacksons, Monk and Rowe"). Finally, some songs are not letters at all. The "graffiti" (in Costello's words) of "Swine," the junk-mail parody that is "This Offer Is Unrepeatable," the report that is "Romeo's Seance" (the title says it all), the diatribe that is "Damnation's Cellar," and the concluding sentiments of "The Birds Will Still Be Singing" resemble letters in the loosest sense. Throughout, Costello's emotive singing and the Brodskys' orchestral structures add depth and feeling to "letters" that are often too sketchy to be meaningful. Costello described the lyrics thus to the *Los Angeles Times*:

> And in this, of course, because we're trying to speak in the voices of the imagined characters of these songs, it behooves us to have them speak in real language. Sometimes they fly into flights of fantasy or fancy, but people do, don't they, in letters? Sometimes they suddenly go from the very matter-of-fact into some dark and quite poetic flight, particularly when they're speaking about their innermost feelings. The curious thing about writing in a three- or four-way collaboration is that I was amazed how much very, very raw autobiographical stuff got into some of these songs. Once we got to know each other more, some of the things that were said in some of the darker, more intense songs, there's some very personal stuff there. Sometimes you find that you do that in a form that isn't so obviously attributable to you.

Just as Costello suggests, *The Juliet Letters* rarely deploys clever metaphors or idiosyncratic symbolism. The *songs* are often cryptic and downright inaccessible, but the *lyrics* use straightforward language. The amount of autobiography is, as always, uncertain and irrelevant. For these reasons, critics wrestled with *The Juliet Letters* and developed love-hate responses to the work. Occasionally, one wonders if they examined *this* record or merely massaged old views from old projects. Consider Stephen Holden's review for the *New York Times*: "Costello's verbal overkill, his fondness for multisyllable words and offbeat images, often seem like a defense against more direct expression. The denser the language, the more it recasts feelings as attitudes and turns stories into puzzles. The quartet's warm, flowing textures only accentuate a tendency that can sabotage melody by weighing it down with too many mouthfuls of verbiage." Although Costello had been guilty of this charge in the past, the collaborative writing on *Letters* restricted such tendencies. The "letters" were puzzles, not their language. Some critics used state-of-the-artist arguments, such as Manuel Mendoza's review for the *Dallas Morning News*: "Returning to his early themes of betrayal, guilt and revenge along with the melancholy and humor he discovered later, Mr. Costello appears to have been reinvigorated by the thirtysomething British quartet." Other writers focused on the project at hand by either praising or damning the results. In cases of the former, Hal Willner claims the record "is an incredible journey, enjoyable without being highbrow"; Elysa Gardner reports that "the singer and his collaborators have created something that is as accomplished as it is moving"; and David Gates concludes, "It's hardly Elvis Costello's most characteristic work, but it may be his purest." On the other side of the aisle, the San Diego Union's George Varga declares the record "fails largely because Costello is over-reaching (while, conversely, the Brodsky Quartet is under-reaching)" and closes with this assessment: "In the final analysis, what 'The Juliet Letters' lacks is joy, be it the joy of creation and discovery or the joy of bringing pop and classical listeners together. Alas, those listeners are more likely to be alienated than enlightened by this grim and clinical musical exercise, and that's a shame." Varga's clairvoyance is as impressive as it is uninformed.

The Juliet Letters provokes a host of responses, an artistic achievement in and of itself. It is in turn enlightening, frustrating, moving, boring—all of which is audience-dependent, for assuredly one person's boredom is another person's delight. With regard to the auteur, Letters is a meaningful moment in the unfolding lifework. As an example of Declan McManus's musical restlessness, Letters offers a fine model of his genre dancing and contributes to his ongoing musical education. As an example of Elvis Costello's commercial recklessness, Letters is as bold an entry as any in the Costello songbook and demonstrates his mission to explore uncharted areas. Elvis Costello's passionate singing reaches yet another emotional plane as its intensity continues to overwhelm, complement, or supplant the song's clarity of expression. Finally, The Juliet Letters provided an opportunity for a well-deserved vacation for Citizen Elvis. There are no editorials or commentaries here. Instead, we observe co-authored fragments that are assembled in sometimes beautiful and sometimes haphazard ways. In all cases, it is a turning point for the auteur, as he explained to Musician's Claudia Buonaiuto:

> I no longer feel that I have to worry about cramming all of the things that I'm interested in into one record. But this isn't a calculated thing to show off my versatility. This was just a collaboration that came by being friendly with some people who happened to be musicians from a completely different world. I mean, I don't see it as my "next step." Nothing's my next step. I think a big mistake of critical or journalistic perspective is to see everything as the next step which denies everything that went before. It's not some 12-step plan, "How to cure yourself of rock 'n' roll."

Elvis Costello had no desire to "cure" himself of any musical form; rather, he was motivated by the challenge, the comradeship, and his commission. That commission is directly tied to his creative impulse and its insistence on musical innovation—even if such challenges threaten his commercial viability. Whether the creative charge involves a multiple-band tour, a spin-ning-songbook show, a trek to Music City, or a blast from his musical past, Costello presses onward. His personal artistic determination was probably a professional hell. Record companies were completely unable to get a handle on their wandering minstrel and his "product." Still, Costello was not uncooperative, just restless. It seems as though every time he ventured out into the musical world for an adventurous project, he would suddenly return to his old haunts and create a "product" that his record company could understand and, therefore, market.

To suggest that Elvis Costello planned to follow the musical adventures that were *Spike*, *Mighty Like a Rose*, and *The Juliet Letters* with an "Attractions" album would be more than misleading, it would be downright inaccurate. *Brutal Youth*'s liner notes (and other sources) indicate the evolutionary quali-ties of a project that started under the name *Idiophone* and gradually incor-porated the various members of The Attractions. Drummer Pete Thomas was the only Attraction to appear on *Spike* and *Rose*. Steve Nieve, Nick Lowe, and Bruce Thomas rejoined Costello as certain musical needs arose. Their re-turn both fueled and deflated the sessions that produced what came to be known as *Brutal Youth*. The results—like *Blood and Chocolate*—represent another blast from the past as Elvis Costello and The Attractions recast sounds and themes from days gone by. Producer Mitchell Froom described the project and its objectives to *Billboard*:

> We worked really hard on Elvis' record to make sure that it didn't sound too good. You don't want a big, polished-up record. Who wants that? The music and the mood is much more important. We tried to get the sound we wanted to hear on the spot, live, and leave it unadorned. Basically, if there was any reverb, it was coming from an instrument's amp. We might add tape slap later on. Tchad [Blake] engineered, and he tends to favor a lot of unusual, and some-times cheap, compression and distortion devices that work particularly well with this band. . . . You can get things a little bit clearer, but something gets lost in the translation. That was the determination of this record. We didn't want to defeat ourselves through the process of making sounds clearer and bigger. We just tried to react to the emotions of the music and the noise the musicians were making.

They were successful. *Youth* features the sonic dynamics first heard on *This Year's Model* and revisited on *Blood and Chocolate* (albeit less successfully). Thomas and Thomas provide a classic Attractions rhythm for Nieve's counterpoints in a fashion that supports the emotional impact of Costello's voice. It was, in every respect, a tried-and-true musical formula—just the kind of thing the auteur despises but record companies adore.

Costello's commentary on *Youth*'s songs is plentiful. His release of an-other "interview disc" that features specific songs and observations about their contents demonstrates his perceived need to communicate with his audience (remember, he used the same strategy with *Blood and Chocolate*). Perhaps all the talk about his wordplay and verbosity weighed heavily on an artist who consistently denounced the need to say any more than what is in the song (he typically announced that if he had more to say, he would have written another song). On the interview disc—*Elvis Costello: Words and Music*—the auteur explains the new project's relationship to previous endeavors: "There's no desire to sound like a rehash of the records that we did then. Anything that's reminiscent of it musically is there because I think it's the right music for the song." The extent to which *Brutal Youth* (released in March 1994) revisits the sounds and themes of yesteryear varies from song to song. Produced by Froom and Costello, the album features 15 songs that stroke traditional Costello songwriting topics. We have four Citizen Elvis editorials (the societal complaints "This Is Hell," "20% Amnesia," "Sulky Girl," and "London's Brilliant Parade"), three relational commentaries ("Kinder Murder," "13 Steps Lead Down," and "Pony Street"), two relational struggles ("You Tripped at Every Step" and "Still Too Soon to Know"), two relational attacks ("Just About Glad" and "All the Rage"), two pieces of narrative impressionism ("Rocking Horse Road" and "Favourite Hour"), a relational plea ("Clown Strike"), and an intrapersonal struggle ("My Science Fiction Twin"). The music is rough and edgy.

The writing, for the most part, is straightforward and clear. Once one ascertains the song's context, the interpretation flows naturally (well . . .). In the absence of that understanding, however, difficulties emerge. For example, the interview disc and media articles clear up the modest chaos in "Rocking Horse" and "Favourite Hour." While both tracks feature Costello's impressionism, their focus is particularly cloudy. In "Hour" the narrator appears to dread an execution as scenes and descriptions that suggest a hanging float in and out of the song. While the liner notes concur with that observation, Costello told Bill Flanagan that the song also embraces his views about college and the life he could have had there. "Rocking Horse" traces the sights and sounds of a long walk down a road bearing that name in Christchurch, New Zealand. The songs are void of homonymic puns or other forms of wordplay that characterize Costello's impressionism; they just avoid any sense of context and, therefore, are evasive. We have, then, shades of *The Juliet Letters* in that in the absence of context, understanding may be limited and interpretation misguided. Nevertheless, this is Costello's songwriting strategy. As he explained to *Vogue*, several of *Youth*'s songs are "little snapshots" of broader events that require some effort by listeners to fill in: "There's a lot left to the imagination. You put a lot of detail in, but you don't want to tell everybody absolutely *everything*."

Citizen Elvis's editorials do not share that trait. "This Is Hell" takes us back to "Clubland" and the vacuous qualities of club life. After announcing the hellish aspects of our location, the song describes cheap clubs with burned-out signs, cheap pickup scenes, cheap clothes, and cheesy music (a clear reiteration of "Pump It Up"). After pausing for scenes of pleasurable fantasy, the song returns to hell, its lost ambitions, and brain-dead occupants. Not only is this a seasoned description of club life, but Costello claims it invokes his idea of "hell," as he explains on the interview disc: "I believe that the repetitive nature of damnation—if such a thing exists—is the boredom of it and the mediocrity of it would be the really horrifying aspect, not these Gothic images of flames and pitchforks." "Sulky Girl" integrates "This Year's Girl" into the "Clubland" scenario with its profile of the enterprising girl, how she's used and abused, and how she endures the ever-present hunt, and closes with a denunciation of her style. The song rotates between sympathy and condemnation as it concludes that our "sulky girl" may, in fact, get what she deserves. Citizen Elvis's commentary expands to broader societal issues via "Amnesia" and "Parade," in which he rails against English society and the mindless populace it fosters. Both songs feature unique twists: "Amnesia" urges perseverance (reminding us that free will exists) and "Parade" rejects suicide as an option. Nevertheless, scenes of losers-in-action dominate these songs that use those activities as symptoms of systemic deterioration.

The tone lightens with the intrapersonal struggle "My Science Fiction Twin" and its tongue-in-check portrayal of the character's alter ego. Here Costello uses autobiographical tidbits to tease us as he presents scenes of strategic marriages, vocational abuses, conceited people, and extremely tall women. He explains the song on *Words and Music*: "It's the lighter look at the delusions that you have about yourself and the way people want to put a hat on you that says something or other, whatever it is if you do music. . . . I wanted to write . . . about the part of you that can juggle while playing the piano and the part of you that can't do anything . . . can't even go to the launderette. And that's really what it's really about: an imaginary character that I can blame it all on."

Costello's emotions run the gamut in the relational portrayals that dominate *Brutal Youth*. In "Clown Strike" he issues a relational plea for simplicity as his character urges his partner to back off all the gamesmanship and sexual gymnastics and just relax (he claims the title came from a newspaper story about an actual clown strike). The relational commentaries and attacks take us back to Citizen Elvis's youth and his biting, snarling observations about relational abuses and disintegration. Whereas "Pony Street" explores a mother-daughter relationship in a playful but slightly critical manner, the commentaries in "Kinder Murder" and "13 Steps" offer darker accounts regarding the sexual beatings "This Year's Girl" consistently endures. The sexual games that violently kill romance constitute a "kinder" form of emotional execution and the victimization that accompanies the "woman-as-object" worldview are the subjects of yet another round of Citizen Elvis editorials. Costello's empathy—with its corresponding disgust—is compelling in these accounts of relational use and abuse. And yet, there is no sign of empathy in the two relational attacks in which characters show their contempt for former partners. In "Just About Glad" the narrator expresses his pleasure over an affair that failed to materialize; taunting the woman and hoping to inflict pain (he could also be rationalizing his failure). In "All the Rage" the narrator bids farewell to a woman he characterizes as a simple-minded, vindictive bitch. These songs are mean-spirited but impressive. Costello's capacity to identify with different emotional states and life conditions demonstrates his songwriting talent in a compelling fashion.

That compassion manifests itself in the relational struggles as well. In "You Tripped" and "Still Too Soon" Costello explores the fight to keep love alive. In the former, he reviews the varied pitfalls of relational life; in the latter, he laments the loss of one's love to another man. In both cases, hope abounds as the narrator in "Tripped" expresses his willingness to work on the relationship, and the central character in "Still Too Soon" exercises patience. "Still Too Soon" features a vocal and instrumental style reminiscent of Cait O'Riordan's "Broken" from *Mighty Like a Rose*. Love is daunting but essential. Such songs indicate that Elvis Costello's compassion is as ferocious as his anger. When he discussed the songs' emotional qualities on *Words and Music* he concluded: "The young people don't have the copyright on rebellion."

The critics either hailed *Brutal Youth*'s back-to-basics approach or derided its songwriting. *Stereo Review* claims the record "refines and clarifies" Costello's art "by focusing sharply on what he does best—boring through the thicket of human interactions with lacerating wit and a musical attack to match . . . time hasn't mellowed Costello and the Attractions—it's made them much more muscular and knowing. . . . This Elvis, I'm pleased to note, has not left the building." The *San Francisco Examiner* concurs and reports that the album "achieves a perfect union between youthful brutality and mature insight." *Esquire* notes that the project "is awash with the old corrosives, or at least an approximation of that classic bile." The *New York Times* assumes a developmental stance by observing that *Youth* "is very much the shrewd creation of a pop pro pushing 40" and that Costello "is also no longer so youthful and self-absorbed," in that his "new goal is to achieve a paradox: exhilarating songs about the misery of others." The lyrics, however, continue to be a source of consternation for many critics. In that vein, *Rolling Stone* contends: "*Brutal Youth* is yet another avalanche of wordplay and woodshedding, of lyrics rushing into each other and instruments vying for musical space . . . [the album] sounds like he's raiding his own catalog." The *Boston Herald* offers a mixed take on the project by praising the band ("Costello and the Attractions are virtuosos of vitality") and damning the writing: "His words, oozing theatrical flair, sound great as they whiz by. But what do they mean? Even if you read the lyrics while you listen, you're seldom sure of what El's going on about. He's too clever for his own— and our—good." Clearly, Costello's "snapshots" are not for everyone.

In 2001, Bob Dylan described his new album—*Love and Theft*—as a "greatest hits" album without the greatest hits. That is, the record features the sounds and textures of American song's "greatest hits" without actually containing a series of accomplished songs. *Brutal Youth* follows a similar logic. The album features classic Attractions sounds with traditional Citizen Elvis lyrics. The societal commentaries, the relational attacks, and the relational commentaries have evolved from his earlier thematic preoccupations to complement his new—perhaps more palatable—approach to impressionism to revise and extend previous songwriting trends. Moreover, *Brutal Youth*—like *Blood and Chocolate*—strives for a sonic edge that once flowed so naturally. Producers such as Mitchell Froom now actively work to cultivate a sound that years ago could not be avoided. That strain joined various personality conflicts to ensure that this reunion would be short-lived. Nevertheless, *Brutal Youth* is a revealing sampler of a specific sound and thematic orientation, and as such, it is a "greatest hits" production of sorts.

The *Kojak Variety* project was, no doubt, a wonderful relief for an artist committed to pushing the musical envelope whenever possible. With Declan McManus's encyclopedic knowledge of music providing one of the pillars upon which Elvis Costello's art rests, an opportunity to assemble some of his "favourite musicians" (according to *Kojak*'s liner notes) to record a series of his "favourite songs" must have been nothing less than a labor of love. Interestingly, the album was released in May 1995, close to five years after it was recorded in Barbados (the album's title reflects the name of a department store near the studio). With Kevin Killen and Costello at the helm, James Burton (guitar), Jim Keltner (drums), Larry Knechtel (keyboards), Marc Ribot (guitar), Jerry Scheff (bass), and Pete Thomas (drums) recorded the album in two weeks. Costello was so pleased with the results that his liner notes label the work "Volume One"—a clear indicator of his intent to repeat the process.

Kojak contains 15 tracks: "Strange" (by Screamin' Jay Hawkins), "Hidden Charms" (Willie Dixon), "Remove This Doubt" (Holland/Dozier/Holland), "I Threw It All Away" (Bob Dylan), "Leave My Kitten Alone" (Little Willie John/Titus Turner), "Everybody's Crying Mercy" (Mose Allison), "I've Been Wrong Before" (Randy Newman), "Bama Lama Bama Loo" (Little Richard), "Must You Throw Dirt in My Face" (Bill Anderson), "Pouring Water on a Drowning Man" (D. Baker/D. McCormick), "The Very Thought of You" (Ray Noble), "Payday" (Jesse Winchester), "Please Stay" (Burt Bacharach/Hal David), "Running Out of Fools" (K. Rogers/R. Ahlert), and "Days" (Ray Davies). Since the project contains no original material, it is essentially outside this study's purview except as evidence of the auteur's creative state of mind and commercial attitude. To those ends, *Kojak* appears to be a positive moment in the songwriter's lifework—regardless of its commercial sales.

Kojak also offers powerful evidence of Elvis Costello's stature as a torch singer. His vocal method embellishes the pain and urgency of these melodramatic romantic portrayals in a unique manner. His sound is like no other. His intensity is unparalleled. Whether he sings his own compositions or those of other writers, Costello brings an emotional dimension to his presentation that is true to his musical origins. The auteur is, without question, the musical world's original punk torch singer.

If a musical career extends beyond six months in duration, there will, without question, be moments of creative, commercial, or personal uncertainty. The ever-present "minstrel's dilemma" may rear its potentially ugly head when artists least expect it—forcing decisions that may involve complicated negotiations and, occasionally, serious compromises. The artistic choice between following a creative inspiration and satisfying an industry, band, management, or audience expectation is, oftentimes, heart-wrenching and, many times, debilitating. Few artists have fought the fight as diligently, as furiously, as Declan McManus. From his name change to his initial image and its marketing, to his genre dancing, to his concerts' formats, to his selection of musical colleagues and elsewhere, the auteur has negotiated his artistic direction through the punk attitude that inspires and sustains his art. For many, this is an admirable trait; for many others, it is an anticommercial nightmare. *All This Useless Beauty* (released in March 1996) features as its final track a song titled "I Want to Vanish." That Costello publicly acknowledged the song's autobiographical qualities indicates his stance regarding his version of the minstrel's dilemma at this particular point in time.

The liner notes for *Beauty* explain the situation in detail. Costello originally planned for a double album, *A Case for Song*, that would represent "a songwriter's compendium, using any ensemble that the music dictated." With Warner Brothers—and the entire music industry—in a state of flux, the auteur's "flawless business acumen" (his words) inspired a project that proved to be rather difficult for his label to accept. Costello reports that he was inspired by his participation in the eclectic 1995 Meltdown Festival— a nine-day musical event that he directed. After performing with rock, jazz, classical, folk, and other diverse artists, Costello proposed an expensive, detailed project that would feature songs he had composed for other singers (e.g., Johnny Cash, Roger McGuinn, June Tabor), written with other writers (e.g., Paul McCartney, Aimee Mann), and new material. Warner Brothers' response to its artist's proposal may be found in the fact that the album never appeared (although a video by that name was issued) and Costello's telling admission, "Any further credit for the fact that this album was ever finished must go to Geoff Emerick and Jon Jacobs [producer and engineer, respectively], who focused the sound on all the strengths and flattered the weaknesses in the playing." Costello's liner notes continue:

> This record exists in the distance between an ideal and the reality. I've read
> that it is simply a collection of songs that I wrote for other singers—usually
> with the implication that this was a bad or inferior thing. True, I had the voice
> of certain singers in mind when many of these songs were composed. How-
> ever, compared to the original blueprint, the final album contains only four
> previously recorded songs. If it was in any way an exercise, then it was one
> in creeping up on yourself in order to trick out a song that would have other-
> wise remained elusive. It was the idealized version of a performer that caused
> me to compose. . . . The title *All this useless beauty* was used in sarcastic
> acknowledgement of the likely fate of the record. I was not being entirely se-
> rious. Amelia Stein's cover photo is of a lovely but tarnished mannequin. I
> recently heard that it had perished in a house fire. I cannot say that I found
> this news very surprising.

Notice how the minstrel's dilemma permeates these remarks: the compromises that shaped the record's final form, the internal negotiations that
enabled the auteur to "trick out" the songs, the sarcastic resignation that
acquiescence inspired. This is the commercial world of popular music from
which the auteur wished to "vanish." Little wonder why.

All This Useless Beauty contains 12 tracks that, from our narrative
interpretation's standpoint, are not as eclectic as the original project proposed. There is, however, a significant innovation among the auteur's traditional songwriting strategies. Along with *Beauty*'s two relational complaints
("The Other End [of the Telescope]" [written with Aimee Mann] and "You
Bowed Down"), a relational commentary ("All This Useless Beauty"), a relational attack ("It's Time"), two personal confessionals ("Distorted Angel"
and "I Want to Vanish"), and three installments of narrative impressionism
("Little Atoms," "Poor Fractured Atlas," and "Starting to Come to Me") is a
new tactic, the sermon. Here Citizen-turned-Reverend Elvis either prescribes
remedies for specific situations ("Complicated Shadows") or embellishes
certain conditions of significance ("Why Can't a Man Stand Alone" and
"Shallow Graves"). In these messages, Citizen Elvis transcends his normal
commentary with moral overtones that venture into the realm of sermonic
lessons. For example, in "Complicated Shadows" (written for Johnny Cash)
our narrator preaches against a perceived sense of invincibility on the part
of a congregation that consists of a bunch of violent gunslinger types who
had better put away their guns, lest they wind up on the wrong end of a
rope. The account is totally prescriptive. The other sermons focus more on
description than prescription. "Why Can't a Man" uses a churchy organ
sound to posit a series of rhetorical questions about individual strength,
personal integrity, relational dishonesty, and personal safety. While listening, you virtually expect him to announce that "faith is the answer," but
that prescription fails to materialize. Instead, the narrator raises the questions and leaves us to contemplate their significance. (In the liner notes
Costello says that this song, as well as "Atlas" and "Useless Beauty," are

"about vanity and the deluded manners of men.") Last, "Shallow Graves" (written with Paul McCartney) invokes a standard sermon about death and final resting places. The difference between these sermons and Citizen Elvis's editorials is merely a matter of degree; nonetheless, the songs do signal a trend toward more prescriptive commentary.

Contributing to the cause are the three pieces of impressionism and the two personal confessionals. In "Starting to Come to Me" one gains a feeling that Costello is having a go at someone or something, but the song shifts gears so quickly that the imagery breezes by. This snapshot requires so much to fill in the details that its interpretation must be restrained for fear of imposition. "Little Atoms" and "Poor Fractured Atlas" appear to form a two-part testimonial that takes us back to *The Juliet Letters'* songwriting style ("Atlas" refers to itself as a letter). The songs' lack of context and shifting pronouns render enigmatic accounts in which clever lines work in isolation to relate the impression of somebody reflecting on something. The songs are anything but superficial; we just do not know their context. This trait holds true for the first of the two confessionals as well. "Distorted Angel" is a haunting, mysterious song. In his liner notes, Costello reports it contains "lighter humour" through its portrayal of an eight-year-old's discovery of "Catholic guilt" at his birthday party. Well, the lyrics seem to me to involve a totally different scenario. I read the lyrics as describing a confession by a child who has been molested (oh, my!). Things happened behind closed doors while the "distorted" angels looked on, inspiring a sense of guilt—and, therefore, repentance—even though the child fails to understand what has transpired. The first verse holds the key to such an interpretation. "I Want to Vanish" contains no such mystery. The song (featuring the Brodsky Quartet) is direct in its confession and seems to represent the resolution of *Might Like a Rose*'s "Couldn't Call It Unexpected, No. 4," in that it was his job to report the truth—as awful as it might be—and now that he has done it, he is finished. So please, leave him alone. It is a powerful piece of autobiography.

Beauty's remaining tracks deploy traditional Costello songwriting strategies. The attack in "It's Time" features our angry older man and his declaration that it is time to move on. Our narrator is ready to dismiss his current interest and search for somebody else to hate (Costello says this is the follow-up to "Tramp the Dirt Down," even though there's no sign of Thatcher in the song). "The Other End" is a quintessential Costello relational complaint (maybe he was too hard-hearted, maybe she overthought everything, maybe they failed to ask the right questions—regardless, it is over), and "You Bowed Down" (written for McGuinn) takes the relational complaint to either a professional or a political context (it seems) as the narrator lambastes the song's target for his or her betrayal. Somebody, somewhere sold the narrator out, and he or she is darned angry about it. Finally, the album's title cut (our first; written for June Tabor) offers a reflective commentary on loving relationships without much praise or blame. The woman is individualistic and, seemingly, capable of dealing with the less-than-ideal man in her life. Costello's comments about how the song portrays the "deluded manners of men" is in clear evidence as he presents how the woman copes with the reality of her situation. The music-lyric interplay reinforces the song's reflective tone.

Virtually all critiques of *Beauty* offer state-of-the-artist assessments that place this work in the context of previous entries. For instance, *Musician* traces the auteur's career and concludes: "*All This Useless Beauty* sounds like the sort of great pop music Elvis Costello was supposed to be making, if, I don't know, he'd only been paying attention or something. Now he is—and we should be, too" ("*supposed to be making*"???). The *Dallas Morning News* states that the album "is an often-stunning work filled with the same spit and spark he showed in the late '70s." *Stereo Review* claims *Beauty* "is spotty but sporadically brilliant," and closes: "It's telling that the best moments all come when the former Declan McManus breaks out of the album's cocktail-lounge ambience." *Melody Maker* uses the album's title as its starting point for analysis: "It's not useless, just awkward—awkward with the dignity of the auteur, awkward with a beauty that yearns for a jaded nod of recognition."

Since my mission involves more than a critique of one album, I, too, must pause to examine recent trends in the oeuvre. Although *Kojak* was recorded long before its release, the "cocktail-lounge ambience" that envelops the ballads on *Beauty* complements *Kojak*'s torch sounds as well as the artist's penchant for singing country love songs and Bacharach/David–style pop standards in a manner that suggests the wave of his songwriting future. That he had composed and recorded the song "God Give Me Strength" with Burt Bacharach just prior to the *Beauty* sessions indicates a prolonged interest that may rescue the auteur from his desire for escape. Ever the punk, Costello has the capacity to aggressively advance his trademark "punishing observation" (in Jim Farber's words) that requires a musical flexibility that was severely restricted by his relationship with The Attractions and their history. For Citizen Elvis's pen to function at optimal levels, Declan McManus's musical restlessness has to be massaged—even if it requires the kind of commercial recklessness that Elvis Costello relishes. It is, quite simply, a law of nature that cannot be denied.

Declan McManus's personal history with Burt Bacharach goes back quite a way. Sarah Vowell reports that their paths first crossed in 1963 when McManus's father performed at the legendary Royal Command Performance featuring The Beatles, Marlene Dietrich, and the Joe Loss Orchestra. As young Declan watched his father sing before the Royal Family and London's elite, he also observed two future collaborators in action: The Beatles' bass player (Paul McCartney) and Marlene Dietrich's musical director (Burt Bacharach). The youngster made sure his father obtained the Fab Four's autographs while, unfortunately, he ignored the other participants. It must have been a grand moment in the young man's life.

As an adult, Elvis Costello performed Bacharach/David tunes from the very outset. For example, the 1978 *Stiffs Live* recording features Costello and The Attractions doing "I Don't Know What to Do with Myself." The first Bacharach/Costello collaboration involved the song "God Give Me Strength," written for the 1996 movie *Grace of My Heart*. Costello told *Musician* that the song was "done by fax machine and telephone" because of a "production deadline" that gave the duo "five days" to write the track. He noted that "having written a song that seems that strong, and having made a record of it, I thought it was fantastic." That success motivated the two musicians to pursue other opportunities. Costello described the situation to *Billboard*: "We wrote ["God Give Me"] over the phone, which is an extraordinary way to begin a collaboration. But we enjoyed recording it so much that I asked Burt if we might get together in the same room sometime." There Bacharach agreed that the initial work "was a very interesting process," but the two men did not connect until they recorded the song: "Working with new writers is like a blind date: You think it will be OK, and then afterward you don't want to go out with them anymore. But it went positive for both of us, and we felt that whether or not it was successful, we should try it again."

From that starting point, a dynamic, fluid collaborative process emerged. Costello explained the procedure to *Musician*: "The formula is different for every song. Two or three songs, I think, are entirely Burt's music. There are some where the larger part of the initial musical information came from me, but then we'd work on it together. And there's quite a good proportion where it was more or less a dialog in music, section by section, with the process of making it work in a flow coming from sitting at the keyboards together." Bacharach joined in, "That is very different for me," and Costello concurred, "totally different from anything I've done." Costello added that the songs "all stopped having that sense of who wrote them because we worked on them together so much," and that his original lyrics endured quite a bit of editing as the process unfolded: "We had songs like this—one was nearly seven minutes long in its original form—that obviously weren't going to work, so there was some serious editing going on in that last week." Costello also told *Newsweek* that the collaborative process was controlled by Bacharach's perfectionism: "He's very precise. . . . Sometimes I tried to steal a couple of notes—you know, 'I've got this great line that would fit if you'd just give me another semiquaver!' But in the end I'd find a different way to say the same thing. It was good discipline."

A major part of that discipline involved adjustments to Costello's traditional mode of expression, as he related to the *New Yorker*: "This idea of keeping the words simple was quite frightening to me. I'm used to hiding behind mannerisms and gestures and rhyme schemes." He elaborated for *Musician*:

On most of these songs, the words are simple enough to keep them compre-
hensible and serve the music clearly, and at the same time still individual
enough to me that people could recognize some of my personality. There aren't
any trick phrases or backflips in the words. There are some individual turns
of phrase, which come from my listening to what the music was telling
me. . . . Ultimately all the songs on this record, however sad they may be, are
about the necessity of feeling something, and the music is about trying to have
those feelings. To be alive means to have feelings, sometimes pain. You can't
have life without pain. . . . Really, our intent was to write eleven songs as good
as but different from "God Give Me Strength." I think we achieved that.

As these remarks indicate, the Bacharach/Costello writing team was firmly
committed to a compositional strategy from the Golden Age of songwriting.
Costello conveyed that objective to *Billboard*: "The grand, dramatic pop
ballad is such an endangered species these days, at least in terms of
sincerity. . . . All these songs and their singers are so hollow. But I feel
strongly that there's still a place for real feeling in the pop ballad. Let's just
say that Burt and I are here to kick Celine Dion's ass."

While the language and style of Costello's writing on *Painted* represent
a marked departure from previous efforts, the songs' emotional intensity
reflects the punk attitude that supports the oeuvre. The aggression may
wane a bit, but the melodrama is rich, moving, and, at times, downright
overwhelming. Images of people sitting by the telephone, praying for it to
ring; walking down streets, observing lovers while pining for lost love; sitting in the dark, alone, desperately trying to gather the strength to survive
another day; and—in that ever-present punk attitude—attempting to muster the resources to exact revenge on a departed lover (but usually unable
to do so) dominate these songs through grand, flowing Bacharach orchestrations that heighten the songs' melodramatic impact. *Painted from Memory*
is a temple to the torch tradition through a writing style that deploys clear,
direct language presented through straightforward narrative structures that
use heavy repetition to drive home their points. This is not *The Juliet Letters*
or even *King of America*, in that the songs openly sacrifice mystery for emotional depth.

The 1998 release (produced by Bacharach/Costello, engineered by Kevin
Killen) contains 12 tracks that use seven narrative strategies. Though the
storytelling tactics vary, emotional depth is achieved through musical and
lyrical continuity. We have five romantic elegies ("This House Is Empty
Now," "Tears at the Birthday Party," "My Thief," "The Long Division," and
"Painted from Memory"), two confessions ("Toledo" and "I Still Have That
Other Girl"), a relational plea ("In the Darkest Place"), a divine plea ("God
Give Me Strength"), a song of relational revenge ("What's Her Name Today?"), a relational celebration ("Such Unlikely Lovers"), and a wonderful
example of relational pugilism ("The Sweetest Punch"). With so much de-

spair roaming through the various songs, the celebration and comedy are a welcome relief. "The Sweetest Punch" chronicles an argument between a married couple in which she tosses her ring off and nails him with a sucker punch (this could involve more metaphor than violence). Clever lines relate how the surprise blow sends the room spinning and stars shining before he decides she should go ahead and leave. Not to endorse domestic violence in any way, but the song is humorous in its portrayal of the pugilistic metaphor resolution to the marital dispute. Our other bright spot is more conventional. "Such Unlikely Lovers" is a sweet tune with a Broadway feel that celebrates the narrator's utter disbelief over his good fortune. Two opposites have bonded, and love is in the house. The narrator's newfound optimism is evident when he announces that everyone has a chance at love, often when you least expect it.

Our other entries explore different emotions. Certainly, the elegies are the album's centerpiece. "This House Is Empty Now" uses the once-happy-now-empty house as a symbol of a once-happy-now-dead relationship which leaves the narrator and his home physically and emotionally vacant. "Tears at the Birthday Party" uses birthday and anniversary celebrations to tell the tale of one extremely miserable loser at love: He lost, and he is sure that her new lover will fail her; nevertheless, all he can do is watch the years go by in regretful remorse. "My Thief" is a heart-wrenching but imaginative account of a man who lost at love but finds comfort in his dreams, where the former lover dwells (the song ends with an interesting twist, in that her voice appears, comforts our dreamer, and states her case). "The Long Division" is a sad story about a man who knows his lover is cheating while he waits for the other shoe to drop, and wonders if friendship is still possible, and "Painted from Memory" depicts a man who worships a photograph of his lost love (he had better rid himself of that picture, or it'll surely be his undoing). The songs are direct, highly repetitive, and extremely melodramatic.

Other narrative strategies appear as well. The relational plea, "In the Darkest Place," is an unbridled appeal for a reunion and a chance to start over—otherwise, nothing is left but darkness. The divine plea, "God Give Me Strength," is self-explanatory as the narrator requests Divine Intervention in his efforts to cope with lost love. While this character would enjoy seeing the other man suffer, he can barely muster the energy to get through his day—he is more than desperate. The confessions, "Toledo" and "I Still Have That Other Girl," admit an affair and an inability to dismiss a former lover, respectively. Our narrator in "Toledo" realizes that he is certainly doomed by his own actions and that forgiveness is unlikely; in "Other Girl," honesty abounds through strength of emotion—the narrator would rather lose his current flame than cheat on his mental relationship with another woman. Shades of young Elvis appear via "What's Her Name Today?", a diabolical tale of mean-spirited revenge. The culprit, it appears, is talking to himself as he discusses the prey of the day and his undying commitment to exacting revenge on innocents. He was burned by a former lover, and he will not be satisfied until he destroys every woman he encounters. Most of *Painted*'s characters are simply unable to muster the strength necessary for such an evil response.

Whether or not Bacharach/Costello "kicked Celine Dion's ass," they certainly created a meaningful contribution to the torch song tradition. The intensely melodramatic accounts of love lost and its aftermath stand tall within the musical world's torch genre. Critics, of course, both agreed and disagreed. All reviews discuss the lush Bacharach orchestrations and their relationship to Costello's singing; some praise the combination, others damn it. Yet, more often than not, the commentary follows *Pulse!* and its view that the collaboration "is a match made in heaven." *Entertainment Weekly* praises the shift in Costello's writing: "He's dumped the tangled, often snide metaphors for the most straightforward set of romantic-heartbreak sentiments he's ever penned." *Rolling Stone* opines that "thanks to Bacharach, Costello's bile has never sounded so sweet," and *Spin* describes the songs in this fashion: "Magnificent bummers such as these transcend khaki ads, transporting listeners into deep worlds of hurt where manly regret over having really, really screwed up is transformed into anguish and, with any luck, action."

That *Painted from Memory* is a crucial addition to the auteur's oeuvre is beyond question. Citizen Elvis's pen achieved new levels of refinement, Declan McManus's musical restlessness explored family tradition, and Elvis Costello's voice and commercial risk-taking pushed through new barriers. All of which operated in a familiar musical context: the love song. Costello's love songs feature a host of emotions as that punk attitude guides his pen, voice, and mode of articulation. His dedication to the love song is complete, as he related to the *San Francisco Chronicle*. When asked if he will ever stop writing love songs, the auteur replied:

> I don't think I can. Love and desire are the reason we're all here. How do you exhaust that as a topic? With these songs we made a decision to look at it, not in a detached way but with cumulative experience to synthesize everything that has happened into something other people can recognize. I want people to see themselves in the picture rather than only me. I'm sure people will. People will recognize these characters. They are universal. There are patterns of behavior, and how we look at them changes, and that's what makes love a never-ending source of inspiration.

Whether expressed through an epistolary chamber music, roots music, new wave/punk, rock, country, or pop standard mode, Elvis Costello's version of the love song assumes a torch point of view. The ever-present punk worldview and its melodramatic imperative fuel a relentlessly aggressive exploration of loving relations and their perils. His response may feature anger, remorse, "revenge and guilt," acquiescence, or a host of other emotions, but it is always aggressively melodramatic.

Anyone who ever writes about anything risks the chance of embarrassment. Something that seems totally innocuous at a given moment may come back as a glaring mistake, a profound over- or understatement, or an undermining false assumption. David Sheppard must know this feeling. When he closes his book on Elvis Costello with a chapter entitled, "The Legacy," he concludes with statements of admiration regarding his subject's eclecticism. Nevertheless, those musical ambitions have limits:

> So while his protean calling is admirable and rare, the parameters within which his muse is played out increasingly date him. However much he attempts to stab forward, he is always restrained by the tendrils of pop classicism with which his enthusiasms have so long been entwined. One Tricky remix and the drum machine dalliance of 'Pills And Soap' aside, Costello has never had much truck with the nominally dance-music-derived underground which is really the last remaining engine of stylistic change in contemporary popular music. Ultimately, perhaps, Costello has more in common with his father's generation than with his son's.

I guess it is safe to say the *When I Was Cruel/Cruel Smile* project must have surprised Sheppard.

As we noted in the biography section, after completing the 200-page score for his orchestral piece, *Il Sogno*, Costello wanted to stretch himself in a different—more rhythmic—direction. He explained his ambitions to Stacy Shapiro of VH1: "I didn't want to make something that I had already made before. . . . I messed around with gadgets I could program with these crazy beats no drummer would ever play, and it got me moving a different way with the electric guitar." The project's foundation invokes the auteur's artistic philosophy in that he wanted the individual *songs* to be the project's musical currency, as he told the *Guardian*: "Songs are important to us, most of us, anyway. . . . They act as signposts, date stamps to our life." With that as his creative signpost, our punk composer frolicked in his technologically driven musical sandbox: "I had a toy drum machine and I played over it with an electric guitar. A drum machine is a great way of getting to the start of something new: you can program it to play in a completely unnatural way, like setting up a big band drum kit and making it play an Egyptian rhythm. You could never ask a real drummer to do that—you would just confuse them." To achieve his ends, he did exactly what Sheppard claims he is incapable of doing. Costello told Alan DiPerma, "Obviously, I'm borrowing techniques that are very familiar to people who make dance records. But they're brand new to me. . . . Also, it was great to be working with younger engineers who don't have a set idea as to who or what I should be. I certainly have no such idea." He elaborated for the *Boston Globe*:

I assembled this team of engineers and producers in Dublin who could work at the speed I like to work at in the studio, but with command of some of the possibilities that the studio has now to bend things and shape the sound more. There's some great live playing from the band, but it's informed by the fact that I set out with a definite idea for the rhythm in most cases, and much of the rhythm was something I had predetermined with some of my little beat boxes at home.

At the heart of the process was his guitar, as he explained—appropriately enough—to Christopher Scapelliti and *Guitar World*: "I see this album as kind of a return to the guitar. This time I felt as if we'd got something fresh on the instrument. The guitar was all new to me again, and the fact that I put it back central to the compositional structure of the songs is something I'm really proud of." After his record company's internal reorganization settled, Costello delivered the project to, of all labels, the hip-hop, dance label Def Jam—a development he relished: "For me it's like being Rare Earth on Motown." The final results pleased our punk composer and—for him—fell neatly into his musical history, as he described to *Time Out*:

It certainly feels like a bolder step. . . . And it came out sounding exactly as I hoped it would. There's no one album of mine that it sounds like, but there is a sort of thread that stems from "Watching The Detectives" and runs through "Chelsea," "New Lace Sleeves," "Pills and Soap," "Clubland," "My Dark Life" and "In The Darkest Place" from the Burt record. They all have the potential to be in this particular bag. They're more rhythmic, swinging, rooted in bass, and not so heavily dominated by harmony. It's darker-hued music. You wouldn't want to stay there the whole time, but I definitely have that bag, and this is the epiphany of it.

Released in April 2002, *When I Was Cruel* (produced by "the imposter"—Elvis Costello, Ciaran Cahill, Leo Pearson, and Kieran Lynch) contains 15 tracks that massage recurrent themes through an innovative sonic strategy. Dedicated to "Cait of the Antarctic," the record represents the pinnacle of punk through its aggressive, melodramatic portrayals that are in turn sermonic, philosophical, celebratory, vituperative, and incomprehensible. The project features eight examples of Costello's famed narrative impressionism that *seem to* embrace a host of topics: "45" (historical), "Tear Off Your Own Head (It's a Doll Revolution)" (relational), "When I Was Cruel No. 2" (marital/societal), "Tart" (relational), "Dissolve" (societal), "Dust 2 . . ." (societal), ". . . Dust" (societal), and "Episode of Blonde" (cosmetology). Joining these narrative follies are an example of the auteur's wordplay ("Daddy Can I Turn This?") and two Citizen Elvis editorials ("Soul for Hire" and "Radio Silence"), a classic Costello personal attack ("Alibi"), a relational plea ("My Little Blue Window"), a relational celebration ("15 Petals"), and the marvelous relational fantasy "Spooky Girlfriend."

There is no question that this project's most striking feature is its sonic impressionism. The sounds demonstrate the cumulative impact of working with Nick Lowe, Billy Sherrill, Langer and Winstanley, T-Bone Burnett, the Brodskys, Burt Bacharach, and The Computer. From the simple "Spooky Girlfriend" groove to the wall of sound that is "Tear Off Your Own Head" to the horns of "15 Petals," ". . . Dust," and "Episode of Blonde" to the guitar work in "Dust 2 . . ." (really, throughout the album) to the subtle harmonica on "Dissolve" to the slight samples from ABBA and Mina, "the imposters" place layer upon layer of live instrumental, voice, and computer-enhanced sounds as required by the *song*. Yet, the Citizen Elvis editorials and attacks deploy sounds quite different from their impressionistic counterparts. For instance, the fierce vitriol of "Alibi" makes sonic room for the verbal assault, whereas the abstract tirades of "Episode of Blonde" roam among other, equally enigmatic, aural happenings. Weird beats, crazed voices, and exotic instrumentals accompany weird metaphors, crazed phrases, and exotic sentiments in ratios that are determined by the *song's* requirements.

With so much happening, one is not surprised that this is the most impressionistic work in the Costello canon to date. The album's nine installments of narrative impressionism and wordplay eclipse *Armed Forces'* and *Punch the Clock's* previous records of seven each. The impressionistic barrage begins with "45" and its rocking historical account that contains lyrics that hint at autobiography through a series of "snapshots" about World War II, youth and music, the music itself, personal frustration, and aging. The song changes topics, it seems, with each beat, leaving many subjects raised and none resolved. The cryptic but systematic imagery in the "Tear Off Your Own Head" sonic bombast describes how people dress up, contort, and generally twist their lovers into dolls that satisfy personal agendas (that Costello reports the song is [a] a reaction to self-help books and [b] a treatment for a television series about Russian models milking the entertainment industry doesn't help at all!). The track "When I Was Cruel No. 2" is a standard piece of narrative impressionism. Here a wedding provides a storytelling context for various forms of snobbery as characters utter snide remarks about the bride and groom, feign different stances, and comment on former wives and acquaintances in a mean-spirited fashion. Still, the song never achieves story status; it—like "45"—deploys Costello's "snapshot" songwriting strategy in which the various fragments ("fractions") are held together by some scenario (the wedding scene "common denominator")—nothing ever happens, just more and more insults. "Tart" uses fruit metaphors to communicate the bittersweet qualities of relationships; "Dissolve" employs a sonic sense of urgency to paint a picture of worldly decline that ranges from personal to global issues (each line contains its own point only to fade into the next line and its idiosyncrasies); the Dust Chronicles ("Dust 2 . . ." and ". . . Dust") use various forms of dustspeak to portray a host of societal abuses (culminating in the "Dust 2" attack on religion), and "Episode of Blonde" is a Dylanesque paean to attention deficit disorder presented in the form of a jazzy, bossa nova rap. The images come in droves. Last, the unbridled wordplay in "Daddy" features words that occasionally rhyme while consistently saying nothing—it does, however, shake the walls.

Not all of these songs use crazy beats to frame enigmatic wordplay. Citizen Elvis's editorials against the legal system ("Soul for Hire") and talk radio ("Radio Silence") drive home their points in a clear, rhythmic fashion. Furthermore, the relational plea ("My Little Blue Window") may be idiosyncratic, but its recurring imagery suggests a person trapped by his or her own devices and seeking some form of relational intervention. Less clear, but relatively coherent, are the "15 Petals" celebration of love (Costello reports the song is for his wife—there do appear to be personal references in the lyrics) and the "Spooky" fantasy (a truly funny song). The emotions bounce around yet somehow run deep in these songs. This emotional commentary peaks in the quintessential Costello composition, "Alibi." The song is a laundry list of personal excuses that provide the narrator's partner the justification for any conceivable act. The narrator uses these excuses to frame his or her love-hate relationship with a lover who has all the answers. The invective is so rich, the singing so emotional, the attack so stinging that you leave the song absolutely certain that the narrator is madly in love with the song's target. This war of the roses will last a very long time—emotions this deep have a substantial shelf life.

The project's sonic qualities extend to new heights in *Cruel*'s companion piece, *Cruel Smile*. The October 2002 release features live versions of old songs (e.g., "Almost Blue," "Watching the Detectives/My Funny Valentine," and "Uncomplicated"), covers of John Turner/Geoffrey Parson/Charles Chaplin's "Smile," and alternative mixes of songs from *When I Was Cruel*. These alternative accounts must really keep David Sheppard up at night with their chaotic beats, crazed overdubs, and unrelenting energy. Throughout it all, we hear the auteur in his musical sandbox, having the time of his life (he laughs, snickers, and jokes with his audience on several live cuts). I just do not think this is his "father's" music. When the Joe Loss Orchestra covers this, well, count me in!

Critical responses to *When I Was Cruel* hail Costello's "return" to rock. Douglas Wolk claims, "You can't write him off—otherwise he wouldn't be so annoying—but Elvis makes you suffer for the good stuff with leaden conceits, overwrought hysterics, a useless reprise." Yet the review concludes that the album's title cut is "the work of somebody who really did learn a lot from being out in the wilderness making records with opera singers and Burt Bacharach and Tricky." Barry Walters describes the album as "a collection of tough tunes and textures that recalls—but doesn't recycle—the records that endeared him to his earliest admirers." Zac Crain argues the record is "literate and livid, vital and vivid, filled with blood and chocolate, bile and forced smiles." Robert Everett-Green looks back on it all: "He's found the way to San Jose, and strolled down Penny Lane. He's written letters with a string quartet and billets-doux for an opera singer. Elvis Costello has done the rounds as no pop musician of his generation has. Now it's time to return to that damp street where he began, flinging curses at doors shut tight to hold the warmth of hypocrisy."

Everywhere, it seems, critics cite the auteur's "return to form" in their commentaries. So much so, in fact, that Costello responded to the trend in an HMV.com interview: "I don't know what they mean by 'form.'. . . If they mean a return to human form after my life as a mermaid. . . . There's a veiled insult in the remark, and I don't know quite how to take it. There's really no 'form' to return to—you just move on to the next thing and try to enjoy the music you're playing as it occurs to you." But that is not how the musical world works. What was once heralded as a new wave gets ridiculed as it crashes onto uncharted—or unrecognized or unacceptable—beaches. That the auteur brings a signature perspective to diverse fields of action evades critics who focus on *their agendas* (among other things). For some reason, critics fail to notice that "the punk" entered the chamber music room or how "the punk" assumed a seat at the piano bar or that "the punk" joined the DJ in the control booth. Instead, they ignore "the auteur" and his quite consistent behavior in favor of an emphasis on his musical context or perceived personality; and in so doing, not only miss the point but confuse everything—including, unfortunately, the record company and its patrons. No wonder "the punk" changes his name, alters his looks, or, in recent years, subjects himself to countless interviews in an effort to frame his work for the market. Yet, if the auteur did what the musical world appears to want, and recycled his sound time and again, commentators would rail against that as well. It would seem that this is a game artists just cannot win. Welcome, then, to the wonderful world of the minstrel's dilemma. If you cannot win the game, you might as well play it on your own terms.

To be sure, Declan McManus has done just that. He has—rightly or wrongly—maintained the courage of his convictions as he negotiates within the world of commercial music. For his is a wandering muse. His creative instincts flow directly from his family influences and their eclectic, open-minded views of music. With a father who abandoned Bing Crosby for the Grateful Dead and a mother with an informed jazz sensibility, McManus developed in a climate that naturally spawned eclecticism. What I find amazing is that the artist never left *any* of these influences behind. They remain with him, actively inspiring the musical instincts that guide his work: A country lyric may coexist with a hip-hop beat to articulate an operatic "snapshot" of a historic event. It is to his credit that he insists on sustaining these diverse interests. Although his rebellion may cost him money and commercial praise, it probably keeps his muse alive and prospering.

As I close this treatment of Elvis Costello's oeuvre, let us turn to tradition and Greil Marcus's "Smithville" as a means of assimilating all that we have learned. Since Marcus changed the name of the book that propagates this idea, it is even more appropriate to this discussion (*different* name, *same* book—sound familiar?). When we look back over the lifework, what characteristics emerge as its guiding principles? Moreover, how would those traits manifest themselves in the McManus/Costello/MacManus version of "Smithville"? Again, I think I know. This Smithville is a curious place where people change their names at systematic intervals—or as a result of a personal whim (today's Romeo is tomorrow's Adolf). It is also a *very* theatrical town where people's lives are directly informed by famous literary and historical characters; thus, people's personalities shift in relation to their current name (today's romantic slave is tomorrow's fascist dictator). Everyone actively steals lines from noted texts because everybody is a magpie and a thief. A given remark may feature a touch of Shakespeare, a bit of Churchill, and the ever-present hint of Hank Williams. These literary personalities come from intensely melodramatic, aggressive stories; as a result, there are no middle-of-the-road personalities—all the citizens display a punk attitude toward daily living. Need I say this is an assertive town? They pogo dance to waltzes (proper waltzes were outlawed because of the gunplay they elicited). They maintain diabolical, vindictive relationships. Kids taunt their parents and the parents threaten the family pets. Politicians remain constantly on edge (lynching elected officials and ecclesiastics is legal). And art flourishes. It is a fantastic place to live if you can learn the rules; if you cannot, be prepared for misunderstanding, condemnation, and ultimate disappointment. This Smithville is a world unto itself, free of outside inhibitions or agendas. The ideas run freely and the art flows naturally. Elvis Costello's Smithville is a dangerous place to live.

CHAPTER 8

The Exemplars

We now turn to a series of exemplars that demonstrate the stylistic tendencies that shape Elvis Costello's oeuvre. Later, I examine his use of homonymic puns, internal rhyme schemes, pronoun gymnastics, and other language-specific aspects of his work in more detail. At this juncture, we explore the songwriter's application of specific storytelling structures that are systematically deployed in service of "Elvis Costello's" creative agenda. As we have seen, from the very outset, this writer has pursued a coherent, methodical mission through an unequivocal set of artistic principles that guide virtually every aspect of his professional life. Elvis Costello is here to shake the tree, rattle your senses, and force you to think. Not ask, not provide the opportunity, but *force* you to endure his point. It is his commitment to that objective that sustains his art.

Again, as we have noted throughout this study, our auteur represents a composite of three distinct entities. "Declan McManus" provides an instinctual ambition that is not just a direct product of his lifelong musical education; it motivates a relentless need for sonic diversity. McManus is incapable of docking in one musical port of call for an extended period; as a result, the oeuvre floats about the musical ocean, visiting diverse locations as mandated by the ship's captain and his adventurous muse. Supporting that creative passage is our composite's second component: Elvis Costello's physical capabilities and professional attitudes. Costello's voice and performance style respond to McManus's stylistic course in a fashion that heightens a given work's emotional qualities. Occasionally, we may not know exactly what Costello *says*, although we rarely have any doubts about how he *feels*. These pronounced emotional outbursts are a direct complement to his professional orientation. Once Captain McManus charts his musical course, Mr. Costello braves whatever industry obstacles appear before him. At times, he is courageous to the point of self-destruction—fiercely fighting a host of elements (e.g., record companies, music critics, band mates) that could easily bring about commercial ruin. The McManus–Costello pairing makes for one artistically ambitious, commercially fearless team. It is every artist's dream, and every record company's nightmare.

Finally, we have the wind that blows the sails; the muscles that row the oars; the nuclear energy that powers the engines: "Citizen Elvis." McManus may chart the creative course and Costello may lead the commercial fight, but Citizen Elvis provides the heart, soul, and intelligence to see the journey through. Citizen Elvis—our aggressive, irreverent, and melodramatic commentator—supplies the material to be delivered at any musical destination. Citizen Elvis and his weapon of choice—what Jim Farber calls "the punishing observation"—provide the creative power for the professional enterprise. Whether he discusses British society, the sociological conditions it fosters, or the varied relationships that operate in that context, Citizen Elvis cuts to the chase through oftentimes brutal assessments of the situations before him.

When we examine the lifework in its entirety, we note that Captain McManus and Mr. Costello fearlessly enter a variety of musical ports, whereas Citizen Elvis remains remarkably focused. A given course may involve a techno-dance destination, a chamber music stopover, or a jazzy lounge port, yet once in dock, Citizen Elvis massages a steady staple of songwriting topics. His editorials probe societal matters, individual issues, or relational situations, or contain piercing "snapshots" that mix and match societal, individual, or relational concerns with considerable regularity. His punishing observations may expose a societal injustice or an individual failure, but ultimately they zero in on human relationships—and more often than not, romantic relationships. Consequently, Citizen Elvis's punishing observations introduce a new dimension to the melodramatic portrayal that is a torch song: the *punk* torch song. It is this aspect of the auteur's oeuvre that makes a unique, innovative contribution to the torch tradition. As McManus and Costello perform their respective duties, Citizen Elvis delivers the narrative goods through a punk attitude that expands the torch song's thematic traditions into an unprecedented realm.

One of the more fascinating yields of an auteur study involves the systematic qualities of the lifework. Creative instincts predicated on specific personality traits shape the work in highly predictable ways. Whether operating on a conscious or an unconscious level, an *agenda*—somehow, someway—controls the art. It could be Pete Townshend's intense interest in personal identity, Bob Dylan's unrestrained rebellion, Joni Mitchell's Earth Mother manifesto, or Bruce Springsteen's obsessive quest for social equality—whatever, there always appears to be a topical glue that holds the lifework together. For Elvis Costello, that agenda involves romantic relationships and the various conditions that facilitate or debilitate the realization of that spiritual, emotional, and physical union.

Providing the context for any interpersonal relationship, as well as the starting point for our analysis, is the societal structure of that particular point in time. When Declan McManus was preparing for his eventual vocation, his views on British society were shaped by a confluence of specific attitudes and socioeconomic conditions. As previously noted, his attitude toward English aristocracy reflected a populist worldview that totally rejected any notion of inherited superiority. His grandmother may respect the "higher ups" and their assumed privileges, but young Declan would have none of that. When combined with the severe socioeconomic constrictions of his day, McManus's outlook turned even harsher as he dismissed more than the Royals or their aristocratic peers; he questioned British government, its policies, and its consequences. It appears as though the young man was nonpartisan in that he seemed to reject—or at least to distrust—the origins of any public policy, whether it emerged from the left or the right. He is, in a word, anti-institutional. Such a worldview fueled Citizen Elvis's internal fire. Much like Bruce Springsteen, McManus intuitively understood the root of the relational evil that plagued his society. Aristocratic traditions, politicians, and industry figureheads would forever be Elvis Costello's archenemy, and he would blame them for the sociological conditions that made trusting friendships and loyal, loving relationships so difficult.

Subsequently, there is a narrative genre within Costello's lifework that I call a "societal complaint" storytelling strategy. Three types of stories emerge within that category: the societal complaint, the social commentary, and the moral complaint. The societal complaint first appears in Costello's debut work, *My Aim Is True*. Songs such as "Welcome to the Working Week," "Blame It on Cain," "Less Than Zero," and "Waiting for the End of the World" communicate a deep distrust of city life, public policies and leaders, and ecclesiastics. It is the pinnacle of punk: totally anti-institutional. That trend continues with the extended treatise *This Year's Model*, in which the emerging Citizen Elvis castigates society for its treatment of women ("This Year's Girl"), laughs at men ("The Beat"), probes romantic relationships ("Lip Service" and "Living in Paradise"), condemns social rituals ("Pump It Up" and "[I Don't Want to Go to] Chelsea"), and warns against political practices ("Night Rally" and "Radio, Radio"). The last two songs feature a dark view of public institutions in which Costello questions commonplace political rituals and the ideological motives of media programmers. Moreover, "Pump It Up" describes the vacuous qualities of the social escapes and relational games that flow from a meaningless existence. Once more, to the extent that Bruce Springsteen places his societal victims in fast cars, Elvis Costello takes them to cheap nightclubs. Everywhere, the writer embellishes the consequences of a social system in a serious state of decline—a demise facilitated by an overbearing aristocratic elite.

Armed Forces expands the societal complaint's scope by taking it to the workplace and transferring the mean-spirited or frivolous attitude that debilitates romantic relationships to the job environment ("Senior Service" and "Busy Bodies," respectively). "Oliver's Army" advances the previously established political rhetoric, and the Nick Lowe tune "(What's So Funny 'Bout) Peace, Love and Understanding" sums up the situation in no uncertain terms. From this starting point, the societal complaint floats in and out of the oeuvre with some frequency, often using relational concerns to articulate a societal stance. *Get Happy!!* features "Opportunity," "Human Touch," and "King Horse." *Trust* presents the pivotal commentary "Clubland," as well as "From a Whisper to a Scream," the quintessential "New Lace Sleeves," and "Fish 'n' Chip Paper." After a break for country tunes and punk introspection, the fully realized Citizen Elvis returns with a vengeance by way of *Punch the Clock*'s "Shipbuilding," "The Invisible Man," the controversial "Pills and Soap," and "The World and His Wife." The Citizen Elvis from the *Punch* project is on top of his game. Following *King of America*'s brief treatment of the genre via "Little Palaces" and "Glitter Gulch," *Spike* explodes with ". . . This Town . . ." as well as "Let Him Dangle," "Satellite," "Last Boat Leaving," and the truly damning "Tramp the Dirt Down." That pace continues with *Might Like a Rose* and "The Other Side of Summer," "Hurry Down Doomsday," "How to Be Dumb," and "Invasion Hit Parade." This genre then takes a ten-year break and returns via *When I Was Cruel*'s "Soul for Hire" and "Radio Silence." Throughout this narrative journey Costello consistently attacks the media for their restricting or abusive policies, the government for its foolhardy initiatives, and the ever-present evil aristocracy—and in so doing, he chronicles how these entities harm families, friendships, and loving relationships. There is a villain in this story, and Citizen Elvis has a *real* go at it.

The social commentaries and moral complaints pursue the same ends with slight twists, in that the "commentaries" assume a more detached stance and the "moral complaints" transcend political and social particulars for universal concerns. Young Citizen Elvis is in the thick of his fight; therefore, the commentaries do not appear until later in his career with *Rose*'s "Harpies Bizarre" and "Couldn't Call It Unexpected No. 4" along with *Brutal Youth*'s seasoned statements, "This Is Hell," "20% Amnesia," "Sulky Girl," and "London's Brilliant Parade." The brief display of moral complaints occurs within *Goodbye Cruel World* via "Room with No Number," "The Deportees Club," and "Peace in Our Time." These songs stand back from their subject matter by propagating less damnation and promoting what could be called punk empathy. Instead of lambasting the cheap, empty hotel rendezvous in "Room," Costello seems to ponder the consequences of the act for his characters' lives. Instead of describing the horrific abuses endured by "This Year's Girl" and her boredom with it all, Costello confronts the victimage in "Sulky Girl" by contemplating her role in that diabolical, unhealthy situation. Instead of denouncing or mocking the "Clubland" lifestyle, Costello reveals that path's ultimate destination in "This Is Hell." Throughout, we observe a systematic, coherent, *punk* attack on the perceived conditions that make life so unnecessarily difficult.

Selecting an exemplar from this formidable list of societal complaints and commentaries is, indeed, difficult. Many songs contain marvelous examples of Citizen Elvis's trademark punishing observation; some songs do not feature our punk commentator at all. So I searched for a song that casts a wide net. A song that brutalizes the aristocracy, the government, and the results of their self-serving elitism. Submitted for your approval, then, is "New Lace Sleeves":

> Bad lovers face to face in the morning.
> Shy apologies and polite regrets.
> Slow dances that left no warning of
> Outraged glances and indiscreet yawning.
> Good manners and bad breath get you nowhere.
> Even presidents have newspaper lovers.
> Ministers go crawling under covers.
> She's no angel.
> He's no saint.
> They're all covered up with whitewash and grease paint.
> And you say. . .
> Chorus: The teacher never told you anything but white lies.
>   But you never see the lies
>   And you believe.
>   Oh you know you have been captured.
>   You feel so civilized
>   And you look so pretty in your new lace sleeves.
> The salty lips of the socialite sisters.
> With their continental fingers that have
> Never seen working blisters.
> Oh I know they've got their problems.
> I wish I was one of them.
> They say daddy's coming home soon.
> With his sergeant stripes and his Empire mug and spoon.
> No more fast buck.
> And when are they gonna learn their lesson.
> When are they gonna stop all of these victory processions.
> And you say. . .
> Chorus

"New Lace Sleeves" conveys the punishing observation: Beware the Big Lie. First, notice the various levels of application. Pretenses and misrepresentations begin with an awakening couple, then move to heads of state, socialites, and into the general population. Everywhere, lies. Aristocratic society, we are told, is populated by people who suffer the same, mundane indignities as everybody else. Poor judgment, physical weakness, and relational ineptitude plague the social and political elite in spite of the propaganda taught in school. Social graces cannot overcome natural embarrassments. Pretty clothes cannot hide unattractive personal characteristics. Military parades cannot transform blatant imperialism into an admirable trait. Simply put, your education propagated a comforting but functionally inaccurate lie. The elites control your education and, therefore, your mental construction of the prevailing social order. Serve their interests, Citizen Elvis warns us, and suffer the consequences. Finally, notice how our narrator inserts himself into the fray, hoping to irritate and disrupt the aristocratic world.

Citizen Elvis is relentless: Social control is ubiquitous. "They" manage the content of the media and anesthetize the populace with silly game shows (e.g., "Glitter Gulch"), stupid television programs (e.g., "The Invisible Man"), empty pop songs (e.g., "Invasion Hit Parade"), insulting talk radio (e.g., "Radio Silence"), and contrived theatricality (everywhere). "They" send you off to war for the Empire's glory and reap the profits of self-declared victories (e.g., "Oliver's Army"). "They" limit the range of your thinking through an educational system that promotes a self-congratulatory social mythology (e.g., "New Lace Sleeves"). For Citizen Elvis, the results are all too clear: deteriorating and abusive family relationships (e.g., "The World and His Wife"), manipulative interpersonal relationships (e.g., "Busy Bodies"), a cheesy adherence to improvised fashion (e.g., "Pump It Up"), intrusive media (e.g., "Fish 'n' Chip Paper"), vocational treachery (e.g., "Senior Service"), and, worst of all, a demoralization of personal faith (e.g., "Human Touch"). As loving relationships become impossible to sustain, family units fall apart and children learn the unfortunate rules that will guide—and subjugate—their lives: The aristocratic system prospers. And Citizen Elvis chronicles it all, never blinking or flinching; itching for a fight. Never forget: What is the best thing you can do with a political song? Start a fight!

But the editorial assault does not end there. These societal conditions have a formidable impact on the individual as well. Subsequently, Citizen Elvis turns his angry pen loose on various individual issues that both harm relationships and inhibit personal growth. These individual issues are addressed through four narrative strategies: the "role issue" editorial, the personal complaint, tales of personal struggle, and the personal confessional. The "role issue" narrative emerges on *My Aim* ("Miracle Man" and "Mystery Dance"), returns briefly in *Armed Forces* ("Big Boys"), and visits *Trust* as well (via "You'll Never Be a Man" and "Watch Your Step"). The "personal complaint" appears but three times: "Mouth Almighty" (from *Punch*), "The Big Light" (*King of America*), and "All Grown Up" (*Rose*). Our tale of "personal struggle" is featured on *Brutal Youth* ("My Science Fiction Twin"), and our "personal confessionals" appear on *All This Useless Beauty* ("Distorted Angel" and "I Want to Vanish") and *Painted from Memory* ("Toledo" and "I Still Have That Other Girl"). Most of these stories anchor their complaints in loving relationships as characters question their *individual* capacity to meet relational needs (e.g., "Miracle Man," "You'll Never Be"), to reach certain performance standards (e.g., "Mystery Dance," "Big Boys"), to restrain unwanted behaviors (e.g., "Mouth Almighty," "Toledo"), or just to survive the day (e.g., "I Want to Vanish"). Costello's humorous accounts of intrapersonal wars ("Fiction Twin") and lifestyle abuses ("Big Light") are offset by the depth of the despair communicated by the confessionals. In all cases, the story emphasizes the individual's internal plight—not the burdens imposed by outside forces. For insight into the strategy, let us consider one of the auteur's signature compositions, "Mystery Dance":

> Romeo was restless, he was ready to kill.
> He jumped out the window 'cause he couldn't sit still.
> Juliet was waiting with a safety net.
> He said "Don't bury me 'cause I'm not dead yet".
> *Chorus*: Why don't you tell me 'bout the mystery dance.
> I wanna know about the mystery dance.
> Why don't you show me,
> 'Cause I've tried and I've tried,
> and I'm still mystified.
> I can't do it anymore and I'm not satisfied.
> I can't do it anymore and I'm not satisfied.
> Well I remember when the lights went out
> And I was tryin' to make it look like it was never in doubt.
> She thought that I knew, and I thought that she knew,
> So both of us were willing, but we didn't know how to do it.
> *Chorus*
> Well I was down under the covers in the middle of the night,
> Tryin' to discover my left foot from my right.
> You can see those pictures in any magazine.
> But what's the use of looking when you don't know what they mean.
> *Chorus*

Notice the song's emphasis on the *individual* and his perceived deficiencies. He blames not his partner, his parents, society, nor his queen for his difficulties; instead, he just wallows in his perceived inadequacy. The punishing observation: the naive admission. This character is merely a victim of inexperience; childishly overthinking the most natural of acts. Perhaps his expectations are too high (too many magazines) or his insecurity is out of control (too much peer pressure); in either case, he remains frustrated and, more than likely, destined never to achieve sexual security. How interesting that later in the oeuvre the auteur will chastise a partner for overthinking and overdramatizing sex ("Clown Strike"). Still, one gains the impression that this character probably had a hard time selecting his outfit for the evening, deciding how to wear his hair, or performing the proper dance steps at the club. Individual insecurity of this nature knows no boundaries.

Citizen Elvis truly excels when he brings the results of these societal and individual conditions to relationships. Discussions of human—and most often romantic—relationships dominate the lifework. There are three major categories of songs addressing relational matters: the relational complaint (the classic elegy), the relational assault or warning, and various relational topics (e.g., relational commentary, relational struggle, relational fantasy, relational plea). Throughout the *entire* oeuvre there are *three* songs of relational celebration: *King of America*'s "Jack of All Parades," *Painted from Memory*'s "Such Unlikely Lovers," and *When I Was Cruel*'s "15 Petals." Cait O'Riordan's relational testimony, the moving "Broken" (from *Rose*), contributes to this very slim series of positive relational songs. The rest, without question, probe relationships from less than positive perspectives.

The relational complaints begin in *My Aim* and the victimage portrayed in "No Dancing," "Alison," "Sneaky Feelings," and "Red Shoes." From there, a more combative stance takes control with *This Year's* "Little Triggers" and *Armed Forces'* "Party Girl." Though somewhat more combative, these songs remain focused on "complaints"—not attacks. The elegies grow more complex in *Happy!!* ("Possession," "Men Called Uncle," "New Amsterdam," "High Fidelity," "Black & White World," "B Movie," and "Motel Matches") and *Trust* ("Strict Time," "Luxembourg," "Different Finger," and "Big Sister's Clothes"), and turn introspective in *Bedroom* ("Tears Before Bedtime," "Shabby Doll," "Long Honeymoon," the beautiful "Almost Blue," " . . . And in Every Home," "Boy with a Problem," and "Town Cryer"). Citizen Elvis's punishing observation is not the controlling factor in most of these songs that, in many cases, follow pop song standards as they lodge their complaint. The elegy returns in *Punch* ("Charm School") and appears in *Goodbye* ("The Only Flame in Town," "Home Truth," "Inch by Inch," "The Comedians," and "Sour Milk-Cow Blues"), *King of America* ("Brilliant Mistake," "Lovable," "Our Little Angel," "American Without Tears," "Poisoned Rose," and "Sleep of the Just"), *Blood and Chocolate* ("Home Is Anywhere You Hang Your Head," the deadly "I Want You," "Blue Chair," "Poor Napoleon," and "Next Time 'Round"), *Spike* ("Chewing Gum," "Pad, Paws and Claws," "Baby Plays Around"), *Rose* ("So Like Candy" and "Sweet Pear"), *All This Useless Beauty* ("Other End of the Telescope" and the professional complaint, "You Bowed Down"), and the Elegiac Temple, *Painted from Memory*: "This House Is Empty Now," "Tears at the Birthday Party," "My Thief," "The Long Division," and "Painted from Memory." Throughout, we have straightforward, heartfelt lamentations (e.g., "This House Is Empty Now," "Motel Matches," "Long Honeymoon," "Almost Blue," "Sleep of the Just"), tongue-in-cheek complaints (e.g., "Different Finger," "Chewing Gum," "Pads, Paws and Claws"), societal-relational hybrids (i.e., songs that use relational matters to probe societal conditions, such as "Party Girl," "Strict Time," "Men Called Uncle," "Charm School," "Our Little Angel"), and rather empty pop songs (e.g., "Possession," "Lovable," "Baby Plays Around"). For our exemplar, we turn to the haunting Citizen Elvis lament "I Want You":

> Oh my baby baby I love you more than I can tell.
> I don't think I can live without you
> And I know that I never will.
> Oh my baby baby I want you so it scares me to death.
> I can't say anymore than "I love you."
> Everything else is a waste of breath.
> I want you.
> You've had your fun you don't get well no more.
> I want you.
> Your fingernails go dragging down the wall.
> Be careful darling you might fall.
> I want you.
> I woke up and one of us was crying.
> I want you.
> You said "Young man I do believe you're dying."
> I want you.
> If you need a second opinion as you seem to do these days.
> I want you.
> You can look in my eyes and you can count the ways.
> I want you.
> Did you mean to tell me but seem to forget.
> I want you.
> Since when were you so generous and inarticulate.
> I want you.
> It's the stupid details that my heart is breaking for.
> It's the way your shoulders shake and what they're shaking for.
> I want you.
> It's knowing that he knows you now after only guessing.
> It's the thought of him undressing you or you undressing.
> I want you.
> He tossed some tattered compliment your way.
> I want you.
> And you were fool enough to love it when he said
> "I want you."
> I want you.
> The truth can't hurt you it's just like the dark.
> It scares you witless
> But in time you see things clear and stark.
> I want you.
> Go on and hurt me then we'll let it drop.
> I want you.

I'm afraid I won't know where to stop.
I want you.
I'm not ashamed to say I cried for you.
I want you.
I want to know the things you did that we do too.
I want you.
I want to hear he pleases you more than I do.
I want you.
I might as well be useless for all it means to you.
I want you.
Did you call his name out as he held you down.
I want you.
Oh no my darling not with that clown.
I want you.
You've had your fun you don't get well no more.
I want you.
No-one who wants you could want you more.
I want you.
Every night when I go off to bed and when I wake up.
I want you.
I want you.
I'm going to say it again 'til I instill it.
I know I'm going to feel this way until you kill it.
I want you.
I want you.

We have here, my friends, a boy with a genuine problem. Our punishing observation: obsessive love. This character—whose demeanor is truly enhanced by Costello's creepy singing—is headed toward God knows what. That he is totally obsessed with his love target is beyond question. The tale opens with a light, romantic folk feel as he pledges his love. Quickly, things turn *very* dark. His obsession is most evident in the repeated lines, "I want you," and gains momentum through brief attacks on the woman ("You've had your fun you don't get well no more"), jealous tirades ("Oh no my darling not with that clown"), and concludes with the obvious resolution, "I know I'm going to feel this way until you kill it." Still, what drives the message home is the simple act of repeating the line "I want you" over and over and over (and over and over—get it?). That simple songwriting tactic brings the punishing observation from the abstract to the concrete. One gets chills just *reading* these lines (and if you get it bad, *never* listen to Costello sing it!).

Yet our character does not overtly attack his love, assault his target, or wallow in his struggle. Instead, he is absorbed in his obsession, thinking in fragments, lost in his sordid images. To *really* attack a love target, Citizen Elvis employs other songwriting methods. The relational assault or warning typically involves a more complicated story that embellishes the rationale for the aggressive response. Then again, there are attacks that merely harp on the target—taunting her in mean-spirited ways. The relational assaults begin with *My Aim*'s "I'm Not Angry" and return via *This Year's* "No Action" and "Lipstick Vogue," *Happy!!*'s powerful "Riot Act," *Trust*'s "White Knuckles," *Chocolate*'s "Uncomplicated" and "I Hope You're Happy Now," *Brutal Youth*'s "Just About Glad" and "All the Rage," *Beauty*'s "It's Time," *Memory*'s spiteful "What's Her Name Today?," and *When I Was Cruel*'s capstone commentary, "Alibi." Some songs are simply childish (e.g., "I Hope You're Happy Now"), others are physically violent (e.g., "White Knuckles"), a few are mean-spirited (e.g., "Just About Glad"), and, of course, there are diabolical entries (e.g., "What's Her Name Today?").

However, not all of Costello's attacks "assault" the target, in that we occasionally observe a "warning" in which he hints at a future course of action, declares a guiding relational philosophy, or urges his target to resolve her situation (often, this involves a love triangle). Our initial warning appears in *My Aim* with "Pay It Back" and continues with *This Year's* "You Belong to Me" and "Hand in Hand," *Happy!!*'s three installments ("Love for Tender," "The Imposter," and "Secondary Modern"), *Trust*'s "Lover's Walk" and "Pretty Words," *Bedroom*'s "You Little Fool," and *Chocolate*'s "Honey, Are You Straight or Are You Blind?" These songs range from him-or-me confrontations (e.g., "Love for Tender," "The Imposter"), to threats of revenge (e.g., "Pay It Back"), to relational danger signs (e.g., "Lover's Walk"), to philosophical pronouncements (e.g., "You Belong to Me"), to advisory commentaries (e.g., "You Little Fool"). At times, Costello warns a specific person; at others, he forewarns lovers young and old of the perils ahead. In all cases, he does not merely complain about a situation or overtly assault a target; he warns either the target or the hearer of the threatening times that accompany loving relationships. For insight into the "warning" and "assault" strategies, we rely on the dark masterpiece that is "Riot Act":

> Forever doesn't mean forever anymore.
> I said forever.
> But it doesn't look like I'm gonna be around much anymore.
> When the heat gets sub-tropical
> And the talk gets so topical.
> *Chorus:* Riot act—you can read me the riot act.
>   You can make me a matter of fact
>   Or a villain in a million.
>   A slip of the tongue is gonna keep me civilian.
> Why do you talk such stupid nonsense?
> When my mind could rest much easier.
> Instead of all this dumb dumb insolence
> I would be happier with amnesia.
> They say forget her.
> Now it looks like you're either gonna be before me or against me.

I got your letter.
Now they say I don't care for the colour that it paints me.
Trying to be so bad is bad enough.
Don't make me laugh by talking tough.
Don't put your heart out on your sleeve.
When your remarks are off the cuff.
Chorus

Here we have a classic Citizen Elvis commentary: Simple, concise, devastating. The punishing observation: Institutional vows are fantasies. From the outset, we are told that words have no permanence; and if words are impermanent, vows, pledges, promises—everything—is worthless. But this character is not content with stating his sense of loss. He attacks! Her conversation is "topical" at best, "stupid" otherwise. If "amnesia" improves your condition, well, things are bad. When Costello launches into the final verse, he is combative beyond belief (once more, his singing sharpens the attack immeasurably): Don't make him laugh with your stance. The extent of the character's pain is evident in his retaliation—another consistent trait in Costello's writing. Many times, the auteur's characters are so far out on the edge that you are certain they will either resolve their difficulty or die trying. Elvis Costello's war of the roses takes few prisoners.

The oeuvre's relational themes extend beyond the complaint, assault, and warning in that we have a mandatory catchall category that embraces songs which probe relational matters through alternative songwriting strategies. These narrative tactics do not appear until *Imperial Bedroom*'s invocation of the innovative genre, punk introspection. There we have our initial relational pleas "Human Hands" and "Kid About It," in which the narrator does not complain or attack; he urges his partner to work with him and resolve whatever is before them. The story form recurs with *America*'s "Indoor Fireworks" and "I'll Wear It Proudly," *Brutal Youth*'s "Clown Strike," *Memory*'s "In the Darkest Place," and *Cruel*'s "My Little Blue Window." In all cases, we witness characters attempting to negotiate with their partners or pleading for relational perseverance. Costello may plead for sincerity (e.g., "Kid About It"), declare his commitment (e.g., "I'll Wear It Proudly"), urge his partner to refrain from unnecessary histrionics (e.g., "Clown Strike"), or beg for mercy (e.g., "In the Darkest Place"). The unrestrained bravado of the warning or assault is nowhere is sight; love is a humbling experience in these songs.

That trait reappears in songs of relational struggle as well. With *Brutal Youth*'s "You Tripped at Every Step" and "Still Too Soon to Know" Costello takes his sentiments beyond the plea strategy as he focuses on the relational strain that accompanies a trial-and-error experience or an attempted recovery. Similarly, the auteur's relational commentaries pull back still further as they offer detached views on romantic or familial happenings. This is not to suggest that these songs are void of emotion; to the contrary, the narrator is simply not in the relationship and, therefore, there is some distance between the narrator and the subject. This genre first appears in *Might Like a Rose* ("After the Fall," "Georgie and Her Rival," and "Playboy to a Man"), returns in *Brutal Youth* ("Kinder Murder," "13 Steps Lead Down," and the mother-daughter exchange in "Pony Street"), and is featured in *All This Useless Beauty*'s title cut. Here Costello discusses relational games (e.g., "Georgie"), points to the irony that occurs when the hunter becomes the prey (e.g., "Playboy"), reports the harm inflicted by the woman-as-object predator mentality (e.g., "Kinder Murder"), and looks back with bemusement on it all (e.g., "All This Useless Beauty"). And then, of course, we have the occasional odd storytelling strategy such as the relational fantasy (*When I Was Cruel*'s hilarious "Spooky Girlfriend"—a song that gains much vigor from Costello's introduction during live performance), the divine plea (*Painted from Memory*'s mournful "God Give Me Strength"), and our lone installment of relational pugilism, *Memory*'s "The Sweetest Punch" (a song that, in all honesty, may involve more metaphor than violence—but I'm a-stickin' to my guns!). Certainly, selecting an exemplar from such varied stories is daunting, but allow me the creative license to present a tale rich in emotion, full of commitment, and *honest* in its approach, "Indoor Fireworks":

> We play these parlour games.
> We play at make-believe.
> When we get to the part where I say that I'm going to leave.
> Everybody loves a happy ending but we don't even try.
> We go straight past pretending
> To the part where everybody loves to cry.
> *Chorus:* Indoor fireworks.
> Can still burn your fingers.
> Indoor fireworks.
> We swore we were as safe as houses.
> They're not so spectacular
> They don't burn up in the sky.
> But they can dazzle or delight
> Or bring a tear
> When the smoke gets in your eyes.
> You were the spice of life.
> The gin in my vermouth.
> And though the sparks would fly
> I thought our love was fireproof.
> Sometimes we'd fight in public darling
> With very little cause.
> But different kinds of sparks would fly
> When we got on our own behind closed doors.
> *Chorus*
> It's time to tell the truth.
> These things have to be faced.

My fuse is burning out.
And all that powder's gone to waste.
Don't think for a moment dear that we'll ever be through.
I'll build a bonfire of my dreams
And burn a broken effigy of me and you.
Chorus

"Indoor Fireworks" is a marked departure from the mean-spirited bra-vado of Citizen Elvis's youth. Here our punishing observation is not very brutal: honesty. This is a clear, direct portrayal of relational strife and an honest response to that condition. No pretenses, no attacks, no alibis. Costello deploys a "house" metaphor to communicate that even the stur-diest home is subject to harm. You can build the sucker out of concrete, but all it takes is one act of nature to send it tumbling down (of course, someone could also blow the place up—not all "threats" are natural). Like so many Costello songs, the emotions are intense—so much so that they erupt in public without provocation or explode in private passion. More-over, as on so many other tracks, this relational war will never, ever end. Passions this deep are not frivolous, subject to whimsy, or easily discarded. When you are in this deep, Citizen Elvis reports, you are most certainly in for the long haul, constitutionally incapable of abandoning the fight. They may play their games. They may border on the brink of ruin. But as long as the narrator can muster the strength to utter this relational plea, they will somehow, someway, survive. I risk getting my name etched in Costello's little black book, but nevertheless, here goes: The song reeks of *maturity*.

As I mentioned before, Captain McManus's musical map may know no boundaries and Mr. Costello is no doubt prepared to engage in any indus-trial struggle, but Citizen Elvis remains surprisingly focused. His applica-tion of societal complaint, individual issue, and relational commentary songwriting strategies is dominant (only his impressionistic work rivals these categories). There are very few exceptions. For example, we have one in-stance of satire (*Spike*'s "God's Comic"), three prescriptive "sermons" (*Beauty*'s "Complicated Shadows," "Why Can't a Man Stand Alone?" and "Shallow Graves"), and two "life sagas" (*Spike*'s touching "Veronica" and "Any King's Shilling"). These songs range from playful images of God's rec-reational agenda to prescriptive commentaries about life matters such as unrestrained violence, role issues, and final resting places, to the only songs that I am absolutely certain involve autobiography: the loving account of his grandmother's sunset years ("Veronica") and the period piece about his grandfather's political difficulties ("Any King's"). Otherwise, the auteur ex-plores his tried-and-true stable of topics, bringing different perspectives and emotions to his subject matter.

Finally, we turn to that part of Elvis Costello's lifework that seems to support the love-hate relationship that has developed with music critics. Our auteur's impressionism and wordplay receive every bit as much praise as they do damnation. Often, from my reading of hundreds of reviews, critical expectations clouded judgments, and lazy critics (or, perhaps, to be fair, rushed journalists) wrote about what they anticipated more than what they received when it comes to this facet of Costello's work. Costello's impressionism and wordplay can be difficult, however. Take, for instance, *The Juliet Letters* and its epistolary mode of songwriting. Without any sense of context or any insight into the communicants' relationship, little meaning emerges from these rhythmic snippets or flowing orchestral ponderings. I omit them here because I have no idea who wrote what, yet they represent the essence of Costello's impressionism: They are private expressions written by and for their author(s).

Costello's impressionism emerged with his third album and its "out the window" approach to songwriting (remember, he reports that these lyrical "snapshots" contain "fragments" gleaned from various road trip observations). *Armed Forces* features five examples of narrative impressionism: "Accidents Will Happen," "Moods for Moderns," "Chemistry Class," "Two Little Hitlers," and "Goon Squad." The practice continues with *Happy!!*'s "Clowntime Is Over," "5ive Gears in Reverse," and "Beaten to the Punch" before taking a brief rest after the piece that foreshadows the Brodsky adventure, *Trust*'s "Shot with His Own Gun." *Imperial Bedroom*'s punk introspection deploys the tactic on "Beyond Belief," "Man Out of Time," "The Loved Ones," "Little Savage," and "Pidgin English." The impressionistic strategy dominates *Punch the Clock* with "Everyday I Write the Book," "The Greatest Thing," "The Element Within Her," "Love Went Mad," "TKO (Boxing Day)," and "King of Thieves." And the strategy floats in and out of *Goodbye* (the beautiful "Love Field," "Joe Porterhouse," and "The Great Unknown"), *King of America* ("Suit of Lights"), *Chocolate* ("Tokyo Storm Warning," "Battered Old Bird," and "Crimes of Paris"), *Spike* ("Deep Dark Truthful Mirror," "Miss Macbeth," and "Coal-Train Robberies"), *Brutal Youth* ("Rocking Horse Road" and "Favourite Hour"), *Useless Beauty* ("Little Atoms," "Poor Fractured Atlas," and "Starting to Come to Me"), and reaches its pinnacle by way of *When I Was Cruel*: "45," "Tear Off Your Own Head," "When I Was Cruel No. 2," "Tart," "Dissolve," "Dust 2 . . .," ". . . Dust," and "Episode of Blonde." Running throughout the oeuvre we have six examples of pure, unadulterated wordplay: "Green Shirt" and "Sunday's Best" (from *Armed Forces*), "Temptation" (*Happy!!*), "Let Them All Talk" (*Punch*), "Worthless Thing" (*Goodbye*), and "Daddy Can I Turn This?" (*When I Was Cruel*).

Costello's impression weaves in and out of topics to the extent that there are times when the song's point is difficult to discern (e.g., "Sunday's Best," "Joe Porterhouse," "Crimes of Paris"). On the other hand, his impressionistic explorations of relational matters appear to be evasively pointed (e.g., "Two Little Hitlers," "Deep Dark Truthful Mirror," "Tart"), and his impressionistic introspection, surprisingly revealing (e.g., "Beyond Belief," "Man

Out of Time"). For insight into Costello's impressionistic strategy, we turn to his initial use of the approach, "Accidents Will Happen":

> Oh I just don't know where to begin.
> Though he says he'll wait forever
> It's now or never.
> But she keeps him hanging on.
> The silly champion.
> She says she can't go home
> Without a chaperone.
> *Chorus:* Accidents will happen.
>   We only hit and run.
>   He used to be your victim.
>   Now you're not the only one.
>   Accidents will happen.
>   We only hit and run.
>   I don't want to hear it
>   'Cause I know what I've done.
> There's so many fish in the sea
> That only rise up in the sweat and smoke like mercury.
> But they keep you hanging on.
> They say you're so young.
> Your mind is made up but your mouth is undone.
> *Chorus*
> And it's the damage that we do
> And never know.
> It's the words that we don't say
> That scare me so.
> There's so many people to see.
> So many people you can check up on
> And add to your collection.
> But they keep you hanging on
> Until you're well hung.
> Your mouth is made up but your mind is undone.
> *Chorus*
> I know, I know, *(repeat . . .)*

Now here we have a song that you just *know* contains a buried treasure. Yes, it is certainly a relational complaint. Yes, it offers the punishing observation that relationships are merely games of "hit and run." Yes, it features clever Citizen Elvis comments that flip their contents as the song unfolds. But can you, in any way, discern who is doing what to whom? As we shall discuss later, this is the song Costello performs on his *Storytellers* episode and follows with a detailed explanation of his lyrical technique that I term "pronoun gymnastics." He flips the story's pronouns around and around, and in so doing, obfuscates everything. When you write for yourself with the expressed goal of keeping your work private, this is one songwriting path that you may follow: Write the song in a direct fashion and then go back through and shift the pronouns around. Still, our impressionistic narrator may jumble his characters and muddy his message, but there is no doubt about how he feels. He is drunk on remorse.

Other instances of Costello's impressionism or wordplay are not as strategic. The crazed, wonderful imagery of "Tokyo Storm Warning" (omitted because it was written with O'Riordan), the rich sarcasm of "Episode of Blonde," the historical musings of "45," and much more demonstrate the breadth of Costello's pen. His words may dress the song set, as in "Any King's Shilling." They may attack a given individual by name, as in "Tramp the Dirt Down." They may fondle a professional vernacular, as in "Everyday I Write the Book." Their range, it appears, is limitless and anchored only by the songwriter's creative intent.

When that intent involves a love song, Elvis Costello may plead, confess, commentate, or celebrate; however, what he does most and what he does best is *complain*. When he complains—or assaults or warns—the auteur takes the melodramatic principles associated with the torch song and expands their scope. When the punk writes of love, he deploys a rich invective, full of irreverent spite and mean-spirited theatricality. But driving home his point more often than not is his trademark punishing observation. Citizen Elvis whips his characters with words that cut, bludgeon, slash, and burn. To be sure, lines such as "your mind is made up but your mouth is undone," "don't make me laugh by talking tough," the simple but haunting phrase "I want you," or the intense desire to become a socialite's "problem" take everyday situations and turn them into battlegrounds. After all, why have an argument when you can have a war? After Captain McManus, his volatile muscle Mr. Costello, and Citizen Elvis, the torch song will never be the same again. Elvis Costello is more than a punk lover—he's Billie Holiday with a bent nail.

PART III

Conclusion

CHAPTER 9

The Auteurs

The concluding chapter of this book's companion piece—*Bob Dylan, Bruce Springsteen, and American Song*—opens with a comparison of those artists' third albums because a musician's third release is almost always a telltale event. Conventional wisdom suggests that most musicians are signed to record labels with about an album and a half of strong material. Once that initial wave of creativity passes through the first two albums, the artist's third project offers indications as to whether or not that individual or band has the staying power to warrant further investment. Moreover, an individual or group's artistic direction often settles by the third album in a fashion that says something about their talent, their ability to negotiate with the industry, and their professional future. So let us follow the same strategy here, and consider Elvis Costello's and Joni Mitchell's third album releases as a starting point for this concluding analysis.

Earth Mother's third album, *Ladies of the Canyon*, is certainly a pivotal record. Not only does it feature her first recording with a backing band (of sorts) and preview her sonic future, but it also solidifies the thematic foundation for her entire lifework. *Ladies of the Canyon* says it all. It contains a trademark opening track, the life celebration "Morning Morgantown." It features the auteur's signature portrait-with-a-point narrative strategy by way of "For Free." It offers a foundational philosophical statement, "The Arrangement." It displays her "doughnut" storytelling strategy in which she introduces one topic with a specific point that is then applied to another, unrelated topic ("Big Yellow Taxi"). It presents the generational anthem/societal complaint, "Woodstock." Finally, it offers two Earth Mother portraits ("Ladies of the Canyon" and "The Circle Game") as well as a host of Mitchell's relational challenge story lines: "Conversation," "Willy," "Rainy

Night House," "The Priest," and "Blue Boy." Just look at how this one record reflects a life's work! And everywhere—I mean *everywhere*—is the Earth Mother manifesto. She opens with a glimpse of The Garden via "Morgantown." She laments the environmental abuses that "progress" brings in "Taxi." She nurtures a current lover and a potential lover in "Willy" and "Conversation," respectively. She chronicles the simple, virtuous lives of the "Ladies of the Canyon." She captures the symbolic significance of the peace and love movement's largest single peaceful event in "Woodstock." *Ladies of the Canyon* is a representative sampling of an entire career with one major exception: The Dream is still alive at this point. "Woodstock" and "The Arrangement" may foreshadow a Gardenless existence and reinforce the need for everyone to get in touch with their First Principles, but the auteur of *Ladies* still *believes*, and she will pay for that.

First Principles were on Elvis Costello's mind as well as he scurried across the United States, scratching down the out-the-bus-window observations that would eventually float in and out of his third album. That record, *Armed Forces*, is also a landmark work. This Nick Lowe production captures the live-in-the-studio sound of Elvis and The Attractions during the band's most outrageous period. Though Costello often speaks of the raw and impulsive qualities of the songwriting on this project, that unrestrained style offers a glimpse of what was *really* on the writer's mind. The album's essence is revealed by way of the cover "(What's So Funny 'Bout) Peace, Love and Understanding?" (written by Lowe in his sarcastic Earth Mother mode). Something is going on here, and our budding auteur is not quite sure what it is; nevertheless, he allows his impulses the freedom to roam on this record, and the results are instructive. Citizen Elvis is gaining his editorial sea legs here as he fondles ideas that represent the foundation of his life's work. English society is bogus (e.g., "Oliver's Army") and, therefore, full of threats for those who dare to challenge the status quo (e.g., "Goon Squad"); aristocratic or institutional structures are self-serving and should be challenged (e.g., the delightful "Senior Service"); romance is hazardous with unpredictable consequences (e.g., "Accidents Will Happen") and occasionally cheap (e.g., "Busy Bodies"); and women are the potential victims of it all (e.g., "Party Girl"). Costello's characters question their personal abilities (e.g., "Big Boys"), wage war on one another (e.g., "Two Little Hitlers"), and suspect everything (e.g., "Green Shirt"). Throughout the project, Costello unveils his personal form of impressionism as songs use musical punctuation and lyrical refrains to create the illusion of narrative structure (e.g., "Accidents," "Moods for Moderns," "Chemistry Class") or his words frolic in their unrestrained symbolic playgrounds (e.g., "Green Shirt" and "Sunday's Best"). The songs demonstrate the auteur's ability to write direct, clear pieces or to generate more evasive, enigmatic works. Citizen Elvis organizes his editorial board on this record that departs from tales of victimage (*My Aim Is True*) or combat (*This Year's Model*), and moves into the participant-observer role that will fuel his evolution into the social commentator that emerges over time. The record may have been assembled in a crazed fashion, but it is remarkably revealing. Third albums are instructive.

Although it would be misleading to suggest that these two albums had a meaningful impact on the torch tradition, they are pivotal moments in these two songwriters' careers, and *that* is significant for the torch song's development. With *Ladies* and *Forces*, the two auteurs' public personalities crystallized in a fashion that would forever affect how they and their work would be received. Earth Mother and Citizen Elvis would from that point forward be considered to be confessional and confrontational, and there would be virtually nothing they could do about it. Their first two albums opened the door to those descriptions, and their third entries slammed it shut. There were times when each played his or her role very, very well. As a result, cookie-cutter critics and formulaic journalists would forever fit whatever they interpreted into these predetermined slots. Mitchell could fight like a lumberjack, and it would be deemed a confession; Costello could cry like a baby, and it would be declared an attack. These two celebrity-singer-songwriters are ensnared by images that permanently framed their work, and *that* was an important development in the torch tradition. That is, they take the torch song out of a context—a bar, lounge, or any smoke-filled room—and associate it with a personality. Their melodramatic accounts of love gained or lost do not exist in isolation; rather, they are considered to be part of an unfolding story—a life, if you will. They may sing about societal issues, historical events, or their pets; nevertheless, those accounts consistently lead to some take on human relations. It is the bread that they butter from two different perspectives. Those perspectives are rarely trite or superficial; to the contrary, they are typically intense and compelling. That takes the torch song into a new realm as it advances the song structure's emotional power through the addition of personality; an emotion with more than a face, the songs embellish a character. And what characters they are.

Joni Mitchell claims songs should nurture their audiences. A song is a potential vehicle to a better understanding of the self and, from there, of others. If the songwriter is incapable of saying "something nice," perhaps he or she should remain silent, she suggests. Mitchell's career, then, is a tale of the nurturing Earth Mother's evolution into the protective Earth Mother. As she evolves, she most assuredly says things that are not very "nice," but she says them because she *has* to protect her flock. Earth Mother is a woman of ways and means—that is for sure. She has achieved success and wealth; consequently, she is in a position to comment on both. Success without freedom is worthless. Wealth without love is worse. So Earth Mother shares the frivolity of materialistic worldviews, shouts down those who propagate such superficial outlooks, and does her damnedest to nurture and protect her constituency. In so doing, she puts herself on the line.

Whether she writes from an autobiographical perspective or deploys a character portrait to illustrate her point, she takes a *stance* in her writing—and that stance is decidedly nurturing.

Elvis Costello claims songs should make people think about life's events. A song is a response to a perceived situation, and the auteur uses whatever musical tools are available to unveil that response. If the song satisfies *him*, it is good enough for the general public. Costello's career, then, is a tale of an angry young social commentator's evolution into an angry, older social commentator. He in no way endeavors to nurture or educate his audience. He attempts to write songs that capture sentiments in a compelling manner, shape those views in a fashion that satisfies his personal agenda, and then, after all is said and done, he walks away from the experience. Throughout the creative-commercial process, he maintains his distance. He changes his name, shifts his sound, and hopscotches his way across the musical spectrum in a way that makes him impossible to pin down. Since we never know who is talking, we never know who said what. To the extent that Mitchell engages, Costello disengages. To the extent that Mitchell protects her audience, Costello protects himself and encourages his audience to do the same. Much like Bob Dylan, Costello's longevity may well be the result of the distance he has systematically imposed between himself and his various publics—including record companies.

Although one artist may embrace her public to the degree that the other dismisses his, they do share one compelling trait: rebellion. Both artists' careers feature a rebellious jaunt across the musical landscape. Whether their sonic innovations are appreciated by their audiences or not, they follow where their rebellious instincts lead, shaping Earth Mother prescriptions or Citizen Elvis editorials in terms of the musical platform du jour. They are fearless, and they have the scars to prove it. That intense rebellion also involves an important player in the complicated game that is commercial music: record companies. If given the choice between wearing a hair shirt for 100 years or succumbing to the demands of the record industry for one single, I believe both of these artists would wind up scratching themselves to death (probably within the first ten minutes). To them, an industrial edict is a note from hell. Few artists hold their record companies in such outright contempt. (In my experience, all artists hate their record companies; this is simply a matter of degree.) Finally, both of these artists are rebellious social commentators. Though they approach that process from different perspectives, both songwriters offer relentless social commentaries on human relations that are informed by a firm understanding of just who the villain is in the never-ending struggle for relational equilibrium. "Commercial greed" and materialism are to Joni Mitchell what "aristocratic abuse" and elitism are to Elvis Costello: the hated enemy. Though Costello says what he is "against" far more than he declares what he is "for," he joins Mitchell in her rebellious assault on the status quo and its self-preserving ways. Giving in to "The Arrangement" or accepting the institutional lies from people with "New Lace Sleeves" will take you to the same dreadful place: subjugation—an enslavement without freedom or populist values. Correspondingly, that subjugation directly threatens the essence of any society, human relationships. The auteurs' rebellious takes on these events chronicle two separate responses to that situation. Their motives differ, but their resolve is shared.

As we examine those various takes on life's events, we instantly note differences in the auteurs' respective approaches. Without question, the fundamental difference between these two writers involves their points of view. The heartfelt, nurturing observation flows from a different songwriting strategy than does its provocative, punishing counterpart. The key to this distinction is the level of involvement between the artist and the audience. While Mitchell labors to embrace her audience and move it toward The Garden and its blissful lifestyle, Costello works to irritate everyone to the extent that they will act on their own. A note from mother reads differently than a letter from an informed stranger—even if he has a famous name. The language, its arrangement, and its tone are so different. Mitchell takes a stance and stands behind it. Costello takes a stance from behind a curtain (BOO!). Mitchell harps on how "she" feels (whether or not "she" is a character reading her script); Costello shifts pronouns in a way that such attribution is impossible (but his editorial point remains). That distance—or lack thereof—is a crucial element in the art that flows from these two writers. Much like Bruce Springsteen and Pete Townshend, Joni Mitchell offers an artistic response to her times in an intensely personal manner. She lays her persona on the line for her views. She—like Townshend and Springsteen—bleeds all over the studio floor. It is most unlikely that she will ever "save anything for herself." Much like Bob Dylan, Elvis Costello offers a professional response to his times in an intensely impersonal fashion. The song's point is there for your personal use; help yourself, but leave the songwriter alone, thank you. He is merely the means to the ends, not the ends themselves. If you crowd him and try to pin him down, he will laugh at you before destroying you with a punishing truth attack or a bent nail. Go ahead, make his day.

All of which leads to the importance of auteur studies. An understanding of an artist's biography, his or her artistic philosophy and creative influences, and the songwriting strategies evidenced in his or her lifework unveils the auteur. You may get to the auteur only through the oeuvre. The auteur Joni Mitchell may *be* her art, but you may examine that only through that art. The auteur Elvis Costello may be many things, but you may ascertain what he is at any given point only through the art. In both cases, we have artists whose intense, melodramatic, stylized accounts of human relations take the torch tradition out of a specific context and associate it with an acknowledged personality. As we conclude with an assessment of the two writers' language use, their narrative strategies, their production methods, and their performance styles, notice how they take tales of love found, love in turmoil, love in decline, and love lost, and spin those stories with a depth of perspective that is just unavailable from a lone singer in a smoke-filled lounge. *Personalities* bring specific *perspectives* to these songs, and that makes them messages from celebrities—whether or not they are accurately attributed. People get to *know* these characters in ways they never thought of knowing Nat King Cole—or the Duke of Aquitaine, for that matter. Those attributions may be as bogus as can be, but the fact that these messages are stylized reinforces the process. The following pages reveal the songwriting strategies that shaped those expressions.

THE AUTEURS: THE LANGUAGE

During our examination of Elvis Costello's *Juliet Letters* we determined that the epistolary mode of communication displays specific characteristics that are unique to that form of expression. A *letter* uses language in a manner distinct from a speech, a poem, or a song. A letter appears in a context that involves a relationship of some type or another. People do not write letters to strangers. You may not actually *know* Sherlock Holmes, but you think you do, and that influences your writing. Joni Mitchell's songs work like letters. Her status as a celebrity-singer-songwriter established the grounds for a relationship with her public that fed audience interpretations of her songwriting. Mitchell and her audience shared a context (real or imagined) that yielded a perceived relationship that made her Earth Mother manifesto content appear personal, directed—virtually like a letter from a caring relative. She engaged her audience whether she praised, condemned, or merely reflected upon her subject matter. That she used language in a fashion that reinforced that relationship contributed mightily to this phenomenon. Joni Mitchell's writings are more than just songs; they are letters from Earth Mother.

Editorials work differently. An editorial's language is contingent upon its context of usage. A *Wall Street Journal* editorial is written in a style quite unlike an editorial in a local paper, a corporate newsletter, or a weekly entertainment magazine. Whether the piece advocates a partisan stance or an unbiased position, the nature of the evidence used to support its claims—the entire content and tone of the commentary—is dependent upon the editorial policies that guide that particular source. Moreover, the editorial's reception by its designated public is influenced by the source's ethos. The medium's reputation plays a crucial role in determining the argument's credibility and its capacity to motivate a targeted public in some manner. But rest assured, editorials are designed to move their audience. They may inspire, irritate, insult, or just inform; in every case, they maintain the communicative goal of arousing their audience. Rarely—if ever—are they designed to *please* an audience, inasmuch as they aspire to *arouse* an audience to consider—and maybe even act upon—a specific situation. Citizen Elvis is one capable editorial writer. He is the Socratic gadfly, picking and probing through particular events in his effort to make sense of the universal principle behind those happenings. As he moved from publication to publication (i.e., musical genre to genre), he deployed narrative devices that fit each context and served his editorial goals. All the while, he maintained his distance, urging his audience to consider his point, not his personality. His aggression cut all ways. He is the musical world's first punk editorial writer.

What makes a Joni Mitchell Earth Mother letter different from any other correspondence? What makes an Elvis Costello Citizen Elvis editorial distinct from other opinion pieces? The consistent use of the literary devices I characterize as the "nurturing observation" and the "punishing observation" separates these two writers from their songwriting peers. Mitchell's peace and love nurturing observations and Costello's shock and awe punishing observations represent signature storytelling strategies that organize their individual opinions into systematic commentaries. These celebrity-singer-songwriters bring personalities to their work—images that influence the creation, production, and reception of their labors. Mitchell's return to The Garden rhetoric and Costello's punk populism provide the observational frameworks upon which they formulate their responses to the events before them. For Mitchell, the Earth Mother manifesto's credo of simplicity, empathy, equality, and personal independence shaped a critical lens through which she viewed the world. When she saw her worldview prosper, she praised that happy day. When she saw it threatened by greed, materialism, and manipulation, she decried that sad condition and, perhaps, damned those responsible. For Costello, Citizen Elvis's editorial board advocated a punk populism that denounced aristocratic institutions and elitist policies. When he saw elites preying on the masses, he attacked with his metaphorical bent nail. Whatever form of fascism he encountered, he pounded it with his populist hammer. He refused be ignored. His aim was persistent, if not true.

Why?

Why did these two writers respond in this fashion? My interpretation indicates that they sincerely believe that greed, materialism, elitism, and fascism of any kind threaten society's most fundamental institution: loving relationships. If "The Arrangement" did not destroy marriages, Mitchell would write about something else. If the "Clubland" mentality did not wreck people's lives through its superficial diversions, Costello might well join in the fun. But no. These two artists did more than write about relational difficulties or social inequities; they understood the evil that supported those conditions and deployed their pens in their individual efforts to denounce that villain—and, in Mitchell's case, advocate an alternative. In so doing, they take the melodramatic imperative of the individual torch song and transform it into a systematic commentary that takes a stance on the proceedings; an artistic position predicated on their celebrity-singer-songwriter images. Fundamental to this creative act is our first topic: the writers' use of language.

These writers' language use is best discussed on three levels: their specific word choices, their applications, and their subsequent manifestations. Costello's editorials use clever language that reflects his punk attitude and maintains distance from his audience. Mitchell's letters use intimate language that generates a personal tone that engages her audience. Costello's use of homonymic puns, double entendres, and his trademark idiosyncratic metaphors allows him to express his commentary through his punk voice and, in turn, attack from a distance. There is little to no *personal* engagement. He explained his technique in considerable detail on VH1's *Storytellers*:

> I was twenty-three when my first record came out and, I have to be honest, the whole business went completely to my head. In the private sense—although I think I was writing pretty good songs—in the private sense, I made a total hash of my life. I spent a long time disguising this in songs and lying about it and then covering my tracks very unsuccessfully after the event. One thing I've noticed in reviewing these songs in order to play them for you tonight, and try to tell you something that isn't a gloss of the background to them, is that I used to deliberately confuse the meaning of the song. If you'll listen to the chorus of "Accidents Will Happen"—"Accidents will happen/We're only hit and run/You used to be your victim/Now you're not the only one"—it's pretty confusing who's doing what to what, you know, in that. The real truth of the matter is I was living a secret life a lot of the time. I mean, how deep do we want to go into this? . . . . I've done this thing throughout, it's as good a time as any because I've lived with the fact that there are people in the world today that think I wrote songs for them. It's clearly impossible that I did this because I'd never met them when I wrote the songs. . . . There are inevitably people in any singer's audience who take maybe the songs a little bit too seriously and start to imagine themselves . . . in the character in the song. In the case of "Accidents Will Happen" the real chorus is "Accidents will happen/I only hit and run/I used to be your victim/Now you're not the only one." Which is quite a different matter, you know. It's saying "I'm doing these things that I shouldn't be doing and you used to be the only one for me, but now you're not." I was uncomfortable—I have to be honest—with it and I felt like I was making it far too personal. And a lot of the time that's what we're supposed to be doing, but I've never subscribed to the idea that you can set your diary to music and make a record. I've been proven very wrong by some people's success . . . it's never suited me . . . I try to be a better songwriter by imagining things that everybody could imagine themselves in. And maybe some of the time I got it right.

What a revealing statement! Once Costello lays his story out with its punishing observation, he systematically shifts basic language (here, pronouns)
in order to obfuscate the specifics. The punishing observation—our Citizen
Elvis editorial—remains, but he creates distance by changing something as
simple as the story's pronouns. How interesting that Costello, once again,
admits how he created havoc in his personal life, used that "material" for
his songs, wrote the songs, and then changed the language in a manner
that shifted the details without forsaking his point. Whether he relied on
crazed metaphors, weird puns, or suggestive language to flavor his views,
he maintained a distance that is a direct invocation of his stated artistic
philosophy: "I've never subscribed to the idea that you can set your diary
to music and make a record."

Joni Mitchell may not have "set her diary to music" as much as everybody thought she did, yet her language use certainly facilitated that interpretation. Her intimate, personal tone comes directly from her language use
and its tendency to frame observations in her Earth Mother, nurturing style.
Often, pundits revealed their sexist orientations by attributing these tendencies to her gender. Mitchell discussed her "confessional" approach and its
relationship to her gender in these comments to Bill Flanagan:

> The things that to me as a writer have the most vitality are those kinds of
> details. Those are the things that would make a novel or screenplay good and
> have some depth as opposed to just being a caricature. I sacrifice myself to
> them. I'd never really say that was easy. I just don't know any other way to
> be. If I could think of a way to change and get consistently strong so that I
> could sing about strong things . . . no, it's a delicate thing. I wouldn't go put-
> ting it into a gender bag at all.

Mitchell strives for neither a uniquely feminine tone nor a specifically confessional result; rather, she pursues *detail*. She "sacrifices" herself to detail.
Mitchell consistently notes how she "acts" and how her lyrics represent a
"script" that enables her to pursue intimate details that may, in fact, be
outside of her personal experience. As she told Flanagan, she seeks some
"kind of identification" with her "subject matter" since, in her view, "you
have to have experienced the emotion" in order to achieve depth. She explained: "To be a great actor you would have to have felt what the character felt and be able to draw it out. It's the same in writing. On that level
you could say it's all autobiographical." Mitchell may be fast and loose with
her notion of autobiography, yet her work reinforces her point. There is no
reason to believe that she is the character in "Marcie" or "Cactus Tree." The
songs use pronouns and scenes that suggest otherwise, but when she told
Karl Dallas that she was "the girl in all of those songs," she opened a can
of worms that Elvis Costello steadfastly avoided. Subsequently, by the time
she wrote songs such as "River," the die was cast. She would forever be

construed as a "confessional" writer simply because of the detail conveyed through her songs—detail that begins with her language use (with a little boost from public comments like those reported by Dallas). Mitchell's plain, intimate language massages the details that make her Earth Mother manifesto accessible and, unfortunately for her, at times attributable. That artistic "sacrifice" proved to be a double-edged sword.

When we turn to our second level of analysis and the strategic application of the artists' language, we note two distinct modes of operation. Costello is an *educated* songsmith. Mitchell is an *intuitive* painter who also happens to write songs. To the degree that Costello applied his lifelong musical education to his craft, Mitchell relied on her lifelong intuitive instincts. One uses craft to shield himself as he issues his punishing editorials; the other relies on artistic intuition to engage her audience through her nurturing impulses. In order to establish my point, let us return to two exemplars that demonstrate the practice.

Costello's "Riot Act" is a quintessential example of his confrontational, punishing observation. The song opens with his lament that the word "forever" has lost its meaning. His slow, emotive singing suggests his character's disappointment over his fading relationship. "Forever" just does not mean "forever anymore." Vows, then, are meaningless (our punishing observation). Notice Costello's internal rhyming schemes as his character declares that his soon-to-be-former lover "can make me a matter of fact/Or a villain in a million/A slip of the tongue is gonna keep me civilian." (His use of the term "civilian" indicates the militaristic qualities of the relational game.) Suddenly, the song's elegiac tone turns confrontational. Her talk is "stupid nonsense," and he would be "happier with amnesia" rather than have to cope with her "insolence." Again, we pause for reflection as the narrator reports his friends "say forget her," and he mentions a "letter" she wrote him. He suddenly turns aggressive once again, denounces her "tough talk" as a joke, and concludes with a trademark Costello pun: "Don't put your heart out on your sleeve/When your remarks are off the cuff." The auteur's use of internal rhymes, strategic pacing, and tactical puns merge "old school" Tin Pan Alley songwriting techniques with a punk sensibility that transforms a raw emotion into a frontal attack. Elvis Costello is a capable, well-educated wordsmith. Citizen Elvis's punk attitude is articulated through a narrative style that synthesizes traditional songwriting techniques and a contemporary voice into one compelling, punishing editorial. In this case, a melodramatic torch song about the deteriorating state of relational commitment provides a starting point for a punk truth attack. It is a spectacular synthesis of styles.

Mitchell's "Don Juan's Reckless Daughter" is a prime example of a different mode of operation. This impressionistic letter from Earth Mother is an intuitive, impulsive exploration of the auteur's personal metaphysics. Though both "Riot Act" and "Reckless Daughter" are written in the first person, "Riot" shares *no personal details* as it launches into its attack, while "Daughter" opens with such knowledge (she instantly identifies her metaphoric father) and proceeds to offer layer upon layer of personal revelation with each stanza. Earth Mother is working through her intrapersonal struggle between her base desires and her noble aspirations. The "snake" and the "eagle" reside in us all, and like Don's daughter, we must seek some reconciliation of those polar opposites in order to maintain The Garden and its magical equilibrium. She shares her emotional responses (she "nearly broke down and cried" when she saw the "ghost" of her "old ideals" on television), her conversation with a "spirit" over her internal conflicts ("He said, 'Your serpent cannot be denied'"), her subsequent battle ("The eagle and the serpent are at war in me"), her restless inner conflicts over lifestyles ("Restless for streets and honky-tonks/Restless for home and routine"), and finally resolves to accept her "twin" and move on with an understanding of her conflicting, yet complementary, dualities ("Self indulgence to self denial/Man to woman/Scales to feathers/You and I"). The song operates on two levels (at least), and in doing so, represents the essence of Mitchell's songwriting. It provided a personal resolution to the idealistic struggle that Earth Mother had endured for well over a decade, and it invited her audience to do the same. In other words, probe the personal as a path to the universal. Classic Earth Mother. Her intuitive self-exploration yields nurturing food for thought for her audience: Accept yourself. She has been arguing this point since "I Think I Understand" and "Roses Blue" on *Clouds* (her *second* album). In all cases, she "sacrifices" herself to detail and engages her audience. She may go on a bit in her letter, but as Costello said, people do that in letters, "don't they?" Besides, "Reckless Daughter" is an example of Mitchell's *impressionism.* Just read "River," "Cactus Tree," and "Come in from the Cold." Just look as the personal, intimate expressions that permeate those songs—whether or not Mitchell is "in character." Joni Mitchell transformed songwriting through these types of songs—so much so that Elvis Costello denounced those who co-opted Mitchell's strategies to superficial ends. It *is* a "delicate thing" that, when mishandled, comes off rather poorly.

All of which leads to our third level of language use and the concrete manifestation of the two writers' individual styles. When you sit back and consider the specific words and their application in Costello's and Mitchell's work, you quickly conclude that Costello is a professional songwriter and Mitchell is a painter. Costello's ability to dress a song in a particular songwriting tradition is a product of his lifelong education and his acute awareness of different songwriting styles. Therefore, he may dress a punishing observation in country attire, lounge apparel, chamber finery, or folk garb, or the Beloved Entertainer may don clown wear. His is a studied craft. He has written with Burt Bacharach, the Brodskys (learning how to write music in the process), T-Bone Burnett, and Paul McCartney, and has secured the assistance of pop, techno-dance, and country producers and engineers.

In every case, he brings his stated artistic philosophy to the creative task at hand. His language drives home his trademark punishing observation while it simultaneously distances him from his editorial. As he shares his observations by reducing them to "fractions" that are held together by the "common denominator" that is the moral of his editorial, he works hard to extract himself from the scenario. Like any self-respecting editorial writer, he is an independent. He is nobody's spokesperson. Elvis Costello is the consummate punk.

Joni Mitchell is a painter who took Arthur Kratzman's advice to heart. If she could paint with colors, she can paint with words. And that is *exactly* what she does. That observation in no way diminishes her songwriting skills; it merely sheds light on how she goes about that task. She is intuitive. She relies on emotions. She places words on her sonic canvas and moves them around until the desired effect is achieved. Once she intuits her nurturing observation, she shares it in intimate terms. She may offer her innermost feelings or she may assume the perspective of a created character and read from her script; either way, she personalizes the account through words that engage her audience. The process is governed by the prevailing feeling that guides her intuitive response to the situation before her—an emotional sentiment that is grounded in her Earth Mother manifesto. Our painter has an agenda, and she willfully "sacrifices" herself to that worldview. All the while, she exposes the various colors that compose our world.

So we have the clever wordsmith who systematically worked as a "thief and magpie" to do whatever needed to be done to achieve his artistic agenda. Once he determined his editorial's context (i.e., its musical genre), he set about the task of appropriating his views within that established framework. Subsequently, he may imagine Johnny Cash is singing a song in order to "trick out" its particulars or he may streamline his sentiments in order to comply with Bacharach's arrangements; in all cases, he is a professional songwriter who deploys the skills of that craft to frame his art. But *this* thief and magpie borrows only frameworks. The details are uniquely his. There is only one Citizen Elvis. The punishing observations that flow from his punk populism may be dressed in country lamé or chamber frippery, yet his melodramatic, aggressive, irreverent language flows from a pen that is uniquely Elvis Costello.

In contrast, we have the sincere painter who systematically constructed nurturing prescriptions for living for her audience. Her peace and love worldview anchored intuitive responses to situations that both reinforced and threatened her heartfelt perspective. She sacrificed herself to narrative details and stood behind them; accepting her audience's praise or blame with the same level of involvement that she used to create her songs. That she refers to her songs as her children says it all. That she refers to her muse as her spouse says even more. Joni Mitchell is married to her Art, and her offspring represent nothing less than her own flesh and blood. Her level of engagement is as much a secret of her success as it is a serious liability. Earth Mother's inability to "save something for herself" injured her irreparably. Adding insult to injury was the fact that The Garden fantasy never had a chance. As her worldview crumbled around her, our polio survivor fought hard—maybe too hard—for her First Principles. When that failed, she focused on the forces that prohibited our return to The Garden, denounced their evil ways, and continued to nurture her audience by attempting to protect it. Always, she embraced the situations before her through language that promoted intimacy, that communicated sincerity, that suggested love. Joni Mitchell's sacrifice was genuine; I only wish she would have listened to Kris Kristofferson.

THE AUTEURS: THE NARRATIVE STYLES

When we consider the narrative styles through which these writers frame their lyrics, we once more observe their artistic philosophies in action. Our auteurs are, indeed, systematic. Earth Mother's nurturing letters follow specific narrative patterns just as Citizen Elvis's editorials adjust to their respective contexts. In both cases, the notion that every picture tells a story gains new meaning. Mitchell's painterly "murals" and Costello's candid "snapshots" provide the narrative frameworks for their individual approaches to storytelling. As we have seen, Mitchell's portrait narrative strategy (i.e., character, scenic, tribute, and self-portrait songs) represents one of her more prominent storytelling forms. However, the practice goes beyond those songs that focus on a character, a scene, or some combination. Virtually all of Mitchell's songs invoke sensory experiences through references to colors, sights, smells, sounds, and other *details* that give so much life to her stories. Her songs paint grand murals that are vast in scope, incorporating as much detail as they can muster and still serve the nurturing observation upon which the account rests. In contrast, Costello deploys a snapshot strategy in which his narrative fractions concentrate on specific focal points that he then ties to the common denominator that is his punishing observation. One approach is vast and all-encompassing; the other is sharp and focused. And it all stands to reason. Letters range far and wide, with each paragraph introducing a new topic or adding another layer to the personal exchange. Editorials are concise, direct, and deliberate, with each paragraph adding another layer of evidence (i.e., Costello's fractions) for the featured argument (i.e., his common denominators). In other words, Mitchell's murals and Costello's snapshots are rhythms of expression that frame their tales of complaint, celebration, struggle, and what have you. We begin with grand portraiture and Earth Mother's letters to her flock.

Most letters open with some sort of greeting—many times, a positive statement or observation. A holiday or date reminded someone of another, an event triggered a memory, a statement sparked an idea, or a location inspired a thought. Perhaps someone traveled somewhere or saw something, and was moved to share it with someone. How interesting that so many of Joni Mitchell's records follow that same pattern. As you look back over her lifework, notice how many albums begin with one of her patented life celebration or travelogue songs. "Part Two" of *Song to a Seagull* opens with "Sisotowbell Lane" and its glimpse of The Garden, "Chelsea Morning" is the second track on *Clouds*, "Morning Morgantown" opens *Ladies*, *Hissing of Summer Lawns* begins with "In France They Kiss on Main Street," *Don Juan's Reckless Daughter* starts with "Cotton Avenue," the biting *Dog Eat Dog* opens with the joyous "Good Friends," *Night Ride Home* starts with the title cut, and *Taming the Tiger* opens with "Harlem in Havana." If an album has a celebration or travelogue song, there is a good chance it will be the opening track. It is almost as if Earth Mother's letters open with a happy face, welcoming you to another installment of peace and love prescriptions.

Contributing to this approach is the tendency for individual songs to open with positive or simple descriptions of some out the window, on the street observation. A person standing on a street corner or a waitress wearing something eye-catching, a scene from a passing car, a license plate, the stars in the night sky, the sound of the beach or wind, how you awaken in the morning (a major motif), someone's appearance (hair, clothes, demeanor), the weather, meeting a child or young person, sitting in a park or a café—the list goes on. Mitchell consistently uses everyday observations as a starting point for her songs in a fashion that establishes the story's context. Like her opening tracks, the first lines of many songs set the tone for the portrayal to follow—much as if she has painted the backdrop for an unfolding scene. She drives down an open road and a thought passes. She is having a coffee and someone catches her eye. She is out for a day or night of shopping and something happens. Mitchell's greetings are a central part of her letters.

Those missives also follow certain patterns of organization that are unique to Mitchell's style. One is the technique I term the portrait-with-a-point narrative strategy. These songs describe a character or scene in detail before pulling back and drawing some point from that description for further embellishment. For instance, in "For Free" she presents the street musician and his joyous, carefree musicmaking before turning that scenario around to her predicament as a professional musician. What he does "for free" brings so much joy, while what she does for a fortune offers little such yield. "Roses Blue" provides a rich account of the gypsy and her mystical ways before shifting gears, dismissing those practices, and urging the hearer to get in touch with his or her laughter and true self. "Free Man in Paris" paints a detailed picture of the music mogul with not-too-subtle jabs at the industry which supports him. "Edith and the Kingpin" and "Otis and Marlena" offer colorful accounts of the two couples before sliding in the morals of the respective stories. This narrative strategy offers depth to the comprehensive mural that is Mitchell's song. The detail, scope, and tone of the expression are established as a preface to the nurturing observation that is the story's point.

A similar strategy is what I call Mitchell's "doughnut" technique (a term from radio advertising in which a product is introduced, a scene depicts its use, and the ad closes with more information). In Mitchell's case, the song opens with one scene, moves to another that embellishes the point or shifts the song's context in some way, and closes by returning to the opening scene. For example, "Paprika Plains" opens with a Canadian dance hall scene, moves to a long instrumental segment (with a parenthetical commentary about the plains), and returns to the dance hall scene as it closes. The dance hall sets the scene for nostalgic recollections that inspire the subsequent dream scenario and its impressionistic account of the plains, the Indians, and assorted visions. Suddenly, the rain stops and she reenters the dance hall to yet another "Down to You" dance partner. The technique reappears in "Ethiopia" as Mitchell speaks of the horrible conditions the African country endures before turning to a brief attack on TV evangelists who use that horror as a fund-raising ploy, and then closes by returning to the original point. Occasionally, the "doughnut" is not as concrete as these examples suggest. In "Amelia," our narrator spots six jets streaking across the sky as she drives through the desert (another example of an everyday observation opening a song) and follows with a comparison of her romantic situation, Amelia Earhart's ambitions, and their mutual frustrations. In "Big Yellow Taxi," Mitchell opens with her environmental observations, notes how you just fail to miss something until it has gone, and applies that notion to her love life in the final stanza. Much like her portrait-with-a-point approach, these stories establish one or more contexts for her nurturing observation and, correspondingly, add depth to the resulting mural.

There are other narrative signatures associated with Earth Mother's letters that make these accounts distinctive. With regard to thematic tendencies, Mitchell's references to dreaming, dancing, or flying represent recurring motifs. So many songs feature daydreams (e.g., "The Dawntreader," "Woodstock," "Paprika Plains"), youthful dance halls or adult party situations (e.g., "Talk to Me," "Let the Wind Carry Me," "In France They Kiss on Main Street"), or scenes from airplanes or sky gazing (e.g., "Both Sides, Now," "This Flight Tonight"). Mitchell's characters lie on decks and dream perfect world scenarios, look wistfully at passing clouds with wonderment, juke and jive with travel partners, or sit in corners, watching partygoers and their diabolical ways. Often, these motifs provide the crucial opening scene that Mitchell uses to contextualize her observations. In her 1974 *MacLean's* interview, Malka pursues a similar point when she notes that Mitchell's songs concentrate on three recurring themes: loneliness, love, and freedom. She has a strong argument. How many songs feature characters sitting alone, daydreaming or pining over a distant memory; attending parties, contemplating some romantic situation or the need for an escape, gazing toward the heavens with notions of personal or professional independence dominating their thoughts? These scenes recur with considerable frequency as Earth Mother relies on a series of tried-and-true images to drive home her nurturing observations.

Finally, there are other recurring narrative trends that we should acknowledge. One interesting habit involves the fact that Mitchell's relational songs seldom feature frontal attacks or mean-spirited accusations; instead, they explain why things failed or offer explanations for the situation. At times, she is downright polite when she considers a failed relationship. Mitchell may go straight after evangelists, politicians, and moneychangers of all sorts with a take-no-prisoners mentality, but she rarely—if ever—deploys that attitude when discussing affairs of the heart. In such interpersonal matters, Mitchell is nurturing to a fault as she seeks understanding over persecution, kindness over revenge.

Another narrative trait involves the use of contrasts or dualities to examine situations. Mitchell's "shadows and light" contrasts indicate the uncertain nature of life events as they contemplate both sides of the situational coin—many times embellishing the narrator's struggle over some point of concern. "Don Juan's Reckless Daughter" is a strong case in point as the "eagle" and the "snake" metaphor is applied to strategic ends. There is a great deal of struggle in Mitchell's oeuvre, and she uses these symbolic contrasts to demonstrate her points. Last, the auteur's use of lyrical repetition and layered vocals represents both her efforts to reiterate a given song's nurturing observation and her painterly approach to songwriting. The layers and layers of voices, instruments, and sound effects offer direct evidence of our musical painter directing the sonic traffic on her canvas. Many of Mitchell's songs are very, very busy. From "The Pirate of Penance" through "Taming the Tiger," her layered vocals, parenthetical asides, crowded instrumentals, and mischievous sound effects demonstrate the painter in the sound studio. At times, the strategy works to great effect; at others, it creates unnecessary distractions. In all cases, they communicate Joni Mitchell's distinctive approach to songwriting.

So much of Elvis Costello's career resembles Bob Dylan's history. Their artistic philosophies, their attitudes about their audiences and the music industry, and their narrative styles share so many traits that seem to bind them, all the while respecting their differences. One major characteristic they share involves their narrative songwriting strategies and their "mission-oriented" approach. That is, Citizen Elvis's editorials—our "snapshots"—serve specific purposes that dictate the content and style of a given expression. Just as Dylan deployed one narrative strategy during his folk period, another during his freewheeling poet stage, another during his Americana era, yet another during his moral phase, and still others as his oeuvre continues to unfold, Costello followed one storytelling strategy in his initial work that evolved into another style in his "making of Citizen Elvis" period, totally shifted approaches during his brief punk tunesmith phase, and relied on the *style du jour* for his subsequent projects. Just look at the narrative diversity in Costello's work. He selected a roots music style for *King of America*, the epistolary mode for his chamber music project, and co-opted soul sounds, lounge attitudes, and country music methods to suit his needs as they arose. The adventurous combination of Declan McManus, Elvis Costello, and Citizen Elvis knows no boundaries as it ranges across the narrative landscape, choosing storytelling structures that serve a particular creative mission.

As he roams wherever his muse leads him, Costello's musical education serves his needs of the moment. Should his mission require a direct, coherent editorial response, he is more than equipped to comply. For example, when he wanted to tell his grandfather's story in "Any King's Shilling," he purposefully dressed the song in the language of his grandfather's day. He explained to Allan Jones how he used instruments and dialogue to systematically re-create the sounds and feel of 1914 in order to tell a story as precisely as he could. In "Tramp the Dirt Down" the auteur carefully used an everyday public relations scenario (a politician kissing a baby for a photograph) as a means of introducing his punishing observation regarding the hypocrisy he associated with Margaret Thatcher's government. Among all the impressionistic folly involved in his innovative techno-dance project (*When I Was Cruel*), he pauses for extremely precise attacks on lawyers ("Soul for Hire"), talk radio ("Radio Silence"), and women with all the answers ("Alibi"). When Citizen Elvis wants to tell you that British imperialism is bogus ("Oliver's Army"), that English housing projects and lifestyles are crumbling ("Little Palaces"), that television game shows are stupid ("Glitter Gulch"), that radio programmers are corrupt ("Radio, Radio"), or that war is a double-edged sword ("Shipbuilding"), he maintains the capacity to deliver his punishing observation in no uncertain terms, guaranteeing that his editorial pierces the heart of his target and conveying the rationale behind his attack for his audience. The resulting snapshot is in full color and 3-D. His lyrical precision is a direct result of his well-rounded musical education and his determined approach to his art.

Not all of Costello's snapshots are in full color. Occasionally, when you don your special 3-D glasses to look into a song, the images collide, the photo is unfocused, and a Citizen Elvis Rorschach test emerges. Gaze all you want, make of the imagery what you please. To the degree that the auteur dresses a song such as "Any King's Shilling," he may also dance around his subject through indirect expressions that are cloudy, evasive, and, at times, darned enigmatic. The "Crimes of Paris" may actually be as coherent a story as "Shilling," but to get to that interpretation you must endure some sort of Rorschach-like experience. (Good luck explaining your analysis to your friends!) Costello may twist the pronouns around to confuse the details (e.g., "Accidents Will Happen"), he may string disjointed images to a merry little tune (e.g., "Sunday's Best"), he may use the vernacular from some recognizable context in a playful manner (e.g., "Everyday I Write the Book"), he may rap along with pointed barbs that go absolutely nowhere (e.g., "Episode of Blonde"), or he may take you on a chaotic magic carpet ride around the world via madcap imagery, convoluted scenery, and intense personal symbolism that, once more, go nowhere (the delightful "Tokyo Storm Warning"). From the beautiful imagery of "Love Field," to the intense impressionism of "Deep Dark Truthful Mirror," to the playful prescriptions of "Tear Off Your Own Head," to the manic introspection of "Man Out of Time," Elvis Costello's narrative snapshots run the storytelling spectrum through prime numbers without common denominators. Here the punishing observation assumes a hit-and-run mission as it darts into the sonic snapshot, delivers its blow, and dashes off as quickly as it appeared.

Complementing his impressionistic gamesmanship is the auteur's penchant for sonic mischief. I know of no other writer who purposefully applies biting, perhaps even mean-spirited, lyrics within the context of a pleasant, sweet tune. Recall his comments to Lisa Traxler about his tendency to create musical contrasts (i.e., "a juxtaposition of quite evil lyrics against a very sweet tune") in an effort to counterbalance "the darker things in the lyrics." Here, my friends, is a songwriter who thinks through his work. He may dash down his observations in a quick, catch-as-catch-can manner— riding that inspiration as far as it will take him; however, once he has his editorial together, he enters his musical photo lab and selects the tones and textures of the subsequent aural snapshot. A light, merry pop tune such as "Tears Before Bedtime" may inspire you to dance across the room in a joyous manner, but all the while the lyrics recount a dark relational scene. You may jump around the disco dance floor to "Pump It Up" without realizing that the song viciously attacks the very setting in which you find yourself. It is sort of like going to church and singing a solemn hymn that praises the devil. There are times when the practice is quite clever. For instance, "I Want You" opens with a light folk tune that carries lyrics praising the narrator's love interest in no uncertain terms. Suddenly, you hear a jangled guitar lick, and it all turns more than blue, transcends indigo, and drifts into a dangerous black. Costello has effectively scored his scene. He delivers his punishing observation and leaves us to shake in its wake. Our auteur is a formidable songwriter.

As our exemplar chapter relates, Costello deploys a host of storytelling structures throughout his lifework. When you pull back from the oeuvre and consider his writing in its totality, two interesting themes emerge that bend and weave throughout the various songs. The first is rather obvious: Costello hates the "Clubland" scene. From day one, he has attacked the vacuous conversation, the cheesy fashion, the dead-end music, the nauseating mating rituals, and every other aspect of club life. But Citizen Elvis is not content to stop there. He understands *why* people lower themselves to the extent that they participate in these practices. Once more, just as Bruce Springsteen placed all those characters into cars as a means of escaping the societal situations that constricted their prosperity, Costello takes his characters to the nightclubs. In their youth, his characters jump around in pursuit of some form of "Human Touch" that makes sense of the "King Horse" bar scene mating rituals. As they age, they continue to play the same game in "Harpies Bizarre" as they transform bar scenes into parlor games. These characters debase themselves to the point of being participants in a spectator sport in which patrons gather in the local bar, watching fool after fool approach their "Little Angel" to no avail. These characters are totally unaware that they are in "Hell," trapped in a redundant lifestyle that assures their continued subjugation. When they go home to their "Little Palaces," Costello's characters experience more mind control as they consume restricted radio programming, dumb movies, stupid soap operas, and silly game shows. If boredom overcomes them, they beat their spouses, kids, and house pets. Just look at the number of songs that feature this scenario! The news media are active participants as well—serving sensational gibberish on tomorrow's "Fish 'n' Chip" paper. None of this is an accident, Citizen Elvis reports. The elite have built a trap specifically designed for their prey. Subsequently, Costello screams at the top of his voice, demanding that the hellish cycle end, denouncing the aristocrats for what they truly are, and delineating his punk populism and its aggressive individualism. And Citizen Elvis *never* gives up his fight. He may twist his funny knobs and play with his drum machine in support of his playful impressionism on *When I Was Cruel*, yet he pauses to attack soulless lawyers and mindless radio talk shows. It is an all-consuming passion.

Our second theme surprised me. Throughout the lifework, Costello displays a genuine concern for women. Among all the "Clubland" relational games and "Lipstick Vogue" histrionics is a consistent interest in the brutal abuses women endure. Now, this is the guy *everybody* deemed a misogynist. Just consider the evidence, and you will quickly see just how *wrong* those people were. "This Year's Girl" suffers through life—the boredom is stifling. Costello may question her role in all the clubland relational games in "Sulky Girl," but his concern over her well-being seems genuine (seeming to warn our sulky one to stop all this foolishness). In "All Grown Up," he encourages his female subject to get over her perceived problems and get on with her life. In "Sleep of the Just" and "Kinder Murder" he attacks the rapist thugs who treat women as objects. In "You Little Fool" and "Big Sister's Clothes" he warns the young lady of her impending doom. "Pony Street" features a mother-daughter dialogue in which they wrestle with different perspectives on the demands of the day. But he does not stop there. To the extent he protects women, he attacks men. The man in "White Knuckles" is a relentless brute, the male characters in *All This Useless Beauty* are rude and useless (e.g., "Poor Fracture Atlas" and the title cut), and the jerk in "Different Finger" is a conniving opportunist. Citizen Elvis understands. He is fully aware of the problem. As aristocratic England advances its subjugation over the populace by fostering useless nightclub diversions and mind-controlling media, it simultaneously places its women in harm's way. Costello's anger protects his female characters as much as it chides them (the former prime minister is, of course, an exception).

All of which once more demonstrates the value of systematic inquiry. To take a snippet here, a line there, a song from this album, or a *Rolling Stone* article from somewhere and use that impression as the basis for interpretation may go beyond a misleading conclusion—it may prove to be downright wrong. The knee-jerk opinion that all of Joni Mitchell's work is autobiographical, that Elvis Costello is a misogynist, that both writers' work is self-centered, or that their sonic wanderlust is pretentious takes an isolated event or opinion and distorts it into inaccuracy. In order to fully appreciate Mitchell's detailed murals or Costello's strategic snapshots, we must disassemble the work, respect its content on its terms, examine the various parts individually and collectively, and build an interpretation that is grounded in the work—not the critic's theoretical worldview, journalistic agenda, or popular opinion. When we dig into the oeuvre, we uncover the auteur free of his or her publicity or celebrity image. What emerges may be pleasing, disturbing, or uninteresting; nevertheless, it is *respectful* of the art. Hopefully, by considering Mitchell's and Costello's language use and narrative styles I have unveiled Earth Mother's letters and Citizen Elvis's editorials as the nurturing murals and the punishing snapshots they really are. Their consistency is their strength—a power that flows directly from their respective artistic philosophies and corresponding creative agendas. The result of our narrative inquiry is, as they say, quite a story.

THE AUTEURS: THE PRODUCTION METHODS

At this point I turn away from narrative interpretations of the auteurs' songwriting in order to consider two important aspects of their art: their production methods and performance styles. How these artists go about the process of recording their nurturing murals and punishing snapshots joins the public presentation of those works as crucial elements of their professional careers. Artistic philosophies, audience attitudes, industry relations, and more are on display in these two areas. Hopefully, by pausing to consider these two important variables, we add a depth of perspective that informs the overall analysis. To be sure, Mitchell and Costello record and perform the way they write. Letters are personal matters, and editorials conform to their context. We begin with the painter in the recording studio.

I enjoy a great many of Joni Mitchell's commentaries, but no remark touched me the way her recollection of her initial piano lessons did. When she recalled how she would cheat during her lessons by faking her reading and memorizing the notes, I thoroughly identified with her ingenuity. However, when she announced *why* she followed those practices, a compelling insight revealed itself. Do you remember what she said? She said she wanted to discover all the colors the piano had buried in it. What a line. The colors are everything to our Earth Mother. Remember her first memory and all of the colors she described? Color has always been Mitchell's artistic currency, as these remarks to *Vanity Fair* reveal:

> I'd say that I was born with a gift of metaphor—which you can translate into any of the arts quite nicely—and a love of color: color for the eyes, color for the ears. And I like colorful people. . . . Color is my first priority in the arts. . . . In the public-school system, I craved to have the box of 24 colors. I only had the box of 8; we couldn't afford the box of 24. But the 24 had magenta and turquoise and chartreuse and gold and silver and blonds in it. Oh, I wanted the 24!

And she has been looking for more and more colors ever since. Why settle for the 8 when you can have the 24 or the 48 or the 64? Searching for life's emotional colors and presenting them through the arts is Mitchell's calling. How she goes about that task demonstrates the wisdom of Arthur Kratzman's advice.

Mitchell is forthright in her description of the recording process. Yet at no time does she ever characterize herself as a professional musician. She is a painter, an architect, a film editor—*anything* but a professional musician. She described her method of music production to Perry Stern in 1986:

> I've always produced my own records so I'm used to being a benign dictator, or free-school teacher. I'll bring players in and give them as much verbal instruction as I can. I don't know what I'm looking for so it's more or less letting them go and waiting until I discover what it is I'm looking for. A lot of my process is intuitive. . . . Sometimes the things I want are so out of synch with fashion, and it appeared that this was happening again. I've been in this business long enough to have bucked these things before. The difficulty is in holding your ground and maintaining confidence in your own ideas against unanimous expertise.

As we have seen, our polio survivor can "hold her ground" with the best of them! Still, fighting for intuitions is a formidable challenge. During this intuitive process, she exercises patience and a firm belief in creative magic. Earth Mother *believes* in nature's power—that is certain. She brings an idea to the studio, encourages the musicians to play around with it, and patiently waits for the magic to strike. Little wonder she found a home in jazz and its improvisational attitudes.

Mitchell explained to Steve Pond that her working process is like "film editing" in that once she gets her "raw material," she likes to "snip and buff and move things around." She reported that she may play the same song "four times with as many different bands" as she looks for the "right balance" or that elusive new color. Pond quotes bassist-producer-husband Larry Klein: "She is a perfectionist. . . . But she has amazing instincts about what can be improved. She can't always articulate what she wants changed, but it always ends up better." There have got to be times when this is a frustrating process. To deal with that problem, Mitchell relies on her metaphorical skills, as she told Matt Resnicoff: "I give a lot of metaphorical instruction, because I'm a painter first; I see music diagrammatically and architecturally in my head." Hence, she provides a metaphorical "diagram" of her idea, encourages the musicians to experiment within that framework, and manipulates those "raw materials" until the "right balance" emerges.

The strongest insights about Mitchell's recording methods come from longtime engineer Henry Lewy. His vast experience with the artist sheds much light on the evolution of her production methods. He had this to say to Blair Jackson:

> I was a teacher and listener at first. When we first got together, she didn't really know anything about the studio, really. When we'd overdub vocals, for instance, she was so insecure that she had to hold a guitar, and that sort of thing. As the years went on, she picked up the engineering aspect more and more and today she knows what a studio can do for her and she knows how to get what she wants. . . . Joni has to be free to try things out. That's how she makes records. She'll come into the studio with a song one way and it'll end up being completely different when the record comes out. In between there are the different ideas she tries out. Some of them are good, some of them aren't. She has the intelligence to know when something is or isn't working out.

Lewy noted that Mitchell will assemble the musicians, record "three or four takes," and just listen to the results. He observed: "She doesn't want to think too much about them [her songs]—she just wants to play, and frequently you get some real magic happening in those takes." In Lewy's seasoned view, "She's essentially a painter . . . and she thinks of her music in painterly terms. She'll talk about adding a colour here or there, or having a skeleton and fleshing it out with more tones." Such an approach directly contributes to the layered qualities of her music. Once she has the various takes, they become paints to be applied to a musical canvas. She selects her sonic hues and moves them around until the desired effect emerges. The musicians play and she searches. It is all intuitive feel, as these comments to Divina Infusino suggest: "People working with you need to know where you're going with an idea. But I don't have an intellectual plan. So there are times when people working with me think I'm lost. But part of my process is to get good and lost. I start to work in random mode and try out crazy ideas. I put my critic to sleep during that process. But if I'm surrounded by minds with their critic wide awake, it's frustrating for me, for everyone."

The key to the process is simple: Mitchell is not afraid to take a risk. She places that "critic" in the closet and lets her "crazy ideas" flow. *That*, in her view, separates her from most producers, as she explained to Alan Jackson: "There's never been a producer. There never was a credit given, and I leaned heavily on artistic contributions from my players. A producer is [a] kind of guy who has the last word. Often he's a formula man. He's trying to make something commercial, and that can be a watering down. I don't think of producers generally speaking—and there are exceptions—as people who play long shots." Most producers, you see, would settle for the big-selling "box of 8," and Joni Mitchell will have none of that. As we noted in the impulse chapter, Mitchell learns from her mistakes and considers all of her work to be steps in her personal journey toward artistic perfection. If a project fails in her view, she never looks back, she seeks to understand the error of her thinking, she files the experience away, and she moves on to the next idea. She is fearless, and *that* is expensive. In 1985, she told *Musician*: "But one of the things I like about being my own producer is that I get to make my own mistakes. I've got no one to blame. I can just chalk it up to experience." Record companies do not share that point of view.

To summarize her production process, Mitchell records in an ensemble fashion. She captures performances on tape, moves them around until she achieves the desired effect, and assembles the various parts into a coherent whole. The results involve songs with layers and layers of voices, instrumentation, and sound effects. Even on her first record with David Crosby and its minimalist sound strategy, she layered voices on songs in a manner that foreshadowed her recording future. Throughout the process, she supervises herself. She depends on her musical colleagues for support, but she makes the decisions. As she related to Charles Gandee: "I have a painter's mentality, much more than a musician's. . . . A producer takes your brush and puts his strokes on." Subsequently, when she worked with Thomas Dolby, problems emerged. Dolby tried to add a stroke here or there as the project unfolded, and Mitchell dutifully donned her Roy Rogers outfit and put an end to that. Letter writing and painting are just not team sports.

There is an inherent danger in this recording strategy. If a recording artist isolates himself or herself too much, the resulting material may enter a state of sonic stagnation. The songs may sound alike, the sound design may become too narrow, and the musicians may work too hard to satisfy a recognizable formula. This can happen to the best bands. When The Who recorded *Who's Next*, producer Glyn Johns did his best to disrupt patterns he felt entrapped the band (this eventually resulted in a fistfight with Roger Daltrey). He heard standard Who sounds and tried to eliminate them wherever possible. He challenged the band to do something different, even if it meant trouble for him personally. This was not your typical "company man."

Regrettably, Mitchell never experienced that type of leadership. Instead, she relied on herself to do it all. Although Larry Klein certainly received production credits for his role as a co-producer, we just do not know the extent of his participation. The purity of expression associated with self-producing may be achieved at the cost of creative longevity. To assume the burden for the entire project requires so much of a recording artist that it may very well threaten ingenuity and creativity. I mean, Mitchell was responsible for the cover art as well. I am certain that she traveled to the pressing plant and supervised that process, too. Still, when you paint personal letters and fill them with detailed, nurturing thoughts, there may be no other alternative.

Editorial writers work in a different fashion. Here the medium dictates the content and form of the subsequent commentary. Should an editorial writer work for an academic publication, language and style must conform to those rigorous standards. Should he or she work for a popular publication, those requirements relax and informality becomes the norm. The context dictates the content's form. Moreover, editorial writers readily accept the division of labor associated with the production process. Headline writers, print/production designers, news anchors, technicians of all stripes, photo/video editors, and more have jobs to do as well. Therefore, diverse participation is accepted. No editorial writer does it all. In fact, it would *never* cross his or her mind.

Elvis Costello is a mission-oriented editorial writer. He may have a particular message he wants to convey, but he articulates that expression in terms of his creative mission. Should the creative goal involve a classical expression, Costello writes, performs, and records the work with those standards in mind. He will even go to the trouble of learning a new language in order to facilitate his communication with his colleagues. Should the mission reflect a techno-dance objective, he shapes his words and sounds accordingly—never fearing the input of professionals from that genre and readily accepting their direction. And I could go on. Costello's work with Nashville veteran Billy Sherrill, his experiences with Geoff Emerick, his projects with Langer and Winstanley, his pivotal work with T-Bone Burnett, and his marvelous collaboration with Burt Bacharach represent direct examples of Costello's capacity to conform to and work with different musical styles and professionals from those fields.

Central to the process is Costello's willingness to learn from producers and incorporate that knowledge into his vast, ongoing musical education. The process began with Nick Lowe, as Costello explained to Timothy White:

Up until then, because I had no experience in recording, I always thought that the more complicated the song was, the more merit it had. To some extent, he [Lowe] was instrumental in making me see the benefit of simplicity—and I adopted that as a creed from there on. As a singer, I always had an understanding with him that he would let me go so far with a vocal, but if he thought I was going past it and becoming too considered and losing the feeling, he'd stop me and use the earlier, imperfect take. He'd always allow me one or two wild takes beyond what he thought was it, in case I did something extraordinary that he wasn't expecting. He taught me a lot about craft *and* non-calculation—and that they needn't be in conflict.

The lesson is a meaningful one, but the willingness to learn is more important. When Costello and The Attractions signed on to work with Langer and Winstanley, Costello's musical education advanced once more. He described his evolution on the interview disc that accompanied the *Blood and Chocolate* reissue: "We'd never conformed to any kind of production design. Nick Lowe's productions had always been just capture what we did. Billy Sherrill's was sort of put up with what we did, and Geoff Emerick's was let us go along until we've sort of exhausted the possibilities and the permutations and then try to make sense of it. So this was the first time that we took a formal approach and, to some extent, it really worked." (Notice how Emerick's method resembles Mitchell's, and then listen to *Bedroom* and all of its layers of sounds.)

Lesson after lesson unfolded as our auteur brought his Citizen Elvis editorials to new aural contexts: T-Bone Burnett reinforced Costello's commitment to the *song* as his musical currency, the Brodskys carried Costello to a different musical planet with its own language and norms, Bacharach taught Costello the value of verbal economy, and the imposter (the production team for *When I Was Cruel*: Ciaran Cahill, Leo Pearson, and Kieran Lynch) taught our auteur what all those funny little knobs on beat boxes are for. Everywhere, new nuances had to be embraced, and Costello readily accepted that challenge. If any producer dared to compromise his standards by placing a bad mark on his editorial, I presume our punk populist was armed with his traditional bent nail, ready to do what he must in the name of free speech.

Again, the mission dictates the production strategy. Punk bands are recorded live—the more warts and raw emotions, the better. Pop bands are recorded in layers, with producers mixing and matching performances and using punch-ins and overdubs as necessary. (The Nashville sound *is* a pop sound.) Classical music is recorded live. Lounge music is tightly orchestrated. Dance music requires computers. Whatever the aural charge, our populist editorial writer was up for the challenge. Why not? A different sound is like a different publication or broadcasting outlet in that it takes the *message* to different audiences. None of the message is lost; it is merely recast in order to meet that medium's particular requirements.

In contrast to our painter, Costello is—first and foremost—a music professional. He was raised by a music professional and, therefore, exposed to the various divisions of labor associated with the musical world at an early age. Producers, engineers, studio musicians, publicists, broadcasters, journalists—any role you care to mention is readily accepted by the artist (well . . . almost). Recall his comments about his music's diversity and how it was his job to make music and the record company's job to sell it. His songs are *not* his children. His muse is *not* his spouse. His detachment is a result of his professional education and its understanding of the various roles involved in the processes of music production, marketing, and sales. Could you imagine Joni Mitchell performing a cold call before a music executive, pitching her heartfelt songs as he ignored her to take a call from his barber? Could you image her singing *louder* in order to get his attention? Or causing a scene outside a record company convention in order to get noticed? Or, better yet, changing her name to the most famous musical personality in the world? I don't think so.

These two artists offer meaningful contributions to the practice of songwriting, but they display very different professional orientations. The painter is an intuitive worker. The professional musician is a pragmatic worker. The painter controls her environment. The professional musician is open to other professional opinions. The painter allows no one to touch her canvas. The professional musician understands the division of labor associated with the recording process and readily accepts direction. The painter creates murals that convey nurturing observations that are designed to improve her audience's life and make the world a better place for all. The professional musician uses the industry to disseminate his editorial snapshots that contain his punishing take on the world around him. His job is to offer his view, not to save the world. He offers his opinion and goes home. Earth Mother, the painter. Citizen Elvis, the editorial writer. Both writers' contributions to the development of the celebrity-singer-songwriter role cannot be minimized.

THE AUTEURS: PERFORMANCE STYLES

The performance dimension of our two auteurs' careers is an interesting—and revealing—component of their art. Rare is the painter who paints before an audience. Rare is the professional musician who does not perform in public. For the painter, public performance was a fun, invigorating part of her musical career when she performed in clubs before 50 people. She was the life of the party. Her Ocean's 11 boys surrounded her, and she hammed it up for everyone's amusement. But take her to a stadium venue or before a huge festival crowd, and the funs stops. The personal sharing of emotions that is well-suited for a small crowd becomes another matter before a large, distant audience. The professional musician does not have this problem. He couldn't care less what his audience is doing or how big it is or how near it is to him on stage. Yet he, too, has a problem. His problem involves keeping *himself* interested in the performance. What can he do to keep the songs alive, to sustain his interest? The performance styles of these two artists, once again, reveal different artistic orientations that hold meaningful consequences for their art.

Joni Mitchell was a sight to behold when she first entered the coffee-houses of Toronto and, later, New York City. Her physical presence, her voice, and those wonderfully funky guitar tunings instantly separated her from Joan Baez and Judy Collins. And she wrote! What a composite. Little wonder David Crosby fell head over heels for her talent. But this scenario was short-lived. She described her evolution to *Musician*'s Bill Flanagan: "I really enjoyed playing clubs for about forty people. I liked being the center of attention. It was like being the life of the party. That I could handle. When it got to the big stage I found that I didn't enjoy it." When she performed before huge audiences and received their praises, it confused her. In 1979, she told *Rolling Stone* that her audiences did not even "know" her, so how could they possibly "worship" her? She continued: "That's why I became a confessional poet. I thought, 'You better know who you're applauding up here.' It was a compulsion to be honest with my audience." She elaborated for Vic Garbarini:

> I would stand up there receiving all this massed adulation and affection and think, "What are you all doing, you don't even know me." Affection like that usually doesn't come without some kind of intimacy, like in a one on one re-lationship. So I thought, you better know who you're grinning at up here, and I began to unveil more and more of my inner conflicts and feelings. Then, after about four years . . . I guess it's just the nature of the press, having built you up, they feel it's time to tear you down. So I began to receive a lot of un-favorable attention. At the same time it became harder and harder to sing these intimate songs at rock festivals. The bigger the audience I drew, the more honest I wanted to be.

With time, however, that attitude changed and she sought some remedy for her predicament. She discussed that situation in a 1972 *Sounds* inter-view:

> Like I gained a strange perspective of performing. I had a bad attitude about it, you know. I felt like what I was writing was too personal to be applauded for. I even thought that maybe the thing to do was to present the songs some different way—like a play or a classical performance where you play every-thing and then run off stage and let them do whatever they want, applaud or walk out. I was too close to my own work. Now I've gained a perspective, a distance on most of my songs. So that now I can feel them when I perform them, but I do have a certain detachment from the reality of the story.

It must be hard to read a personal letter in public. The larger the crowd, the more awkward the experience must be. But Mitchell's reaction! As the crowds grew bigger, she opened up more. As she opened up more, she resented the fact that she felt she had to open up more. This is one vicious cycle with no apparent end. Fortunately, Mitchell skated north on that river and returned to Canada for a break. From that, her anxieties relaxed for the time being.

Just what was the problem here? Why did performance affect Mitchell in this manner? Consider these remarks to Malka and *MacLean's* in 1974: "That's the wonderful thing about being a successful playwright or an author: you still maintain your anonymity, which is very important in order to be somewhat of a voyeur, to collect your observations for your material. And to suddenly often be the center of attention was . . . it threatened the writer in me. The performer threatened the writer." *Here* lies the answer to our question: Joni Mitchell is not a professional musician. She is a painter. Although she made her living—and earned much fame—as a professional musician, in her creative heart she is a painter. Perhaps if her first public performance had been before a sleeping Ewan MacColl, she would have developed the skills to dismiss her audience and follow her own instincts. But that did not happen. She developed a painter's mentality. And, as you may have noticed, painters do not follow patrons around galleries and absorb their praise or blame for each visual offering. There is a natural distance present. Mitchell longed for that situation. During a break between songs on the *Miles of Aisles* live recording, fans begin to scream out song titles in the hopes Mitchell will would perform them. Suddenly, she stops and remarks that this practice just does not happen in the visual arts. She cleverly notes that nobody ever yelled at Picasso, "Paint another 'Starry Night,' man!" This was Joni Mitchell's predicament. Though a multitalented artist of considerable skill, she was essentially out of her element.

As time passed, another consideration emerged. With age, Mitchell's medical history began creeping up on her. Standing for extended periods holding her guitar became too demanding for her physically. The rigors of touring, the physical strain of performing, and an increasingly deteriorating view of her audience and industry mechanisms virtually killed any desire to perform. When she recorded *Painting with Words and Music* in 1998, she discovered a compromise as she placed her paintings around the studio, furnished the set with couches and lamps for her audience, and performed in those intimate surroundings. Now, this is a set designer's nightmare if such an arrangement were extended to a touring situation. Simply, the performance dimension of Mitchell's art died quickly. The incongruity between personal statements and public settings, the ever-growing size of the venues, the mounting tensions within the performer, and the physical drain of it all guaranteed that this would be the one aspect of Mitchell's art to decay over time.

Professional musicians do not have that problem. In fact, they often write songs in order to have something to perform. When you grow up on stage, you become accustomed to all sorts of distractions from technicians, news media, and audiences. Experience provides distance, and distance facilitates longevity. Audience expectations have to be kept in perspective. Costello discussed this situation with *Newsweek*'s Jim Miller: "It's a bit of a dilemma. . . . You've got to play what they came to see. But I'm not a one-dimensional sort of paper tiger. You can make songs so crass that everyone can understand them, or complicated enough that they're interesting. I'm afraid that the preconceptions of the audience outweigh my powers of communication. Most of the time that we're onstage, I feel like a man from Mars." If audience "preconceptions" can be kept in their place, the performer is free to explore all of the possibilities that the stage offers—creating new sounds, using different theatrical devices, invigorating the art through a diversity of expression.

For Elvis Costello, the key to his performance style is that diversity. Although his mid-1990s tours with The Attractions relied on conventional staging techniques, most of Costello's performance history reflects a carelessly expensive, but hilariously innovative, commitment to musical theatricality. He has run the proverbial gauntlet. Shows include a cappella vocals without amplification (Costello standing center stage, belting out a song, demonstrating his voice's power); spinning wheels that contain song titles or "deadly sins" that audience members sling to determine the next song (afterward, the participant entered an onstage lounge or a disco dancing cage); theatrical chamber pieces, again without amplification; wacky games of musical chairs in which musicians vie for seats with different instruments, requiring the participants to play whatever instrument they "land on" for the following number; multiple-night residencies in which each night featured a different band or act; fronting full-fledged orchestras; and more. Costello played with one of Elvis Presley's bands (the TCB Band), Count Basie, Tony Bennett, the Swedish Symphony Orchestra, the Jazz Passengers, Irish folk acts, punk bands, what have you—often recasting old songs in new ways. His damn-the-cost (or minimalist) approach to staging has delighted fans, puzzled critics, angered record company executives, and rewarded venues in varying degrees at various times. Although it sounds trite, the man rarely did the same thing twice!

One compelling case in point involves the powerfully innovative project, *The Juliet Letters*. Here musicians from different parts of the musical world assembled to push each other into new creative realms. The Brodsky Quartet wrote its initial song lyrics; Elvis Costello learned to write music (certainly no moment's task). Once the record was issued, the artists promoted their work with a small tour. Two of the tour's limited number of stops were Boston and the San Francisco Bay area. Journalistic responses to the shows reflect the utter confusion this creative union produced. First, we consider the Bay area show, and Dave Becker's comments for the *Oakland Tribune*:

> Suppose you gave Aunt Bee a couple of pounds of ground sirloin, some imported black truffles and a bounty of fresh herbs. Chances are Mayberry's favorite chef would still turn out a meat loaf. Meat loaf is what she knew, what she did best, and no amount of top-shelf ingredients is going to substitute for basic technique. . . . Pop music is what Costello knows and what he does best. While he has the wherewithal these days to enlist classical artists like the Brodskys in his quest for musical glory, knowing how to utilize artists properly is an entirely different proposition. Time and again during Monday's performance . . . Costello demonstrated how far out of his element he has wandered with "Juliet."

The *San Jose Mercury News*'s Harry Sumrall responds to the same production:

> If rock really is about adventure and rebellion—and not a cliché involving cavorting buffoons in leather—then the show that Elvis Costello and the Brodsky Quartet gave . . . was the rock show of the decade. It was the best concert—period—to hit the Bay Area in ages. Performing songs from the recent album "The Juliet Letters," Costello and the Brodsky Quartet cut across the boundaries separating "rock" and "classical" and headed straight into new, provocative territory. They did it with wit and intelligence and a cocksure rebellion against musical stereotypes that earned them ovation after ovation from the capacity crowd. . . . No one who saw the show wanted it to end.

Two days later, the New England media interpreted the same event for their readers. Roger Catlin writes for the *Hartford Courant*: "The quieter format not only highlighted the lyrics but also Costello's voice, which was astonishing in its power and vibrato. . . . But his success in this venture has whetted the appetite for more intelligent, challenging music in venues where you needn't stand on chairs all night or show your appreciation by flicking a lighter." After viewing the same show, Jim Sullivan reports for the *Boston Globe*: "It seemed all their hearts were in the right place, but it rarely jelled. . . . While Costello and the Brodskys moved from loneliness to despair to madness to whimsy to folly to playfulness to heartbreak to a hint of redemption, it all added up to, well, not quite less than zero, but not a lot more. . . . Costello's vocalizing often seemed more like showboating than genuine emoting." Record reviews and sales (forget about radio airplay) followed similar, confused patterns: What is viewed as artistic achievement by one is considered to be commercial "showboating" by another.

Since his controversial American debut and its rigorous commitment to a preconceived style, Costello has floated from musical domain to musical domain with yesterday's folk singer becoming today's lounge singer becoming tomorrow's rock star and next week's chamber musician. Costello explained his diversity to *Billboard*: "There are all these things flying off in different directions for me, which, far from being dilettantish as some cynical people like to think, is the way I work. This is what I do . . . I am interested in all these things, and I'm passionate about each of them in turn." (There is nothing "dilettantish" about learning to write chamber music!) That passion yields hilarious moments, such as the spinning wheel tour, or the musical chairs act, or a quiet evening with The Coward Brothers. In all cases, regardless of the staging, Costello's singing controlled the show. The band may change, the sound may vary, the musical approach may differ, but his melodramatic voice defines his performance. At times, his voice's sheer power overcomes the words—taking the slightest sentiment and elevating its emotional impact. Just as Declan McManus's restless musical mind and Citizen Elvis's punishing editorials contribute to his career's distinctive qualities, so Elvis Costello's voice is a defining element of his art.

Interestingly, as time passed, it appears Costello became more and more comfortable with his role as an entertainer. His performances with Burt Bacharach, his 2002 tour with The Imposters in support of the *Cruel* projects, and, in one of his grandest moments, his appearance as the guest host on *Late Night with David Letterman* revealed an artist at peace with himself. Ever the punk, he brought his personality to the event—fearlessly tackling the performance task before him. He may wear a tuxedo and perform with a backing orchestra, he may sit on a stool and fondle the various buttons on his little beat boxes, he may perform jokes during an opening monologue, or he may scream and dance to 25-year-old songs—in all cases, the artist who watched the most important member of his audience sleep during his first performance takes measures to make sure that will never, ever happen again. The key, once more, is distance and diversity. Elvis Costello's musical teachers taught him well.

What a fascinating entity this "auteur" thing is. From his or her language use, to that language's arrangement within songs, to the means through which the songs are recorded, to their performance in public, we note compelling similarities and differences in the content and style of the two artists' work. The synthesis of biography, creative influence, artistic philosophy, and stylistic tendency that produces the auteur is a situation-specific phenomenon. Just look at what we have learned. A determined polio survivor with a penchant for the visual arts brings that determination and eye for detail to the musical context. Like all painters, she works alone as she takes personal prescriptions for living and creates sonic murals that convey her worldview. Her ambitions are grand. She is the consummate flower child. The simplicity of her peace and love prescriptions assumes an intensely personal tone. They revolutionize songwriting, but have little impact on the world around her. Her disappointment was devastating. Her eventual withdrawal was predictable. She was simply unable to "save something for herself." In contrast, a child raised in a musical family learns to play the phonograph before he can walk. He accompanies his father to live shows and radio and TV performances, and soaks up the situation. He listens intensely to his mother's jazz recordings. Everything feeds his musical education—including his attitude toward British aristocracy and institutional elitism. He becomes a professional musician and markets his work. He develops a punk attitude that enables him to distance himself from anything that debilitates his ability to ply his trade. That attitude is not a public façade or a publicity ploy, but a genuine extension of his personality. It fuels his pen. He develops as a songwriter and brings those abilities to the wide world of musical possibilities that he has been exposed to since his birth. He knows no creative boundaries, his commercial attitude is fearless, and his musical experiences are vast. His lifelong education created him, sustained him, and, ultimately, defined him.

What a fascinating entity this auteur thing is.

THE AUTEURS: JONI MITCHELL, ELVIS COSTELLO, AND THE TORCH TRADITION

When Billie Holiday strolled across the stage belting out Brown, Stept, and Tobias's "Comes Love" or Frank Sinatra cruised down the aisle crooning Arlen and Mercer's "One for My Baby (and One More for the Road)," their audiences were no doubt taken aback by the range and depth of the emotions conveyed by their performances. Holiday's demeanor and Sinatra's style were especially suited to the torch song's melodramatic tone. They sang from their hearts, playing their roles to their fullest. But it is unlikely that anybody in either audience took the songs as personal messages from Holiday or Sinatra. Nobody attributed the songs' contents to the life and times of the two singers. Yes, the performers personified the songs in their own unique ways. But the idea that those sentiments represented personal points of view just did not dawn on the audience. Popular music did not work that way. Singers sang songs that were written by professional songwriters, and *that* task was divided into at least two roles, the lyricist and the composer. Professional musicians were employed to accompany the singer, who performed the song under tightly orchestrated conditions. It was a complex process that followed tried-and-true formulas that were under the direct control of the music industry.

Then came Jimmie Rodgers, Woody Guthrie, Hank Williams . . . and Bob Dylan.

When Robert Allen Zimmerman invented his "Bob Dylan" character, he changed songwriting forever. While the Brill Building/Nashville/Hollywood tunesmiths continued to pen their faceless songs to fit their needs, Bob Dylan represented a musical hybrid that was a direct extension of Guthrie's image, Williams's poetry, Rodgers's sensibility, Little Richard's fire, and James Dean's rebellion (later, with a dash of Phil Spector's eyewear tossed in for good measure). Dylan was a *character* who delivered *messages* through an *image* and a *style* that made his writings more than songs from a singer; they represented a *text* delivered by an *author* with a public *personality*. When Bob Dylan stood before his audience, he was a man with a message. His looks, stage demeanor, media image, personal history (real or contrived), and song content joined his performance style to produce a musical celebrity with a highly publicized attitude. Whether rightly or wrongly attributed, that image influenced the entire creative commercial process. This was a long way from Nat King Cole, Patsy Cline, or the troubadours of southern France.

With the celebrity-singer-songwriter's arrival, the music industry changed. The technological and economic explosion that took the recording industry, radio, television, film, and print media to unimagined heights facilitated this evolution. From the mid-1950s on, the cult of celebrity emerged as a powerful cultural force. Movie stars, politicians, ecclesiastics, television personalities, musicians, and perfect strangers rode the new wave of personality-driven media. In terms of the music, though there was certainly some dilution of technical quality, the new self-contained artist was a potential gold mine for the industry, and a fresh musical experience for the listening public.

Once the musical world experienced Dylan, it was obviously just a matter of time before Joni Mitchell would follow. Like Dylan, she was a celebrity pioneer. With Mitchell, the celebrity-singer-songwriter composite discovered another dimension: the female personality. Although the auteur's writing, singing, and instrumental style transcend any "gender bag," she was most certainly an innovation. Like Dylan, she synthesized all that traveled before her through her personality, and generated something the musical world had yet experienced. She may decry the dilution of the process due to the lack of expertise the lone singer-songwriter brings to the musical process, but she was a major influence in the development of that creative composite. She told *Mojo*:

> Everybody's a singer-songwriter now, but not everybody should be, not everybody can do all of these things, and yet everybody does. And that's why I think music has gone downhill. It used to take three—a great lyricist and a great musician and then a great singer. Like with Frank [Sinatra], and that's why that stuff is so enduring—because you had three gifted people doing it. Now you've got people, they're not really a great singer or a great writer or a great musician doing it, so the standards have dropped severely. And ironically, at the same time that the standards dropped, the machines have increased. These people have 20 times the distribution, so the bad stuff is really everywhere.

Indeed, the "bad stuff" was "everywhere" by the summer of hate. By 1977, the celebrity-singer-songwriter had achieved ubiquity. There were the "next"

Bob Dylans, the "next" Joni Mitchells. If you were born in the late 1950s or early 1960s, you were inundated with pop sounds, celebrity images, and corporate propaganda. Music celebrities indulged themselves in every way, and the public thoroughly absorbed the publicity. The summer of hate produced a much-anticipated backlash. Joni Mitchell's complaint echoed around the musical world, and the response was intensely negative.

The British punk scene, for example, spat on the success that passed before it. For virtually all of these bands, however, that reaction was sociological, not musical. There was *one* character who offered the world an informed, grounded *musical* response to the situation before him, but nobody listened as much as they looked. The sight of a gangly, bespectacled, nervy guy with a guitar was so distinctive in an age of rock pretension that it became a distraction. (Of course, name him "Elvis" and that will seal the deal, right?) Elvis Costello carefully watched the cult of personality have its way with Bob Dylan, Joni Mitchell, The Beatles, and more. He also observed his father's career. He listened to *everything*. From that education, he molded a character, shaped a sound, and entered the fray. *Nobody* thought his career would turn out the way it has.

With Joni Mitchell and Elvis Costello we have the state of the art of the celebrity-singer-songwriter composite. One was a pioneer, the other a student. Both brought personalities, worldviews, and talent to the musical world. When Joni Mitchell strolled across the stage belting out "River" or Elvis Costello cruised down the aisle crooning "Alison," the audience was no doubt taken aback by the range and depth of the emotions conveyed by the performance. Mitchell's demeanor and Costello's style were especially suited to the torch song's melodramatic tone. They sang from their hearts, playing their roles to their fullest. It is most likely that everybody in each audience took the songs as personal messages from Mitchell and Costello, and little doubt that everybody attributed the songs' contents to the life and times of the two singers. Not only did the performers personify the songs in their own unique ways, they wrote them. The idea that these sentiments represented personal points of view was the principal basis of the audiences' relationship with the songs. Popular music now works that way.

Hopefully, this book has demonstrated how the cult of personality that accompanies the celebrity-singer-songwriter composite has transformed a musical genre that is most often associated with a context, and attached it to a personality. Initially, torch singers were like characters in a movie. You attended the film, absorbed the performance, and praised or condemned the experience. With Mitchell and Costello, the process became more like a long-running television series. You returned to the characters week after week for another round of performances. You got to *know* the characters, their points of view, and their personalities. And *that* influenced how you responded to their work. A rich, moving, melodramatic love song—a *torch* song—was no longer an isolated experience when performed by these two personalities. No. It was yet another episode from an unfolding story.

And what stories they are.

References

GENERAL

Chaytor, H. (1912). *The troubadours*. Cambridge: Cambridge University Press.

Clarke, D. (1995). *The rise and fall of popular music*. New York: St. Martin's.

Crawford, R. (2001). *America's musical life: A history*. New York: W.W. Norton.

Davis, F. (1995). *The history of the blues: The roots, the music, the people from Charley Patton to Robert Cray*. New York: Hyperion.

Flanagan, B. (1986). *Written in my soul: Rock's great songwriters talk about creating their music*. New York: Contemporary.

Furia, P. (1992). *The poets of Tin Pan Alley: A history of America's great lyricists*. New York: Oxford University Press.

Gillett, C. (1996). *The sound of the city: The rise of rock and roll*. New York: Da Capo.

Guralnick, P. (1986). *Sweet soul music: Rhythm and blues and the southern dream of freedom*. New York: HarperPerennial.

Guralnick, P. (1989). *Feel like going home*. New York: Perennial Library.

Guralnick, P. (1989). *Lost highway: Journeys and arrivals of American musicians*. New York: HarperPerennial.

Hilburn, R. (2002, February 10). Cheatin' hearts, faithful history. *latimes.com*.

The history of rock 'n' roll. (1995). Time-Life Video.

Jasen, D., and Jones, G. (1998). *Spreadin' rhythm around: Black popular songwriters, 1880–1930*. New York: Schirmer.

Malone, B. (1985). *Country music USA*. Austin: University of Texas Press.

Marcus, G. (1997). *Invisible republic: Bob Dylan's basement tapes*. New York: Henry Holt.

Palmer, R. (1978). *Baby, that was rock and roll: The legendary Leiber and Stoller*. New York: Harcourt Brace Jovanovich.

Pollock, B. (1975). *In their own words*. New York: Macmillan.

Rock 'n' Roll. (1995). Public Broadcasting System. Boston: WGBH.

Santelli, R., George-Warren, H., and Brown, J. (Eds.). (2001). *American roots music.* New York: Abrams.

Smith, L. (1999). *Pete Townshend: The minstrel's dilemma.* Westport, CT: Praeger.

Smith, L. (2002). *Bob Dylan, Bruce Springsteen and American Song.* Westport, CT: Praeger.

Taylor, G. (1989). *Reinventing Shakespeare: A cultural history from Restoration to the present.* New York: Oxford Univerity Press.

Webb, J. (1998). *Tunesmith: Inside the art of songwriting.* New York: Hyperion.

White, T. (1990). *Rock lives: Profiles and interviews.* New York: Henry Holt.

Wilder, A. (1972). *American popular song: The great innovators, 1900–1950.* New York: Oxford University Press.

Wilhelm, J. (1970). *Seven troubadours: The creators of modern verse.* University Park: Penn State University Press.

Zollo, P. (1997). *Songwriters on songwriting.* New York: Da Capo.

JONI MITCHELL

Anderman, J. (2000, May 30). Mitchell and her songs age with grace and class. *Boston Globe* (NEWSBANK).

Barol, B. (1985, November 4). Grown-up James, adult Joni. *Newsweek*, pp. 79–81.

Bell, C., and Sexton, P. (1998, August 22). Mitchell unleashes "Tiger' on Reprise. *Billboard*, p. 1.

Bishop, E. (1988, April 9). "Chalk Mark in a Rain Storm." *The Keene Sentinel* (NEWSBANK).

Blair, I. (1988, April 17). Joni Mitchell goes back to basics. *Boston Herald* (NEWSBANK).

Boyd, J., and George-Warren, H. (1992). *Musicians in tune.* New York: Fireside.

Breskin, D. (1987, February). Joni Mitchell. *Musician*, pp. 49, 54.

Brinn, D. (2000, March 28). Joni's reckless sister. *Jerusalem Post*, p. 10.

Brown, J. (1988, April 6). Two voices' middle-aged renaissance. *Washington Post*, p. B7.

Brown, L. (1968, July 6). Joni Mitchell. *Rolling Stone*, jmdl.com.

Clark, M. (2000, February 13). A long look back for Joni. *Houston Chronicle*, p. 6.

Cocks, J. (1991, March 4). Navigator of the deep. *Time*, p. 74.

Considine, J. (1988, April 21). Records: *Chalk Mark in a Rain Storm. Rolling Stone*, p. 110.

Considine, J. (1998, September 29). Legends don't have to play the MTV game. *The* [Baltimore] *Sun*, p. 1E.

Coppage, N. (1979, October). Joni's "Mingus." *Stereo Review*, p. 100.

Coppage, N. (1983, March). Joni Mitchell: *Wild Things Run Fast. Stereo Review*, pp. 101–2.

Crouse, T. (1971, August 5). *Blue. Rolling Stone*, jmdl.com.

Crowe, C. (1979, July 26). The Rolling Stone interview: Joni Mitchell. *Rolling Stone*, pp. 47–53.

Cullman, B. (1982, December). Record reviews: Joni Mitchell: *Wild Things Run Fast. Musician*, p. 100.

Dallas, K. (1968, September 28). Joni, the seagull from Saskatoon. *Melody Maker*, jmdl.com.

Davis, S. (1975, February 13). Records: *Miles of Aisles. Rolling Stone*, p. 78.

DeLuca, D. (1994, October 25). Joni Mitchell: Melancholy music, but not by design. *Philadelphia Inquirer* (NEWSBANK).

DeVoss, D. (1974, December 16). Rock 'n' roll's leading lady. *Time*, pp. 63–66.

DiMartino, D. (1998, August). The unfiltered Joni Mitchell. *Mojo*, jmdl.com.

Dunn, J. (1994, December 15). Q&A: Joni Mitchell. *Rolling Stone*, p. 32.

Emerson, K. (1974, April). Records: *Court and Spark. Creem*, p. 65.

Ephland, J. (1996, December). Joni Mitchell and Cassandra Wilson. *Down Beat*, pp. 18–25.

Escott, C. (1991). *Good rockin' tonight: Sun Records and the birth of rock 'n' roll*. New York: St. Martin's.

Farber, J. (1994, October 27). They repaved paradise. *New York Daily News* (NEWSBANK).

Farley, C. (1998, November 2). Burning bright. *Time South Pacific*, p. 72.

Feather, L. (1979, September 6). Joni Mitchell makes *Mingus. Down Beat*, pp. 16–17, 49, 52–53, 56.

Feldman, J. (1983, February). Records: Joni Mitchell: *Wild Things Run Fast. Creem*, pp. 53–54.

Flanagan, B. (1985, December). Joni Mitchell loses her cool. *Musician*, pp. 64–74.

Flanagan, B. (1997, June). Joni Mitchell. *Vanity Fair*, pp. 167–79.

Flanagan, B. (1988, May). Secret places: Joni Mitchell builds shelter from the rainstorm. *Musician*, pp. 65–79.

Gandee, C. (1995, April). Triumph of the will. *Vogue*, pp. 191, 194, 196–200.

Garbarini, V. (1983, January). Joni Mitchell. *Musician*, pp. 42–52.

Garcia, G. (1994, November 28). A deeper shade of blue. *Time*, p. 83.

Gilbert, J. (1970, January 10). Joni still feels the pull of the country. *Melody Maker*, jmdl.com.

Gilbert, M. (1991, March 17). Joni Mitchell comes in from the cold. *Boston Globe* (NEWSBANK).

Givens, R. (1991, June). Joni Mitchell updates her life and times. *Stereo Review*, p. 73.

Goldberg, J. (1979, November). Records: Wrong ring, wrong classification. *Creem*, pp. 50–51.

Graff, G. (1988, March 27). Joni Mitchell brushes up her style. *Detroit Free Press* (NEWSBANK).

Gundersen, E. (1998, September 29). Joni Mitchell, still untamed. *USA Today*, pp. D1–2.

Hall, C. (1979, August 25). The new Joni Mitchell. *Washington Post*, pp. B1, 3.

Harrington, R. (2000, February 20). 'Both Sides Now'—and then Joni Mitchell, taking a swing through pop standards of the '30s and '40s. *Washington Post* (NEWSBANK).

Harrington, R. (2002, December 4). Joni Mitchell gets back to the garden. *Washington Post*, jmdl.com.

Heckman, D. (1978, March). Joni Mitchell: She soars, she orbits, she never lands. *High Fidelity Magazine*, pp. 123–24.

Hilburn, R. (1991, February 24). Out of the canyon. *Los Angeles Times* (NEWSBANK).

Hilburn, R. (1994, October 27). "Your life should affect your direction." *Los Angeles Times* (NEWSBANK).

Hilburn, R. (1996, December 8). Both sides, later. *Los Angeles Times* (NEWSBANK).

Hilburn, R. (1998, September 26). Mitchell brings perspective and wit to "Taming the Tiger." *Los Angeles Times* (NEWSBANK).

Hilburn, R. (2000, February 6). Checking in with . . . Joni Mitchell. *Los Angeles Times* (NEWSBANK).

Hilburn, R. (2000, May 15). Mitchell's truly fusing Both Sides Now. *Los Angeles Times*, p. F5.

Himes, G. (1979, August 19). Joni Mitchell: Music makes the world go round. *Washington Post*, p. L3.

Himes, G. (1982, August 26). Journeys into jazz. *Washington Post*, p. D12.

Himes, G. (1991, March 3). The last of the literary. *Washington Post* (NEWSBANK).

Hinton, B. (1996). *Joni Mitchell: Both sides now*. London: Sanctuary.

Holden, S. (1976, January 15). Records: A 'Summer' garden of verses. *Rolling Stone*, p. 50.

Holden, S. (1980, November 13). Records: Joni Mitchell's live album is a surprise and a triumph. *Rolling Stone*, pp. 57–58.

Holden, S. (1985, October 16). Joni Mitchell takes up topicality. *New York Times*, p. 16.

Holden, S. (2000, February 13). Something's lost and something's gained. *New York Times*, p. 2:29.

Hoskyns, B. (1994, December). Our lady of the sorrows. *Mojo*, jmdl.com.

Howell, D. (1994, July 11). "Just me and my guitar": Joni Mitchell. *Vancouver Sun* (NEWSBANK).

Hunter, J. (2002, November 28). Joni Mitchell: *Travelogue*. *Rollingstone.com*.

Infusino, D. (1988, April 3). A "Chalk" talk with Joni Mitchell. *San Diego Union* (NEWSBANK).

Jackson, A. (1985, November 30). Joni Mitchell. *New Music Express*, jmdl.com.

Jackson, A. (2000, February 26). The new Joni Mitchell. *London Times Magazine*, jmdl.com.

Jackson, B. (1983, April 22). Subject—Henry Lewy. *BAM*, jmdl.com.

Jennings, N. (1988, April 4). Portrait of an artist in her prime. *MacLean's*, pp. 54–55.

Jennings, N. (1988, April 4). A voice in the spirits. *MacLean's*, pp. 54–55.

Jennings, N. (1994, October 31). Lady of the canyon. *MacLean's*, p. 66.

Johnson, B. (1997, April 21). Joni's secret: When a pop legend found her long-lost daughter, a musical prophecy came true. *Maclean's*, pp. 49–52.

Kart, L. (1979, August 26). Mitchell and Mingus. *Chicago Tribune*, pp. 6:6–7.

Kernis, M. (1978, January 11). "Daughter": Bitterness with a steely edge. *Washington Post*, p. B4.

King, P. (1988, April 17). Joni Mitchell still poppin' with "Chalk Mark in a Rainstorm." *Pittsburgh Press* (NEWSBANK).

King, P. (1991, March 24). At 47, Joni Mitchell takes a look back. *Pittsburgh Press* (NEWSBANK).

Klein, L. (2000). Liner notes to *Both Sides Now*. Reprise Records.

Landau, J. (1974, February 28). Records: Joni Mitchell: A delicate balance. *Rolling Stone*, pp. 54–55.

Levitin, D. (2000). A conversation with Joni Mitchell. In S. Luftig (Ed.), *The Joni*

Mitchell companion: Four decades of commentary (pp. 177–88). New York: Schirmer.

The Life and Times of Joni Mitchell: A Woman of Heart and Mind. (2003). *American Masters*. PBS.

Lowman, R. (2000, May 15). Performance shows new side of Mitchell. *Los Angeles Daily News* (NEWSBANK).

Luftig, S. (Ed.) (2000). *The Joni Mitchell companion: Four decades of commentary.* New York: Schirmer.

MacDonald, P. (2000, February 10). Joni Mitchell looks back. *Seattle Times* (NEWSBANK).

Malamut, B. (1974, April). Records: Red roses for a blue lady of the canyon. *Crawdaddy*, pp. 65–66.

Maron, Malka. (1974, June). Self-portrait of a superstar. *MacLean's*, jmdl.com.

Maslin, J. (1978, March 9). Joni Mitchell's reckless and shapeless "Daughter." *Rolling Stone*, p. 54.

McCardell, C. (1983, April). Joni Mitchell: *Wild Things Run Fast. Trouser Press*, pp. 44–45, 49.

McKenna, K. (1982, November 14). Mitchell makes habit of change. *Los Angeles Times* (NEWSBANK).

McKenna K. (1988, March 27). Chalking it up to experience. *Los Angeles Times* (NEWSBANK).

Meisel, P. (1977, January). An end to innocence: How Joni Mitchell fails. *Village Voice*, jmdl.com

Milward, J. (1982, November 25). Records: More songs about love from Joni Mitchell. *Rolling Stone*, pp. 70–72.

Milward, J. (1994, December 15). Joni Mitchell: *Turbulent Indigo. Rolling Stone*, p. 98.

Mitchell, J. (1975). Liner notes to *The Hissing of Summer Lawns*. Asylum Records.

Mitchell, J. (1979). Liner notes to *Mingus*. Asylum Records.

Mitchell, J. (1997). *Joni Mitchell: The complete poems and lyrics*. New York: Crown.

Mitchell, J. (2002). Liner notes to *Travelogue*. Nonesuch Records.

Mitchell, J. (2003, April 8). *Travelogue*. VH1.com.

Mitchell masters nuances of melancholy. (1994, December 9). *Winston-Salem Journal* (NEWSBANK).

Moon, T. (1991, March 5). New joy of Joni Mitchell. *Philadelphia Inquirer* (NEWSBANK).

Moon, T. (1996, December 4). Compilations "Hits" and "Misses" work to Joni Mitchell's disadvantage. *Philadelphia Inquirer* (NEWSBANK).

Murphy, M. (1972, November 21). Joni Mitchell's new "For the Roses." *Los Angeles Times*, p. 12.

Murthi, R. (1999, January 20). Mitchell still works her spell. *New Straits Times*, p. 4.

Nash, A. (1986, March). Joni Mitchell. *Stereo Review*, pp. 69–71.

Newman, M. (1996, August 24). Joni Mitchell offers "Hits" and "Misses." *Billboard*, p. 1.

O'Brien, K. (2001). *Joni Mitchell: Shadows and light*. London: Virgin.

O'Connor, R. (1988, August). Talking to: Joni Mitchell. *Vogue*, pp. 273, 276.

Ouellette, D. (1991, June). Joni Mitchell: *Night Ride Home. Down Beat*, p. 31.

Pareles, J. (1978, February). Four sides now. *Crawdaddy*, p. 63.

Phillips, S. (1977, February). Joni Mitchell interview. *ZigZag,* jmdl.com.

Point, M. (1988, April 7). Erratic album is Mitchell on an upswing. *Austin American-Statesman* (NEWSBANK).

Pond, S. (1982, November 25). Joni Mitchell: Wild things run fast. *Rolling Stone,* pp. 27–29, 87.

Pond, S. (1988, April 21). Mitchell 'storms' back. *Rolling Stone,* p. 20.

Purvis, A. (1997, April 21). Joni, no longer blue. *Time,* p. 101.

Reginato, J. (2002, December). The diva's last stand. *W,* jmdl.com.

Resnicoff, M. (1991, March). Front woman: Joni Mitchell. *Musician,* p. 7.

Resnicoff, M. (1992, February). Joni Mitchell on tunings. *Musician,* p. 70.

Rising folksinger from Saskatoon discusses career. (1966, July 28). *Saskatoon StarPhoenix,* jmdl.com.

Robins, W. (1975, March). Records: *Miles of Aisles. Creem,* pp. 68–69.

Rockwell, J. (2003, January 5). Joni Mitchell's long and restless journey. *New York Times,* jmdl.com.

Rodgers, J. (2000). Setting the stage: The vocal and lyrical craft of Joni Mitchell. In S. Luftig (Ed.), *The Joni Mitchell companion: Four decades of commentary* (pp. 255–60). New York: Schirmer.

Rohter, L. (1975, December 3). Capturing California's essence. *Washington Post,* pp. C1, 4.

Rohter, L. (1976, December 8). Self-centered fantasy. *Washington Post,* p. B8.

Rowland, M. (1985, November). Record reviews: Joni Mitchell: *Dog Eat Dog. Musician,* p. 105.

Ruhlmann, W. (1988, May 10). Joni Mitchell and her music have played a "Circle Game." *New York Tribune* (NEWSBANK).

Ruhlmann, W. (1995, February 17). From blue to indigo. *Goldmine,* jmdl.com.

Salamon, J. (1996, December). Spins: Joni Mitchell: *Misses, Hits. Spin,* p. 145.

Sanders, L. (1991, March 1). The grown-up game. *Entertainment Weekly,* jmdl.com.

Schruers, F. (1977, February). Records: Joni drones, Melanie finds new key. *Crawdaddy,* pp. 71–72.

Selvin, J. (2000, May 15). Joni Mitchell's dull twist on standards. *San Francisco Chronicle* (NEWSBANK).

Shuster, F. (1994, November 22). These "Turbulent" times. *Los Angeles Daily News* (NEWSBANK).

Sinclair, T. (1991, March 21). *Night Ride Home. Rolling Stone,* p. 79.

Small, M. (1985, December 6). She's looked at life from up and down, so Joni Mitchell has new ways to write about both sides now. *People Weekly,* pp. 93–98.

Smith, P. (1985, November 24). Joni Mitchell turns on the juice. *St. Petersburg Times* (NEWSBANK).

Songwriter returns to pop after jazz fling. (1983, June 17). *Arizona Republic* (NEWSBANK).

Stern, C. (1995, January/February). Songs to aging children: Joni Mitchell pulls your ear. *Musician,* pp. 22–30.

Stern, P. (1986, February). Joni Mitchell—The benign dictator. *Canadian Musician,* jmdl.com.

Sumrall, H. (1985, November 24). Joni Mitchell. *San Jose Mercury News* (NEWSBANK).

Sutherland, S. (1977, March). Joni Mitchell's "Hejira." *High Fidelity Magazine*, pp. 138–39.

Sutherland, S. (1979, September). Mitchell and Mingus. *High Fidelity Magazine*, pp. 141–42.

Swartley, A. (1977, February 10). Records: Mitchell: The siren and the symbolist. *Rolling Stone*, pp. 99–100.

Swartley, A. (1979, September 6). The babe in bopperland and the great jazz composer. *Rolling Stone*, pp. 53–55.

Tannenbaum, R. (1986, January 16). Records: Joni Mitchell: *Dog Eat Dog. Rolling Stone*, p. 47.

Tucker, K. (1977, March). Records: *Hejira. Creem*, p. 59.

Tucker, K. (1985, December 1). Renaissance for Joni Mitchell. *Philadelphia Inquirer* (NEWSBANK).

Valentine, P. (1972, June 3). Joni Mitchell interview, part 1. *Sounds*, jmdl.com.

Valentine, P. (1972, June 10). Joni Mitchell interview, part 2. *Sounds*, jmdl.com.

Van Matre, L. (1972, February 22). Joni's inward journeys. *Chicago Tribune*, p. 2:3.

Varga, G. (1998, September 24). New stripes: Joni Mitchell returns—and roams free—with subtle, nuanced "Tiger." *San Diego Union-Tribune* (NEWSBANK).

Walls, R. (1978, February). Records: Don Juan says he doesn't know you. *Creem*, p. 60.

Ward, E. (2000). Charles, Joni, and the circle game. In S. Luftig (Ed.), *The Joni Mitchell companion: Four decades of commentary* (pp. 103–106). New York: Schirmer.

Weinstein, N. (2000, February 25). Joni Mitchell's new look at "Both Sides Now." *Christian Science Monitor*, p. 19.

White, T. (1994, August 27). Joni Mitchell's many shades of "Indigo." *Billboard*, p. 5.

White, T. (1995, December 9). Joni Mitchell—A portrait of the artist. *Billboard*, jmdl.com.

White, T. (2001, September 8). Words from a woman of heart and mind. *Billboard*, jmdl.com.

Whyte, M. (2002, November 19). Joni Mitchell not "sour," will keep making music. *Toronto Star*, thestar.com.

Wild, D. (1979, December). Caught! Joni Mitchell, The Persuasions. *Down Beat*, pp. 68–69.

Wild, D. (1991, May 30). A conversation with Joni Mitchell. *Rolling Stone*, pp. 63–67.

Wild, D. (1992, October 15). Joni Mitchell. *Rolling Stone*, pp. 167–69.

Wild, D. (1995, March 23). Performance: Joni Mitchell. *Rolling Stone*, p. 46.

Wild, D. (1997, March 6). Melancholy meets the infinite sadness. *Rolling Stone*, pp. 46–47, 84.

Wild, D. (2000, April 13). Q&A: Joni Mitchell. *Rolling Stone*, p. 48.

Wild, D. (2002, October 31). Women in rock: Join Mitchell. *Rolling Stone*, pp. 115–16.

Willis, E. (1973, March 3). Joni Mitchell: Still travelling. *New Yorker*, pp. 104–5.

Woodard, J. (1994, December). Reviews: Joni Mitchell: *Turbulent Indigo. Musician*, pp. 92–94.

ELVIS COSTELLO

Alkyer, F. (1991, June). *Mighty Like a Rose. Down Beat*, pp. 37–38.

Altman, B. (1980, December). Records: Costello's inventory closeout: B-sides, "A" material. *Creem*, p. 52.

Aquilante, D. (1991, June 24). Mellow Costello still aims true. *New York Post* (NEWSBANK).

Aquilante, D. (1995, August 4). Short on "Variety." *New York Post* (NEWSBANK).

Baird, J. (1983, October). Elvis Costello: *Punch the Clock. Musician*, p. 93.

Bambarger, B. (1996, May 18). New Elvis Costello set stars Attractions. *Billboard*, pp. 11, 74.

Bambarger, B. (1998, February 7). Costello signs unorthodox multi-label P'gram pact. *Billboard*, pp. 1, 89.

Barton, D. (1987, April 17). Costello puts his best points forward. *Sacramento Bee* (NEWSBANK).

Becker, B. (1993, March 17). Elvis Costello way out of his element with "Juliet Letters." *Oakland Tribune* (NEWSBANK).

Berger, A. (1998, November 26). Performance: Elvis Costello and Burt Bacharach. *Rolling Stone*, p. 42.

Bessman, J. (1993, February 6). Costello project has strings attached. *Billboard*, pp. 14–15.

Bessman, J. (1993, August 7). Rykodisc nabs Costello catalog. *Billboard*, pp. 8, 73.

Bessman, J. (1997, October 25). Elvis Costello ends WB stint with compilation. *Billboard*, pp. 9, 54.

Bessman, J. (1998, August 29). Bacharach, Costello team their talents on new Mercury set. *Billboard*, pp. 5, 93.

Binelli, M. (1998, October 29). The buddy system. *Rolling Stone*, pp. 64–65.

Blair, I. (1989, March 5). Elvis is back! *Chicago Tribune*, p. 13:6.

Blair, I. (1989, March 8). Costello in a classy comeback. *Boston Herald* (NEWSBANK).

Booth, D. (1996, May 18). *All This Useless Beauty. Melody Maker*, p. 49.

Branigan, T. (1996, July 13). Singles: Little Atoms. *Melody Maker*, p. 54.

Britt, B. (1989, September 14). Slow start, but Costello comes through in the end. *Los Angeles Daily News* (NEWSBANK).

Britt, B. (1993, March 16). Costello takes a different tack with strings. *Los Angeles Daily News* (NEWSBANK).

Brogan, D. (1986, October 14). Costello shatters the mold. *Chicago Tribune* (NEWSBANK).

Brown, M. (1993, January 17). Elvis Costello's latest is one few will hear. *Orange County Register* (NEWSBANK).

Browne, D. (1989, March 26). A kinder, gentler Elvis. *New York Daily News* (NEWSBANK).

Browne, D. (1994, March 18). Four angry men. *Entertainment Weekly*, p. 100.

Browne, D. (1998, October 2). Charmed forces. *Entertainment Weekly*, pp. 71–72.

Buonaiuto, C. (1993, February). Elvis Costello. *Musician*, p. 7.

Byrne, D. (1998). Elvis Costello with Burt Bacharach interview. Sessionsatwest54th.com.

Carson, T. (1980, April 17). Records: Elvis Costello happy? Of course not. *Rolling Stone*, pp. 53–55.

Catlin, R. (1989, April 3). Costello, up to new tricks, is good as gold. *Hartford Courant* (NEWSBANK).

Catlin, R. (1989, August 17). Elvis Costello gets happy in concert at Compounce. *Hartford Courant* (NEWSBANK).

Catlin, R. (1993, March 19). Elvis Costello's pop flirts well with classical. *Hartford Courant* (NEWSBANK).

Catlin, R. (1993, October 27). The king and his namesake. *Hartford Courant* (NEWSBANK).

Cavanagh, D. (2002, May). 10 questions for Elvis Costello. *Mojo*, n.p.

Charlie Rose Show. (2002, May 24). Elvis Costello interview. PBS.

Chin, B. (1986, September 18). No sweetness in Elvis' "Chocolate." *New York Post* (NEWSBANK).

Christensen, T. (1986, October 19). Elvis Costello's fun and games. *Milwaukee Journal* (NEWSBANK).

Christensen, T. (1996, May 12). Power surges in Costello's new album. *Dallas Morning News* (NEWSBANK).

Clark, R. (1994, March 12). Froom's sensitivity keeps acts coming back. *Billboard*, pp. 69–70.

Clayton-Lea, T. (1998). *Elvis Costello: A biography*. New York: Fromm International.

Cohen, D. (1980, December 11). Elvis Costello holds a rummage sale. *Rolling Stone*, p. 56.

Cohen, M. (1978, February). Records: *My Aim Is True*. *Creem*, p. 59.

Cohen, M. (1984, September). Elvis's sticky wickets. *Creem*, p. 57.

Coleman, M. (1986, March 27). Elvis Costello's crown of thorns. *Rolling Stone*, pp. 113–14.

Coleman, M. (1993, March 4). Elvis Costello's classical gas. *Rolling Stone*, p. 23.

Connelly, C. (1982, February 18). Costello cheery, generous at three U.S. shows. *Rolling Stone*, p. 41.

Connelly, C. (1983, September 1). Records: Costello: too much yakety-yak. *Rolling Stone*, pp. 47–49.

Considine, J. D. (1989, March 5). Elvis Costello cuts a new path without his band. *The* [Baltimore] *Sun* (NEWSBANK).

Costello, E. (1993). Liner notes to *The Juliet Letters*. Warner Bros. Records.

Costello, E. (1995). Liner notes to *Goodbye Cruel World*. Rykodisc.

Costello, E. (1995). Liner notes to *King of America*. Demon Records.

Costello, E. (1995). Liner notes to *Kojak Variety*. Warner Bros. Records.

Costello, E. (1995). Liner notes to *Punch the Clock*. Rykodisc.

Costello, E. (2001). Liner notes to *All This Useless Beauty*. Rhino Entertainment Company.

Costello, E. (2001). Liner notes to *Spike*. Rhino Entertainment Company.

Costello, E. (2002). Liner notes to *Armed Forces*. Rhino Entertainment Company.

Costello, E. (2002). Liner notes to *Blood and Chocolate*. Rhino Entertainment Company.

Costello, E. (2002). Liner notes to *Brutal Youth*. Rhino Entertainment Company.

Costello, E. (2002). Liner notes to *Imperial Bedroom*. Rhino Entertainment Company.

Costello, E. (2002). Liner notes to *Mighty like a Rose*. Rhino Entertainment Company.

Costello, E. (2002). Liner notes to *This Year's Model*. Rhino Entertainment Company.

Crain, Z. (2002, May 2). Elvis Costello: *When I Was Cruel*. *Houston Press*, n.p.

Cromelin, R. (1980, October 4). Costello at his most candid. *Los Angeles Times*, pp. 5, 8.

Cromelin, R. (1983, August 7). Costello clocks out. *Los Angeles Times*, p. 69.

Cromelin, R. (1989, February 5). Costello opens floodgates in "Spike." *Los Angeles Times*, p. C72.

Crook, D. (1986, October 4). Costello and the rock photo wars. *Los Angeles Times*, pp. VI:1, 7.

Darnall, S. (1998, October 16). First person: Elvis Costello. *Chicago Tribune*, p. 7:3.

De Barros, P. (2002, May 17). Elvis Costello pumps it up with new album, outlook. *Seattletimes.com.*

DeCaro, F. (1998, October 11). What's it all about? Simply Burt. *New York Times*, pp. 9:1, 4.

DiMartino, D. (1991, May). Recordings: I'm okay, you're a jerk: Elvis Costello gets his dander up. *Musician*, pp. 88–90.

DiMartino, D. (1996, July). Records: Elvis Costello: *All This Useless Beauty. Musician*, pp. 86–87.

Di Perma, A. (2002, May). Jesus of cruel. *Pulse*, n.p.

Doerschuk, R., and Kubernik, H. (1999, January). The harmony of opposites. *Musician*, pp. 30–40.

Duffy, T. (1995, May 27). Costello's "Variety" show gets worldwide attention. *Billboard*, p. 45.

Duffy, T. (1996, October 26). Collaborations spur U.K.'s Elvis Costello, Lush. *Billboard*, pp. 1, 48.

Edwards, G. (2003, June 26). In the studio: Elvis Costello. *Rolling Stone*, p. 18.

Ehrlich, D. (2002, May). Music's master craftsman shares his songwriting secrets. *Interview*, n.p.

Elvis blasts Bruce! (1986, October 12). *Los Angeles Times*, pp. C:80–81.

Elvis Costello: An overview disc. (1995). Rykodisc.

Elvis Costello and the Brodsky Quartet. (1993, May). Reviews: Popular music. *Stereo Review*, p. 83.

The Elvis Costello that no one knows. (1977, November 3). *Rolling Stone*, p. 39.

England's Elvis: Gut emotions. (1977, December 26). *Time*, p. 60.

Everett-Green, R. (2002, April 25). The aim is truer than ever. *Toronto Globe and Mail*, p. R7.

Farber, J. (1991, April 28). Anger's away and Elvis sails. *New York Daily News* (NEWSBANK).

Farber, J. (1995, May 23). Elvis "Kojak" makes bald mistakes. *New York Daily News* (NEWSBANK).

Farber, J. (2002, April 14). Why Elvis Costello's aim is still true. *New York Daily News*, n.p.

Fissinger, L. (1983, November). Records: Elvis Costello: *Punch the Clock. Creem*, pp. 51–52.

Flaherty, M. (1998, October 2). Committed to "Memory." *Entertainment Weekly*, p. 72.

Flanagan, B. (1986, March). The last Elvis Costello interview you'll ever need to read. *Musician*, pp. 36–53.

Flanagan, B. (1994, March). Elvis Costello and his invisible twin. *Musician*, pp. 22–34, 97.

Fortune, R. (2002, March 27). Cruel intentions. *Time Out*, n.p.

Franklin, N. (1998, October 19). Dept. of give and take. *The New Yorker*, pp. 28–29.

Friar, W. (1996, September 1). Concert a testimony to the attraction of Elvis Costello. *Oakland Tribune* (NEWSBANK).

Fricke, D. (1986, April 10). This year's model. *Rolling Stone*, pp. 23–24.

Fricke, D. (1998, December 24). Elvis Costello with Burt Bacharach: *Painted from Memory*. *Rolling Stone*, p. 159.

Gallo, P. (1989, August 18). Elvis Costello's mixed bag of styles. *New Haven Register* (NEWSBANK).

Garbarini, V. (1991, May 16). *Mighty Like a Rose*. *Rolling Stone*, pp. 112–13.

Gardner, E. (1993, March 18). *The Juliet Letters*. *Rolling Stone*, pp. 39–40.

Gates, D. (1993, February 22). String along with Elvis. *Newsweek*, p. 65.

Gehr, R. (1998, December). Reviews: *Painted from Memory*. *Spin*, p. 183.

Get Happy!! (1989, November 16). *Rolling Stone*, p. 75.

Gilmore, M. (1979, April 5). Two sides of Elvis Costello. *Rolling Stone*, p. 84.

Gilmore, M. (1986, March 2). After some mediocre work, he regains his aim and name. *Los Angeles Herald Examiner* (NEWSBANK).

Goldstein, P. (1978, May). Can Elvis Costello cure acne? *Creem*, pp. 36–37, 65–66.

Goodman, T. (1996, May 17). Elvis proves his voice to be king. *Contra Costa Times* (NEWSBANK).

Gouldstone, D. (1989). *Elvis Costello: God's comic*. New York: St. Martin's.

Graff, G. (1989, April 21). The acid voice of Elvis Costello. *Detroit Free Press* (NEWSBANK).

Graff, G. (1993, January 31). Elvis Costello, classics quartet join forces for chamber pop. *Detroit News and Free Press* (NEWSBANK).

Hampton, H. (1994, April). Elvis Costello: *Brutal Youth*. *Spin*, pp. 88, 90.

Harrington, R. (1998, October 11). "Painted": Brushes with heartache. *Washington Post*.com.

Harris, M. (1994, July 14). Performance: Elvis Costello and the Attractions. *Rolling Stone*, p. 36.

Heaton, M. (1989, August 13). Singer's aim proves true during boffo Nautica show. *Cleveland Plain Dealer* (NEWSBANK).

Hewitt, P. (1981, March 7). Pumping up this green and pleasant land. *Melody Maker*, pp. 14–15, 35.

Hewitt, P. (1981, October 17). Fast forward: Elvis grilled. *Melody Maker*, p. 3.

Hilburn, R. (1977, November 22). A reluctant Elvis Costello. *Los Angeles Times*, pp. IV:1, 8.

Hilburn, R. (1978, January 8). 1977 music roundup: The top of the pop. *Los Angeles Times*, p. 58.

Hilburn, R. (1978, April 23). Costello, Lowe: The power in pop. *Los Angeles Times*, p. 72.

Hilburn, R. (1978, May 30). Rock's "Bad Boy" takes on the media. *Los Angeles Times*, pp. IV:1, 8.

Hilburn, R. (1978, June 1). Tantrum mars Costello date. *Los Angeles Times*, p. 19.

Hilburn, R. (1979, January 14). Elvis Costello: Rock's soldier of the mind. *Los Angeles Times*, p. 62.

Hilburn, R. (1979, February 13). Costello crests the new wave. *Los Angeles Times*, pp. 1, 8.

Hilburn, R. (1979, February 20). A second great Elvis in rock. *Los Angeles Times*, pp. 10–11.

Hilburn, R. (1981, January 10). Costello: Storm center of rock. *Los Angeles Times*, pp. 6, 13.

Hilburn, R. (1981, February 2). Elvis to Elvis: The name is still in good hands. *Los Angeles Times*, p. 63.

Hilburn, R. (1981, October 24). Costello cuts conventional country LP. *Los Angeles Times*, pp. 3, 7.

Hilburn, R. (1981, December 31). Tensing in the dark: An evening with Costello. *Los Angeles Times*, pp. V:5, 10.

Hilburn, R. (1982, July 18). Elvis Costello: Shedding the image of an angry young man. *Los Angeles Times*, pp. C:1, 60–61.

Hilburn, R. (1982, July 20). Fanning Costello's new image. *Los Angeles Times*, pp. 1, 4.

Hilburn, R. (1983, September 16). Costello's aim is still true. *Los Angeles Times*, pp. VI:1, 14.

Hilburn, R. (1983, September 20). Elvis Costello acquits himself again. *Los Angeles Times*, p. VI:4.

Hilburn, R. (1984, May 3). Costello climbs back off a limb. *Los Angeles Times*, pp. VI:1, 4.

Hilburn, R. (1984, December 23). Court's in session on pop violations. *Los Angeles Times*, p. 62.

Hilburn, R. (1986, September 28). Costello redux: Mixing blood, chocolate and rock 'n' roll. *Los Angeles Times*, p. C3.

Hilburn, R. (1986, October 3). Costello not quite off the cuff enough. *Los Angeles Times*, pp. VI:1, 16.

Hilburn, R. (1986, October 7). The Costello watch: Night 5: A great moment in L.A. rock. *Los Angeles Times*, p. VI: 7.

Hilburn, R. (1990, November 11). Costello's true aim. *Los Angeles Times*, p. 64.

Hilburn, R. (1991, May 28). Costello retains his fury and bite. *Los Angeles Times*, pp. F1, 6.

Hilburn, R. (1996, May 16). Costello's still the bard of the bittersweet. *Los Angeles Times* (NEWSBANK).

Himes, G. (1980, April 6). The other Elvis. *Washington Post*, p. E8.

Himes, G. (1981, November 5). Country road. *Washington Post*, p. C12.

Himes, G. (1982, August 22). Retain the rock, revive the refined. *Washington Post*, p. K7.

Himes, G. (1989, February 5). Costello and Cockburn: Two dazzling returns. *Washington Post*, pp. G6, 7.

Hinckley, D. (1986, February 24). The new and improved Elvis Costello. *New York Daily News* (NEWSBANK).

Hinton, B. (1999). *Let them all talk: The music of Elvis Costello*. London: Redwood Books.

Hodgins, P. (1993, January 17). Clash of musical aesthetics, not poor writing, dooms "Letters." *Orange County Register* (NEWSBANK).

Hodgkinson, W. (2002, April 5). Elvis Costello. GuardianUnlimited.co.uk.

Hoekstra, D. (1989, August 11). Forget the jive as Elvis Costello joins the Rude Five live. *Chicago Sun Times* (NEWSBANK).

Holden, S. (1983, August 9). Rock: Elvis Costello and his band. *New York Times*, p. C13.

Holden, S. (1983, September 14). Elvis Costello has first hit in the U.S. *New York Times*, p. C18.

Holden, S. (1984, July 8). Elvis Costello strives toward grown-up pop. *New York Times*, pp. B19, 22.

Holden, S. (1991, May 15). The pop life: Elvis Costello, the believing skeptic. *New York Times*, p. C13.

Holden, S. (1991, June 24). A softer image for Elvis Costello. *New York Times*, p. C9.

Holden, S. (1993, January 31). Elvis Costello laces punk with grand ambitions. *New York Times*, p. B24.

Holden, S. (1993, March 22). Song cycle unites musical opposites. *New York Times*, p. C15.

Holden, S. (1995, June 4). Recycled pop: New life from old songs? *New York Times*, p. B28.

Holden, S. (1998, October 4). Pop classicists leave the crowd behind. *New York Times*, pp. 33–34.

Hughley, M. (1996, August 30). Elvis lives! *The Oregonian* (NEWSBANK).

Hume, M. (1981, December 10). Costello goes country. *Rolling Stone*, pp. 91, 94.

Irwin, C. (1989, July). Floor singer's revenge. *Folk Roots*, pp. 44–49.

Jacobson, M. (1994, April). His aim is still true. *Esquire*, p. 36.

Jones, A. (1977, June 25). The Elvis (Costello, that is) interview. *Melody Maker*, p. 14.

Jones, A. (1986, March 1). Crown time is over. *Melody Maker*, pp. 16–18.

Jones, A. (1989, May 13). Elvis Costello: Songs of love and hate. *Melody Maker*, pp. 32–34.

Jones, A. (1989, May 20). Elvis Costello: The beloved entertainer, part two. *Melody Maker*, pp. 30–31.

Jones, A. (1997, June). Armed forces: The full story of Elvis Costello's calamitous 1979 American tour. *Uncut*, pp. 56–65.

Kalogerakis, G. (1994, April). Elvis revived. *Vogue*, pp. 206–7.

Katz, L. (1986, October 18). Costello: King of surprise. *Boston Herald* (NEWSBANK).

Katz, L. (1989, February 7). Elvis Costello at his best in risky album. *Boston Herald* (NEWSBANK).

Katz, L. (1993, January 22). Costello dares mix classical and rock in "Juliet Letters." *Boston Herald* (NEWSBANK).

Katz, L. (1993, March 14). Elvis Costello changes focus for Symphony Hall. *Boston Herald* (NEWSBANK).

Katz, L. (1994, March 10). Elvis Costello proves he's not your average rocker. *Boston Herald* (NEWSBANK).

Katz, L. (1998, October 9). Naked truths and Elvis citings: What's new Bacharach? A collaborator named Costello. Boston Herald.com.

Kehoe, P. (2002, April 12). Interview about *When I Was Cruel*. *RTE Guide*, n.p.

Kelp, L. (1986, October 10). Elvis Costello: Good rock but no surprises. *Oakland Tribune* (NEWSBANK).

Kelp, L. (1989, February 26). Elvis Costello: A rock renaissance for punk's angry young man. *Oakland Tribune* (NEWSBANK).

Kelp, L. (1989, September 18). Wet weather fails to foil Elvis. *Oakland Tribune* (NEWSBANK).

Kelp, L. (1991, June 3). He's a little hoarse, but Elvis lives. *Oakland Tribune* (NEWSBANK).

Kent, N. (1978, February). Revenge! Guilt! Frustration! Welcome to the working of Elvis Costello's mind. *Creem*, pp. 27, 69–72.

Kent, N. (1978, March 25). Elvis Costello. *New Musical Express*, pp. 27–29.

Kent, N. (1979, September). Murder on the Liverpool express. *Creem*, pp. 18, 21.

Kent, N. (1994). *The Dark Stuff: Selected writings on rock music, 1972–1995.* New York: Da Capo.

Kenton, G. (1980, October 5). Elvis Costello and John Hiatt. *Washington Post*, p. M5.

Kot, G. (1991, June 2). The last word from Elvis Costello. *Chicago Tribune*, pp. 13: 4–5.

Kot, G. (1998, October 15). *Painted from Memory. Rolling Stone*, pp. 130–31.

Lababedi, I. (1987, February). Elvis Costello and the Attractions: *Blood and Chocolate. Creem*, p. 15.

Laswell, M. (1989, October 5). Elvis Costello and the SNL weenies. *Rolling Stone*, p. 69.

Leiby, R. (1994, June 16). Elvis lives! *Washington Post* (NEWSBANK).

Leland, J. (1991, July 8). Time is on their side. *Newsweek*, pp. 54–56.

Leland, J. (2002, April 28). Questions for Elvis Costello. *New York Times*, n.p.

Levin, E. (1986, June 9). Elvis Costello. *People*, pp. 61–65.

Lioce, T. (1983, August 19). Elvis on Elvis. *Providence Journal* (NEWSBANK).

Live! Regis & Kathie Lee. (1998, September 29). Interview with Elvis Costello and Burt Bacharach. WTHR: Indianapolis, IN.

Lloyd, J. (1979, April 10). Elvis Costello plays a "tune" full of slurs. *Chicago Tribune*, p. 5.

Lustig, J. (1991, August 12). Costello turns on the talent, anger, tenderness. (Newark) *Star-Ledger* (NEWSBANK).

Marcus, G. (1977, December 1). Records: Don't tread on me. *Rolling Stone*, pp. 69–73.

Marcus, G. (1978, January 12). Elvis: His aim is off. *Rolling Stone*, p. 68.

Marcus, G. (1982, September 2). Elvis Costello explains himself. *Rolling Stone*, pp. 12–17, 56.

Marcus, G. (1993). *Ranters and crowd pleasers: Punk in pop music 1977–92.* New York: Doubleday.

Marcus, G. (1997, March). Elvis Costello's warmth in cold places. *Interview*, p. 80.

Margasak, P. (1998, October 16). Critic's choice: Elvis Costello and Burt Bacharach. *The Reader's Guide*, p. 52.

Marine, C. (1996, May 16). Costello: Unplugged and sounding good. *San Francisco Examiner* (NEWSBANK).

Marsh, D. (1978, May 18). Hate conquers. *Rolling Stone*, p. 38.

Maslin, J. (1979, March 22). Elvis Costello in love and war. *Rolling Stone*, pp. 59–60.

Mayer, I. (1986, October 23). Elvis Costello's anger arouses a powerful, haunting heartache. *New York Post* (NEWSBANK).

Maynard, J. (1983, September). Portrait: Elvis Costello. *Life*, pp. 21–22.

McKenna, K. (1984, June 24). Costello: The Picasso of pop. *Los Angeles Times*, p. 63.

McLeese, D. (1989, March 5). Elvis Costello. *Chicago Sun Times* (NEWSBANK).

Mendoza M. (1986, October 19). Costello goes beyond punk. (Woodbridge) *News Tribune* (NEWSBANK).

Mendoza, M. (1993, January 28). Elvis Costello can take a few bows for his new album's classical tone. *Dallas Morning News* (NEWSBANK).

Mendoza, M. (1993, October 14). Discs affirm Costello's importance. *Dallas Morning News* (NEWSBANK).

Milano, B. (1996, September). Elvis Costello and the Attractions: *All This Useless Beauty*. *Stereo Review*, p. 107.

Miller, J. (1981, February 23). Riding the new wave. *Newsweek*, p. 77.

Miller, J. (1982, August 9). No more Mr. Bad Guy. *Newsweek*, p. 41.

Miller, J. (1984, June 18). Return of rock heroes. *Newsweek*, p. 100.

Miller, J. (1989, March 13). Getting back on track: Elvis Costello. *Newsweek*, p. 68.

Mitchell, J. (1989, September 7). Grown-up Costello puts on a show. *Rocky Mountain News* (NEWSBANK).

Moon, T. (1986, March 6). Elvis Costello shows his serious side. *Miami Herald* (NEWSBANK).

Moon, T. (1989, February 9). Costello mixes art and pop. *Philadelphia Inquirer* (NEWSBANK).

Moon, T. (1989, August 21). A new Elvis Costello with greater finesse. *Philadelphia Inquirer* (NEWSBANK).

Moon, T. (1996, August 9). For Elvis Costello, the aim is to remain true to himself. *Philadelphia Inquirer* (NEWSBANK).

Morse, S. (2002, April 21). Elvis Costello's aim returns to rock with a definite rhythm. *Boston Globe*, p. L9.

Moses, M. (1989, April 24). Wise guys. *New Yorker*, pp. 84–85, 87.

Musicians. (2002, April 29). Elvis Costello. Bravo.

Nesin, J. (1980, June). Records: Elvis Costello seeks the window up above. *Creem*, p. 52.

Nesin, J. (1986, June). Records: Imperial margarine. *Creem*, p. 26.

Norris, C. (1995, May 22). *Kojak Variety*. *New York*, pp. 126–27.

O'Connor, R. (1994, March 24). *Brutal Youth*. *Rolling Stone*, p. 96.

Okrent, D. (1998, November 23). An unusual Elvis sighting. *Fortune*, p. 48.

Palmer, R. (1981, February 2). Rock: Elvis Costello shows range and consistency. *New York Times*, p. C13.

Pareles, J. (1978, June). Below the belt. *Crawdaddy*, p. 70.

Pareles, J. (1984, August 20). Elvis Costello in Forest Hills concert. *New York Times*, p. C21.

Pareles, J. (1989, February 19). Elvis Costello's happy marriage of lyrics and music. *New York Times*, p. B29.

Pareles, J. (1989, April 13). Elvis Costello, still taking risks. *New York Times*, p. C19.

Pareles, J. (1995, August 4). Costello sings of romance and betrayal. *New York Times*, p. C2.

Pareles, J. (1998, October 15). From roots of lilt and punk. *New York Times*, p. E5.

Perone, J. E. (1998). *Elvis Costello: A bio-bibliography*. Westport, CT: Greenwood.

Philbrook, E. (2003, May). Beyond belief: Elvis Costello's astonishing career. ASCAP.com.

Pond, S. (1986, December 4). The many moods of Elvis Costello. *Rolling Stone*, p. 20.

Puterbaugh, P. (1982, August 5). Elvis: His "Bedroom" is more like a mansion. *Rolling Stone*, 46–48.

Puterbaugh, P. (1994, July). Elvis Costello, 1994's model. *Stereo Review*, p. 77.

Puterbaugh, P. (1995, July). Elvis Costello, cover boy. *Stereo Review*, pp. 75–76.

Rachlis, K. (1978, June 29). Records: Who's afraid of Elvis Costello? *Rolling Stone*, pp. 53–54.

Rein, R. (1979, April 23). It's Elvis Costello v. Bonnie Bramlett in rock's vituperative battle of Britain. *People Weekly*, pp. 43–44.

Robbins, I. (1989, August 29). Still skillful Costello falls short. *New York Post* (NEWSBANK).

Robins, W. (1989, March 12). His aim is still true. *Newsday* (NEWSBANK).

Robins, W. (1989, April 13). A solo Elvis Costello pumps it up. *Newsday* (NEWSBANK).

Robinson, L. (1996, May 17). Costello's aim still true. *New York Post* (NEWSBANK).

Rogers, F. (1989, March 10). Elvis Costello's big musical wheel keeps on turning. *Atlanta Journal* (NEWSBANK).

Rosenburg, S. (1994, May 9). Elvis still angry, but more mature. *San Francisco Examiner* (NEWSBANK).

Rowland, M. (1989, March). Elvis Costello in love and war. *Musician*, pp. 62–79, 98.

Ruhlmann, W. (1989, September 1). The return of Elvis Costello. *New York Tribune* (NEWSBANK).

St. Michael, M. (1986). *Elvis Costello: An illustrated biography*. London: Omnibus Press.

Samuels, L. (1986, March 16). Elvis Costello hits top form in "King of America" album. *Dallas Morning News* (NEWSBANK).

Samuels, L. (1986, November 9). Costello's new LP will have fans rocking. *Dallas Morning News* (NEWSBANK).

Sandora, M. (1998, October 19). Talking with . . . Elvis Costello. *People*, p. 46.

Sandow, G. (1989, September 14). Costello makes power play. *Los Angeles Herald Examiner* (NEWSBANK).

Santoro, G. (1994, May 30). This year's model. *The Nation*, pp. 762–764.

Sasfy, J. (1977, December 25). Elvis: The new king of rock 'n' roll. *Washington Post*, p. H7.

Saturday Early Show. (2002, April 27). Elvis Costello interview. New York: CBS.

Scapelliti, C. (2002, June). Cruel inventions. *Guitar World*, n.p.

Scheuer, D. (1986, December 15). The unconventional Elvis Costello. *Scholastic Update*, p. 15.

Schinder, S. (1998, October). Reviews: *Painted from Memory*. *Pulse!* p. 66.

Schoemer, K. (1991, May 12). A word or two (or three) on love, death and insects. *New York Times*, p. B30.

Schoemer, K. (1998, October 5). The odd couple. *Newsweek*, pp. 80–81.

Schruers, F. (1979, May 17). What'd I say? *Rolling Stone*, pp. 9, 24.

Schruers, F. (1984, August). Elvis Costello and the Attractions: *Goodbye Cruel World*. *Musician*, pp. 90–91.

Schulps, D. (1977, November). Separate ways. *Crawdaddy*, pp. 98–99.

Schulps, D. (1977, December). Elvis Costello: I fought the law! *Trouser Press*, pp. 10–12, 33.

Shapiro, S. (2002, April 16). Elvis Costello: All this useful chatter. VH1.com.

Sheppard, D. (2000). *Elvis Costello*. New York: Thunder Mouth Press.

Shewey, D. (1984, July 5). Records: Elvis Costello: *Goodbye Cruel World*. *Rolling Stone*, p. 44.

Shuster, F. (1991, August 15). Elvis Costello: Thrill is gone. *Los Angeles Daily News* (NEWSBANK).

Silverman, D. (1989, April 24). Elvis Costello still a riveting rocker, but 3rd set's a dud. *Chicago Tribune*, p. 14.

Simels, S. (1986, June). "King of America." *Stereo Review*, p. 113.

Snyder, M. (1983, September 18). Elvis Costello still rues racist gaffe. *San Francisco Chronicle* (NEWSBANK).

Snyder, M. (1989, September 10). Mellow Costello in comeback. *San Francisco Examiner* (NEWSBANK).

"Spike" drives home Costello's cosmic vision. (1989, March 5). (Newark) *Star-Ledger* (NEWSBANK).

Strauss, N. (1996, May 25). A songwriter's odyssey to points of view he once observed. *New York Times*, pp. 13, 17.

Storytellers. (1996, June 20). Elvis Costello. New York: VH1.

Sullivan, J. (1989, March 31). This year's Elvis Costello. *Boston Globe* (NEWSBANK).

Sullivan, J. (1993, March 19). Weight of his latest reinvention drags Costello down. *Boston Globe* (NEWSBANK).

Sullivan, J. (1996, August 16). Elvis Costello: Happy people's punk. *Boston Globe* (NEWSBANK).

Sumrall, H. (1993, March 17). This decade's model. *San Jose Mercury News* (NEWSBANK).

Swartley, A. (1978, June 29). Costello wins his game of risk. *Rolling Stone*, p. 68.

Tannenbaum, R. (1986, November 6). Records: *Blood and Chocolate*. *Rolling Stone*, p. 74.

Teller. (1993, June). Name that tune. *The New Yorker*, p. 100.

This Year's Model. (1987, August 27). *Rolling Stone*, p. 72.

Traxler, L. (1985, February). Elvis Costello's cruel world blues. *Creem*, pp. 36–39, 60.

Tucker, K. (1981, April 2). "Trust" never sleeps. *Rolling Stone*, pp. 58–59.

Tucker, K. (1994, March 13). Elvis Costello, a shrewd pop pro pushing 40. *New York Times*, p. 33.

Van Matre, L. (1978, April 24). Costello gains confidence with softer punk. *Chicago Tribune*, p. 2:5.

Van Matre, L. (1979, March 12). Elvis Costello is witty but still resistible, alas. *Chicago Tribune*, p. 2:5.

Van Matre, L. (1981, January 19). Stripped of his affectations, Costello far more effective. *Chicago Tribune*, p. 2:8.

Van Matre, L. (1984, April 26). Costello as solo act: Bring back the band. *Chicago Tribune*, p. 5:13.

Varga, G. (1993, January 28). Costello experiment "Juliet Letters" won't qualify as a classic. *San Diego Union* (NEWSBANK).

Varga, G. (2002, May 23). Elvis, unchained. *San Diego Union Tribune*, n.p.

Vaziri, A. (1998, October 4). Q&A with Elvis Costello. *San Francisco Chronicle*, p. 41.

Vowell, S. (1998, November). My aim is blue. *GQ*, pp. 161–66.

Walls, R. (1982, November). Records: E.C.'s emotional rescue. *Creem*, p. 56.

Walls, R. (1989, May). E.C. is here there and everywhere. *High Fidelity*, pp. 71, 73.

Walls, R. (1995, June 29). *Kojak Variety. Rolling Stone*, p. 43.

Walsh, B. (2002, May 1). The importance of being Elvis. HMV.com.

Walters, B. (1989, February 9). Elvis Costello's subtle "Spike." *San Francisco Examiner* (NEWBANK).

Walters, B. (1989, September 18). Mellow Costello. *San Francisco Examiner* (NEWSBANK).

Walters, B. (2002, May 9). Elvis Costello *When I Was Cruel*. Rolling Stone.com.

Whitall, S. (1991, June 7). Costello has a new look, but he's the same old skeptic. *Detroit News* (NEWSBANK).

White, T. (1994, February 4). Elvis Costello's sweet bird of "Youth." *Billboard*, p. 3.

Wild, D. (1989, March 9). What's so funny about peace, love and Elvis. *Rolling Stone*, pp. 103–4.

Wild, D. (1989, June 1). Interview: Elvis Costello. *Rolling Stone*, pp. 62–68, 94.

Wild, D. (1991, August 8). Performance: Elvis Costello. *Rolling Stone*, p. 24.

Wild, D. (1998, September 17). Burt Bacharach and Elvis Costello. *Rolling Stone*, p. 25.

Willman, C. (1986, February 16). Elvis roots into America. *Los Angeles Times*, p. 63.

Willman, C. (1986, October 4). The Costello watch: Night 2: Subdues 'n' sensitive. *Los Angeles Times*, p. VI:7.

Willman, C. (1986, October 6). The Costello watch: Nights 3, 4: Witty and wonderful. *Los Angeles Times*, p. VI:3.

Willman, C. (1989, March 26). God, as seen by Elvis Costello. *Los Angeles Times*, p. C67.

Willman, C. (1993, February 14). Greetings from Elvis. *Los Angeles Times* (NEWSBANK).

Willner, H. (1993, February). Platter du Jour: The Brodsky Quartet and Elvis Costello. *Spin*, p. 77.

Willwerth, J. (1978, March). Angry new Elvis: "My Rage Is True." *Crawdaddy*, pp. 12–14.

Winner, L. (1982, December). A gentle Costello. *Atlantic Monthly*, pp. 94–95.

Wolk, D. (2002, May 1). Sneer and loathing. *Village Voice*, n.p.

Words and music: Elvis Costello and Brutal Youth. (1994). Warner Bros. Records.

Wright, C. (1994, June 13). Bringing it all back home. *New York*, pp. 68–69.

WXRT-Radio Chicago. (1999, October 10). Interview with Elvis Costello.

Young, J. (1986, December). Elvis Costello and the Attractions: *Blood & Chocolate. Musician*, pp. 115–16.

Zeller, C. (1982, March). Records: *Almost Blue*. *Creem*, pp. 54–55.

Zibart, E. (1982, August 26). Elvis Costello. *Washington Post*, p. D26.

Zito, T. (1977, November 26). Style's the thing in rock as art. *Washington Post*, pp. C1, 7.

Zito, T. (1977, December 9). Elvis!! Elvis!! *Washington Post*, pp. B1, 7.

Zito, T. (1978, March 1). Performing arts: Elvis Costello. *Washington Post*, p. B12.

Index

About the Author

LARRY DAVID SMITH is an independent writer and lecturer specializing in narrative critiques of popular media. His previous books include *Bob Dylan, Bruce Springsteen, and American Song* (Praeger, 2002) and *Pete Townshend: The Minstrel's Dilemma* (Praeger, 1999).